JONES & BARTLETT LEARNING

CDX Automotive

We support ASE
program certification
through

D1484078

FUNDAMENTALS OF

Medium/Heavy Duty Commercial Vehicle Systems

STUDENT WORKBOOK

JONES & BARTLETT
LEARNING

World Headquarters
Jones & Bartlett Learning
5 Wall Street
Burlington, MA 01803
978-443-5000
info@jblearning.com
www.jblearning.com

Jones & Bartlett Learning books and products are available through most bookstores and online booksellers. To contact Jones & Bartlett Learning directly, call 800-832-0034, fax 978-443-8000, or visit our website, www.jblearning.com.

Substantial discounts on bulk quantities of Jones & Bartlett Learning publications are available to corporations, professional associations, and other qualified organizations. For details and specific discount information, contact the special sales department at Jones & Bartlett Learning via the above contact information or send an email to specialsales@jblearning.com.

Copyright © 2017 by Jones & Bartlett Learning, LLC, an Ascend Learning Company

All rights reserved. No part of the material protected by this copyright may be reproduced or utilized in any form, electronic or mechanical, including photocopying, recording, or by any information storage and retrieval system, without written permission from the copyright owner.

The content, statements, views, and opinions herein are the sole expression of the respective authors and not that of Jones & Bartlett Learning, LLC. Reference herein to any specific commercial product, process, or service by trade name, trademark, manufacturer, or otherwise does not constitute or imply its endorsement or recommendation by Jones & Bartlett Learning, LLC and such reference shall not be used for advertising or product endorsement purposes. All trademarks displayed are the trademarks of the parties noted herein. *Fundamentals of Medium/Heavy Duty Commercial Vehicle Systems Student Workbook* is an independent publication and has not been authorized, sponsored, or otherwise approved by the owners of the trademarks or service marks referenced in this product.

There may be images in this book that feature models; these models do not necessarily endorse, represent, or participate in the activities represented in the images. Any screenshots in this product are for educational and instructive purposes only. Any individuals and scenarios featured in the case studies throughout this product may be real or fictitious, but are used for instructional purposes only.

Production Credits

Chief Executive Officer: Ty Field
President: James Homer
Chief Product Officer: Eduardo Moura
Executive Publisher—CDX and Electrical: Vernon Anthony
Acquisitions Editor—CDX: Ian Andrew
Managing Editor—CDX Automotive: Amanda J. Mitchell
Editorial Assistant: Jamie Dinh
Vendor Manager: Nora Menzi
Senior Marketing Manager: Brian Rooney
VP, Manufacturing and Inventory Control: Therese Connell
Composition: diacriTech
Cover Design: Kristin E. Parker
Cover Image: © Max Popov/123RF.com
Printing and Binding: Edwards Brothers Malloy
Cover Printing: Edwards Brothers Malloy

ISBN: 978-1-284-09148-9

6048

Printed in the United States of America
19 18 17 16 15   10 9 8 7 6 5 4 3 2 1

Contents

Tire Tread:
© AbleStock

Introduction to Heavy-Duty Commercial Vehicles

Chapter Review

The following activities have been designed to help you refresh your knowledge of this chapter. Your instructor may require you to complete some or all of these activities as a regular part of your training program. You are encouraged to complete any activity that your instructor does not assign as a way to enhance your learning.

Matching

Match the following terms with the correct description or example.

A. A-train

B. B-train

C. C-train

D. Federal Bridge Gross Weight Formula

E. Full trailer

F. Gross vehicle weight (GVW)

G. Gross weight limits

H. Semi-trailer

I. Torque rise

J. Upper coupler

_____ **1.** Laws that limit the weight-to-length ratio of heavy trucks with the goal of protecting roads and bridges from the damage caused by the concentrated weight of shorter trucks.

_____ **2.** The maximum design weight of a vehicle including a full tank of fuel, fully loaded to its capacity, and with all passengers.

_____ **3.** A steel plate and a kingpin fastened to the underside of the forward portion of a semi-trailer frame and designed to tow and support the weight of the trailer.

_____ **4.** A combination vehicle similar to an A-train but using a dolly that has two parallel drawbars.

_____ **5.** The maximum legal weight of a vehicle that can travel on roads and bridges.

_____ **6.** A trailer that is supported at both ends with an axle and does not rest on a fifth wheel.

_____ **7.** The difference between engine torque produced at rated speed (maximum engine RPM under load) and peak torque.

_____ **8.** A combination vehicle in which the second trailer is a full trailer unit connected by a draw bar to a single hitch point on the lead (first) trailer.

_____ **9.** A trailer that has some of its load carried by the tractor through a hitching device.

_____ **10.** A combination vehicle in which the tractor pulls a semi-trailer and a third, full trailer behind the semi-trailer.

Multiple Choice

Read each item carefully, and then select the best response.

_____ **1.** A commercial vehicle with a gross vehicle weight of 32,000 lbs. would be classified as a _____ vehicle.

    A. class 5

    B. class 6

    C. class 7

    D. class 8

_____ **2.** General freight trucks and refrigerated food trucks are examples of _____ trucks that are capable of traveling long distances with heavy loads at high speeds.

    A. heavy haul

    B. line-haul

    C. pick-up and delivery

    D. intercity

_____ **3.** Belly dump trailers and semi-end dump hopper trailer combinations are examples of vehicles used for _____ applications.
  A. refuse collection
  B. logging
  C. mining
  D. heavy haul

_____ **4.** All of the following are examples of urban transit coaches, *except*: _____.
  A. school buses
  B. airport shuttle buses
  C. city transit buses
  D. articulated buses

_____ **5.** A(n) _____ axle is used on heavy-duty commercial vehicles to help increase maximum gross vehicle weight ratings.
  A. pusher
  B. articulated
  C. tag
  D. Both A and C

_____ **6.** The name _____ comes from the coupling method where some of the trailer's load is actually carried by the tractor through a connection known as a fifth wheel.
  A. A-train
  B. B-train
  C. semi-trailer
  D. combination vehicle

_____ **7.** The _____ does not use a converter dolly. Instead, the lead trailer has a sliding section of frame to which a fifth wheel is attached.
  A. A-train
  B. B-train
  C. C-train
  D. D-train

_____ **8.** The _____ is a plate-type coupling device designed to support the weight of a semi-trailer.
  A. fifth wheel
  B. lunette
  C. pintle
  D. coupler

_____ **9.** Ball hitches are classified by _____.
  A. gross trailer weight (GTW)
  B. gross vehicle weight (GVW)
  C. tongue weight (TW)
  D. Either A or C

_____ **10.** The vehicle identification number (VIN) is usually located on the _____.
  A. frame
  B. engine
  C. inside the driver's door on an information sticker
  D. All of the above

True/False

If you believe the statement to be more true than false, write the letter "T" in the space provided. If you believe the statement to be more false than true, write the letter "F".

_____ **1.** Regional operations dispatch vehicles on trips lasting days—and even weeks—before returning them to a dispatch or maintenance facility.

_____ **2.** A pick-up and delivery vehicle typically travels three miles between starts/stops with a 100% load capacity going and 40% load on return.

_____ **3.** Intercity coaches will travel on highway and in urban conditions accumulating high mileage on routes exceeding 30 miles (48.3 km) between start and stop.

_____ **4.** Belly dump trailers, better known as garbage trucks, are used for pick-up and transportation of residential garbage or recycling materials.

_____ **5.** Rescue vehicles are specialized vehicles designed for rapid acceleration to crash sites on highways or airport tarmacs away from hydrant hookups.

_____ **6.** Peak torque describes how fast the engine can turn while producing torque.

_____ **7.** High-torque-rise engines are ideal for stop-start traffic and varying speed/load conditions.

_____ **8.** Regardless of design, most truck cabs include some type of aerodynamic fairings and wind deflectors to improve fuel economy.

_____ **9.** The conventional cab configuration enables the use of a longer trailer and has greater maneuverability than a cab-over-engine configuration when a small turning radius is needed.

_____ **10.** Suspension systems commonly use air for springs.

_____ **11.** The Federal Bridge Formula allows motor vehicles to be loaded to maximum weight only if each group of axles and their spacing also satisfy the requirements of the formula.

_____ **12.** A semi-trailer has axles at the front and rear of the trailer, which carry the entire load.

_____ **13.** A-trains are often called Western doubles, Rocky Mountain doubles, or Road Trains.

_____ **14.** The fifth wheel is the point of articulation between the trailer and the tractor.

_____ **15.** The first digit of a vehicle identification number identifies the original equipment manufacturer.

Fill in the Blank

Read each item carefully, and then complete the statement by filling in the missing word(s).

1. Road _____ is expressed as a percentage and refers to the steepness of a hill.

2. Vehicles in the _____ classification face operating conditions that are primarily within cities and suburban areas.

3. Vehicles in the _____ _____ category move equipment or materials at legal maximums for length, width, and weight.

4. A _____ truck is used to move shipments of wood, chips, and pulp to and from paper mills.

5. A vehicle's backbone or _____ must be sized and built appropriately to be capable of supporting loads applied to it while adapting to forces that bend and twist.

6. Torque _____ is expressed as a percentage of torque at the rated speed.

7. A vehicle's _____ system is needed to support the load on the chassis, absorb road shock, and enable movement of the axles to adapt to road conditions.

8. The Federal Bridge _____ _____ Formula is also known as Bridge Formula B and the Federal Bridge Formula.

9. The upper coupler contains a _____, which is coupled to the tractor's fifth wheel.

10. The _____ _____ _____ is a unique serial number composed of 17 characters—letters and digits—that is assigned to each vehicle produced.

Labeling

Label the following diagrams with the correct terms.

1. Identify the following chassis and wheel configurations:

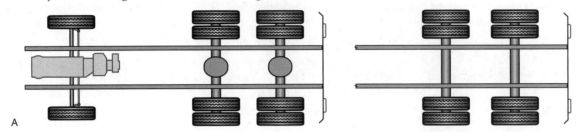

A

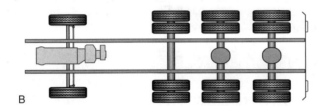

B

A. _____

B. _____

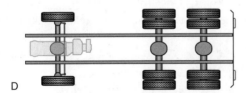

C

C. _____

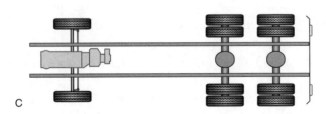

D

D. _____

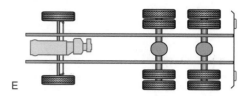

E.

E. _____

F.

F. _____

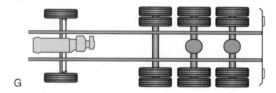

G.

G. _____

2. Identify the aerodynamic features of cabs:

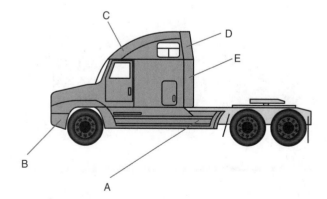

A. _____

B. _____

C. _____

D. _____

E. _____

3. Decode the vehicle identification numbers:

North American VIN System

1	2	3	4	5	6	7	8	9	10	11	12	13	14	15	16	17
A			B					C	D	E	F					

ISO Standard 3779

1	2	3	4	5	6	7	8	9	10	11	12	13	14	15	16	17
G		H							I							

A. _____

B. _____

C. _____

D. _____

E. _____

F. _____

G. _____

H. _____

I. _____

Common Terms and Conventions

Match the following terms and acronyms with their correct definitions.

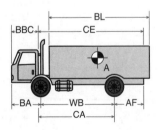 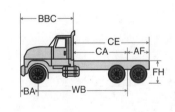 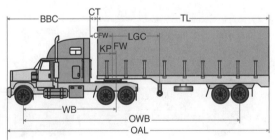

_____ **1.** CE

_____ **2.** LGC

_____ **3.** AF

_____ **4.** Chassis

_____ **5.** FH

A. Bumper to back of cab

B. Body length

C. Back of cab to centerline or rear axle or tandem suspension

D. Weight of chassis only

E. Centerline of rear axle or tandem to center point of fifth wheel

_____ **6.** Curb weight

_____ **7.** BL

_____ **8.** OWB

_____ **9.** Payload

_____ **10.** KP

_____ **11.** BBC

_____ **12.** CT

_____ **13.** GVW

_____ **14.** FW

_____ **15.** CA

F. Overall wheelbase of tractor and trailer

G. Landing gear clearance—center point of kingpin to nearest interface point of landing gear assembly

H. Gross Vehicle Weight—total of curb, body, and payload weights

I. Center of rear axle, or tandem, to end of frame

J. Basic vehicle—cab, frame, and running gear

K. Back of cab to front of semi-trailer in straight-ahead relationship

L. Kingpin setting—front of semi-trailer to center point of kingpins on semi-trailer

M. Back of cab to end of frame

N. Commodity to be carried

O. Frame height

Skill Drills

Test your knowledge of skill drills by filling in the correct words in the photo captions.

1. Decoding the VIN:

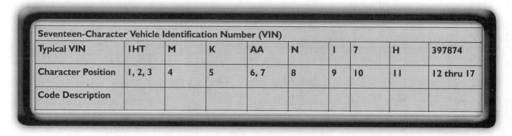

Seventeen-Character Vehicle Identification Number (VIN)									
Typical VIN	1HT	M	K	AA	N	1	7	H	397874
Character Position	1, 2, 3	4	5	6, 7	8	9	10	11	12 thru 17
Code Description									

Step 1:   The VIN is 1HTMKAAN17H397874. The first character is the _____ of _____.

Step 2:   The second character is usually a _____; it tells you the name of the _____, which is International in this case.

Step 3:   The third character tells you the _____ _____; in this case, "_____."

Step 4:   The fourth character indicates the type of _____.

Step 5:   The fifth character describes the _____ _____ and _____. This is a Durastar 4400.

Step 6:   The sixth and seventh characters tell you the _____ _____ and _____ range. In this case, it's a DT 466.

Step 7:   The eighth character provides the vehicle recommended _____ _____ _____ _____ (GVWR), which is 26,001 to 33,000 lbs. (11,818 to 15,000 kg.) in this case.

Step 8:   The ninth character is the _____ character. It is used internally by the _____.

Step 9:   The tenth character tells you the _____ of _____. You can decode this character according to a model year _____ _____, which in this example shows us that the vehicle was assembled for the 2007 model year.

Step 10: The eleventh character tells you the _____ _____ or _____ where the vehicle was put together.

Step 11: The final six numbers make up the sequential number of the vehicle as it comes off the _____ _____, starting at a _____ number, which is usually one hundred thousand (100000). So the _____ vehicle to be produced will usually, but not always, have the number 100001.

Crossword Puzzle

Use the clues in the column to complete the puzzle.

Across

2. Bars used to connect tow vehicles to a tractor or lead towing unit.

6. Trailer hitching device similar to pintle hooks but in which the towing horn pivots and is not fixed.

7. The design rating specified by a manufacturer as the recommended maximum weight of a vehicle when fully loaded.

8. Two or more combined or coupled vehicle units.

Down

1. The capability of a vehicle to maintain forward motion on a specified grade while sustaining a minimum speed.

3. The capability of a vehicle to commence moving forward on a specified grade.

4. Movement of axles.

5. A unit of measure of power that conveys how fast the engine can turn while producing torque.

ASE-Type Questions

Read each item carefully, and then select the best response.

_____ **1.** Technician A says each application of commercial vehicles will be purpose built according its own specialized requirements. Technician B says each application's vehicle being purpose built includes the ability to carry people, products, or perform services. Who is correct?
   A. Technician A
   B. Technician B
   C. Both Technician A and Technician B
   D. Neither Technician A nor Technician B

_____ **2.** Technician A says the operating condition of off-highway includes 20% of the total operating time on secondary roads made from good concrete or asphalt. Technician B says the operating condition of off-highway includes intermittent grades of up to 12%. Who is correct?
   A. Technician A
   B. Technician B
   C. Both Technician A and Technician B
   D. Neither Technician A nor Technician B

_____ **3.** While discussing construction vehicles, Technician A says operation is primarily movement of material to and from a job site. Technician B says operating conditions are 90% of loaded operation on road surfaces made of concrete, asphalt, gravel, crushed rock, or hard packed dirt. Who is correct?
   A. Technician A
   B. Technician B
   C. Both Technician A and Technician B
   D. Neither Technician A nor Technician B

_____ **4.** Technician A says the intercity coach is a category of vehicles that transports people and occasionally light freight between cities and/or suburban areas. Technician B says typical vehicle types in this category are tour coaches and cross country coaches. Who is correct?
   A. Technician A
   B. Technician B
   C. Both Technician A and Technician B
   D. Neither Technician A nor Technician B

_____ **5.** Technician A says refuse vehicles encounter steep grades of up to 20% when travelling into landfill, transfer, or recycling sites. Technician B says refuse vehicles typically have a high frequency of accelerations and stops for every mile travelled. Who is correct?
   A. Technician A
   B. Technician B
   C. Both Technician A and Technician B
   D. Neither Technician A nor Technician B

_____ **6.** Technician A says a frame must be sized and built appropriately to be capable of supporting the loads applied to it. Technician B says the frame has the additional task of adapting to the forces that bend and twist the frame. Who is correct?
   A. Technician A
   B. Technician B
   C. Both Technician A and Technician B
   D. Neither Technician A nor Technician B

_____ **7.** Technician A says start-ability refers to the capability to commence forward motion on a specified grade. Technician B says an engine's torque output and powertrain gear ratios will determine the steepest grade a truck can begin to climb from a standing stop. Who is correct?
   A. Technician A
   B. Technician B
   C. Both Technician A and Technician B
   D. Neither Technician A nor Technician B

_____ **8.** Technician A says auxiliary braking devices: compression release, exhaust-based, or driveline retarders are not considered to be in the category of special equipment. Technician B says aerodynamic fairings are considered special equipment. Who is correct?

   A. Technician A

   B. Technician B

   C. Both Technician A and Technician B

   D. Neither Technician A nor Technician B

_____ **9.** Technician A says GVW class 8 vehicles are usually considered heavy trucks. Technician B says trucks or power units (tractors) are classified primarily into a class between 2 and 8 based on their GVW.

   A. Technician A

   B. Technician B

   C. Both Technician A and Technician B

   D. Neither Technician A nor Technician B

_____ **10.** Technician A says the gross combination weight rating is a specific maximum weight limit determined by the manufacturer. Technician B says tractors and trucks can also be classified according to their drive and non-drive axle configurations. Who is correct?

   A. Technician A

   B. Technician B

   C. Both Technician A and Technician B

   D. Neither Technician A nor Technician B

Careers, Employability Skills, and Workplace Practices

Chapter Review

The following activities have been designed to help you refresh your knowledge of this chapter. Your instructor may require you to complete some or all of these activities as a regular part of your training program. You are encouraged to complete any activity that your instructor does not assign as a way to enhance your learning.

Matching

Match the following terms with the correct description or example.

A. Operator's manual

B. Parts specialist

C. Primary sources

D. Secondary sources

E. Service campaign and recall

F. Shop or service manual

G. Supporting statement

H. Technical service bulletin (TSB)

I. Vehicle emission control information (VECI) label

J. Vehicle safety certification (VSC) label

_____ **1.** A statement that urges the speaker to elaborate on a particular topic.

_____ **2.** A label certifying that the vehicle meets the Federal Motor Vehicle Safety, Bumper, and Theft Prevention Standards in effect at the time of manufacture.

_____ **3.** Secondhand information compiled from a variety of sources.

_____ **4.** A label used by technicians to identify engine and emission control information for the vehicle.

_____ **5.** The person who serves customers at the parts counters.

_____ **6.** Information issued by manufacturers to alert technicians of unexpected problems or changes to repair procedures.

_____ **7.** A document that contains information about a vehicle, which is a valuable source of information for both the owner and the technician.

_____ **8.** A corrective measure conducted by manufacturers when a safety issue is discovered with a particular vehicle.

_____ **9.** People who have direct experience with the same or a similar problem.

_____ **10.** Manufacturer's or after-market information on the repair and service of vehicles.

Multiple Choice

Read each item carefully, and then select the best response.

_____ **1.** To gain the Automotive Service Excellence (ASE) qualifications, candidates need a minimum of _____ year's working experience before taking an exam for each area of specialization.

    A. one

    B. two

    C. three

    D. four

_____ **2.** The _____ administers technician certification procedures throughout the United States.

    A. Competitive Automotive Regulatory System

    B. National Highway Traffic Safety Administration

    C. National Institute for Automotive Service Excellence

    D. National Automotive Technical Association

_____ **3.** H-series Automotive Service Excellence (ASE) certification is designed specifically for _____.
  A. medium/heavy-duty truck technicians
  B. transit bus certification
  C. truck equipment
  D. school bus certification

_____ **4.** Making an attempt to see a situation from someone else's point of view is called _____.
  A. empathy
  B. active listening
  C. nonverbal feedback
  D. validation

_____ **5.** Body position, eye contact, and facial expression are all examples of _____.
  A. verbal feedback
  B. empathy
  C. nonverbal feedback
  D. defensive listening

_____ **6.** Which of the following phrases is an example of a supporting statement?
  A. "I understand."
  B. "I see."
  C. "Give me an example."
  D. "That must be frustrating for you."

_____ **7.** Speaking is a three-step process that includes all of the following, _except_: _____.
  A. thinking about the message
  B. providing feedback
  C. checking whether the message is correctly understood
  D. accurately presenting the message

_____ **8.** When asking a customer an open question, you would begin with the word _____.
  A. why
  B. when
  C. where
  D. who

_____ **9.** When you read through the table of contents, introduction, conclusion, headings, and index until you find what we are looking for you are using a(n) _____ reading method.
  A. open
  B. selective
  C. comprehending
  D. absorbing

_____ **10.** Information from _____ sources tends to be more reliable since it is more generic and objective.
  A. primary
  B. direct
  C. secondary
  D. human

_____ **11.** A complete repair order should contain all of the elements of the three Cs; this includes all of the following, _except_: _____.
  A. concern
  B. correction
  C. cause
  D. complication

_____ **12.** Which of the following determines the use of our personal space?
  A. Familiarity
  B. Gender
  C. Culture
  D. All of the above

_____ **13.** Manufacturers supply every new vehicle with a(n) _____, which is usually kept in the glove compartment.
- **A.** service bulletin
- **B.** operator's manual
- **C.** service manual
- **D.** service information program

_____ **14.** A(n) _____ lists how much time will be involved in performing a standard or warranty-related service or repair.
- **A.** labor guide
- **B.** technical service bulletin
- **C.** parts program
- **D.** inspection report

_____ **15.** In order to determine the total cost of the service, you need to know all of the following, *except*: _____.
- **A.** the labor cost
- **B.** the tax amount
- **C.** the cost of gas and consumables you used to service the vehicle
- **D.** the service history

True/False

If you believe the statement to be more true than false, write the letter "T" in the space provided. If you believe the statement to be more false than true, write the letter "F".

_____ **1.** In the United States, ASE certification is a mandatory requirement to work in the trade.

_____ **2.** All ASE's heavy-duty certifications are designed in a way that the number represents the subject matter and the letter represents the classification of the vehicle type.

_____ **3.** Nonverbal feedback includes thoughts and feelings that interfere with our listening, such as our own assumptions, emotions, and prejudices.

_____ **4.** In order to empathize with someone you must first agree with him or her.

_____ **5.** A closed question only allows an individual to answer with a simple yes or no.

_____ **6.** Instructions should contain information about who, what, when, where, why, and directions for how a task should be completed.

_____ **7.** The first step of the researching process is to look for information or clues that can help solve the problem.

_____ **8.** Technical assistance hotlines put you in contact with professionals who can assist you in diagnosing a particularly difficult problem over the phone.

_____ **9.** If a problem is noticed with a piece of workshop equipment such as a defective automotive lift, a lockout/tagout procedure should be followed.

_____ **10.** A service information program is specific to one year and make/model of a particular vehicle.

Fill in the Blank

Read each item carefully, and then complete the statement by filling in the missing word(s).

1. Skilled _____ are vital to ensure commercial vehicles stay on the road, operating efficiently, safely, and reliably.

2. Health and safety legislation demand strict adherence by employers to _____ in the use of certified personal and shop safety equipment for all workers.

3. The active _____ focuses all of his or her attention on the speaker, including verbal and nonverbal messages.

4. A _____ statement such as "I see" or "Tell me more" indicates to the customer that you are paying attention.

5. A _____ question requires a specific answer, and there is usually only one answer.

6. When taking a _____ message, make sure you get the person's name and organization, contact details, the date and time, and a summary of the message.

7. Being part of a _____ allows us to share ideas, knowledge, and resources and complement each other's strengths and weaknesses.

8. A repair order can become a _____ document in a lawsuit and can be used by the court to determine if the shop has any liability in the situation.

9. Most shops should have a _____ inspection form that needs to be completed on a regular basis, typically weekly or monthly, although some tasks may need to be performed daily.

10. By following the checklist on a vehicle _____ form a technician can check all of the components in a systematic way and ensure that they are operational or serviceable.

11. All aspects of our physical appearance, including our clothes, jewelry, hairstyle, posture, and outward demeanor, culminate to create the _____ _____ made in any encounter.

12. Being _____, clocking in on time, for example, demonstrates a good work attitude and professionalism.

13. The quality of _____ _____ influences people to choose us over our competitors and makes people feel good about continuing to buy our products or services.

14. A typical _____ _____ _____ is issued by manufacturers and contains step-by-step procedures and diagrams on how to identify if there is a fault and perform an effective repair.

15. A fault within the locking mechanism of a seatbelt that results in the seatbelt not operating as a restraint when it should would cause a manufacturer to issue a mandatory _____.

Labeling

Label the following diagrams with the correct terms.

1. Identifying vehicle information labels:

A. _____

B. _____

C. _____

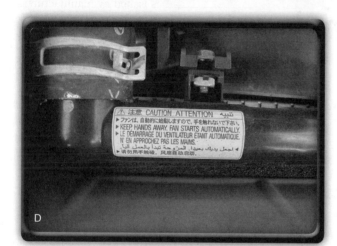

D. _____

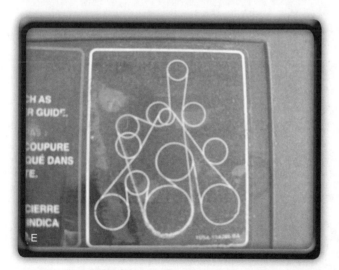

E. _____

Skill Drills

Test your knowledge of skill drills by filling in the correct words in the photo captions.

1. Locating Parts Information on the Computer:

Step 1:   Log in to the application using the appropriate _____ and _____.

Step 2:   Enter the _____, make, _____, and engine and _____ number information into the system in the appropriate places.

Step 3:   Search for the _____ you require to conduct the _____ or _____.

Step 4:   The _____ _____ will provide a list of possible matches for you to select from. If the initial search does not produce what you are looking for, try changing the _____ _____. Keep searching until you find the information.

Step 5:   Gather information on the identified parts, including _____ _____, _____, _____, and _____.

Step 6:   Print, _____ down, or directly _____ an _____ for the desired parts.

2. Identifying Information Needed and Service Requested:

Step 1:   Locate a _____ _____ used in your shop.

Step 2:   Familiarize yourself with the repair order, and _____ the following _____ on the repair order:

    a.   _____

    b.   Customer details: _____ and _____, daytime _____ number

    c.   Vehicle details: _____, make, model, _____, _____ reading, VIN

    d.   Customer _____ _____: Note any additional information that is required on your shop's _____ _____.

Step 3:   Following the shop _____, determine the _____ for the tasks that are listed.

Step 4:   Use the repair order to carry out the requested _____ or _____. Fill in the repair order with _____ of the cause of the customer concern(s) and the _____(s) conducted.

3. Reviewing a Vehicle Service History:

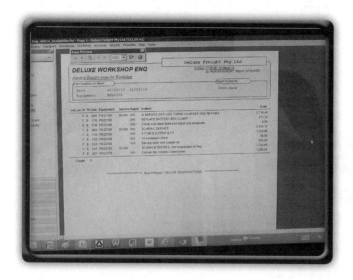

Step 1:   Locate the service _____ for the vehicle. This may be in shop _____ or in the service history _____ within the vehicle glove compartment. Some shops may keep the vehicle's service history on a _____.

Step 2:   Familiarize yourself with the _____ _____ of the vehicle.

   a. On what _____ was the vehicle first serviced?

   b. On what date was the vehicle _____ serviced?

   c. What was the most _____ _____ performed?

   d. Was the vehicle ever serviced for the _____ _____ more than _____?

Step 3:   Compare the vehicle service history to the manufacturer's _____ maintenance requirements and list any _____.

   a. Have all the services been _____?

   b. Have all the _____ been checked?

   c. Are there any _____ items?

Crossword Puzzle

Use the clues in the column to complete the puzzle.

Across

4. A complete list of all the servicing and repairs that have been performed on a vehicle.
5. A statement that shows common interest in the topic being discussed.

Down

1. A form used by shops to collect information regarding a vehicle coming in for repair, also referred to as a work order.
2. A computer software program for identifying and ordering replacement vehicle parts.
3. A label that lists the type of coolant installed in the cooling system.
6. A guide that provides information to make estimates for repairs.

ASE-Type Questions

Read each item carefully, and then select the best response.

_____ 1. Technician A says that maintaining an appearance of neatness is important as it conveys to the customer the idea of careful, professional technicians. Technician B says that a dirty and cluttered shop indicates that the shop gets a lot of quality work done. Who is correct?

  A. Technician A

  B. Technician B

  C. Both Technician A and Technician B

  D. Neither Technician A nor Technician B

_____ 2. Technician A says researching the service information is a waste of time. Technician B says that researching the service information saves time. Who is correct?

  A. Technician A

  B. Technician B

  C. Both Technician A and Technician B

  D. Neither Technician A nor Technician B

_____ 3. Technician A says that an example of an open question is: "What are the conditions like when your A/C is not working?" Technician B says that an example of an open question is: "Does your A/C work at all?" Who is correct?

  A. Technician A

  B. Technician B

  C. Both Technician A and Technician B

  D. Neither Technician A nor Technician B

_____ 4. Technician A says that labor guides are necessary for the service writer to quote prices for a customer on the repair bill. Technician B says that labor guides are what the customer pays and that warranty pays more for labor using a different labor guide. Who is correct?

  A. Technician A

  B. Technician B

  C. Both Technician A and Technician B

  D. Neither Technician A nor Technician B

_____ 5. Technician A says joining the commercial vehicle service industry in its repair and service sector as a service technician is the most popular trade pathway. Technician B says the position of a service technician allows for maximum exposure to the most recent technological developments and advancements in the industry. Who is correct?

  A. Technician A

  B. Technician B

  C. Both Technician A and Technician B

  D. Neither Technician A nor Technician B

_____ 6. Technician A says that hybrid vehicle is a specialized area in commercial vehicle service and repair in which a technician can specialize. Technician B says that the manufacturing of parts is a specialized area in commercial vehicle service and repair in which a technician can specialize. Who is correct?

  A. Technician A

  B. Technician B

  C. Both Technician A and Technician B

  D. Neither Technician A nor Technician B

_____ 7. Technician A states that it is a lifelong learning process to perfect your communication skills. Technician B states that learning and applying good communication skills will not save you time but it will help you avoid or get through tricky situations.

  A. Technician A

  B. Technician B

  C. Both Technician A and Technician B

  D. Neither Technician A nor Technician B

_____ 8. While discussing effective writing, Technician A says a repair order can never be considered a legal document. Technician B says writing is one of the most important tasks a technician does on a daily basis. Who is correct?

A. Technician A

B. Technician B

C. Both Technician A and Technician B

D. Neither Technician A nor Technician B

_____ **9.** Technician A says you should always escort customers in the shop to keep them safe and continue any conversation in the customer write-up area as soon as possible. Technician B says customers should be given safety glasses to enter a shop, and the shortest amount of time possible should be spent with the customer in the shop. Who is correct?

A. Technician A

B. Technician B

C. Both Technician A and Technician B

D. Neither Technician A nor Technician B

_____ **10.** Technician A says being focused on customer service means you are fully engaged in providing the highest level of service that you can. Technician B says one of the most important parts of customer service is repairing the vehicle correctly the first time. Who is correct?

A. Technician A

B. Technician B

C. Both Technician A and Technician B

D. Neither Technician A nor Technician B

Safety, Personal Protection Equipment, and First Aid

Chapter Review

The following activities have been designed to help you refresh your knowledge of this chapter. Your instructor may require you to complete some or all of these activities as a regular part of your training program. You are encouraged to complete any activity that your instructor does not assign as a way to enhance your learning.

Matching

Match the following terms with the correct description or example.

A. Double-insulated
B. Ear protection
C. First aid
D. Hazardous material
E. Heat buildup

F. Internal bleeding
G. Occupational Safety and Health Administration (OSHA)
H. Shock
I. Strain
J. Threshold limit value (TLV)

_____ **1.** The maximum allowable concentration of a given material in the surrounding air.

_____ **2.** The loss of blood into the body cavity from a wound; there is no obvious sign of blood.

_____ **3.** An injury caused by the overstretching of muscles and tendons.

_____ **4.** Protective gear worn when the sound levels exceed 85 decibels, when working around operating machinery for any period of time, or when the equipment you are using produces loud noise.

_____ **5.** Any material that poses an unreasonable risk of damage or injury to persons, property, or the environment if it is not properly controlled during handling, storage, manufacture, processing, packaging, use and disposal, or transportation.

_____ **6.** Government agency created to provide national leadership in occupational safety and health.

_____ **7.** The immediate care given to an injured or suddenly ill person.

_____ **8.** A dangerous condition that occurs when the glove can no longer absorb or reflect heat and heat is transferred to the inside of the glove.

_____ **9.** Tools or appliances that are designed in such a way that no single failure can result in a dangerous voltage coming into contact with the outer casing of the device.

_____ **10.** Inadequate tissue oxygenation resulting from serious injury or illness.

Multiple Choice

Read each item carefully, and then select the best response.

_____ **1.** The federal agency that provides regulations and procedures designed to help prevent worker fatalities and workplace injuries and illnesses is called the _____.
   A. Occupational Safety and Health Administration
   B. Environmental Protection Agency
   C. National Transportation Safety Board
   D. Automotive Safety Council

_____ **2.** The federal government agency that deals with issues related to environmental safety is called the _____.
   A. National Association for Environmental Management
   B. National Environmental Health Association
   C. Environmental Protection Agency
   D. Occupational Safety and Health Administration

_____ 3. The signal word _____ indicates a potentially hazardous situation, which, if not avoided, may result in minor or moderate injury.
   A. alert
   B. danger
   C. warning
   D. caution

_____ 4. A _____ background is used for emergency-type signs, such as for first aid, fire protection, and emergency equipment.
   A. red
   B. blue
   C. green
   D. yellow

_____ 5. Running engines produce dangerous exhaust gases, including _____.
   A. carbon dioxide
   B. hydrogen dioxide
   C. carbon monoxide
   D. Both A and C

_____ 6. A _____ fire involves flammable liquids or gaseous fuels.
   A. class A
   B. class B
   C. class C
   D. class K

_____ 7. A fire extinguisher marked with a green triangle is approved to fight a _____ fire.
   A. class A
   B. class B
   C. class C
   D. class D

_____ 8. If you are cleaning up dust after a repair, you should use a(n) _____.
   A. low-pressure wet cleaning method
   B. dry sweeping method
   C. HEPA vacuum cleaner
   D. Either A or C

_____ 9. What type of gloves should be used to protect your hands from exposure to greases and oils?
   A. Chemical gloves
   B. Light-duty gloves
   C. Cloth gloves
   D. Leather gloves

_____ 10. Safety glasses must be marked with "_____" on both the lens and frame.
   A. polarized
   B. UV protection
   C. Z87
   D. heavy duty

_____ 11. When you approach the scene of an accident or emergency, you should _____.
   A. make sure there are no other dangers, and assist only if it is safe to do so
   B. check to see if the victim is responsive and breathing
   C. have a bystander call 9-1-1
   D. All of the above

_____ 12. If a chemical splashes into the eye, hold the eye wide open and flush with warm water for at least _____, continuously and gently.
   A. 5 minutes
   B. 10 minutes
   C. 15 minutes
   D. 20 minutes

_____ **13.** A _____ fracture involves bleeding or the protrusion of bone through the skin.
- **A.** simple
- **B.** open
- **C.** complicated
- **D.** All of the above

_____ **14.** A _____ occurs when a joint is forced beyond its natural movement limit causing stretching or tearing in the ligaments that hold the bones together.
- **A.** dislocation
- **B.** strain
- **C.** sprain
- **D.** simple fracture

_____ **15.** A _____ burn involves blistering and damage to the outer layer of skin.
- **A.** first-degree
- **B.** second-degree
- **C.** third-degree
- **D.** All of the above

True/False

If you believe the statement to be more true than false, write the letter "T" in the space provided. If you believe the statement to be more false than true, write the letter "F".

_____ **1.** Almost all accidents are avoidable or preventable by taking a few precautions.

_____ **2.** Danger is usually indicated by black text with a yellow background.

_____ **3.** A pictorial message allows a safety message to be conveyed to people who are illiterate or who do not speak the local language.

_____ **4.** Gasoline engines fitted with a catalytic converter can be run safely indoors.

_____ **5.** All electric tools must be equipped with a ground prong or double-insulated. If they are not, do not use them.

_____ **6.** Three elements must be present at the same time for a fire to occur: fuel, oxygen, and heat.

_____ **7.** The shop should have a material safety data sheet for each hazardous substance or dangerous product.

_____ **8.** You should always use compressed air to blow dust from components or parts before attempting to work on them.

_____ **9.** Coming into frequent or prolonged contact with used engine oil can cause dermatitis and other skin disorders, including some forms of cancer.

_____ **10.** Over-the-ear style hearing protection has a higher noise-reduction rating than in-the-ear style protection.

_____ **11.** Safety glasses should only be worn when there is a chance of direct impact or debris damage to the eyes.

_____ **12.** Gas welding goggles can be worn instead of a welding mask when assisting a person using an electric welder.

_____ **13.** It is necessary to use a full face shield when using solvents and cleaners, epoxies, and resins or when working on a battery.

_____ **14.** You should always remove watches, rings, and jewelry before starting work.

_____ **15.** If an object punctures the victim's skin and becomes embedded in the victim's body you should remove the object and apply a sterile dressing.

Fill in the Blank

Read each item carefully, and then complete the statement by filling in the missing word(s).

1. Personal _____ equipment refers to items of safety equipment like safety footwear, gloves, clothing, protective eyewear, and hearing protection.

2. _____ routes are a safe way of escaping danger and gathering in a safe place where everyone can be accounted for in the event of an emergency.

3. A _____ is anything that could hurt you or someone else, and most workplaces have them.

4. To prevent accidents, a machinery guard or a _____ painted line on the floor usually borders large, fixed machinery such as lathes and milling machines.

5. Poor _____ safety practices can cause shocks and burns, as well as fires and explosions.

6. The _____ used in electric droplights are very vulnerable to impact and must not be used without insulating cage protection.

7. All flammable items should be kept in an approved _____ storage container or cabinet, with firefighting equipment close at hand.

8. The acronym _____ should be followed when operating a fire extinguisher.

9. A fire _____ is designed to smother a small fire and is very useful in putting out a fire on a person.

10. Most shops use _____ materials daily, such as cleaning solvents, gasket cement, brake fluid, and coolant.

11. A(n) _____ _____ _____ is used to flush the eye with clean water or sterile liquid in the event that you get foreign liquids or particles in your eye.

12. Used oil and fluids will often contain dangerous chemicals and impurities and need to be safely _____ or disposed of in an environmentally friendly way.

13. A shop safety _____ is a valuable way to identify unsafe equipment, materials, or activities so they can be corrected to prevent accidents or injuries.

14. Before you undertake any activity, think about all potential hazards and select the correct _____ _____ _____ based on the risk associated with the activity.

15. The proper _____ provides protection against items falling on your feet, chemicals, cuts, abrasions, and slips.

16. _____ cream looks and feels like a moisturizing cream, but it has a specific formula to provide extra protection from chemicals and oils.

17. A disposable _____ _____ is made from paper with a wire-reinforced edge that is held to your face with an elastic strip.

18. Safety _____ must be worn when servicing air-conditioning systems or any other system that contains pressurized gas.

19. Good _____ is about always making sure the shop and your work surroundings are neat and kept in good order.

20. _____ bleeding is the loss of blood from a wound where the blood can be seen escaping.

Labeling

Label the following diagrams with the correct terms.

1. Identify the following fire extinguisher types:

 A

 B

 C

 D

A.

B.

C. _____

D. _____

2. Identify the following forms of hand protection:

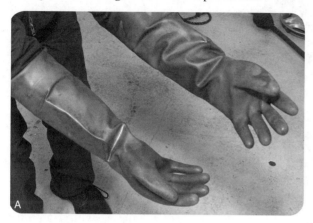

A. _____

B. _____

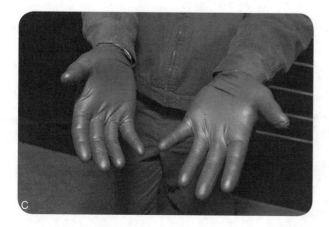

C. _____

D. _____

3. Identify the following forms of eye protection:

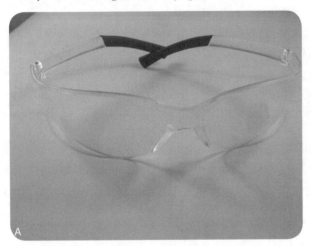

A. _____

B. _____

C. _____

D. _____

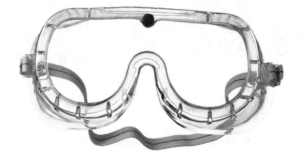

E

E. _____

Skill Drills

Test your knowledge of skill drills by filling in the correct words in the photo captions.

1. Identifying Hazardous Environments:

Step 1: Familiarize yourself with the shop _____. Study and understand the various _____ _____ around your shop. Identify _____ and plan your _____ route. Know the designated _____ point and go there in an emergency.

Step 2: Check for air _____. Locate the extractor _____ or _____ outlets and make sure they are not obstructed in any way. Locate and observe the operation of the exhaust _____ hose, pump, and outlet used on the vehicle's _____ pipes.

Step 3: Check the _____, _____, and _____ of fire extinguishers in your shop. Be sure you know when and how to use each type of _____ _____.

Step 4: Find out where _____ materials are kept, and make sure they are _____ properly.

Step 5: Check the _____ and _____ on the air compressor and air guns for any _____ or excessive wear. Be particularly careful when troubleshooting _____ _____. Never pull the _____ while inspecting one. Severe _____ damage can result.

Step 6: Identify _____ _____ and _____ associated with activities in your shop. Ask your supervisor for information on any special _____ in your particular shop and any special avoidance _____, which may apply to you and your working environment.

2. Identify Information on a Safety Data Sheet:

Step 1: Once you have studied the information on the _____ _____, find the _____ for that particular material. Always check the _____ _____ to ensure that you are reading the most recent update.

Step 2: Note the _____ and _____ names for the material, its manufacturer, and the emergency _____ _____ to call.

Step 3: Find out why this material is potentially _____. It may be _____, it may _____, or it may be _____ if inhaled or touched with your bare skin. Check the threshold _____ _____ (TLVs). The concentration of this material in the air you _____ in your shop must not exceed these figures. There could be physical symptoms associated with breathing harmful _____. Find out what will happen to you if you suffer _____ to the material, either through breathing it or by coming into physical _____ with it. This will help you take safety precautions, such as eye, face, or skin _____, wearing a mask or _____ while using the material, or _____ your skin afterwards.

Step 4: Note the _____ _____ for this material so that you know at what temperature it may catch fire. Also note what kind of _____ _____ you would use to fight a fire involving this material. The _____ fire extinguisher could make the emergency even worse.

Step 5: Study the _____ for this material to identify the _____ conditions or other materials that you should _____ when using this material. It could be _____, moisture, or some other chemical.

Step 6: Find out what special _____ you should take when working with this material. This will include personal protection for your _____, _____, or _____ and storage and use of the material.

Step 7: Be sure to _____ your _____ of your SDS from time to time. Be confident that you know how to _____ and _____ the material and what action to take in an _____, should one occur.

Crossword Puzzle

Use the clues in the column to complete the puzzle.

Across

4. A list of the steps required to get the same result each time a task or activity is performed.

6. A fracture that involves no open wound or internal or external bleeding.

7. The displacement of a joint from its normal position; it is caused by an external force stretching the ligaments beyond their elastic limit.

8. An injury in which a joint is forced beyond its natural movement limit.

Down

1. A place where hazards exist.

2. Protective gear that includes items like hairnets, caps, or hard hats.

3. Protective gear used to protect the wearer from inhaling harmful dusts or gases.

5. A guiding principle that sets the shop direction.

ASE-Type Questions

Read each item carefully, and then select the best response.

_____ 1. Technician A says that exposure to solvents may have long-term effects. Technician B says that accidents are almost always avoidable. Who is correct?
   A. Technician A
   B. Technician B
   C. Both Technician A and Technician B
   D. Neither Technician A nor Technician B

_____ 2. Technician A says that both OSHA and the EPA can inspect facilities for violations. Technician B says that a shop safety rule does not have to be reviewed once put in place. Who is correct?
   A. Technician A
   B. Technician B
   C. Both Technician A and Technician B
   D. Neither Technician A nor Technician B

_____ 3. Technician A says that both caution and danger indicate a potentially hazardous situation. Technician B says that an exhaust extraction hose is not needed if the vehicle is only going to run for a few minutes. Who is correct?
   A. Technician A
   B. Technician B
   C. Both Technician A and Technician B
   D. Neither Technician A nor Technician B

_____ 4. Technician A says that firefighting equipment includes safety glasses. Technician B says that a class A fire extinguisher can be used to fight an electrical fire only. Who is correct?
   A. Technician A
   B. Technician B
   C. Both Technician A and Technician B
   D. Neither Technician A nor Technician B

_____ 5. Technician A says that a good way to clean dust off brakes is with compressed air. Technician B says that asbestos may be in current auto parts. Who is correct?
   A. Technician A
   B. Technician B
   C. Both Technician A and Technician B
   D. Neither Technician A nor Technician B

_____ 6. Technician A says that personal protective equipment (PPE) does not include clothing. Technician B says that the PPE used should be based on the task you are performing. Who is correct?
   A. Technician A
   B. Technician B
   C. Both Technician A and Technician B
   D. Neither Technician A nor Technician B

_____ 7. Technician A says that appropriate work clothes include loose-fitting clothing. Technician B says that you should always wear cuffed pants when working in a shop. Who is correct?
   A. Technician A
   B. Technician B
   C. Both Technician A and Technician B
   D. Neither Technician A nor Technician B

_____ 8. Technician A says that a hat can help keep your hair clean when working on a vehicle. Technician B says that chemical gloves may be used when working with solvent. Who is correct?
   A. Technician A
   B. Technician B
   C. Both Technician A and Technician B
   D. Neither Technician A nor Technician B

_____ **9.** Technician A says that barrier creams are used to make cleaning your hands easier. Technician B says that hearing protection only needs to be worn by people operating loud equipment. Who is correct?
  A. Technician A
  B. Technician B
  C. Both Technician A and Technician B
  D. Neither Technician A nor Technician B

_____ **10.** Technician A says that tinted safety glasses can be worn when working outside. Technician B says that welding can cause a sunburn. Who is correct?
  A. Technician A
  B. Technician B
  C. Both Technician A and Technician B
  D. Neither Technician A nor Technician B

Basic Tools and Lubricants

Tire Tread:
© AbleStock

Chapter Review

The following activities have been designed to help you refresh your knowledge of this chapter. Your instructor may require you to complete some or all of these activities as a regular part of your training program. You are encouraged to complete any activity that your instructor does not assign as a way to enhance your learning.

Matching

Match the following terms with the correct description or example.

A. Air-impact wrench

B. Alkalis

C. Bench vice

D. Chassis dynamometer

E. Coolant

F. Copper

G. Double flare

H. Flashback arrestor

I. Hygroscopic

J. Impact driver

K. Lockout/tagout

L. Morse taper

M. Non-ferrous metals

N. Peening

O. Ratchet

P. Rattle gun

Q. Socket

R. Telescoping gauge

S. Tin snips

T. Vernier caliper

_____ **1.** A term used to describe the action of flattening a rivet through a hammering action.

_____ **2.** A non-ferrous, pure metal that can be alloyed (combined) with other metals but is not combined with iron.

_____ **3.** An enclosed metal tube commonly with 6 or 12 points to remove and install bolts and nuts.

_____ **4.** A seal that is made at the end of metal tubing or pipe.

_____ **5.** A safety system designed to ensure that faulty equipment or equipment in the middle of repair is not used.

_____ **6.** A generic term to describe a handle for sockets that allows the user to select direction of rotation.

_____ **7.** Chemical compounds that have a pH value greater than 7. They are commonly used in toy batteries and bleaches.

_____ **8.** When brake fluid absorbs water from the atmosphere.

_____ **9.** Cutting device for sheet metal, works in a similar fashion to scissors.

_____ **10.** A device that securely holds material in jaws while it is being worked on.

_____ **11.** Tool used for measuring distances in awkward spots such as the bottom of a deep cylinder.

_____ **12.** A fluid that contains special anti-freezing and anti-corrosion chemicals mixed with water.

_____ **13.** A tool powered by compressed air designed to undo tight fasteners.

_____ **14.** Pure metals such as copper; can also be used in alloys.

_____ **15.** A tool that is struck with a blow to provide an impact turning force to remove tight fasteners.

_____ **16.** An accurate measuring device for internal, external, and depth measurements that incorporates fixed and adjustable jaws.

_____ **17.** A machine with rollers that allows a vehicle to attain road speed and load while sitting still in the workshop.

_____ **18.** The most common air tool in an automotive workshop; also called the air-impact wrench.

_____ **19.** A spring-loaded valve installed on oxyacetylene torches as a safety device to prevent flame from entering the torch hoses.

_____ **20.** A tapered mounting shaft for drill bits and chucks in larger drills and lathes.

Multiple Choice

Read each item carefully, and then select the best response.

_____ **1.** Stainless steel rulers are commonly _____ in length.
   A. 12"
   B. 24"
   C. 36"
   D. All of the above

_____ **2.** To measure the precise diameter of a part or item such as a valve stem, you would use a(n) _____.
   A. outside micrometer
   B. inside micrometer
   C. feeler gauge
   D. depth micrometer

_____ **3.** To measure the trueness of a rotating disc brake rotor or camshaft, you would use a(n) _____.
   A. outside micrometer
   B. vernier caliper
   C. dial indicator
   D. feeler gauge

_____ **4.** A _____ is used to check the flatness of a surface, often used to measure the amount of warpage the surface of a cylinder head has.
   A. feeler gauge
   B. straight edge
   C. dial indicator
   D. depth micrometer

_____ **5.** The most common type of drill bit is the _____. It has a point with cutting flutes that form a common angle of 118 degrees.
   A. morse taper
   B. SDS bit
   C. brad point bit
   D. twist drill

_____ **6.** A _____ is designed not to bounce back when it hits something.
   A. ball-peen hammer
   B. dead-blow hammer
   C. club hammer
   D. rubber mallet

_____ **7.** Technicians sometimes use a _____ to remove bolts whose heads have rounded off.
   A. cold chisel
   B. pry bar
   C. cross-cut chisel
   D. gasket scraper

_____ **8.** A _____ has the coarsest teeth, with approximately 20 teeth per 1 inch (25 mm). It is used when a lot of material must be removed quickly.
   A. coarse bastard file
   B. rough file
   C. second-cut file
   D. warding file

_____ **9.** The name for the _____ comes from its shape; it is used to hold parts together while they are being assembled, drilled, or welded.
   A. D-clamp
   B. F-clamp
   C. G-clamp
   D. P-clamp

_____ **10.** To cut a brand-new thread on a blank rod or shaft, you would use a(n) _____.
   A. tap
   B. die
   C. puller
   D. extractor

_____ **11.** When marks need to be drawn on an object such as a steel plate to help locate a hole to be drilled, a _____ is used to mark the points so they will not rub off.
   A. starter punch
   B. pin punch
   C. wad punch
   D. prick punch

_____ **12.** A(n) _____ is a device able to communicate electronically with and extract data from the vehicle's one or more on-board computers.
   A. scan tool
   B. dynamometer
   C. multimeter
   D. oscilloscope

_____ **13.** A waste recovery system is incorporated into _____ where contaminated washer fluids can be captured for environmentally friendly disposal.
   A. spray-wash cabinets
   B. brake washers
   C. solvent tanks
   D. pressure washers

_____ **14.** A _____ uses high pressure to blast small abrasive particles to clean the surface of parts.
   A. pressure washer
   B. spray-wash cabinet
   C. sand or bead blaster
   D. cleaning gun

_____ **15.** A(n) _____ is a break in the electrical circuit where either the power supply or earth circuit has been interrupted.
   A. open circuit
   B. short circuit
   C. grounded circuit
   D. All of the above

_____ **16.** Batteries are filled with a dangerous and corrosive liquid called _____.
   A. sulphuric acid
   B. hydrochloric acid
   C. muriatic acid
   D. nitric acid

_____ **17.** The purpose of engine oil is to _____.
   A. reduce unwanted friction
   B. cool the engine
   C. absorb shock loads
   D. All of the above

_____ **18.** Also known as mineral oil, _____ is used mainly as a cleaning agent in the automotive industry.
   A. petrol oil
   B. paraffin
   C. PAO oil
   D. ethylene

_____ **19.** An alloy of zinc and copper, _____ is used to make some metal nuts, bolts, and bushes.
   A. chrome
   B. brass
   C. tin
   D. cast iron

_____ **20.** When carbon and other materials are alloyed with iron they form _____.
   A. aluminum
   B. chrome
   C. graphite
   D. steel

True/False

If you believe the statement to be more true than false, write the letter "T" in the space provided. If you believe the statement to be more false than true, write the letter "F".

_____ **1.** Tools are identified as metric or imperial by markings identifying their sizes, or by the increments on measuring instruments.

_____ **2.** A micrometer should always be stored with its measuring surfaces touching in order to maintain its calibration.

_____ **3.** Morse taper is a system for securing drill bits to drills.

_____ **4.** Grinding wheels and discs usually have a maximum safe operating speed printed on them.

_____ **5.** An air hammer is not as efficient as a hand chisel and hammer for driving and cutting.

_____ **6.** Combination wrenches usually have either different-sized heads on each end of the wrench, or heads the same size but with different angles.

_____ **7.** Six- and 12-point sockets fit the heads of hexagonal-shaped fasteners. Four- and 8-point sockets fit the heads of square-shaped fasteners.

_____ **8.** Waterpump pliers are often called Channellocks, after the company that first made them.

_____ **9.** The most common screwdriver is the Phillips or Pozidriv screwdriver.

_____ **10.** A pry bar is designed to remove a gasket without damaging the sealing face of the component.

_____ **11.** A warding file is thinner than other files and comes to a point; it is used for working in narrow slots.

_____ **12.** A taper tap, known as a plug tap, is used to tap a thread into a hole that does not come out the other side of the material.

_____ **13.** A tube-flaring tool is used to flare the end of a tube so it can be connected to another tube or component.

_____ **14.** Blind rivets are so named because there is no need to see or reach the other side of the hole in which the rivet goes to do the work.

_____ **15.** The engine dynamometer measures engine performance through a vehicle's driven wheels.

_____ **16.** Pneumatic foot controls are usually used on a tire changer to allow both hands of the technician to be free to work on the tire.

_____ **17.** Oxyacetylene torches are used by technicians to heat, braze, weld, and cut metal.

_____ **18.** Slow battery chargers incorporate microprocessors to monitor and control the charge rate so that the battery receives the correct amount of charge according to its state of charge.

_____ **19.** Propylene glycol is a chemical that resists freezing but is very toxic to people and animals.

_____ **20.** Gear oil is the lubricant used in transmissions, transfer cases, and differentials.

Fill in the Blank

Read each item carefully, and then complete the statement by filling in the missing word(s).

1. A measuring _____ is a flexible type of ruler that is useful for measuring longer distances and is accurate to a millimeter or fraction of an inch.

2. A _____ ball gauge is good for measuring small holes where telescoping gauges cannot fit.

3. A _____ tool may be stationary, such as a bench grinder, or portable, such as a portable electric drill.

4. A drill _____ is a device for gripping drill bits securely in a drill.

5. A(n) _____ grinder uses discs rather than wheels.

6. The _____ wrench has an open-end head on one end and a closed-end head on the other. Both ends are usually the same size.

7. A speed _____ is the fastest way to spin a fastener on or off a thread by hand, but it cannot apply much torque to the fastener.

8. The traditional _____ wrench is a hexagonal bar with a right-angle bend at one end.

9. The _____ screwdriver fits into spaces where a straight screwdriver cannot and is useful where there is not much room to turn it.

10. Magnetic pickup tools and mechanical _____ are very useful for grabbing items in tight spaces.

11. The _____ is used for the general cutting of metals. The frames and blades are adjustable and rated according the number of teeth and hardness of the saw.

12. When materials are too awkward to grip vertically in a plain vice, it may be easier to use an offset _____.

13. Screw _____ are devices designed to remove screws, studs, or bolts that have broken off in threaded holes.

14. Gear _____ consist of three main parts: jaws, a cross-arm, and a forcing screw.

15. A typical _____ or blind rivet has a body, which forms the finished rivet, and a mandrel, which is discarded when the riveting is completed.

16. Pressure _____ gauges are a particular type of pressure gauge that measures "negative" pressure below atmospheric pressure.

17. Wheel _____ systems are often incorporated into a special-purpose vehicle hoist and use light beams with calibration equipment.

18. Automatic transmission fluid must lubricate the internal gears, bearings, and bushes of the transmission, yet have a large enough _____ of friction to allow the clutches to grab and not slip.

19. Diesel fuel oil is a derivative of _____ oil that is used to power diesel engines, also known as compression ignition or CI engines.

20. Like stainless steel, _____ is a bright, shiny corrosion-resistant metal and is used mostly for decorative purposes, such as on hubcaps.

Labeling

Label the following diagrams with the correct terms.

1. Identify the types of air tools:

A. _____

B. _____

C. _____

D. _____

E. _____

2. Identify the components of a socket:

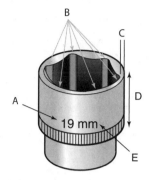

A. _____

B. _____

C. _____

D. _____

E. _____

F. _____

3. Identify the types of pliers:

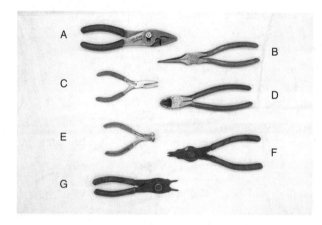

A. _____

B. _____

C. _____

D. _____

E. _____

F. _____

G. _____

4. Identify the types of hammers:

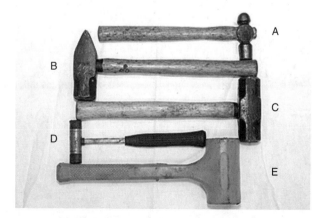

A. _____

B. _____

C. _____

D. _____

E. _____

5. Identify the components of a flare tool:

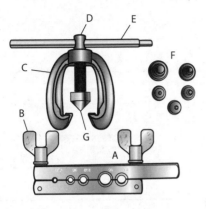

A. _____

B. _____

C. _____

D. _____

E. _____

F. _____

G. _____

Materials Used in the Vehicle Industry

Match the following materials used in the automotive industry with the correct description.

A. Bakelite
B. Cork
C. Fiberglass
D. Glass
E. Graphite

F. Melamine
G. Nylon
H. Perspex
I. Rubber
J. Silicone rubber

_____ **1.** A metal glass that is used in some timing belts.

_____ **2.** A synthetic rubber that is used for spark plug high-tension leads, seals, and gaskets.

_____ **3.** Used for windscreens, windows, and headlight coverings.

_____ **4.** A synthetic resin that was used primarily in the construction of distributor caps and rotors.

_____ **5.** A tough, clear plastic used as partitions on instrument panels. It resembles glass by its transparency.

_____ **6.** A black substance that is often used as an additive to grease or sprayed on, used as a lubricant in automotive applications.

_____ **7.** Used in the manufacture of tires.

_____ **8.** A synthetic plastic material that is used in the construction of some bushings.

_____ **9.** Often used in combination with rubber to form gaskets for engine blocks.

_____ **10.** A compound used to make synthetic resins and used for moulding some lightweight vehicle body parts.

Skill Drills

Test your knowledge of skill drills by filling in the correct words in the photo captions.

1. Measuring Using an Outside Micrometer:

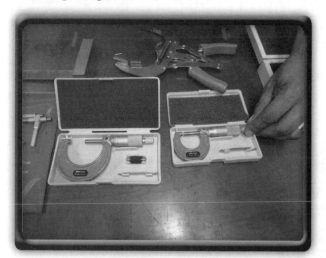

Step 1: Select the correct _____ of micrometer. Verify that the _____ and _____ are _____ and that it is _____ properly.

Step 2: _____ the _____ of the part you are measuring.

Step 3: In your _____ hand, hold the _____ of the micrometer between your little finger, _____ finger, and palm of your hand, with the _____ between your thumb and forefinger.

Step 4: With your _____ hand, hold the part you are measuring and place the _____ over it.

Step 5: Using your _____ and forefinger, lightly _____ the ratchet. It is important that the correct amount of force is applied to the _____ when taking a measurement. The spindle and _____ should just _____ the component, with a slight amount of _____ when the micrometer is removed from the measured piece. Be careful that the part is _____ in the micrometer so the reading is correct. Try _____ the micrometer in all directions to make sure it is square.

Step 6: Once the micrometer is properly _____, tighten the _____ mechanism so the _____ will not turn.

Step 7: Read the micrometer and _____ your reading.

Step 8: When all readings are finished, _____ the micrometer, position the spindle so it is _____ _____ from the anvil and return it to its protective case.

2. Measuring Using a Dial Bore Gauge:

Step 1: Select the correct _____ of the dial bore gauge you will use and fit any _____ to it.

Step 2: Check the _____ and adjust it as necessary.

Step 3: Insert the dial bore gauge into the _____. The accurate measurement will be at exactly _____ degrees to the bore. To find the accurate measurement, _____ the dial bore gauge _____ slightly back and forth until you find the centered position.

Step 4: Read the _____ to determine the bore _____.

Step 5: Always _____ the dial bore gauge and return it to its _____ _____ when you have finished using it.

3. Measuring Using Vernier Callipers:

Step 1: Verify that the vernier calliper is _____ (zeroed) before using it. If it is not zeroed, _____ your mentor, who will get you a _____ vernier calliper.

Step 2: Position the _____ correctly for the measurement you are making. Internal and external readings are normally made with the vernier calliper positioned at _____ degrees to the _____ of the component to be measured. Length and _____ measurements are usually made _____ to or in line with the object being measured. Use your thumb to press or withdraw the _____ _____ to measure the outside or inside of the part.

Step 3: Read the _____ of the vernier calliper, being careful not to change the position of the _____ _____. Always read the dial or face _____ on. A view from the _____ can give a considerable parallax error. Parallax error is a visual error caused by viewing measurement markers at an incorrect _____.

4. Measuring Using a Dial Indicator:

Step 1: Select the gauge type, size, attachment, and _____ that fit the part you are measuring. Mount the dial indicator _____ to keep it _____.

Step 2: Adjust the _____ so that the _____ is at 90 degrees to the part you are measuring and _____ it in place.

Step 3:   _____ the part one complete turn and locate the _____ spot. _____ the indicator.

Step 4:   Find the point of maximum _____ and note the reading. This will indicate the _____-_____ value.

Step 5:   Continue the _____ and make sure the _____ does not go below zero. If it does, _____ the indicator and remeasure the point of _____ variation.

Step 6:   Check your readings against the manufacturer's _____. If the _____ is _____ than the specifications allow, consult your supervisor.

Crossword Puzzle

Use the clues in the column to complete the puzzle.

Across

3. The shaft of a pop rivet.

5. Precise measuring tools designed to measure small distances and are available in both millimeter (mm) and inch calibrations.

6. A term used to generically describe an internal thread-cutting tool.

8. Tools powered by electricity or compressed air.

9. A generic term to describe tools that tighten and loosen fasteners with hexagonal heads.

10. A device that converts and stores electrical energy through chemical reactions.

Down

1. A renewable fuel made by chemically combining natural oils from soybeans (or cottonseeds, canola, etc.; animal fats; or even recycled cooking oil) with an alcohol such as methanol (or ethanol).

2. Also called feeler blades; flat metal strips used to measure the width of gaps, such as the clearance between valves and rocker arms.

4. Pliers designed to cut protruding items level with the surface.

7. A highly flammable liquid that can dissolve other substances.

ASE-Type Questions

Read each item carefully, and then select the best response.

_____ **1.** Technician A says that you would use an outside micrometer to measure the bottom of a cylinder. Technician B says that you would use a telescoping gauge to measure the bottom of a cylinder. Who is correct?
   A. Technician A
   B. Technician B
   C. Both Technician A and Technician B
   D. Neither Technician A nor Technician B

_____ **2.** Technician A says to use nippers to cut through soft metal. Technician B says to use an Allen key. Who is correct?
   A. Technician A
   B. Technician B
   C. Both Technician A and Technician B
   D. Neither Technician A nor Technician B

_____ **3.** Technician A says pressure compression gauges are used to measure the compression pressures inside an engine cylinder. Technician B says pressure compression gauges can identify overall condition and pressure leakage situations that could be caused by a range of engine faults. Who is correct?
   A. Technician A
   B. Technician B
   C. Both Technician A and Technician B
   D. Neither Technician A nor Technician B

_____ **4.** Technician A says the most commonly used pair of pliers in the shop is the needle-nosed plier. Technician B says the most common is the snap-ring plier. Who is correct?
   A. Technician A
   B. Technician B
   C. Both Technician A and Technician B
   D. Neither Technician A nor Technician B

_____ **5.** Technician A says bolt cutters cut hardened rods. Technician B says tin snips can cut thin sheet metal. Who is correct?
   A. Technician A
   B. Technician B
   C. Both Technician A and Technician B
   D. Neither Technician A nor Technician B

_____ **6.** Technician A says that a drift punch is also named a starter punch because you should always use it first to get a pin moving. Technician B says a center punch centers a drill bit at the point where a hole is required to be drilled. Who is correct?
   A. Technician A
   B. Technician B
   C. Both Technician A and Technician B
   D. Neither Technician A nor Technician B

_____ **7.** Technician A states that a tap handle has a right angled jaw that matches the squared end that all taps have. Technician B states that to cut a thread in an awkward space, a T-shaped tap handle is very convenient. Who is correct?
   A. Technician A
   B. Technician B
   C. Both Technician A and Technician B
   D. Neither Technician A nor Technician B

_____ **8.** Technician A states that there are many applications for blind rivets, and various rivet types and tools may be used to do the riveting. Technician B states that a typical pop or blind rivet has a body, which will form the finished rivet, and a mandrel, which is discarded when the riveting is complete. Who is correct?
   A. Technician A
   B. Technician B
   C. Both Technician A and Technician B
   D. Neither Technician A nor Technician B

_____ **9.** Technician A says a battery could discharge if the vehicle is not started for as little as one month due to normal vehicle drains. Technician B says slow charging a battery is less stressful on a battery than fast charging. Who is correct?
   A. Technician A
   B. Technician B
   C. Both Technician A and Technician B
   D. Neither Technician A nor Technician B

_____ **10.** Technician A says engine oil reduces wear on moving parts. Technician B says engine oil absorbs shock loads. Who is correct?
   A. Technician A
   B. Technician B
   C. Both Technician A and Technician B
   D. Neither Technician A nor Technician B

Fasteners, Locking Devices, and Lifting Equipment

Chapter Review

The following activities have been designed to help you refresh your knowledge of this chapter. Your instructor may require you to complete some or all of these activities as a regular part of your training program. You are encouraged to complete any activity that your instructor does not assign as a way to enhance your learning.

Matching

Match the following terms with the correct description or example.

- **A.** Allen head screw
- **B.** Bolt
- **C.** Fasteners
- **D.** Flat washers
- **E.** Screws

- **F.** Taper key
- **G.** Tensile strength
- **H.** Torque
- **I.** Torx bolt
- **J.** Vehicle hoist

_____ **1.** Devices that securely hold items together, such as screws, cotter pins, rivets, and bolts.

_____ **2.** In reference to fasteners, the amount of force it takes before a fastener breaks.

_____ **3.** A type of vehicle lifting tool designed to lift the entire vehicle.

_____ **4.** Spread the load of a bolt head or a nut as it is tightened and distribute it over a greater area.

_____ **5.** A type of threaded fastener with a thread on one end and a hexagonal head on the other.

_____ **6.** Often found in vehicle engines in places such as cylinder heads to blocks, where particular tightening sequences are required.

_____ **7.** Usually smaller than bolts and are sometimes referred to as metal threads. They can have a variety of heads and are used on smaller components.

_____ **8.** Sometimes called a cap screw, it has a hexagonal recess in the head, which fits a hex wrench.

_____ **9.** Used to prevent the free rotation of gears or pulleys on a shaft; used to anchor a pulley to a shaft or a disc to a driving shaft.

_____ **10.** The twisting force applied to a shaft that may or may not result in motion.

Multiple Choice

Read each item carefully, and then select the best response.

_____ **1.** A self-locking or _____ nut is highly resistant to being loosened by the kind of vibration that engines and vehicles experience.
- **A.** torx
- **B.** castellated
- **C.** nylock
- **D.** spring

_____ **2.** When a _____ nut is screwed onto a bolt that has been drilled in the right spot, a split pin can be passed through them both and then spread open to lock the nut in place.
- **A.** castellated
- **B.** spring
- **C.** nylock
- **D.** shake proof

_____ 3. The external version of a _____ has teeth on the outside and the internal version has teeth on the inside; one type has both.
  A. tab washer
  B. serrated edge shake-proof washers
  C. castellated washer
  D. torx washer

_____ 4. Bolts, nuts, and studs are designated by their _____.
  A. thread diameter
  B. grade
  C. pitch
  D. All of the above

_____ 5. The coarseness of any thread is called its _____.
  A. depth
  B. pitch
  C. grade
  D. tensile strength

_____ 6. Torque value is specified in _____.
  A. foot pounds
  B. megapascals
  C. newton meters
  D. Either A or C

_____ 7. As long as a bolt is not tightened too much, it will return to its original length when loosened. This is called _____.
  A. yield
  B. torque
  C. elasticity
  D. stretch

_____ 8. A torqueing procedure called _____ is considered a more precise method to tighten torque-to-yield bolts using a multistep process.
  A. torque angle
  B. sequencing
  C. torque gauging
  D. pitch gauging

_____ 9. Used to keep components in place where shearing forces are high _____ are used in high-pressure pumps to keep valve plates anchored in position.
  A. taper pins
  B. rawl pins
  C. dowel pins
  D. split pins

_____ 10. A _____ is usually attached to levers that have to slide along a shaft to allow engagement of a part.
  A. feather key
  B. parallel key
  C. taper key
  D. gibb-head key

_____ 11. A _____ is designed to be pulled out easily and is used when a gear or a pulley has to be attached to a shaft.
  A. taper key
  B. feather key
  C. gibb-head key
  D. parallel key

_____ 12. A(n) _____ is designed to conduct heat laterally to transfer heat from the combustion chamber to the coolant faster.
  A. sealing bead
  B. anisotropic gasket
  C. O-ring
  D. fire ring

_____ **13.** Mechanical seals called _____ are used to seal holes in the engine block that were left during original manufacture to remove the sand core during the casting process.
- **A.** welch plugs
- **B.** stopper plugs
- **C.** core plugs
- **D.** Either A or C

_____ **14.** Slings are normally made out of _____.
- **A.** webbing material
- **B.** wire rope
- **C.** chain
- **D.** All of the above

_____ **15.** A(n) _____ is a common type of hydraulic jack that is mounted on four wheels, two of which swivel to provide a steering mechanism.
- **A.** sliding-bridge jack
- **B.** floor jack
- **C.** bottle jack
- **D.** air jack

True/False

If you believe the statement to be more true than false, write the letter "T" in the space provided. If you believe the statement to be more false than true, write the letter "F".

_____ **1.** Bolts are always threaded into a nut or hole that has an identical thread cut inside.

_____ **2.** Studs can have different threads on each end.

_____ **3.** On both metric and imperial bolts the size indicates the diameter of the bolt head.

_____ **4.** The higher a bolt's grade number, the lower the tensile strength.

_____ **5.** Torque-to-yield bolts cannot be reused because they have been stretched into their yield zone and would very likely fail if re-torqued.

_____ **6.** A helical insert is used to repair damaged bolt holes.

_____ **7.** Parallel keys are used to anchor a pulley to a shaft or a disc to a driving shaft.

_____ **8.** The most widely used seal for rotating parts is the lip-type dynamic oil seal.

_____ **9.** O-rings are generally effective at sealing high pressures where the differential speed between the opposing surfaces is minimal.

_____ **10.** In engines that use a timing chain or timing gears the front main seal is located in a housing bolted to the front of the engine block.

_____ **11.** For cork, felt, or neoprene gaskets, a light coat of adhesive spray is used on each surface of the block and the gasket.

_____ **12.** Sliding-bridge jacks are specialized jacks for lifting and lowering transmissions during removal and installation.

_____ **13.** Every vehicle hoist in the workshop must have a built-in mechanical locking device so the vehicle hoist can be secured at the chosen height after the vehicle is raised.

_____ **14.** Once you drive a vehicle over an inspection pit you can inspect and service the vehicle underside without fear of the vehicle toppling over.

_____ **15.** A crane is only as good as the slings connecting it to the equipment to be moved.

Fill in the Blank

Read each item carefully, and then complete the statement by filling in the missing word(s).

1. A(n) _____-_____ screw is made of a hard material that cuts a mirror image of itself into the hole as you turn it.

2. A(n) _____ nut does not need to be held when started but it is not as strong as a conventional nut.

3. A flat _____ is used to protect the surface underneath from being marked by the nut or head as it turns and tightens down.

4. The metric system uses _____ stamped on the heads of metric bolts and on the face of metric nuts.

5. A(n) _____-_____ compound neutralizes the chemical reaction that causes some metals to react with each other and bind together.

6. If a bolt continues to be tightened and stretched beyond its _____ point, it will not return to its original length when loosened.

7. _____ pins are often used to hold components on rotating shafts.

8. The _____ gasket seals and contains the pressures of combustion within the engine, between the cylinder head and the engine block.

9. To seal the rotating parts of an engine, a(n) _____ seal is needed.

10. Room temperature _____ oxygen-safe silicone is used to help seal fiber gaskets and gasket joints.

11. The maximum operating capacity of lifting equipment is usually expressed as the safe _____ _____.

12. Chain blocks and mobile _____ are often used together to lift larger components inside heavy vehicle workshops.

13. Jack _____ are adjustable supports used with vehicle jacks designed to support a vehicle's weight once a vehicle has been raised by a vehicle jack.

14. A(n) _____ lifting hoist provides workshop flexibility as they can be easily moved to any area of a standard workshop floor.

15. An engine _____, or mobile floor crane, is capable of lifting very heavy objects, such as engines while they are being removed from a vehicle.

Labeling

Label the following diagrams with the correct terms.

1. Identify the bolt dimensions:

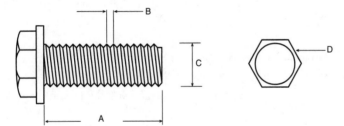

A. _____

B. _____

C. _____

D. _____

2. Identify the washer types:

A. _____

B. _____

C. _____

D. _____

3. Identify the types of locking keys:

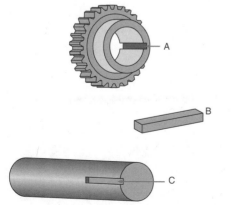

A. _____

B. _____

C. _____

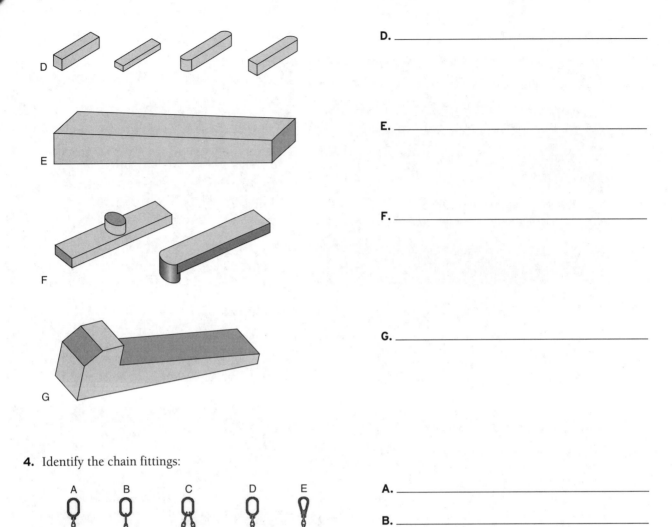

D. _____

E. _____

F. _____

G. _____

4. Identify the chain fittings:

A. _____

B. _____

C. _____

D. _____

E. _____

Skill Drills

Test your knowledge of skill drills by filling in the correct words in the photo captions.

1. Using a Torque Wrench and Torque Angle Gauge:

Step 1:   Identify the _____ _____ either through the manufacturer's specifications or, in some cases, stretch bolts themselves have a specific _____ on the head of the bolt. In addition, the diameter of the _____ of the bolt is _____ than the threaded diameter.

Step 2:   Check the specifications. Determine the correct _____ value and _____ for the bolts or fastener you are using. This will be in _____ -pounds (ft-lb). Also check the torque _____ specifications for the bolt or fastener, and whether the procedure is one step or more than one step.

Step 3:   Tighten the _____ to the specified torque. If the component requires _____ bolts or fasteners, make sure to _____ them all to the same _____ _____ in the sequence and follow the _____ that are specified by the manufacturer. Some torqueing procedures could call for _____ or more steps to complete the torqueing process.

2. Fitting a Formed Head Gasket:

Step 1:   Obtain an assembly that will need a gasket _____, in this case the _____ gasket.

Step 2:   Remove the _____ _____ and keep track of the head _____.

Step 3:   Remove the old _____.

Step 4:   Clean the mating _____ with the proper cleaning _____.

Step 5:   Select a _____ according to the manufacturer's _____.

Step 6:   Inspect the gasket for _____ or other _____.

Step 7:   Select a _____ that is manufacturer recommended.

Step 8:   Spread the _____ on the _____ surfaces according to the manufacturer's specifications.

Step 9:   Align the _____ with the mating surface.

Step 10: Assemble the components and tighten the _____ to their _____ specification and tightening _____.

3. Removing and Replacing Lip-Type Seals:

Step 1:   Use a component that requires a _____-_____ seal, usually a _____.

Step 2:   Inspect the assembly for _____, sharp _____, or _____.

Step 3:   _____ the assembly and assess seal _____.

Step 4:   Seal failure can include a broken _____ _____ or a _____ component at the sealing surface.

Step 5:   Remove the seal with an oil seal _____.

Step 6:   Measure and record the housing _____ diameter, the _____ diameter, and _____ of the seal landing.

Step 7:   Select the recommended _____ seal.

Step 8:   Compare the _____ seal with the _____ to make sure they are the same _____.

Step 9:   Lubricate the _____ and the seal with clean _____ before fitting the new _____ over the shaft, making sure that the seal _____ faces into the housing.

Step 10: Locate the seal in the _____ according to the manufacturer's specifications.

Step 11: Press the seal into the housing with the sealing lip _____ the fluid being sealed.

Step 12: Use a _____to make sure the seal is snugly fit.

Step 13: Check the installation and make sure the _____ _____ is correct.

4. Lifting a Vehicle Using a Hydraulic Hoist:

Step 1:   Read and follow the safety instructions that are provided with the four-post hoist. They should be displayed near the lift operating _____. Also verify the vehicle's _____ and compare it against the hoist's safe load _____. Check the hydraulic system for any _____ and the steel cables for any sign of _____. Make sure there are no oil _____ around or under the hoist. The four-post hoist should be completely _____ before you attempt to drive the vehicle onto it.

Step 2:   The platform may have built-in wheel _____ or attachments for wheel _____ equipment. A set of bars is normally mounted at the _____ of each ramp to prevent the vehicle from being _____ off the front of the four-post hoist. At the back will be _____ that allow the vehicle to be driven onto the four-post hoist. The back of the ramps will _____ upwards when the hoist is _____ and prevent the vehicle from _____ off the back.

Step 3:   Prepare to use the vehicle hoist _____. With the aid of an assistant _____ the driver, or a large _____ in front of the hoist, drive the vehicle _____ and _____ onto the four-post hoist and position it centrally. If the vehicle has front wheel _____, drive the vehicle forward until the _____ lock into the _____.

Step 4:   Get out of the vehicle and check that it is correctly _____ on the platform. If it is, apply the _____ _____.

Step 5:   Make sure the hydraulic hoist area is _____. Move to the controls and _____ the vehicle until it reaches the appropriate _____ height. If the four-post hoist has a manual _____ mechanism, lock it in place to _____ whatever _____ device is used.

Step 6:   Before the four-post hoist is _____, remove all _____ and _____ from the area and _____ up any spilled _____. Remove the safety device or _____ the lift before lowering it. Make sure no one is near the area. Once the four-post hoist is fully lowered, carefully _____ the vehicle off the hoist with the help of a _____.

5. Using Engine Hoists and Stands:

Step 1:   Prepare to use the engine _____. Lower the _____ _____ and position the lifting end and chain over the _____ of the engine.

Step 2:   Wear appropriate PPE, such as _____ _____, during the entire operation, beginning with _____ the chain, steel cable, or sling, and bolts to make sure they are in good condition. Before you use the crane, make sure the chain/sling is rated _____ than the weight of the item to be lifted. Also _____ that the lifting arm is only extended to the length of its lifting _____ applicable to the weight of the item to be lifted. Only use _____ lifting equipment, nothing homemade. Look carefully around the component that is about to be lifted to determine if it has _____ _____ or other anchor points.

Step 3:   If the engine or component has _____ _____, attach the _____ with D-_____ or chain _____. If you need to screw in _____ and spacer _____ to lift the engine, make sure you use the correct bolt and spacer _____ for the chain or cable. Screw the bolts until the _____ is held _____ against the component.

Step 4:   Attach the hoist's _____ under the _____ of the sling and raise the engine hoist just enough to lift the engine to take the _____ up on the cable, chain, or sling. Double-check the sling and attachment points for _____. The engine's or component's _____ _____ _____ should be directly under the engine hoist's hook, and there should be no _____ or _____ in the chain or sling.

Step 5:   _____ the engine hoist until the engine is clear of the _____ and any obstacles. Slowly and _____ move the engine hoist and lifted component to the new location with _____ ground clearance to prevent _____ and potential _____ of the whole crane.

Step 6:   Make sure the engine is _____ correctly. You may need to place _____ under the engine to stabilize it. Once you are sure the engine is _____, lower the engine hoist and _____ the _____ and any securing fasteners. Finally, return the equipment to its _____ area.

Crossword Puzzle

Use the clues in the column to complete the puzzle.

Across

1. A tool used to measure the rotational or twisting force applied to fasteners.
2. Usually smaller than bolts and are sometimes referred to as metal threads. They can have a variety of heads and are used on smaller components. The thread often extends from the tip to the head so they can hold together components of variable thickness.
5. A washer that compresses as the nut tightens; the nut is spring loaded against this surface, which makes it unlikely to work loose.
6. A type of vehicle jack that uses oil under pressure to lift vehicles.
7. Helps prevent fasteners from loosening; it is applied to one thread, then the other fastener is screwed onto it. This creates a strong bond between them, but one that stays plastic, so they can be separated by a wrench.

Down

1. A certificate issued when lifting equipment has been checked and deemed safe.
3. A metal spring wrapped circularly around the inside of a lip seal to keep it in constant contact with the moving shaft.
4. Used to prevent the free rotation of gears or pulleys on a shaft and can be used to secure a gear wheel on its shaft.
5. A type of threaded fastener with a thread cut on each end, as opposed to having a bolt head on one end.

ASE-Type Questions

Read each item carefully, and then select the best response.

_____ **1.** Technician A says seals are usually used on stationary components and gaskets are used on rotating parts. Technician B says seals are usually used on rotating parts whereas gaskets are used for stationary components. Who is correct?
   A. Technician A
   B. Technician B
   C. Both Technician A and Technician B
   D. Neither Technician A nor Technician B

_____ **2.** Technician A says the purpose of gaskets and seals is to keep critical fluids from leaking and to keep contaminants out. Technician B disagrees. Who is correct?
   A. Technician A
   B. Technician B
   C. Both Technician A and Technician B
   D. Neither Technician A nor Technician B

_____ **3.** Technician A says a garter spring is used in lip-type seals. Technician B says it is used to maintain high pressure without fluid leaking. Who is correct?
   A. Technician A
   B. Technician B
   C. Both Technician A and Technician B
   D. Neither Technician A nor Technician B

_____ **4.** Technician A says that hoists should be inspected and certified periodically. Technician B says that safety locks do not need to be applied before working under a vehicle, unless you will be working for more than 10 minutes. Who is correct?
   A. Technician A
   B. Technician B
   C. Both Technician A and Technician B
   D. Neither Technician A nor Technician B

_____ **5.** Technician A says that an engine sling should have an angle greater than 90 degrees. Technician B says that all slings and lifting chains should be inspected for damage prior to use. Who is correct?
   A. Technician A
   B. Technician B
   C. Both Technician A and Technician B
   D. Neither Technician A nor Technician B

_____ **6.** Technician A says that you should have a co-worker help guide you onto an inspection pit. Technician B says that all lights should be on in the pit before driving over it. Who is correct?
   A. Technician A
   B. Technician B
   C. Both Technician A and Technician B
   D. Neither Technician A nor Technician B

_____ **7.** Technician A says if a fastener is overtightened, it could become damaged or could break. Technician B says if a fastener is undertightened, it is likely to be satisfactory. Who is correct?
   A. Technician A
   B. Technician B
   C. Both Technician A and Technician B
   D. Neither Technician A nor Technician B

_____ **8.** Technician A says torque specifications for bolts and nuts in vehicles will usually be contained within workshop manuals. Technician B says that in practice, most torque specifications call for the nuts and bolts to have oiled threads prior to tightening. Who is correct?
   A. Technician A
   B. Technician B
   C. Both Technician A and Technician B
   D. Neither Technician A nor Technician B

_____ **9.** Technician A says one of the tools used to repair damaged bolt holes is the helical insert, more commonly known by its trademark, Heli-coil. Technician B says Heli-coils are made of coiled wire and are inserted into a tapped hole that is larger than the desired hole. Who is correct?

    A. Technician A

    B. Technician B

    C. Both Technician A and Technician B

    D. Neither Technician A nor Technician B

_____ **10.** Technician A says a MLS head gasket has multiple layers that provide superior combustion sealing. Technician B says one of the most critical gaskets in automotive applications is the head gasket. Who is correct?

    A. Technician A

    B. Technician B

    C. Both Technician A and Technician B

    D. Neither Technician A nor Technician B

Principles of Electricity

Chapter Review

The following activities have been designed to help you refresh your knowledge of this chapter. Your instructor may require you to complete some or all of these activities as a regular part of your training program. You are encouraged to complete any activity that your instructor does not assign as a way to enhance your learning.

Matching

Match the following terms with the correct description or example.

A. Ampere (amp)   **D.** Ohm

B. Ground   **E.** Volt

C. Hertz

_____ **1.** The return path for electrical current in a vehicle chassis, other metal of the vehicle, or dedicated wire.

_____ **2.** The unit for measuring electrical resistance.

_____ **3.** The unit for measuring the quantity of electron flow past one point in a circuit per unit of time.

_____ **4.** The unit used to measure potential difference or electrical pressure.

_____ **5.** The unit for electrical frequency measurement, in cycles per second.

Multiple Choice

Read each item carefully, and then select the best response.

_____ **1.** The theory that negative charges are attracted to positive charges, and like charges are repelled by one another is known as _____.

    A. electrical resistance theory

    B. electrostatic theory

    C. Ohm's law

    D. conventional current theory

_____ **2.** The nucleus of an atom is composed of _____.

    A. neutrons and protons

    B. neutrons and electrons

    C. protons and electrons

    D. electrons, protons, and neutrons

_____ **3.** Materials that hold electrons tightly and prevent electron movement are called _____.

    A. conductors

    B. insulators

    C. resistors

    D. ions

_____ **4.** Electrons can be moved on or off of an atom using force created by _____.

    A. light

    B. friction

    C. chemical energy

    D. All of the above

_____ **5.** Anything that slows down the speed of electron movement is considered a(n) _____.
   A. insulator
   B. restrictor
   C. resistor
   D. isolator

_____ **6.** The _____ determines the amount of resistance in a circuit.
   A. diameter of the conductor
   B. temperature of the conductor
   C. length of the conductor
   D. All of the above

_____ **7.** Voltage = Resistance × Amperage represents the mathematical relationship known as _____.
   A. Ohm's law
   B. Kirchhoff's law
   C. Watt's law
   D. Joule's law

_____ **8.** When electrons move only in one direction in a circuit, the current is described as being _____.
   A. positive voltage
   B. direct current
   C. negative voltage
   D. grounded

_____ **9.** The transformation that occurs during the heating effect of current is measured in _____.
   A. joules
   B. ohms
   C. volts
   D. amperes

_____ **10.** A basic semiconductor is made from a _____.
   A. P-type material
   B. MOS-type material
   C. N-type material
   D. Both A and C

True/False

If you believe the statement to be more true than false, write the letter "T" in the space provided. If you believe the statement to be more false than true, write the letter "F".

_____ **1.** Today's electrical system components are no longer separated into distinct systems.

_____ **2.** A proton (+) charge attracts another proton (+) charge.

_____ **3.** Neutrons are the electrical glue that prevents the electrostatic forces of repulsion between the protons from bursting away from the nucleus.

_____ **4.** If an atom loses or gains an electron, it is called an ion.

_____ **5.** Atoms with the highest number of electrons in its outer shell are the best conductors.

_____ **6.** When describing the flow of electricity, a circuit's voltage and amperage together is called electric current.

_____ **7.** The higher the temperature the lower the resistance.

_____ **8.** One volt of electrical pressure is required to push one amp of current through a circuit if the circuit has a resistance of one ohm.

_____ **9.** If resistance is held constant in a circuit then amperage will increase if voltage increases.

_____ **10.** Electrons will always move toward a negative pole.

Fill in the Blank

Read each item carefully, and then complete the statement by filling in the missing word(s).

1. Electricity is the movement of particles from one place to another pushed or pulled by _____ force.

2. Electrons travel in different layers or _____ around the nucleus.

3. Electrical _____ is a material's property that reduces voltage and amperage in an electrical current.

4. Only _____ can be moved on and off an atom to create either a negative or positive electric charge.

5. The idea that electric current movement takes place when positive charges move to a negative pole is called _____ current theory.

6. When electrons are alternately pulled and pushed, the type of current flow produced is described as _____ current.

7. Plotting AC voltage on a graph produces what is called a(n) _____.

8. A device known as a(n) _____ is used to change direct current into alternating current.

9. A(n) _____ can have properties of both conductors and insulators and can switch back and forth between either state using small electrostatic charges.

10. Field effect transistors made from metal oxides are abbreviated _____ and are one of the most common types of transistors used in circuit boards.

Labeling

Label the following diagrams with the correct terms.

1. Identify the architecture components of a contemporary truck electrical system:

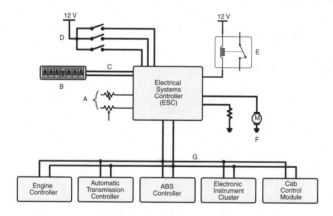

A. _____

B. _____

C. _____

D. _____

E. _____

F. _____

G. _____

2. Identify the concepts of electrical current flow.

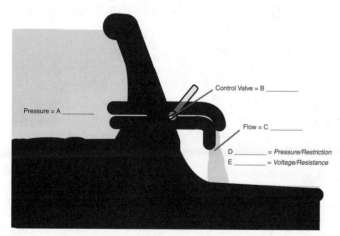

A. _____

B. _____

C. _____

D. _____

E. _____

Crossword Puzzle

Use the clues in the column to complete the puzzle.

Across

1. The state of charge, positive or negative.

5. A material that can have properties of both conductors and insulators and that can switch back and forth between either state using small electrostatic charges.

6. The measurement of the quantity of electrons in electric current movement.

Down

2. A component designed to produce electrical resistance.

3. A material that easily allows electricity to flow through it. It is made up of atoms with very few outer shell electrons, which are loosely held by the nucleus.

4. The speed at which electrons travel from atom to atom.

ASE-Type Questions

Read each item carefully, and then select the best response.

_____ 1. Technician A says there are two theories of current flow: the electron theory and the conventional theory. Technician B says it is important to remember that current flow is described by both concepts. Who is correct?

A. Technician A

B. Technician B

C. Both Technician A and Technician B

D. Neither Technician A nor Technician B

_____ 2. Technician A says AC circuits are used in virtually all chassis circuits because a battery can easily store and supply AC current. Technician B says DC current is used to power hybrid drive electric motors. Who is correct?

A. Technician A

B. Technician B

C. Both Technician A and Technician B

D. Neither Technician A nor Technician B

_____ 3. Technician A says AC current's main advantage is that it can be transmitted farther distances with less resistance and little voltage drop. Technician B says the term resistance is used with AC circuits as well as DC circuits. Who is correct?

A. Technician A

B. Technician B

C. Both Technician A and Technician B

D. Neither Technician A nor Technician B

_____ 4. Technician A says when an electric current travels through a bulb filament or electric heating element, the filament or resistive element heats. Technician B says resistance in the elements converts electrical energy into heat energy. Who is correct?

A. Technician A

B. Technician B

C. Both Technician A and Technician B

D. Neither Technician A nor Technician B

_____ 5. Technician A says electronic circuits use less amperage and often process signals rather than perform the work of lighting, heating, and moving. Technician B says electrical circuits usually conduct higher amounts of current through heavier conductors and commonly operate devices such as solenoids, relays, motors, lights, and more. Who is correct?

A. Technician A

B. Technician B

C. Both Technician A and Technician B

D. Neither Technician A nor Technician B

_____ 6. Technician A says metal oxide semiconductors are used in MOS-type transistors and microprocessors. Technician B says MOS types have less resistance and conduct more current than the older semiconductor materials. Who is correct?

A. Technician A

B. Technician B

C. Both Technician A and Technician B

D. Neither Technician A nor Technician B

_____ 7. Technician A says two types of materials make up a basic semiconductor. Technician B says the two types are R-type and M-type. Who is correct?

A. Technician A

B. Technician B

C. Both Technician A and Technician B

D. Neither Technician A nor Technician B

_____ **8.** Technician A says today's electrical system components are no longer separated into distinct systems. Technician B says networking electrical system components add new vehicle features that can enhance safety, performance, and passenger comfort. Who is correct?

    A. Technician A

    B. Technician B

    C. Both Technician A and Technician B

    D. Neither Technician A nor Technician B

_____ **9.** Technician A says all questions about the nature of electricity lead to the composition of matter. Technician B says the movement of electrons from one atom to another is called electricity. Who is correct?

    A. Technician A

    B. Technician B

    C. Both Technician A and Technician B

    D. Neither Technician A nor Technician B

_____ **10.** Technician A says metal typically have lots of easily moved electrons, which make them good conductors. Technician B says liquids cannot function as a conductor. Who is correct?

    A. Technician A

    B. Technician B

    C. Both Technician A and Technician B

    D. Neither Technician A nor Technician B

Generating Electricity

Chapter Review

The following activities have been designed to help you refresh your knowledge of this chapter. Your instructor may require you to complete some or all of these activities as a regular part of your training program. You are encouraged to complete any activity that your instructor does not assign as a way to enhance your learning.

Matching

Match the following terms with the correct description or example.

A. Electromagnetic induction

B. Fuel cell

C. Photovoltaic (PV) effect

D. Piezoelectric effect

E. Secondary winding

_____ **1.** A type of electricity produced by bending or squeezing a unique type of quartz crystal.

_____ **2.** The production of an electrical current in a conductor when it moves through a magnetic field or a magnetic field moves past it.

_____ **3.** The coil of wire in which high voltage is induced in a step-up transformer.

_____ **4.** An electrochemical device that combines hydrogen and oxygen to produce electricity and water.

_____ **5.** The conversion of light into electricity.

Multiple Choice

Read each item carefully, and then select the best response.

_____ **1.** Which of the following methods can be used to produce electron flow?
   A. Light
   B. Heat
   C. Friction
   D. All of the above

_____ **2.** Producing electricity using friction is known as _____.
   A. triboelectricity
   B. electrolysis
   C. piezoelectricity
   D. induction

_____ **3.** Which of the following materials is most likely to lose electrons?
   A. Rubber
   B. Silicon
   C. Glass
   D. Copper

_____ **4.** Commercially available _____ cells are sometimes used as trickle chargers for batteries.
   A. electromagnetic
   B. thermoelectric
   C. photovoltaic
   D. piezoelectric

_____ **5.** A thermocouple works by measuring the incremental increase in exhaust temperature through _____ changes produced by the pyrometer.
- **A.** voltage
- **B.** amperage
- **C.** resistance
- **D.** wattage

_____ **6.** Examples of the application of _____ energy include microphones, speaker tweeters, and the sparking lighters that ignite the gas in barbecue grills.
- **A.** photovoltaic
- **B.** piezoelectric
- **C.** thermoelectric
- **D.** electromagnetic induction

_____ **7.** The creation of an electrical voltage by moving a conductor through a magnetic field is known as _____.
- **A.** piezoelectric energy
- **B.** electrolysis
- **C.** transformer action
- **D.** electromagnetic induction

_____ **8.** Opposition or resistance to magnetic lines of force is known as _____.
- **A.** flux
- **B.** friction
- **C.** reluctance
- **D.** induction

_____ **9.** The phenomenon of _____ explains why network data bus wires use a twisted pair of wires to carry low-voltage serial data.
- **A.** mutual induction
- **B.** variable reluctance
- **C.** transformer action
- **D.** piezoelectric effect

_____ **10.** Corrosion is an example of a(n) _____ reaction.
- **A.** inductive
- **B.** galvanic
- **C.** reactive
- **D.** Both A and C

True/False

If you believe the statement to be more true than false, write the letter "T" in the space provided. If you believe the statement to be more false than true, write the letter "F".

_____ **1.** Static electricity can be induced by rubbing two materials together.

_____ **2.** Grounding oneself using a special bracelet or anklet is a standard practice while handling unconnected integrated circuits.

_____ **3.** One of the most common ways electricity is produced on a heavy-duty vehicle is through the use of thermoelectric induction.

_____ **4.** Magnetism can produce electricity, and electricity can produce magnetism.

_____ **5.** Alternators, generators, and speed sensors use electromagnetic induction to produce electrical current.

_____ **6.** The polarity of induced current flow is the same as that of the current that induced the original magnetic field.

_____ **7.** The primary winding is the coil of wire in which voltage is induced.

_____ **8.** Tap water would be considered an electrolyte if it contains minerals or chlorine.

_____ **9.** Just like a battery, a fuel cell requires periodic recharging to produces energy.

_____ **10.** The high cost of fuel cells removes them from practical consideration as a viable auxiliary power supply.

Fill in the Blank

Read each item carefully, and then complete the statement by filling in the missing word(s).

1. When two materials rub together _____ transfer from one material to the other creating an electric charge.

2. When fuel and powdered products such as flour or cement are removed from a tanker trailer a _____ clamp is connected to the chassis to minimize the likelihood of an explosion.

3. Electrostatic charging though _____ occurs when rubber-based air bags for air suspension systems move up and down over aluminum pedestals.

4. When two dissimilar metals are brought together and heated, _____ is produced at the junction points.

5. When used in common rail injectors, _____ crystals produce the fastest rate of injector response when switching the injection event on and off.

6. The higher the _____ density the higher the number of magnetic lines of force per square inch.

7. The number of conductors that are cutting across the lines of force changes induced _____.

8. A(n) _____ is any liquid that conducts electric current.

9. A(n) _____ _____ is an electrochemical device that combines hydrogen and oxygen to produce water.

10. A fuel _____ operates along with a fuel cell to remove hydrogen from diesel fuel, natural gas, methanol, or gasoline.

Labeling

Label the following diagrams with the correct terms.

1. Identify the components of a fuel cell:

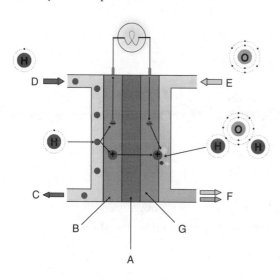

A. _____

B. _____

C. _____

D. _____

E. _____

F. _____

G. _____

Crossword Puzzle

Use the clues in the column to complete the puzzle.

Across

3. A thermoelectric device consisting of two dissimilar metals that produce voltage when heated.

4. A transformer used to reduce voltage in the secondary coil. A battery charger would use this to change 120 volts into 12 to charge a 12-volt battery.

5. The force that attracts or repels magnetic charges; or the property of a material to respond to a magnetic field.

Down

1. A conductor wound in a coil that produces a magnetic field when current flows through it.

2. The coil of wire in the low-voltage circuit, which creates the magnetic field in a step-up transformer.

ASE-Type Questions

Read each item carefully, and then select the best response.

_____ **1.** Technician A says electric charges are produced when two materials rub together. Technician B says static electricity is another name given to triboelectricity because objects can develop stationary high voltage charges. Who is correct?
   A. Technician A
   B. Technician B
   C. Both Technician A and Technician B
   D. Neither Technician A nor Technician B

_____ **2.** Technician A says solar cells that can produce electricity are widely used in commercial vehicle applications. Technician B says commercially available cells are used as trickle chargers for batteries. Who is correct?
   A. Technician A
   B. Technician B
   C. Both Technician A and Technician B
   D. Neither Technician A nor Technician B

_____ **3.** Technician A says thermoelectric devices (TED) are solid-state heat pumps formed from several layers of semiconductor materials. Technician B says TEDs are used for cooling or heating small areas, including seats, steering wheels, cup holders, or beverage storage compartments. Who is correct?
   A. Technician A
   B. Technician B
   C. Both Technician A and Technician B
   D. Neither Technician A nor Technician B

_____ **4.** Technician A says one of the most common ways electricity is produced in a heavy-duty vehicle is through the use of the energy found in magnetic fields. Technician B says magnetism is the force that attracts or repels magnetic charges, or the property of a material to respond to a magnetic field. Who is correct?
   A. Technician A
   B. Technician B
   C. Both Technician A and Technician B
   D. Neither Technician A nor Technician B

_____ **5.** Technician A says magnetism can produce electricity. Technician B says electricity cannot produce magnetism. Who is correct?
   A. Technician A
   B. Technician B
   C. Both Technician A and Technician B
   D. Neither Technician A nor Technician B

_____ **6.** Technician A says the principle of producing electrical current flow using electromagnets is known as electromagnetic induction. Technician B says alternators, generators, and speed sensors use this electrical principle to produce electrical current. Who is correct?
   A. Technician A
   B. Technician B
   C. Both Technician A and Technician B
   D. Neither Technician A nor Technician B

_____ **7.** Technician A says the current that is induced when the magnetic field collapses after a circuit is opened can have much lower voltage than the voltage in the closed circuit. Technician B says any coil of wire in an electrical system can produce hundreds of volts when it is de-energized. Who is correct?
   A. Technician A
   B. Technician B
   C. Both Technician A and Technician B
   D. Neither Technician A nor Technician B

_____ **8.** Technician A says suppression of the voltage spike from magnetic coils is accomplished using diodes, capacitors, resistors, or induction coils. Technician B says without suppression, the voltage spike can travel back in a circuit to its source and damage any sensitive electronic component. Who is correct?
   A. Technician A
   B. Technician B
   C. Both Technician A and Technician B
   D. Neither Technician A nor Technician B

_____ **9.** Technician A says the primary winding is where current is induced. Technician B says the secondary winding is supplied current. Who is correct?
   A. Technician A
   B. Technician B
   C. Both Technician A and Technician B
   D. Neither Technician A nor Technician B

_____ **10.** Technician A says dozens of varieties of fuel cells exist, but they all fundamentally work in the same manner. Technician B says like a battery, a fuel cell requires recharging. Who is correct?
   A. Technician A
   B. Technician B
   C. Both Technician A and Technician B
   D. Neither Technician A nor Technician B

Electric Circuits and Circuit Protection

Chapter Review

The following activities have been designed to help you refresh your knowledge of this chapter. Your instructor may require you to complete some or all of these activities as a regular part of your training program. You are encouraged to complete any activity that your instructor does not assign as a way to enhance your learning.

Matching

Match the following terms with the correct description or example.

A. Combination circuit
B. Grounded circuit
C. Parallel circuit

D. Series circuit
E. Short circuit

_____ **1.** A circuit characterized by an unwanted low resistance connection between battery positive power and chassis ground.

_____ **2.** The simplest type of electrical circuit with multiple loads but only one path for current to flow.

_____ **3.** A circuit in which all components are connected directly to the voltage supply.

_____ **4.** An electrical circuit that is formed between two points, allowing current to flow through an unintended pathway.

_____ **5.** A circuit that uses elements both of series and parallel circuits.

Multiple Choice

Read each item carefully, and then select the best response.

_____ **1.** The working devices that turn electrical energy into some other form of energy, such as lamps or motors, are called _____ and are considered the resistance of a circuit.
  A. controls
  B. conductors
  C. loads
  D. power sources

_____ **2.** The force in a circuit that impedes or slows the transfer of electrons from one atom to the next is called _____.
  A. voltage
  B. resistance
  C. amperage
  D. pressure

_____ **3.** The observation that the sum of the voltage drop across all loads is equal to the source voltage is referred to as _____.
  A. Ohm's law
  B. Tesla's law
  C. Kirchhoff's law
  D. Edison's law

_____ **4.** If one branch of a _____ circuit is broken, current will continue to flow in the other branches.
  A. series
  B. parallel
  C. combination
  D. simple

_____ **5.** The most common circuits used in a commercial vehicle chassis are _____ circuits.
   A. parallel
   B. series
   C. resistance
   D. combination

_____ **6.** The relationship between current, resistance, and voltage is explained in mathematical language by _____.
   A. Ohm's law
   B. Watt's law
   C. Tesla's law
   D. Kirchhoff's law

_____ **7.** Power (Watts) = Voltage × Amperage is an example of _____.
   A. Kirchhoff's law
   B. Ohm's law
   C. Watt's law
   D. Tesla's law

_____ **8.** A device requiring 120 watts of power would use _____ amps at 24 volts.
   A. 5
   B. 6
   C. 10
   D. 12

_____ **9.** A(n) _____ uses strips of metal made in various thicknesses that are enclosed in a glass tube.
   A. blade type fuse
   B. cartridge type fuse
   C. inline type fuse
   D. circuit breaker

_____ **10.** A _____ circuit breaker must be reset by depressing a reset button.
   A. Type 1
   B. Type 2
   C. Type 3
   D. Type 4

True/False

If you believe the statement to be more true than false, write the letter "T" in the space provided. If you believe the statement to be more false than true, write the letter "F".

_____ **1.** The power source creates the electrons that cause movement in the conductors of a circuit.

_____ **2.** In a parallel circuit each device is connected like a chain, with all current flowing through one device after another.

_____ **3.** At any given point in a series circuit, the amperage is the same.

_____ **4.** Total circuit resistance in a parallel circuit is always less than the resistance of the smallest resister.

_____ **5.** Reducing the amperage not only increases resistance and may require an increase in the size of the conductor.

_____ **6.** Amperage = Watts × Volts.

_____ **7.** An open circuit will not burn the fuse, but the fuse may be open if the circuit was overloaded by a short to ground.

_____ **8.** Intermittent current flow through circuits is often attributed to vibration from a moving vehicle.

_____ **9.** Blade type fuses do not require replacement when they trip. Instead, they may either automatically reset or require a manual reset.

_____ **10.** A polymeric positive temperature coefficient device is commonly known as a resettable fuse.

Fill in the Blank

Read each item carefully, and then complete the statement by filling in the missing word(s).

1. Pathways made by electrical conductors that enable the flow of electrons are called _____.

2. A(n) _____ circuit has a complete electrical pathway for current to flow between the negative and positive terminal.

3. On paper, the schematic diagram of a(n) _____ circuit resembles a ladder.

4. Connecting batteries together in parallel increases available cranking amperage, but the _____ stays the same.

5. One volt is required to push one _____ of current through a circuit that has a resistance of one ohm.

6. A(n) _____ may draw a higher or lower than normal amperage and simply be an unintended connection between two wires or circuits.

7. A(n) _____ circuit is sometime called "dead short."

8. Dirty, corroded, or loose connections result in _____ circuits that do not allow components to properly operate.

9. A(n) _____ fuse may be used when adding electrical accessories to a circuit.

10. Protection devices are designed to prevent excessive _____ from flowing in the circuit.

Labeling

Label the following diagrams with the correct terms.

1. Identify the components of a simple series circuit:

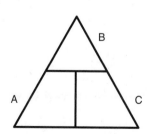

A. _____

B. _____

C. _____

D. _____

E. _____

2. Identify the variables in the "Tradesperson Triangle":

Ohm's Law states: Voltage = Amperage × Resistance

A. _____

B. _____

C. _____

3. Identify the various types of thermal fuses:

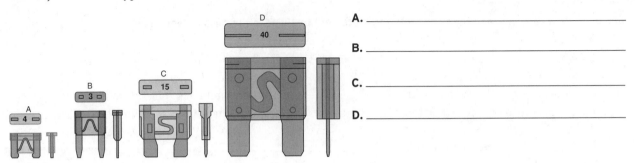

A. _____

B. _____

C. _____

D. _____

4. Identify the components of a cycling circuit breaker:

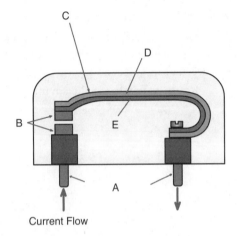

Current Flow

A. _____

B. _____

C. _____

D. _____

E. _____

Skill Drills

Test your knowledge of skill drills by filling in the correct words in the photo captions.

1. Inspecting and Testing Circuit Protection Devices:

Step 1:   Identify the _____ _____ to be inspected and tested. A _____ or _____ _____ is most commonly checked at a _____ _____ box or _____ _____.

Step 2:   Turn the _____ _____ to the _____ or _____ position to supply _____ to the fuse.

Step 3:   Using a _____ _____, probe the fuse or circuit breaker on each side (_____ and _____) to determine whether _____ is supplied to the device and whether current is available to the _____ in the circuit.

Step 4:   If there is only power available to the circuit protection _____ and not to the _____, the device is _____. This requires _____ if it is a _____ or _____ the _____ _____ if possible. Fuse replacement is performed after identifying the _____ for the overloaded circuit.

2. Identifying a Resistive Ground Connection:

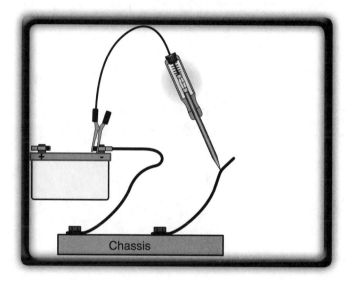

Chassis

Step 1:   Locate a suspected _____ connection. This is usually a _____ on a _____ or _____ on a _____ _____ attached to a _____.

Step 2:   Using a voltmeter, place one _____ of the voltmeter onto the _____ _____.

Step 3:   Place the other _____ on the _____ connection to the _____ that is _____ _____ correctly.

Step 4:   Energize the _____ or _____ the _____.

Crossword Puzzle

Use the clues in the column to complete the puzzle.

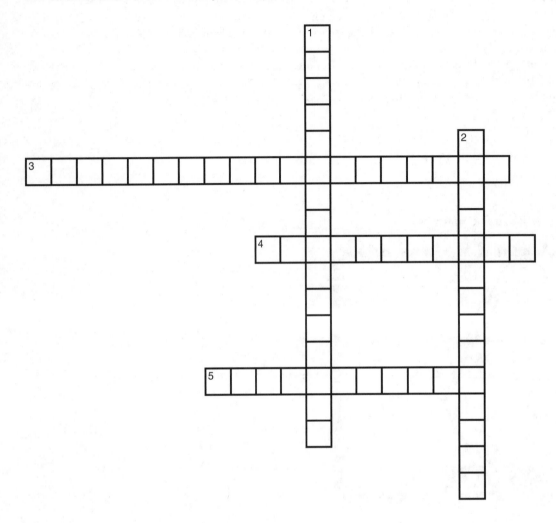

Across

3. A circuit characterized by uneven current flow.

4. A type of fuse opened by heat produced from resistance caused by high amperage flow.

5. A software-controlled fuse that uses field effect transistors for the circuit control device. Also called e-fuses.

Down

1. A circuit in which grounds and power connections cannot properly function due to overly high resistance.

2. A device that trips and opens a circuit, preventing excessive current flow in a circuit. It is resettable to allow for reuse.

ASE-Type Questions

Read each item carefully, and then select the best response.

_____ 1. Technician A says circuits are pathways made by electrical conductors that enable the flow of electrons. Technician B says a variety of classifications are used to describe circuit configurations and failures. Who is correct?
   A. Technician A
   B. Technician B
   C. Both Technician A and Technician B
   D. Neither Technician A nor Technician B

_____ 2. Technician A says resistance is electrical friction. Technician B says resistance will lower voltage, but in a circuit, will not proportionately lower amperage to the amount of resistance. Who is correct?
   A. Technician A
   B. Technician B
   C. Both Technician A and Technician B
   D. Neither Technician A nor Technician B

_____ 3. Technician A says circuits found in commercial vehicles are classified in an operational state of open and closed. Technician B says circuits found in commercial vehicles are classified in the failure mode of blocked as well as shorted or open. Who is correct?
   A. Technician A
   B. Technician B
   C. Both Technician A and Technician B
   D. Neither Technician A nor Technician B

_____ 4. Technician A says a series circuit is a circuit with multiple loads and only one path for current to flow. Technician B says in a series circuit total circuit resistance is equal to the sum of the individual resistances. Who is correct?
   A. Technician A
   B. Technician B
   C. Both Technician A and Technician B
   D. Neither Technician A nor Technician B

_____ 5. Technician A says Watt's law, which is related to Ohm's law, explains the relationship between resistance and amperage. Technician B says increasing amperage through a circuit produces proportionally more resistance. Who is correct?
   A. Technician A
   B. Technician B
   C. Both Technician A and Technician B
   D. Neither Technician A nor Technician B

_____ 6. Technician A says a grounded circuit should not be confused with a "dead short," which is a different condition. Technician B says a common example of a grounded circuit would be a battery or power cable insulation rubbing against the negative ground chassis frame. Who is correct?
   A. Technician A
   B. Technician B
   C. Both Technician A and Technician B
   D. Neither Technician A nor Technician B

_____ 7. Technician A says when circuits are overloaded with current, hungry components, or grounded circuits, it is the quickest way to cause damage to wiring, or even start fires. Technician B says a 20-amp fuse will open at 32 to 33 amps of current. Who is correct?
   A. Technician A
   B. Technician B
   C. Both Technician A and Technician B
   D. Neither Technician A nor Technician B

_____ **8.** Technician A says fuse links are short sections of wire installed in series with larger diameter conductors. Technician B says when the gauge on the main conductor is at halfway, the fuse link will overheat and melt as excessive amperage passes through the wire. Who is correct?
   A. Technician A
   B. Technician B
   C. Both Technician A and Technician B
   D. Neither Technician A nor Technician B

_____ **9.** Technician A says a polymeric positive temperature coefficient device (PPTC) is a thermistor-like electronic device used to protect against circuit overloads. Technician B says PPTCs are commonly known as resettable fuses. Who is correct?
   A. Technician A
   B. Technician B
   C. Both Technician A and Technician B
   D. Neither Technician A nor Technician B

_____ **10.** Technician A says virtual fuses, or e-fuses, are a recent innovation in a circuit protection. Technician B says virtual fuses are software-controlled fuses that use Field Effect Transistors (FET) as the circuit control device. Who is correct?
   A. Technician A
   B. Technician B
   C. Both Technician A and Technician B
   D. Neither Technician A nor Technician B

Circuit Control Devices

Chapter Review

The following activities have been designed to help you refresh your knowledge of this chapter. Your instructor may require you to complete some or all of these activities as a regular part of your training program. You are encouraged to complete any activity that your instructor does not assign as a way to enhance your learning.

Matching

Match the following terms with the correct description or example.

A. Capacitor

B. Forward bias

C. Potentiometer

D. Rheostat

E. Zener point

_____ **1.** A variable resistor with three connections—one at each end of a resistive path, and a third sliding contact that moves along the resistive pathway.

_____ **2.** A circuit-control device made up of two plates separated by an insulating material.

_____ **3.** The voltage at which a diode will conduct current in both directions instead of just one.

_____ **4.** A situation in which a diode conducts current.

_____ **5.** A variable resistor constructed of a fixed input terminal and a variable output terminal, which vary current flow by passing current through a long resistive tightly coiled wire.

Multiple Choice

Read each item carefully, and then select the best response.

_____ **1.** A switch with a _____ contact arrangement is sometimes called a changeover relay.
   A. single pole single throw
   B. single pole double throw
   C. double pole single throw
   D. double pole double throw

_____ **2.** The horn and the starter button are both examples of _____ switches.
   A. toggle
   B. proximity
   C. momentary contact
   D. pressure

_____ **3.** A switch connecting a positive voltage to the ECM is called a _____ switch.
   A. pull-up
   B. common
   C. pull-down
   D. magnetic

_____ **4.** Colored bands around a _____ resistor identify its numerical resistance in ohms.
   A. variable
   B. fixed
   C. stepped
   D. All of the above

_____ **5.** Throttle pedal position sensors are a common application for _____.
   A. rheostats
   B. fixed resistors
   C. potentiometers
   D. thermistors

_____ **6.** A _____ is ideal for using a small current to control a larger current.
   A. capacitor
   B. solenoid
   C. transistor
   D. relay

_____ **7.** The unit of capacitance is the _____, which is a measure of the ability of a capacitor to store an electrical charge.
   A. ampere
   B. farad
   C. coulomb
   D. pascal

_____ **8.** A _____ is an electronic device that operates as a one-way electrical check valve.
   A. diode
   B. relay
   C. capacitor
   D. resistor

_____ **9.** A _____ is an example of a bipolar transistor.
   A. PNP transistor
   B. potentiometer
   C. NPN transistor
   D. Both A and C

_____ **10.** A _____ is an integrated circuit containing arithmetic logic core, limited memory, and programmable input and output pins.
   A. field effect transistor
   B. microprocessor
   C. microcontroller
   D. MOSFET

True/False

If you believe the statement to be more true than false, write the letter "T" in the space provided. If you believe the statement to be more false than true, write the letter "F".

_____ **1.** If a switch closes a circuit in its resting position, it is called normally closed.

_____ **2.** Once the operator removes pressure from the mechanism of a smart switch the switch turns off.

_____ **3.** Fixed resistors function as current limiters because they become more resistive when connected in series and amperage increases.

_____ **4.** As the temperature increases the resistance value of a negative temperature coefficient thermistor increases.

_____ **5.** The relay is standardized to be used across all vehicle manufacturers, having standard pin numbers, functions, and dimensions to fit into a power distribution box.

_____ **6.** Magnetic switches are identical in function to relays except that mag switches are designed to switch smaller amounts of current.

_____ **7.** Capacitors are often used as timers in circuits such as wiper delay modules or dimming of dome lights.

_____ **8.** One important application of a capacitor is to suppress high-voltage spikes caused by self-induction in coils.

_____ **9.** Transistors primarily function as electronic switches, amplifiers, and voltage-controlled resistors.

_____ **10.** Field effect transistors are the most common transistor used in digital and analog circuits today.

Fill in the Blank

Read each item carefully, and then complete the statement by filling in the missing word(s).

1. Electric circuits use _____ _____ to direct the flow of current.

2. Because switches can be in only one of two states, switch inputs are _____ inputs.

3. A typical _____ has a control circuit and a load circuit.

4. A(n) _____ resistor is made from two or more wire-wound resistors.

5. Capacitors are simple devices made up of three components—two plates and an insulating material separating the plates. The insulation is called a(n) _____.

6. A(n) _____ can be useful for smoothing out voltage fluctuations that interfere with the operation of sensitive electronic components.

7. Sandwiching a P- and N- semiconductor material produces a(n) _____.

8. Rather than using minerals, the silicon or germanium material in _____ light-emitting diodes is replaced with carbon-based semiconductors.

9. To achieve the greatest current flow across the emitter-collector circuit, the P and N materials are _____ differently.

10. A _____ uses integrated circuitry and is formed from vast numbers of transistors, resistors, and capacitors in multiple layers.

Labeling

Label the following diagrams with the correct terms.

1. Identify the common contact arrangements:

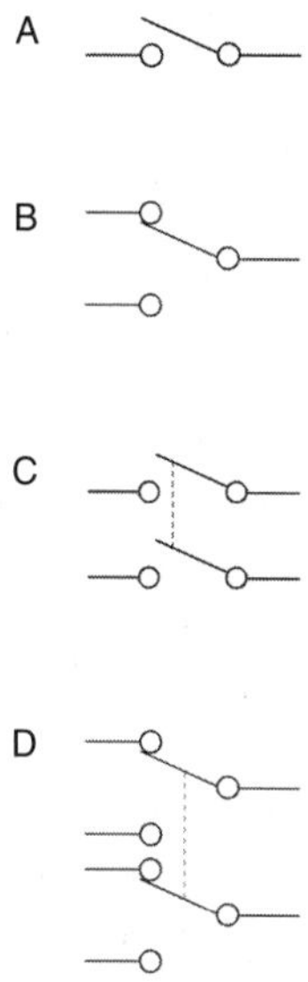

A   A. _____

B   B. _____

C   C. _____

D   D. _____

2. Identify the circuit symbols for various switch types:

 A

 D

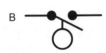 B

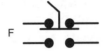 E

C

F

A. _____

B. _____

C. _____

D. _____

E. _____

F. _____

3. Identify the components of a potentiometer:

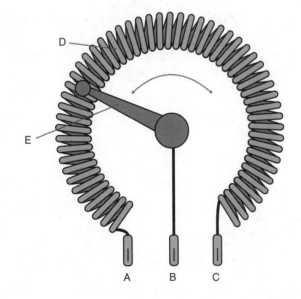

A. _____

B. _____

C. _____

D. _____

E. _____

4. Identify the schematic symbols for various types of diodes:

A. _____

B. _____

C. _____

Crossword Puzzle

Use the clues in the column to complete the puzzle.

Across

3. A type of diode that behaves like a typical silicon diode up to a precise voltage threshold. After the diode reaches its threshold voltage, it conducts in both directions.

4. A material with a movable negative charge.

5. A situation in which a diode blocks current flow.

Down

1. A material with a movable positive charge.

2. A semiconductor-type of resistor in which resistance decreases as light intensity increases.

ASE-Type Questions

Read each item carefully, and then select the best response.

_____ 1. Technician A says simple switches are categorized by the number of input terminals they have. Technician B says input terminals are called throws, and output terminals called poles. Who is correct?
   A. Technician A
   B. Technician B
   C. Both Technician A and Technician B
   D. Neither Technician A nor Technician B

_____ 2. Technician A says smart switches can function as digital inputs to electronic control systems. Technician B says because switches can be in only one of two states, switch inputs are binary inputs. Who is correct?
   A. Technician A
   B. Technician B
   C. Both Technician A and Technician B
   D. Neither Technician A nor Technician B

_____ 3. Technician A says fixed-type resistors are designed to conduct either heavy or light amount of current. Technician B says colored bands around the resistor identify its numerical resistance in amps. Who is correct?
   A. Technician A
   B. Technician B
   C. Both Technician A and Technician B
   D. Neither Technician A nor Technician B

_____ 4. Technician A says a relay is a switch that uses a small amount of current to switch a larger amount of current. Technician B says locating a relay closer to a load requiring large amounts of current eliminates voltage drop caused by resistance from long runs of wires. Who is correct?
   A. Technician A
   B. Technician B
   C. Both Technician A and Technician B
   D. Neither Technician A nor Technician B

_____ 5. Technician A says magnetic switches have a different function as compared to a relay. Technician B says magnetic switches can be classified as continuous or intermittent duty service. Who is correct?
   A. Technician A
   B. Technician B
   C. Both Technician A and Technician B
   D. Neither Technician A nor Technician B

_____ 6. Technician A says capacitors are devices that act like electric shock absorbers and are capable of storing and discharging current much like a battery or hydraulic accumulator. Technician B says capacitors are simple devices made up of three components—two plates and an insulating material. Who is correct?
   A. Technician A
   B. Technician B
   C. Both Technician A and Technician B
   D. Neither Technician A nor Technician B

_____ 7. Technician A says capacitors never wear out, but they can short out. Technician B says an ohmmeter connected to each lead of the capacitor should show continuity. Who is correct?
   A. Technician A
   B. Technician B
   C. Both Technician A and Technician B
   D. Neither Technician A nor Technician B

_____ 8. Technician A says sandwiching a P- and N- semiconductor material produces a diode. Technician B says diodes are electronic devices that operate as one-way electrical check valves. Who is correct?
   A. Technician A
   B. Technician B
   C. Both Technician A and Technician B
   D. Neither Technician A nor Technician B

_____ **9.** Technician A says "virtual fusing" is the description given to the use of FETs, which replace a fuse or circuit breaker in the individual high-side controlled circuits. Technician B says virtual fusing is also designed to imitate the characteristics of SAE type 2 and 3 circuit breakers. Who is correct?
  A. Technician A
  B. Technician B
  C. Both Technician A and Technician B
  D. Neither Technician A nor Technician B

_____ **10.** Technician A says microprocessors contain memory and logic circuits that enable them to operate using sophisticated programmed sets of stored instructions. Technician B says actuators supply processors with data, and an arithmetic unit performs calculations using algorithms based on programmed instructions. Who is correct?
  A. Technician A
  B. Technician B
  C. Both Technician A and Technician B
  D. Neither Technician A nor Technician B

Electrical Test Instruments

Chapter Review

The following activities have been designed to help you refresh your knowledge of this chapter. Your instructor may require you to complete some or all of these activities as a regular part of your training program. You are encouraged to complete any activity that your instructor does not assign as a way to enhance your learning.

Matching

Match the following terms with the correct description or example.

A. Analog meter

B. Circuit (wire) tracer

C. Data link adapter

D. Digital multimeter

E. High-impedance multimeter

_____ **1.** A device used to translate serial data from the DLC into a format readable by a desktop or laptop computer.

_____ **2.** A meter that samples very little of a circuit's own current to take a measurement.

_____ **3.** An electronic service tool used to trace a single wire over a distance where multiple wires are bundled, shorted, or open.

_____ **4.** A meter that uses a sweeping needle that continuously measures electrical values.

_____ **5.** A type of multimeter that provides numerical displays of electrical data.

Multiple Choice

Read each item carefully, and then select the best response.

_____ **1.** Self-powered test lights can be used to check for _____ when either chassis power or ground is removed from the circuit.

   A. open circuits

   B. high impedance circuits

   C. grounded circuits

   D. Both A and C

_____ **2.** A lit green light on a self-powered test light with two LEDs would indicate _____.

   A. circuit voltage

   B. positive polarity

   C. negative polarity

   D. Both A and C

_____ **3.** A(n) _____ is an electrical measuring instrument that combines the functions of at least voltage, resistance, and amperage measurement into a single compact instrument.

   A. scan tool

   B. inductive clamp

   C. multimeter

   D. oscilloscope

_____ **4.** The term _____ refers to a meter's internal resistance to current flowing from a live circuit into the meter when measuring voltage and amperage.

   A. shunt

   B. high impedance

   C. microfarad

   D. capacitance

_____ **5.** Multimeters are used to perform _____ measurements.
   A. duty cycle
   B. frequency
   C. capacitance
   D. All of the above

_____ **6.** A(n) _____ uses a small amount of electrical current from an internal battery and sends it through a circuit or component.
   A. ohmmeter
   B. voltmeter
   C. ammeter
   D. All of the above

_____ **7.** When measuring _____, the meter should be connected in parallel with the voltage source.
   A. ohms
   B. volts
   C. amps
   D. Both A and C

_____ **8.** When measuring _____, the circuit should be broken and the meter placed in series with the circuit so that all the current flows through the meter shunts.
   A. amps
   B. volts
   C. ohms
   D. All of the above

_____ **9.** An inductive amp clamp measures the strength of the magnetic field around a conductor using a _____.
   A. potentiometer
   B. thermistor
   C. photodiode
   D. Hall effect sensor

_____ **10.** Multimeters use a _____ as a low-cost, general-purpose, temperature-sensing element.
   A. diode scale
   B. Hall effect sensor
   C. type K thermocouple
   D. thermistor

True/False

If you believe the statement to be more true than false, write the letter "T" in the space provided. If you believe the statement to be more false than true, write the letter "F".

_____ **1.** A blown fuse will light up a test light on both sides when probed with the key on.

_____ **2.** High voltage from hybrid drives, the latest common rail injectors, and other electric systems can easily kill or cause serious physical harm if pierced by a technician.

_____ **3.** One advantage of LED lights is they provide an indication of a circuit's voltage.

_____ **4.** Analog multimeters are the most common category of multimeters and provide numerical displays of electrical data.

_____ **5.** Auto-ranging multimeters can be slower to measure electrical values because they need time to adjust the operating range.

_____ **6.** A larger amperage shunt will have a lower resistance than a low amperage shunt.

_____ **7.** Connecting an ohmmeter into a powered circuit will blow the fuse or battery in the meter or otherwise damage the meter.

_____ **8.** When connecting a voltmeter to an AC circuit the polarity of the meter and circuit must be matched.

_____ **9.** Inductive amp clamps cannot be used to measure DC amperage.

_____ **10.** The low-voltage settings of an ohmmeter may not be able to properly evaluate a diode.

Fill in the Blank

Read each item carefully, and then complete the statement by filling in the missing word(s).

1. A(n) _____ _____ is the simplest piece of electrical test equipment used to determine the presence or absence of current.

2. When connected in _____ with a circuit, test lights can indicate bad grounds or parasitic current drawn from a battery.

3. Measuring _____ drops in a circuit can help evaluate resistance in high amperage circuits such as the starting circuit.

4. Most measurements of amperage are performed at levels higher than multimeters can typically handle, so an inductance _____ _____ is used instead.

5. A(n) _____-_____ multimeter must be set to the correct range first based on anticipated values measured.

6. A(n) _____ measures the difference in electrical pressure or electron velocity between two different points in the circuit.

7. A(n) _____ measures the quantity of electrons flowing through a circuit per second of time.

8. The SAE has developed on-board diagnostic (OBD) standards for hand-held _____ tools.

9. Using _____ control, a scan tool can control selected vehicle components or initiate systems actuator or diagnostic tests on command.

10. The most basic diagnostic scanner is a(n) _____ _____

Labeling

Label the following diagrams with the correct terms.

1. Identify the features of a basic DVOM:

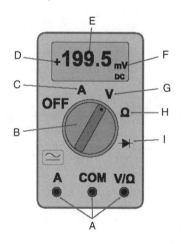

A. _____

B. _____

C. _____

D. _____

E. _____

F. _____

G. _____

H. _____

I. _____

Symbols and Meanings for Electrical Units of Measurement

Match the following symbols to their correct meaning or electrical unit of measurement.

_____ **1.** Ω   **A.** Amperage

_____ **2.** dB   **B.** Voltage

_____ **3.** M   **C.** Out of range

_____ **4.** OL   **D.** Milli or one thousandth

_____ **5.** K   **E.** Capacitance

_____ **6.** Hz   **F.** Resistance

_____ **7.** V   **G.** Kilo or thousand

_____ **8.** F   **H.** Sound

_____ **9.** A   **I.** Mega or million

_____ **10.** m   **J.** Frequency

Skill Drills

Test your knowledge of skill drills by filling in the correct words in the photo captions.

1. Checking Meter Shunts:

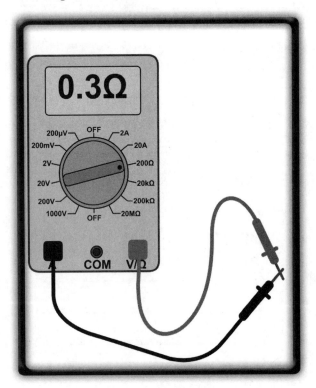

Step 1: Plug test _____ in volts/ohms _____.

Step 2: Select _____ range.

Step 3: Insert _____ _____ into mA input and read value. A small amount of _____ should be noted when probing the _____ inputs with the _____ volt/ohm probe.

Step 4: Insert probe tip into _____ input and read value. It should have a _____ amount of _____ than the mA input.

Crossword Puzzle

Use the clues in the column to complete the puzzle.

Across

3. Internal conductors with small calibrated resistance and that direct current flow into the meter while measuring amperage.

4. An electrical test instrument used to analyze waveforms and graphically plot an electrical value of a signal over time.

5. A device used to identify the root cause of vehicle vibration.

Down

1. A device that measures amperage by measuring a conductor's magnetic field strength, which is proportional to amperage.

2. A 12- or 24-volt incandescent light bulb connected to an insulated lead and a sharpened metal probe.

ASE-Type Questions

Read each item carefully, and then select the best response.

_____ 1. Technician A says that a test light is the simplest piece of electrical test equipment used to determine the presence or absence of current. Technician B says that a test light consists of either an 18- or 36-volt incandescent light bulb connected to an insulated lead and a sharpened metal probe. Who is correct?
   A. Technician A
   B. Technician B
   C. Both Technician A and Technician B
   D. Neither Technician A nor Technician B

_____ 2. Technician A says that a popular type of LED test light is battery powered and has two LEDs—one red and the other green. Technician B says that the LED light will change brightness depending on the circuit's voltage. Who is correct?
   A. Technician A
   B. Technician B
   C. Both Technician A and Technician B
   D. Neither Technician A nor Technician B

_____ 3. Technician A says that multimeters are electrical measuring instruments combining features of at least voltage, resistance, and amperage measurement into a single compact instrument. Technician B says that digital multimeters are the most common category of multimeters and provide numerical displays of electrical data. Who is correct?
   A. Technician A
   B. Technician B
   C. Both Technician A and Technician B
   D. Neither Technician A nor Technician B

_____ 4. Technician A says that a multimeter measures resistance, continuity, voltage, and amperage. Technician B says that the multimeter can be used to measure circuit resistance in amps to determine whether amperage is within specifications. Who is correct?
   A. Technician A
   B. Technician B
   C. Both Technician A and Technician B
   D. Neither Technician A nor Technician B

_____ 5. Technician A says that before using a digital multimeter, the first task is to check that its shunts and fuses are in place and functioning. Technician B says that shunts do not operate like fuses and do not have a maximum rating. Who is correct?
   A. Technician A
   B. Technician B
   C. Both Technician A and Technician B
   D. Neither Technician A nor Technician B

_____ 6. Technician A says that the multimeter is connected in series with the circuit or component to measure the voltage dropped by the circuit resistance. Technician B says that the ohmmeter works well in testing semiconductors. Who is correct?
   A. Technician A
   B. Technician B
   C. Both Technician A and Technician B
   D. Neither Technician A nor Technician B

_____ 7. Technician A says that ammeters measure the quantity of electrons flowing through a circuit per second of time. Technician B says that measuring amperage requires that the circuit be broken and the meter placed in series with the circuit so that all the current flows through the meter shunts. Who is correct?
   A. Technician A
   B. Technician B
   C. Both Technician A and Technician B
   D. Neither Technician A nor Technician B

_____ **8.** Technician A says multimeters use a thermocouple accessory to measure temperature by contact. Technician B says that heating the thermocouple produces amperage proportional to temperature. Who is correct?
  A. Technician A
  B. Technician B
  C. Both Technician A and Technician B
  D. Neither Technician A nor Technician B

_____ **9.** Technician A says that circuit tracers, also called wire tracers, are electronic service tools used to trace a single wire over a distance where multiple wires are bundled, shorted, or open. Technician B says that circuit tracers can identify wires deeply buried behind walls or in tightly bundled harness. Who is correct?
  A. Technician A
  B. Technician B
  C. Both Technician A and Technician B
  D. Neither Technician A nor Technician B

_____ **10.** Technician A says the vibration analyzers are used to identify the root cause of vehicle vibration. Technician B says that, typically, flywheel speed and road speed sensors are used along with data collected from a three-axis accelerometer placed under the driver's seat using a magnet. Who is correct?
  A. Technician A
  B. Technician B
  C. Both Technician A and Technician B
  D. Neither Technician A nor Technician B

Commercial Vehicle Batteries

Tire Tread:
© AbleStock

Chapter Review

The following activities have been designed to help you refresh your knowledge of this chapter. Your instructor may require you to complete some or all of these activities as a regular part of your training program. You are encouraged to complete any activity that your instructor does not assign as a way to enhance your learning.

Matching

Match the following terms with the correct description or example.

A. Amp-hour
B. Cold cranking amps (CCA)
C. Cranking amps (CA)

D. Electrical capacity
E. Reserve capacity

_____ **1.** A measurement of the load, in amps, that a battery can deliver for 30 seconds while maintaining a voltage of 1.2 volts per cell or higher at 32°F (–0°C).

_____ **2.** The time, in minutes, that a new, fully charged battery at 80°F (26.7°C) will supply a constant load of 25 amps without its voltage dropping below 10.5 volts for a 12-volt battery.

_____ **3.** A measurement of the load, in amps, that a battery can deliver for 30 seconds while maintaining a voltage of 1.2 volts per cell or higher at 0°F (–18°C).

_____ **4.** The amount of electrical current a lead acid battery can supply.

_____ **5.** A measure of how much amperage a battery can continually supply over a 20-hour period without the battery voltage falling below 10.5 volts.

Multiple Choice

Read each item carefully, and then select the best response.

_____ **1.** Water containing _____ would be considered an electrolyte.
   A. salt
   B. acids
   C. alkaline solutions
   D. All of the above

_____ **2.** The first battery was built by _____, who alternately stacked copper and zinc plates separated with a piece of saltwater-soaked cardboard.
   A. Galvani
   B. Tesla
   C. Volta
   D. Joule

_____ **3.** Batteries used for cranking purposes have unique construction features and are commonly called _____.
   A. starting, lighting, and ignition (SLI) batteries
   B. absorbed glass mat (AGM) batteries
   C. valve-regulated lead acid (VRLA) batteries
   D. recombinant batteries

_____ **4.** Current demands on the battery when the ignition is switched off are called _____.
   A. key-off electrical loads
   B. stray currents
   C. parasitic draw
   D. Either A or C

_____ **5.** Rechargeable batteries used for propulsion in hybrid electric vehicles are called _____.
   A. deep cycle batteries
   B. traction batteries
   C. recombinant batteries
   D. valve-regulated lead acid (VRLA) batteries

_____ **6.** The electrodes and electrolyte of a lead acid battery cell produce _____ volts.
   A. 2.1
   B. 3.2
   C. 6
   D. 12

_____ **7.** A squeeze bulb and float type _____ is an instrument used to measure the density or the specific gravity of batteries.
   A. hygrometer
   B. dielectric tester
   C. hydrometer
   D. refractometer

_____ **8.** A specific gravity reading of 1.155 and an open circuit voltage of 12.06 would indicate that the battery was at a _____ state of charge.
   A. 25%
   B. 50%
   C. 75%
   D. 100%

_____ **9.** Battery Council International group numbers are established according to _____.
   A. physical case size
   B. terminal type
   C. terminal placement
   D. All of the above

_____ **10.** Automotive battery capacity is rated by _____.
   A. cranking amps (CA)
   B. cold cranking amps (CCA)
   C. reserve capacity
   D. All of the above

True/False

If you believe the statement to be more true than false, write the letter "T" in the space provided. If you believe the statement to be more false than true, write the letter "F".

_____ **1.** Primary batteries are the most practical for use in automotive applications because they can be used over and over again.

_____ **2.** Tap water will not conduct current.

_____ **3.** Lead acid batteries are the most common battery used in the transportation industry.

_____ **4.** Flooded lead acid batteries refer to battery cell construction where the electrodes are made from thin lead (Pb) plates submersed in liquid electrolyte.

_____ **5.** Plates are connected together in series to increase the amperage or capacity of a battery.

_____ **6.** The primary difference between deep cycle batteries and SLI batteries is the thickness of the plates.

_____ **7.** During charging and discharging, the specific gravity of the electrolyte changes.

_____ **8.** The common battery capacity ratings used by North American manufacturers are established by the International Electrotechnical Commission.

_____ **9.** In cold weather, battery power drops drastically because the electrolyte thickens and cold temperatures slow chemical activity inside the battery.

_____ **10.** The only way galvanic reaction will stop in a battery is if the electrical load is removed.

Fill in the Blank

Read each item carefully, and then complete the statement by filling in the missing word(s).

1. The single direction electrons flow during discharge means a battery is a source of _____ current.

2. In a _____ battery, chemical reactions are not reversible, and the battery cannot be recharged.

3. Corrosion is one example of a _____ reaction.

4. A(n) _____ consists of two dissimilar metals: an insulator material separating the metals and an electrolyte, which is an electrically conductive solution.

5. A(n) _____ _____ battery is used to deliver a lower, steady level of power for a much longer period of time than an SLI-type battery.

6. Connecting cells together in _____ allows batteries to be produced in a variety of output voltage.

7. To prevent the battery positive and negative plate from touching and short circuiting, _____ plates are placed between each plate in every cell.

8. Lead acid battery _____ is a mixture of 36% sulfuric acid and 64% water.

9. A battery's internal _____ determines how quickly a battery can be charged or discharged.

10. Introduced in the middle 1970s, no- and low-maintenance batteries reduce or eliminate the _____ content in grids.

Labeling

Label the following diagrams with the correct terms.

1. Identify the components of a wet cell battery:

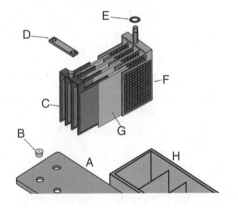

A. _____

B. _____

C. _____

D. _____

E. _____

F. _____

G. _____

H. _____

2. Identify the various types of battery terminals with their correct identification:

1. _____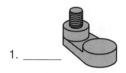

2. _____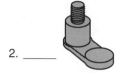

3. _____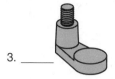

4. _____

5. _____

6. _____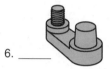

7. _____

8. _____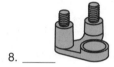

9. _____

A. Universal terminal (UT)

B. Low profile terminal (LPT)

C. Stud terminal (ST)

D. Wingnut terminal (WNT)

E. Automotive post and stud terminal (DT)

F. Dual wingnut terminal (DWNT)

G. High profile terminal (HPT)

H. L-terminal (LT)

I. Automotive post terminal (AP)

Crossword Puzzle

Use the clues in the column to complete the puzzle.

Across

3. An electrically conductive solution.

4. A chemical reaction that produces electricity when two dissimilar metals are placed in an electrolyte.

5. A situation that occurs when overcharging or rapid charging causes some gas to escape from the battery.

Down

1. The use of electricity to break down water into hydrogen and oxygen gases.

2. A chemical reaction that results in the soft sulfate turning to a hardened crystalline form that cannot be driven from the plates in the battery.

ASE-Type Questions

Read each item carefully, and then select the best response.

_____ 1. Technician A says that hybrid electric vehicles are not commonplace in urban transit but are likely to be in the future. Technician B says that commercial equipment, particularly diesel-powered equipment, will use multiple batteries connected in series or parallel to produce adequate starting current. Who is correct?
  A. Technician A
  B. Technician B
  C. Both Technician A and Technician B
  D. Neither Technician A nor Technician B

_____ 2. Technician A says that a spiral cell (Optima battery) is not considered a sealed lead acid (SLA) battery. Technician B says that an absorbed glass mat (AGM) battery is not considered a sealed lead acid (SLA) battery. Who is correct?
  A. Technician A
  B. Technician B
  C. Both Technician A and Technician B
  D. Neither Technician A nor Technician B

_____ 3. Technician A says that a fully charged 12-volt battery is 12.00 volts. Technician B says that connecting cells together in series allow batteries to be produced in a variety of output voltage. Who is correct?
  A. Technician A
  B. Technician B
  C. Both Technician A and Technician B
  D. Neither Technician A nor Technician B

_____ 4. Technician A says that the primary difference between deep cycle batteries and SLI is the thickness of the plates. Technician B says that deeply discharging SLI batteries dramatically shortens their service life. Who is correct?
  A. Technician A
  B. Technician B
  C. Both Technician A and Technician B
  D. Neither Technician A nor Technician B

_____ 5. Technician A says that lead acid battery electrolyte is a mixture of 64% sulfuric acid and 36% water. Technician B says that sulfuric acid has a specific gravity of 1.835, which means it is much heavier than water. Who is correct?
  A. Technician A
  B. Technician B
  C. Both Technician A and Technician B
  D. Neither Technician A nor Technician B

_____ 6. Technician A says that the battery case is usually made of polypropylene. Technician B says that ribbing and irregular features on the outside of the case add to the appearance of the battery and make it sturdy. Who is correct?
  A. Technician A
  B. Technician B
  C. Both Technician A and Technician B
  D. Neither Technician A nor Technician B

_____ 7. Technician A says that battery plates are made of two different compositions of lead that is fabricated from paste and bonded to lead-alloy grids. Technician B says that the negative plate uses lead peroxide (PbO_2) and the positive plate uses lead (Pb). Who is correct?
  A. Technician A
  B. Technician B
  C. Both Technician A and Technician B
  D. Neither Technician A nor Technician B

_____ **8.** Technician A says that both soft and hard sulfate can be driven from the plates, bringing the battery back into service. Technician B says that the latest innovation to lead acid battery technology incorporates black-carbon graphite foam into the plate paste to prevent sulfation damage. Who is correct?
   A. Technician A
   B. Technician B
   C. Both Technician A and Technician B
   D. Neither Technician A nor Technician B

_____ **9.** Technician A says that during charging and discharging, water in the electrolyte is broken apart into its constituent hydrogen and oxygen in a process called electrolysis. Technician B says if battery electrolyte is too low, the plates dry out, and the increased acid concentration of electrolyte permanently damages the grids. Who is correct?
   A. Technician A
   B. Technician B
   C. Both Technician A and Technician B
   D. Neither Technician A nor Technician B

_____ **10.** Technician A says that the latest and most advanced commercial vehicle battery technology are absorbed glass mat (AGM) batteries. Technician B says that the AGM battery can deliver more cranking amperage and absorb up to 10% more charging current than conventional lead acid. Who is correct?
   A. Technician A
   B. Technician B
   C. Both Technician A and Technician B
   D. Neither Technician A nor Technician B

Advanced Battery Technologies

Chapter Review

The following activities have been designed to help you refresh your knowledge of this chapter. Your instructor may require you to complete some or all of these activities as a regular part of your training program. You are encouraged to complete any activity that your instructor does not assign as a way to enhance your learning.

Matching

Match the following terms with the correct description or example.

A. Absorbed glass mat (AGM) battery

B. Gel cell battery

C. Lithium–ion (Li-ion) battery

D. Nickel–metal hydride (NiMH) battery

E. Spiral-wound cell battery

_____ **1.** A type of battery that does not use a galvanic reaction and in which a gel, salt, or solid material replaces the electrolyte solution.

_____ **2.** A type of lead acid battery that uses a thin fiberglass plate to absorb the electrolyte.

_____ **3.** A type of AGM battery in which the positive and negative electrodes are coiled into a tight spiral cell with an absorbent micro-glass mat placed between the plates.

_____ **4.** A type of battery to which silica has been added to the electrolyte solution to turn the solution to a gel-like consistency.

_____ **5.** A battery in which metal hydroxide forms the negative electrode and nickel oxide forms the positive electrode.

Multiple Choice

Read each item carefully, and then select the best response.

_____ **1.** The ability to convert charging current into storage capacity is known as _____.
   A. energy density
   B. deep cycling
   C. energy efficiency
   D. life span

_____ **2.** What type of batteries are used in consumer electronics and are also the preferred battery chemistry for hybrid drive vehicles?
   A. Lead acid
   B. Nickel–metal hydride (NiMH)
   C. Lithium–ion
   D. Nickel–cadmium (NiCad)

_____ **3.** Which type of battery chemistry produces the highest amount of voltage per cell?
   A. Lithium–ion
   B. Nickel–metal hydride (NiMH)
   C. Lead acid
   D. Ultra capacitors

_____ **4.** Which type of battery is used primarily in laptops, cell phones, and other consumer electronic devices?
   A. Nickel–cadmium (NiCad)
   B. Lithium–ion
   C. Spiral-wound
   D. Absorbed glass mat

_____ **5.** One lithium cell can replace _____ NiCad or NiMH cells, which have a cell voltage of only 1.2 volts.
  A. two
  B. three
  C. four
  D. five

_____ **6.** What is the advantage to using valve-regulated lead acid batteries?
  A. No need to add distilled water
  B. The fastest recharge possible
  C. No corrosive gas in battery compartment
  D. All of the above

_____ **7.** The battery case of a(n) _____ battery is pressurized constantly to between 1–4 psi (6.9–27.6 kPa).
  A. lead acid
  B. lithium–ion
  C. absorbed glass mat
  D. nickel–cadmium (NiCad)

_____ **8.** A deep cycle spiral cell battery will have a _____ top cover.
  A. blue
  B. red
  C. yellow
  D. green

_____ **9.** A(n) _____ is used to assist batteries for the first 1.5 seconds during cranking to supply an additional 2,000 amps of current to supplement the starter batteries.
  A. smart charger
  B. split charge relay
  C. ultra capacitor
  D. battery isolator

_____ **10.** A(n) _____ will sense battery voltage and drive a higher charge rate into weaker batteries and less current into stronger batteries.
  A. equalizer
  B. isolator
  C. balancer
  D. Either A or C

True/False

If you believe the statement to be more true than false, write the letter "T" in the space provided. If you believe the statement to be more false than true, write the letter "F".

_____ **1.** Energy efficiency is expressed in watt-hour per kilogram (Wh/kg) and watt-hour per liter (Wh/l).

_____ **2.** Nickel–metal hydride batteries provide twice the energy storage of lead acid batteries by weight, but only half the power output.

_____ **3.** Lithium-ion batteries are identical in construction as disposable lithium batteries.

_____ **4.** Cold temperatures slow down the nongalvanic reactions in lithium-ion batteries.

_____ **5.** Lithium-ion batteries cost eight times more than conventional lead acid batteries for each kilowatt of power produced per hour.

_____ **6.** There are two common types of valve-regulated lead acid batteries—absorbed glass mat and gel.

_____ **7.** Absorbed glass mat batteries can charge up to 10 times the rate of conventional lead acid batteries.

_____ **8.** The deeper the discharge between charges, the shorter the life cycle of the battery.

_____ **9.** Ultra capacitors are not worn out by continuous charge and discharge cycles.

_____ **10.** Battery equalizers enable charging of an auxiliary battery by the vehicle charging system and electrical separation of the auxiliary battery from the starting circuit when the engine shuts down.

Fill in the Blank

Read each item carefully, and then complete the statement by filling in the missing word(s).

1. The _____ _____ of a battery is measured by the number of charge/discharge cycles as a function of depth of discharge.

2. Lithium-ion batteries have low internal _____ and can discharge their current four times faster when compared to lead acid batteries.

3. _____ _____ _____ batteries eliminate water loss through a process called oxygen recombination.

4. Absorbed glass mat cells are extremely sensitive to damage from overcharging and should be charged using a(n) _____ charger.

5. A(n) _____-_____ cell battery is an absorbed glass mat battery in every way except that the electrodes for each cell are not made of rectangular plates.

6. In the mid-1960s, spill-proof batteries were introduced using _____ cells.

7. A(n) _____ _____ is capable of supplying large bursts of energy and quickly recharging, which makes them ideal for use in modern vehicles.

8. Components of the battery _____ system include battery isolators, low-voltage disconnects, battery balancers and equalizers, and battery monitors.

9. Devices that monitor battery voltage and disconnect noncritical electrical loads when the battery voltage level falls below a preset threshold value are called low-voltage _____.

10. Hybrid commercial vehicles use battery _____ to collect battery data for display to the operator and service technician.

Labeling

Label the following diagrams with the correct terms.

1. Identify the components of a flooded absorbed glass mat battery:

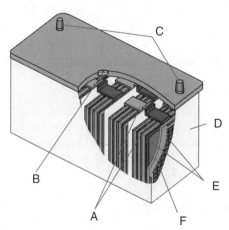

A. _____

B. _____

C. _____

D. _____

E. _____

F. _____

2. Identify the components of a spiral cell battery:

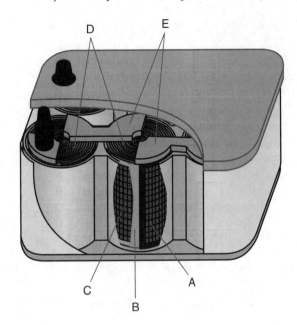

A. _____

B. _____

C. _____

D. _____

E. _____

3. Identify the components of a fully charged ultra capacitor:

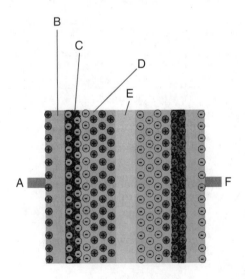

A. _____

B. _____

C. _____

D. _____

E. _____

F. _____

Crossword Puzzle

Use the clues in the column to complete the puzzle.

Across

3. A system designed to separate the main starting battery and the auxiliary battery. Also called a battery isolator system.

4. A new generation of high-capacity and high-energy density capacitors.

5. A system of electrical devices used to manage battery performance.

Down

1. A battery charger with microprocessor-controlled charging rates and times.

2. Devices designed to adjust battery voltage to compensate for unequal charges in multiple batteries. Also called battery equalizers.

ASE-Type Questions

Read each item carefully, and then select the best response.

_____ 1. Technician A says that the demand for advanced battery technology in commercial vehicles is growing. Technician B says that, not only do the increasing popular hybrid electric vehicles require advanced batteries, heavy-duty commercial vehicles also have a greater need for electrical storage capacity to run accessories. Who is correct?
   A. Technician A
   B. Technician B
   C. Both Technician A and Technician B
   D. Neither Technician A nor Technician B

_____ 2. Technician A says that nickel–metal hydride (NiMH) is one type of battery used in commercial vehicles. Technician B says that lithium and lead acid batteries are also used in commercial vehicles. Who is correct?
   A. Technician A
   B. Technician B
   C. Both Technician A and Technician B
   D. Neither Technician A nor Technician B

_____ 3. Technician A says that lithium–ion cells maintain a constant voltage for over 90% of their discharge curve as compared to conventional lead acid batteries maintaining voltage until only 60% discharged. Technician B says that once charged, lithium–ion batteries self-discharge at very low rate. Who is correct?
   A. Technician A
   B. Technician B
   C. Both Technician A and Technician B
   D. Neither Technician A nor Technician B

_____ 4. Technician A says that one disadvantage of current lithium–ion battery technology is cost. Technician B says that lithium–ion batteries cost four times more than conventional lead acid batteries for each kilowatt of power produced per hour. Who is correct?
   A. Technician A
   B. Technician B
   C. Both Technician A and Technician B
   D. Neither Technician A nor Technician B

_____ 5. Technician A says that a VRLA battery has the highest cranking amps—even at low temperature. Technician B says that a VRLA battery has triple the life of traditional lead acid batteries. Who is correct?
   A. Technician A
   B. Technician B
   C. Both Technician A and Technician B
   D. Neither Technician A nor Technician B

_____ 6. Technician A says that no vents are used on AGM batteries. Technician B says that AGM batteries will be damaged if charged at greater than 13.2 volts. Who is correct?
   A. Technician A
   B. Technician B
   C. Both Technician A and Technician B
   D. Neither Technician A nor Technician B

_____ 7. Technician A says that a smart charger is a battery charger in which microprocessors control charging rates and times. Technician B says that AGM state of charge can be tested with a battery hydrometer. Who is correct?
   A. Technician A
   B. Technician B
   C. Both Technician A and Technician B
   D. Neither Technician A nor Technician B

_____ **8.** Technician A says that ultra capacitors supplement increases to starter torque and speed. Technician B says that ultra capacitors are currently used to assist batteries for the first 3.5 seconds during cranking, during which time they can supply an additional 1,000 amps of current to supplement the starter batteries. Who is correct?

  A. Technician A

  B. Technician B

  C. Both Technician A and Technician B

  D. Neither Technician A nor Technician B

_____ **9.** Technician A says that battery management systems (BMS) are designed to protect the cells or the battery from damage. Technician B says that battery management systems (BMS) are designed to prolong the life of the battery. Who is correct?

  A. Technician A

  B. Technician B

  C. Both Technician A and Technician B

  D. Neither Technician A nor Technician B

_____ **10.** Technician A says that battery balancers attempt to adjust battery voltage to compensate for unequal charges in multiple batteries. Technician B says that equalizers are found in many commercial applications using 24-volt charging systems, including transit and tour buses, private coaches, and off-highway equipment. Who is correct?

  A. Technician A

  B. Technician B

  C. Both Technician A and Technician B

  D. Neither Technician A nor Technician B

Servicing Commercial Vehicle Batteries

Tire Tread:
© AbleStock

Chapter Review

The following activities have been designed to help you refresh your knowledge of this chapter. Your instructor may require you to complete some or all of these activities as a regular part of your training program. You are encouraged to complete any activity that your instructor does not assign as a way to enhance your learning.

Matching

Match the following terms with the correct description or example.

A. Constant-current charger

B. Constant-voltage charger

C. Intelligent charger

D. Taper-current charger

E. Trickle charger

_____ **1.** A direct current (DC) power that is a step-down transformer with a rectifier to provide the DC voltage to charge.

_____ **2.** A battery charger that charges at a low amperage rate.

_____ **3.** A battery charger that applies either constant voltage or constant amperage to the battery through a manually adjusted current selection switch.

_____ **4.** A battery charger that automatically varies the voltage applied to the battery to maintain a constant amperage flow into the battery.

_____ **5.** A battery charger that varies its output according to the sensed condition of the battery it is charging.

Multiple Choice

Read each item carefully, and then select the best response.

_____ **1.** Any voltage exceeding _____ volts between the negative battery post and the top of the battery indicates that the battery is leaking current due to excessive dirt or grime.
   A. 0.25
   B. 0.3
   C. 0.4
   D. 0.5

_____ **2.** Never wear _____ when working on or near batteries, as they may provide an accidental short-circuit path for high currents.
   A. neck chains
   B. watches
   C. rings
   D. Any of the above

_____ **3.** Subjecting a battery to prolonged undercharge conditions can cause _____.
   A. oxidation
   B. sulfation
   C. grid corrosion
   D. shedding

—— **4.** A condition called ——— takes place primarily in the positive grid and is accelerated by overcharging and high temperatures.
   A. grid corrosion
   B. sulfation
   C. shedding
   D. calcification

—— **5.** A fully charged battery should have an open-circuit voltage of ——— volts.
   A. 2.1
   B. 6.25
   C. 12.65
   D. 24

—— **6.** The state of charge is best evaluated by measuring the density of electrolyte in each cell using a ———.
   A. refractometer
   B. spectrometer
   C. bulb-type hydrometer
   D. Either A or C

—— **7.** If a battery has an open circuit voltage of 12.24 and a specific gravity reading of 1.190 it would indicate that the battery has a ——— state of charge.
   A. 100%
   B. 75%
   C. 50%
   D. 25%

—— **8.** A ——— test performs a measurement of the amount of active plate surface area available for chemical reaction.
   A. state of charge
   B. conductance
   C. discharge
   D. load

—— **9.** A(n) ——— charger can be left connected indefinitely without overcharging since it can maintain a float charge.
   A. intelligent
   B. pulsed
   C. trickle
   D. taper-current

—— **10.** The voltage threshold of a low-voltage disconnect systems is normally set between ———.
   A. 2.1 and 2.3 volts
   B. 6.2 and 6.4 volts
   C. 12.2 and 12.4 volts
   D. 24.2 and 24.4 volts

True/False

If you believe the statement to be more true than false, write the letter "T" in the space provided. If you believe the statement to be more false than true, write the letter "F".

—— **1.** To clean dirt and grime from the top of a battery you should use a mixture of diluted ammonia and baking soda.

—— **2.** An explosive gas mixture consisting of hydrogen and oxygen is produced during the charging and discharging of a battery.

—— **3.** To minimize self-discharge, batteries are best stored in cool, dry places.

—— **4.** Although voltage and electrolyte readings may be satisfactory, contaminants even in one cell will cause the battery to self-discharge quickly.

—— **5.** The readings from a refractometer must be corrected for electrolyte temperature.

—— **6.** All manufacturers require the use of a state of charge test in order for warranty coverage to be considered.

_____ **7.** The most sophisticated testers today can identify not only the type and condition of a battery, but also the manufacturer and other battery details.

_____ **8.** If a battery fails a load test after it has had its state of charge properly qualified, the battery should be recharged and tested again.

_____ **9.** Vehicle computer systems require a small amount of power to maintain the computer memory while the vehicle is off.

_____ **10.** The recycling of batteries is mandatory.

Fill in the Blank

Read each item carefully, and then complete the statement by filling in the missing word(s).

1. A(n) _____ drain of battery current should be no more than 0.5 amps of current.
2. Always wear _____ clothing such as rubber gloves and goggles or full-face shields when handling batteries.
3. Always remove the _____ or ground terminal first when disconnecting battery cables.
4. A three-minute battery charge test can be used to verify a diagnosis of _____.
5. Excessive _____ can cause open circuits in the internal battery connections and "shed" or shake loose plate material, which settles to the bottom of the battery case.
6. Batteries should be given a _____ inspection before proceeding with any other significant tests.
7. A(n) _____ _____ _____ test will tell you how charged or discharged a battery is, not how much capacity it has.
8. The _____ _____ of electrolyte indicates the state cell charge.
9. A(n) _____ test determines the ability of a battery to deliver cranking amperage and is based on the battery CCA rating.
10. Batteries connected in _____ are connected side by side, with positive connected to positive and negative to negative.

Skill Drills

Test your knowledge of skill drills by filling in the correct words in the photo captions.

1. Performing a Battery State of Charge Test:

Step 1: If the battery is not a _____ unit, it will have individual or combined removable _____ on top. Remove them and look inside to check the level of the _____. If the level is below the tops of the _____ and their _____ inside, add _____ water or water with a low _____ content until it

covers them. Be careful not to overfill the cells; they could "boil" over when charging. If water is added, the battery will need to be _____ to ensure the newly added water mixes with the electrolyte before measuring the _____ _____.

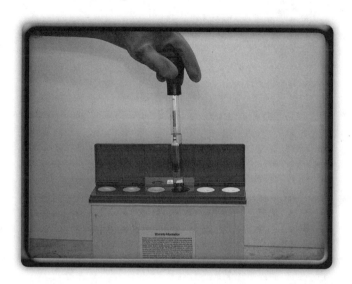

Step 2: Using a _____ designed for battery testing, draw some of the electrolyte into the tester and look at the float inside it. A scale indicates the battery's relative _____ of _____ by measuring how high the float sits in relation to the _____ level. A very _____ overall reading (1.150 or below) indicates a low state of charge. A _____ overall reading (about 1.280) indicates a high state of charge. The reading from each _____ should be the same. If the variation between the highest and lowest cell exceed 0.050, the battery is _____ and should be _____. Be sure to consult temperature _____ _____ if the battery electrolyte temperature is not at or around 80°F (27°C).

Step 3: Using the _____, place one or two _____ of electrolyte on the specimen window and lower the cover plate. Make sure the liquid completely _____ the _____ window. If not, add another drop of electrolyte:

- Look into the _____ with the refractometer under a bright _____.
- Read the scale for _____ _____. The point where the _____ area meets the _____ area is the reading. Compare the _____ with the values given in step 2.

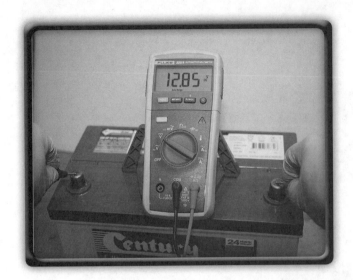

Step 4: For open circuit _____ testing with a _____, perform the following actions:

    a. With the engine not running, select the "_____ _____" position on your _____ and attach the _____ to the battery terminals (red to _____, black to _____).

    b. With all vehicle _____ switched _____ and the battery near 80°F (27°C), the voltage reading should be _____ volts if the battery is fully charged. This may be slightly lower at _____ temperatures.

2. Conductance Testing a Battery:

Step 1: Consult manufacturers' procedures and guidelines for the _____ being tested and _____ being used.

Step 2: Isolate batteries if they are _____ in a _____ so that they can be individually tested.

Step 3: Identify the type of _____, _____, and _____ for input into the test unit.

Step 4: Save information and _____ as required into the _____ _____.

Step 5: _____ the _____.

Step 6: Analyze the result by _____ them to manufacturer _____.

Step 7: Print or record _____ of the _____ _____. Repeat steps if _____ batteries are to be _____.

3. Load Testing a Battery:

Step 1:   With the tester controls _____ and the _____ _____ turned to the off position, connect the tester _____ to the battery. Observe the correct _____ and be sure the _____ fully contact the battery _____.

Step 2:   Place the inductive _____ _____ around either the _____ or the _____ tester _____ in the correct orientation.

Step 3:   Verify that the battery's _____ _____ _____ is more than _____% before beginning the test. Also measure the battery's _____ to make any correction to the cut-off _____ threshold.

Step 4:   If you are using an automatic _____ _____, enter the battery's _____ and select "test" or "start." If you are using a _____ load tester, calculate the _____ _____, which is _____ of the CCA. Turn the _____ _____ or press the "_____" button.

Step 5:   Maintain _____ _____ of 1/2 the CCA rating for _____ seconds while watching the _____. At the end of the _____-second test load, read the voltmeter and immediately turn the control knob _____. At room temperature, the voltage must be _____ volts or higher at the end of the _____-second load. If the battery is _____ than room temperature, correct the battery failure _____ _____ against temperature. Close to 1/10 volt lower is allowed for every _____°F (12°C) below _____°F (21°C). Using the results from the test, determine any necessary action.

4. Jump-Starting Commercial Vehicles:

Step 1:   Position the _____ battery close enough to the _____ battery that it is within comfortable range of your _____ _____. If the charged battery is in another vehicle, make sure the two vehicles are not _____.

Step 2:   Always connect the leads in this order:

- First, connect the _____ jumper lead to the _____ terminal of the _____ battery in the vehicle you are trying to start. The _____ terminal is the one with the _____ sign.
- Next, connect the other end of this lead to the _____ _____ of the _____ battery.
- Then connect the _____ jumper lead to the _____ terminal of the _____ battery. The _____ terminal is the one with the _____ sign.
- Connect the other end of the _____ lead to a good _____ on the _____ of the vehicle with the _____ battery, and as far away as possible from the battery.
- DO NOT connect the lead to the _____ terminal of the _____ battery itself; doing so may cause a dangerous _____.

Step 3:   Try to _____ the vehicle with the discharged battery. If the _____ battery does not have enough _____ or the jumper cables are too _____ in diameter to do this, _____ the _____ in the booster vehicle and allow it to partially _____ the discharged battery for several _____. Try starting the first vehicle again with the booster vehicle's engine _____.

Step 4:   Disconnect the leads in the _____ _____ of connecting them. Remove the _____ lead from the chassis _____ away from the battery. Then disconnect the _____ lead from the _____ _____. Next remove the _____ lead from the booster battery, and lastly, disconnect the other _____ end from the battery in the vehicle you have just _____. If the _____ _____ is working correctly and the battery is in good condition, the battery will be _____ while the engine is running. Note, a deeply _____ set of batteries can cause the _____ to charge at an excessively high rate for too long and _____ the alternator.

5.   Measuring Parasitic Draw on a Battery:

Step 1:   Research the _____ _____ specifications in the appropriate service information for the vehicle you are diagnosing. Typically this is between _____ amps and _____ amps (_____–_____ milliamps).

Step 2:   Connect the low-current _____ around (or insert the ammeter in _____ with) the _____ battery cable and _____ the parasitic draw. Compare the parasitic draw with _____.

Step 3:   Disconnect the circuit fuses _____ at a time to determine the _____ of excessive parasitic _____ draw. Determine any necessary actions.

Crossword Puzzle

Use the clues in the column to complete the puzzle.

Across

3. A battery test that subjects the battery to a high rate of discharge, and the voltage is then measured after a set time to see how well the battery creates that current flow.

5. A battery charger that sends current into the battery in pulses of one-second cycles; used to recover sulfated batteries.

Down

1. A type of battery test that determines the battery's ability to conduct current.

2. A device that claps around a conductor to measure current flow. It is often used in conjunction with a digital volt-ohm meter (DVOM).

4. A process that reduces the plate surface area and therefore reduces capacity. This process may also produce short circuits between the bottom of positive and negative plates.

ASE-Type Questions

Read each item carefully, and then select the best response.

_____ 1. Technician A says that batteries should be the starting point when diagnosing complaints such as hard starting, slow cranking, or no start. Technician B says that dirt on top of the battery does not cause premature self-discharge of the battery. Who is correct?
   A. Technician A
   B. Technician B
   C. Both Technician A and Technician B
   D. Neither Technician A nor Technician B

_____ 2. Technician A says you should never create a low-resistance connection or short across the battery terminals. Technician B says to always wear protective clothing such as rubber gloves and goggles or full-face shields when handling batteries. Who is correct?
   A. Technician A
   B. Technician B
   C. Both Technician A and Technician B
   D. Neither Technician A nor Technician B

_____ 3. Technician A says that a low electrolyte level is a common reason for sulfation. Technician B says that high ambient temperature is a common reason for sulfation. Who is correct?
   A. Technician A
   B. Technician B
   C. Both Technician A and Technician B
   D. Neither Technician A nor Technician B

_____ 4. Technician A says that batteries may slowly fail over time through due to the loss of a cell or open circuits within the internal connections. Technician B says that batteries may slowly fail over time through the gradual loss of capacity caused by plate deterioration. Who is correct?
   A. Technician A
   B. Technician B
   C. Both Technician A and Technician B
   D. Neither Technician A nor Technician B

_____ 5. Technician A says that, if electrolyte is lost due to spillage, then the battery should be topped up with electrolyte. Technician B says that, if electrolyte level is lost through evaporation, then tap water should be added. Who is correct?
   A. Technician A
   B. Technician B
   C. Both Technician A and Technician B
   D. Neither Technician A nor Technician B

_____ 6. Technician A says to always coat battery terminals with chassis grease to prevent corrosion. Technician B says that all slide mechanisms on battery trays should work properly. Who is correct?
   A. Technician A
   B. Technician B
   C. Both Technician A and Technician B
   D. Neither Technician A nor Technician B

_____ 7. Technician A says that a fully charged battery should have an open-circuit voltage of 12.25 volts. Technician B says that, if the battery has been recently charged, a light load applied to the battery for a few minutes will remove a surface charge. Who is correct?
   A. Technician A
   B. Technician B
   C. Both Technician A and Technician B
   D. Neither Technician A nor Technician B

_____ 8. Technician A says that a conductance test determines the battery's ability to conduct current. Technician B says that batteries must be fully charged to test battery conductance. Who is correct?
   A. Technician A
   B. Technician B
   C. Both Technician A and Technician B
   D. Neither Technician A nor Technician B

_____ **9.** Technician A says that the load test determines the ability of a battery to deliver cranking amperage and is based on the battery CCA rating. Technician B says that a battery must be at least 95% charged to perform a capacity test, so SOC must be first evaluated before proceeding. Who is correct?

   A. Technician A
   B. Technician B
   C. Both Technician A and Technician B
   D. Neither Technician A nor Technician B

_____ **10.** Technician A says that all modern vehicles have a small amount of current draw when the ignition is turned off. Technician B says that this charge is used to run some of the vehicle systems, such as various modules making up the onboard vehicle network. Who is correct?

   A. Technician A
   B. Technician B
   C. Both Technician A and Technician B
   D. Neither Technician A nor Technician B

Chapter Review

The following activities have been designed to help you refresh your knowledge of this chapter. Your instructor may require you to complete some or all of these activities as a regular part of your training program. You are encouraged to complete any activity that your instructor does not assign as a way to enhance your learning.

Matching

Match the following terms with the correct description or example.

- **A.** Automatic disengagement lockout (ADLO)
- **B.** Counter-electromotive force (CEMF)
- **C.** Overcrank protection (OCP) thermostat
- **D.** Planetary gear reduction drive
- **E.** Reduction gear drive

_____ **1.** A device that monitors the temperature of the motor and opens a relay circuit to interrupt the current to the solenoid if prolonged cranking causes the motor temperature to exceed a safe threshold.

_____ **2.** A type of gear reduction system in which a planetary gear set reduces the starter profile to multiply motor torque to the pinion gear.

_____ **3.** An electromagnetic force produced by the spinning magnetic field of the armature, which induces current in the opposite direction of battery current through the motor.

_____ **4.** A starter motor drive system in which the motor multiplies torque to the starter pinion gear by using an extra gear between the armature and the starter drive mechanism.

_____ **5.** A device that prevents the starter motor from operating if the engine is running.

Multiple Choice

Read each item carefully, and then select the best response.

_____ **1.** A _____ type of electric starter can be identified by an offset drive housing to the motor housing.
- **A.** direct drive
- **B.** reduction gear drive
- **C.** planetary gear reduction drive
- **D.** pneumatic

_____ **2.** Often used as blower motors, _____ -type DC motors develop less torque but maintain a constant speed.
- **A.** shunt
- **B.** compound
- **C.** stepper
- **D.** series

_____ **3.** What type DC motors are used in instrument clusters' gauges, turbochargers, and EGR actuators where high precision movement is required?
- **A.** Series
- **B.** Compound
- **C.** Stepper
- **D.** Shunt

_____ **4.** Low-voltage burn-out can be prevented by using _____.
- **A.** ultra-capacitors
- **B.** correctly sized battery cables
- **C.** overcrank protection switches
- **D.** All of the above

_____ **5.** A(n) _____ winding is made of heavy, flat, copper strips.
   A. shunt motor
   B. armature
   C. commutator
   D. field coil

_____ **6.** It is the role of the _____ to switch the direction of current flow through each armature coil as the armature rotates.
   A. commutator
   B. pole shoes
   C. field coil
   D. starter housing

_____ **7.** The pinion drive gear is attached to a roller-type _____ that is splined to the starter armature.
   A. one-way clutch
   B. two-way clutch
   C. overrunning clutch
   D. Either A or C

_____ **8.** Pinion clearance is adjusted using _____.
   A. an eccentric shift fork pin
   B. shims
   C. a screw or nut on the solenoid core
   D. Any of the above

_____ **9.** The automatic disengagement lockout relay contacts are connected in _____ with the starter motor control circuit.
   A. series
   B. parallel
   C. series-parallel
   D. None of the above

_____ **10.** Intermittent starter operation or starter operation that resumes after it is tapped with a hammer may indicate _____.
   A. a damaged armature
   B. worn bushings or bearings
   C. worn brushes
   D. damaged field coils

True/False

If you believe the statement to be more true than false, write the letter "T" in the space provided. If you believe the statement to be more false than true, write the letter "F".

_____ **1.** Adding more batteries increases the amount of amperage available for cranking, but the system voltage remains the same.

_____ **2.** Gear reduction starters can reduce starter weight by more than 50%.

_____ **3.** Like magnetic poles attract one another and unlike poles repel one another.

_____ **4.** The compound and stepper motor are the two most common types of DC motors found in the automotive industry.

_____ **5.** Battery current and counter-electromotive force current both flow through a motor at the same time but in opposite directions.

_____ **6.** Starters will use any combination of voltage and amperage to produce the necessary output power.

_____ **7.** Field coils are connected in parallel with the armature windings through the starter brushes.

_____ **8.** Safety switches can be located in either of two places in the control circuit—interrupting either the ground or battery positive of the starter relay.

_____ **9.** Ignition switches normally have five separate positions.

_____ **10.** Slow-crank and no-crank conditions can be caused by both electrical and mechanical faults.

Fill in the Blank

Read each item carefully, and then complete the statement by filling in the missing word(s).

1. To supply more cranking amperage in a 12-volt system, batteries are connected in _____.

2. The only gear torque multiplication in a _____ drive starter is between the pinion gear and the ring gear.

3. A(n) _____, or air starting system, consists of a geared air motor, starting valve, and a pressure tank.

4. Heavy-duty starter motors use _____ in their field and armature windings.

5. Most starter motors are _____ -wound motors because they develop the greatest amount of torque at zero rpm.

6. The _____ assembly presses onto the armature shaft.

7. A(n) _____ is an electromagnet that is used to perform work and has mechanical action.

8. The _____ _____ circuit allows the operator to use a small amount of battery current provided by the ignition switch to control the flow of a large amount of current in the starting circuit.

9. Series-parallel electrical systems, or _____ _____ as it is generally called, use two, four, or six 12-volt batteries connected in series through an equalizer to supply most of the vehicle's electrical systems.

10. Testing starter motor _____ draw is the best indicator of overall cranking system performance.

Labeling

Label the following diagrams with the correct terms.

1. Identify the components of a direct drive starter motor:

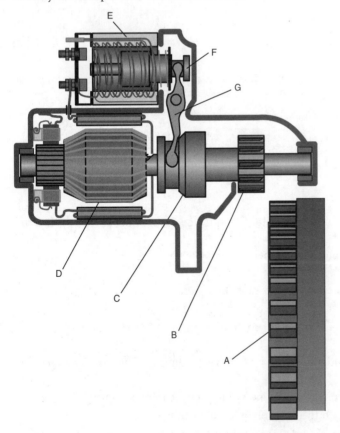

A. _____

B. _____

C. _____

D. _____

E. _____

F. _____

G. _____

2. Identify the components of a typical planetary gear reduction drive starter motor:

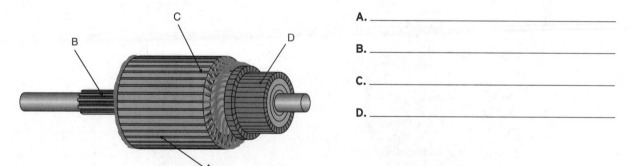

A. _____

B. _____

C. _____

D. _____

3. Identify the features of an armature:

A. _____

B. _____

C. _____

D. _____

4. Identify the components of a simple single-loop motor:

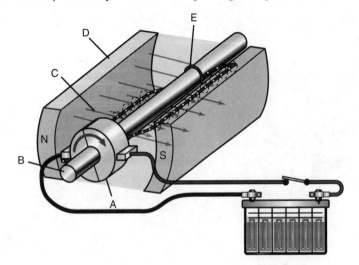

A. _____

B. _____

C. _____

D. _____

E. _____

5. Identify the components of a starter drive one-way clutch:

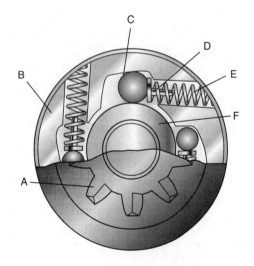

A. _____

B. _____

C. _____

D. _____

E. _____

F. _____

Skill Drills

Test your knowledge of skill drills by filling in the correct words in the photo captions.

1. Testing Starter Draw:

Step 1: Research the specifications for the starter draw test. Place an inductive type _____ _____ over either the positive or negative cable. It doesn't matter which starter cable is measured, as it is a _____ circuit, so _____ will be the same at any point in the circuit.

Step 2: Connect the AVR voltmeter leads to the _____ or at the _____.

Step 3: Make sure all of the appropriate wires are _____ the clamp and the clamp is completely _____.

Step 4: Disable the engine from starting by removing a _____ from the engine _____ or disabling the _____ system shut-off _____.

Step 5: With the engine disabled, _____ the engine and record the _____ and _____ as soon as the _____ stabilize.

Step 6: Compare the readings with the _____ and determine any necessary actions.

2. Testing Starter Circuit Voltage Drop:

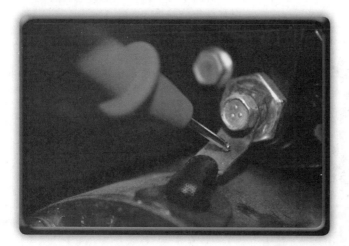

Step 1: Set the DVOM to _____. Connect the _____ lead to the _____ battery post and the _____ lead to the positive _____ _____ on the starting motor.

Step 2: Crank the engine and read the maximum _____ _____ for the _____ side of the circuit. Connect the _____ lead to the _____ battery post and the _____ lead to the _____ terminal or starting motor _____ _____. Crank the engine and read the voltage drop.

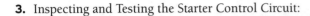

Step 3: If the voltage drop is more than _____ volts on either side of the circuit, use the voltmeter and wiring diagram to _____ the voltage drop. Conduct further _____ _____ tests across individual components and cables. Determine any necessary actions.

3. Inspecting and Testing the Starter Control Circuit:

Step 1: Use a _____ to measure _____ between the solenoid control circuit terminal on the solenoid (R) terminal and the _____ of the starter while the engine is _____.

Step 2: If the voltage is less than _____ volts, measure the voltage drop between the _____ terminal and the _____.

Step 3: If the voltage drop is less than _____ volts, measure the voltage drop on the _____ side of the _____ control circuit.

Step 4: If the voltage drop is higher than _____ volts on either side of the circuit, use the _____ _____ to guide you in isolating the _____ _____ on that side of the circuit. Continue conducting voltage drop tests across individual components and cables.

Step 5: If the _____ _____ are within specifications on both sides of the circuit, the _____ of the solenoid pull-in and hold-in _____ will need to be _____. If out of specifications, the solenoid or _____ _____ and solenoid will need to be _____.

4. Inspecting and Testing Relays and Solenoids:

Step 1: To test a relay, measure the _____ of the relay _____ and compare with specifications. If the relay is out of specifications, _____ it.

Step 2: Use a relay _____ to mount the relay on top of the relay _____ so you can check the _____ _____ wiring and perform _____ _____ tests on the contacts.

Step 3: Activate the relay while measuring the _____ across the relay _____. If it is near _____ voltage, the control circuit wiring is _____.

Step 4: Measure the voltage across the _____ with the relay not activated. This should read near _____ _____ if both sides of the _____ circuit are OK. If not, perform _____ _____ tests on each side of the switch circuit.

Step 5: Activate the relay while measuring the _____ _____ across the _____. If it is more than _____ volts, the relay will need to be _____.

Step 6: To test a starter solenoid, measure the _____ _____ across the solenoid _____ _____ with the key in the _____ position. If it is more than _____ volts, replace the solenoid or starter assembly.

Step 7: If the solenoid does not _____ with the key in the _____ position, remove the electrical connection for the _____ _____ at the solenoid.

Step 8: Use a _____ _____ to apply battery voltage to the control circuit terminal on the solenoid and see if the solenoid _____. If it does, then there is likely a _____ in the control circuit wiring. If the solenoid still does not click (and the circuit is grounded), then the solenoid _____ or starter _____ are likely worn (sometimes _____ on the starter while the key is turned to the crank position will free up the brushes enough that the pull-in winding can operate). Determine any necessary actions.

5. Removing and Replacing a Starter Motor and Inspecting the Ring Gear or Flex Plate:

Step 1: Locate and follow the appropriate procedure in the _____ _____.

Step 2: Disconnect the battery _____ and electrical connections to the _____ _____.

Step 3: Loosen the _____ _____, leaving them in place until you are ready to remove the _____ _____.

Step 4: Remove the _____ _____ by supporting its weight while the _____ _____ are removed. You may need _____ to support the weight of the starter while this step is being conducted.

Step 5: Examine the starter _____ for any wear to the drive _____.

Step 6: Using a work light, inspect the _____ _____ or flex plate _____ for damage. Slowly turn the engine over while checking the _____ _____ or _____ _____, ensuring the circumference is inspected. In difficult-to-see locations, an engine _____ may provide assistance. Report any damage to the ring gear.

Step 7: Reinstall the _____ _____ by _____ the steps used in steps 1 through 4 above.

Crossword Puzzle

Use the clues in the column to complete the puzzle.

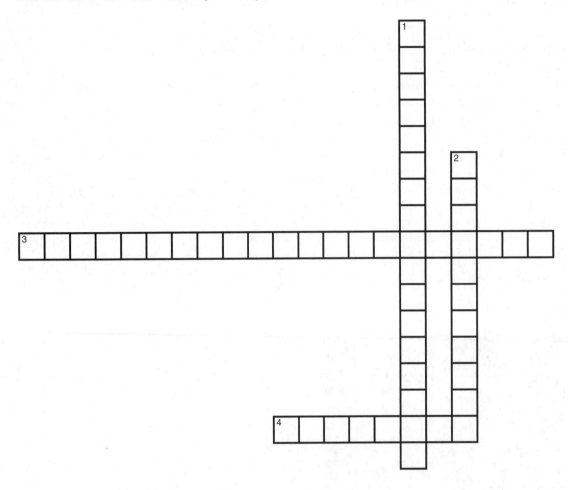

Across

3. A relay connected to the alternator that detects alternating current only when the alternator is charging.

4. The only rotating component of the starter; has three main components: the shaft, windings, and the commutator.

Down

1. A damaging condition for starter motors in which excess current flows through the starter, causing the motor to burn out prematurely.

2. A starter motor drive system in which the motor armature directly engages the flywheel through a pinion gear.

ASE-Type Questions

Read each item carefully, and then select the best response.

_____ 1. Technician A says that dozens of electric motors are found in heavy vehicles operating a variety of devices from electric seats, fuel and coolant pumps, fan blower motors, and even instrument gauges. Technician B says that the largest of all these electric motors is the starter motor. Who is correct?
   A. Technician A
   B. Technician B
   C. Both Technician A and Technician B
   D. Neither Technician A nor Technician B

_____ 2. Technician A says that all electric motors operate using principles of magnetic attraction and repulsion. Technician B says that because like magnetic poles attract one another and unlike poles repel, it is possible to arrange magnetic poles within the motor to be continuously in a state repulsion and attraction. Who is correct?
   A. Technician A
   B. Technician B
   C. Both Technician A and Technician B
   D. Neither Technician A nor Technician B

_____ 3. Technician A says that the series and shunt motor are the two most common types of motor found in the automotive industry. Technician B says that series motors are called "series" because the field and armature windings are connected in series. Who is correct?
   A. Technician A
   B. Technician B
   C. Both Technician A and Technician B
   D. Neither Technician A nor Technician B

_____ 4. Technician A says that series-wound motors also are self-limiting in speed due to the development of a counter-electromotive force (CEMF). Technician B says that CEMF is produced by the spinning magnetic field of the armature, which induces current in the same direction of battery current through the motor. Who is correct?
   A. Technician A
   B. Technician B
   C. Both Technician A and Technician B
   D. Neither Technician A nor Technician B

_____ 5. Technician A says that cranking an engine with low battery voltage causes one of the most damaging conditions for a starter. Technician B says that low-voltage burn-out occurs when excess amperage flows through the starter, causing the motor to burn out prematurely. Who is correct?
   A. Technician A
   B. Technician B
   C. Both Technician A and Technician B
   D. Neither Technician A nor Technician B

_____ 6. Technician A says that the starter housing, or frame, encloses and supports the internal starter components, protecting them and intensifying the magnetic fields produced in the field coils. Technician B says that in the starter housing field coils and their pole shoes are securely attached to the inside of the iron housing. Who is correct?
   A. Technician A
   B. Technician B
   C. Both Technician A and Technician B
   D. Neither Technician A nor Technician B

_____ 7. Technician A says that different from the thin wire used in shunt motors, armature windings are made of heavy, flat, copper strips that can handle the heavy current flow of the series motor. Technician B says that in a four-brush motor, each half of a coil is wound at 60 degrees to each other. Who is correct?
   A. Technician A
   B. Technician B
   C. Both Technician A and Technician B
   D. Neither Technician A nor Technician B

_____ **8.** Technician A says that solenoid on the starter motor generates the high current flow required by the starter motor on and off. Technician B says that the solenoid on the starter motor engages the starter drive with the pinion gear. Who is correct?

   A. Technician A
   B. Technician B
   C. Both Technician A and Technician B
   D. Neither Technician A nor Technician B

_____ **9.** Technician A says that the starter drive transmits the rotational force from the starter armature to the engine via the ring gear that is mounted on the engine flywheel or torque converter. Technician B says that in the past gear reduction starters were used but that today, direct-drive starters have replaced them. Who is correct?

   A. Technician A
   B. Technician B
   C. Both Technician A and Technician B
   D. Neither Technician A nor Technician B

_____ **10.** Technician A says that some starter motors are equipped with an overcrank protection (OCP) thermostat. Technician B says that the thermostat monitors the temperature of the motor. Who is correct?

   A. Technician A
   B. Technician B
   C. Both Technician A and Technician B
   D. Neither Technician A nor Technician B

Charging Systems

Chapter Review

The following activities have been designed to help you refresh your knowledge of this chapter. Your instructor may require you to complete some or all of these activities as a regular part of your training program. You are encouraged to complete any activity that your instructor does not assign as a way to enhance your learning.

Matching

Match the following terms with the correct description or example.

A. Alternator ripple

B. Delta windings

C. Load-dumping

D. Rectification

E. Wye windings

_____ **1.** A process of converting alternating current (AC) into direct current (DC).

_____ **2.** The top of the waveform.

_____ **3.** Stator windings in which one end of each phase winding is taken to a central point where the ends are connected together.

_____ **4.** A feature that allows temporary suppression of high-voltage spikes.

_____ **5.** Stator windings in which the windings are connected in the shape of a triangle.

Multiple Choice

Read each item carefully, and then select the best response.

_____ **1.** The development of low-cost solid-state _____ in the 1950s made the use of alternating current "generators" (alternators) possible.

    A. batteries

    B. rectifiers

    C. solenoids

    D. capacitors

_____ **2.** The alternator converts mechanical energy into electrical energy by _____.

    A. electromagnetic induction

    B. rectification

    C. kinetic unification

    D. recombination

_____ **3.** The amount of current produced from an alternator is proportional to _____.

    A. the strength of the magnetic field in the rotor

    B. the speed at which the magnetic field rotates

    C. the angle between the magnetic field and conductors in the stator

    D. All of the above

_____ **4.** The two halves of the rotor's soft iron core are arranged into _____.

    A. claws

    B. rings

    C. pole pieces

    D. Either A or C

_____ **5.** The _____ is made of loops of coiled wire wrapped around a slotted metal alternator frame.
   A. stator
   B. rectifier
   C. rotor
   D. regulator

_____ **6.** A _____ - wound alternator is best adapted to supply higher amperage output to charge multiple batteries and the heavy electrical loads found in trucks and buses.
   A. Wye
   B. Delta
   C. Delta-Wye
   D. Wye-Delta

_____ **7.** A minimum of _____ diodes is required to completely rectify all three phases of alternating current into DC current.
   A. 3
   B. 6
   C. 9
   D. 12

_____ **8.** A(n) _____ voltage regulator regulates the field current by controlling the resistance through to ground.
   A. "A" type
   B. "B" type
   C. isolated field type
   D. All of the above

_____ **9.** Charging at voltages above 15 volts (12-volt system) and 31 volts (24-volt system) will cause _____.
   A. bulb and LED failure
   B. batteries to gas excessively
   C. battery plates to shed grid material
   D. All of the above

_____ **10.** Connecting alternators in _____ requires the output of each to be properly balanced so one will not work harder than the other and wear out.
   A. series
   B. parallel
   C. Wye
   D. Delta

True/False

If you believe the statement to be more true than false, write the letter "T" in the space provided. If you believe the statement to be more false than true, write the letter "F".

_____ **1.** The 12-volt electrical system load for a late model highway tractor averages 45 amps of current.

_____ **2.** DC generators are much more efficient at producing current than alternators.

_____ **3.** Alternators will produce current when rotated in either direction.

_____ **4.** Maximum amperage output of an alternator is limited by the speed at which an alternator rotates.

_____ **5.** Most heavy-duty alternators typically contain between four and six claws.

_____ **6.** Residually magnetized rotors will begin to induce current in the stator windings when the alternator starts rotating without any current passing through the rotor coil.

_____ **7.** Combination Wye and Delta stators are commonly found in heavy-duty alternators.

_____ **8.** Capacitors can be used to smooth alternator AC ripple and prevent electromagnetic interference (EMI).

_____ **9.** Larger 24-volt alternators, such as the Delco 50DN used by buses, circulate engine coolant through the alternator to remove heat from the rectifier and stator windings.

_____ **10.** Alternators that require external excitation will have an ignition excite or "I" connection.

Fill in the Blank

Read each item carefully, and then complete the statement by filling in the missing word(s).

1. In a(n) _____, the magnetic field is created by the rotor, which rotates within the stationary stator windings to generate electricity.

2. The voltage _____ circuit maintains optimal battery state of charge by sensing and maintaining a required charging system output voltage.

3. Several pairs of diodes, referred to as the _____ bridge, have the job of converting AC current to usable DC current.

4. The _____ contains a spinning electromagnet that induces current flow in the stator winding, which is made up of numerous coils of wire.

5. Regulated current to the alternator rotor is supplied through a pair of graphite _____ sliding against slip rings on the rotor shaft.

6. A(n) _____ - _____ alternator does not use a circuit connected to the ignition switch to switch on the voltage regulator and supply current to the rotor.

7. Each stator winding will produce one of three _____ of AC current.

8. A(n) _____ voltage regulator uses a pulse-width-modulated signal to control the magnetic field strength.

9. Voltage regulation for 12-volt systems will establish a maximum charging voltage, known as the _____ _____.

10. A(n) _____ _____ _____ pulley uses an internal spring and clutch system that allows it to rotate freely in one direction and provide limited, springlike movement in the other direction.

Labeling

Label the following diagrams with the correct terms.

1. Identify the parts of an alternator:

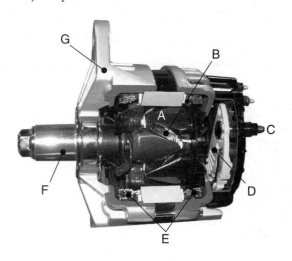

A. _____

B. _____

C. _____

D. _____

E. _____

F. _____

G. _____

Skill Drills

Test your knowledge of skill drills by filling in the correct words in the photo captions.

1. Performing a Charging System Output Test:

Step 1: Connect a charging system _____ to the battery with the _____ lead to the _____ post, the _____ lead to the _____ post, and the _____ _____ around the alternator _____ wire.

Step 2: Start the engine, turn off all _____, and measure the regulated voltage at around _____ rpm. The regulated voltage is the _____ voltage the system achieves once the battery is relatively _____, as evidenced by the _____ reading less than about _____–_____ amps when the amps clamp is around the alternator output cable. Typical regulated voltage specifications are wider than they used to be due to the ability of the _____ to adjust the _____ _____ for a wide range of conditions.

Step 3: Operate the engine at about _____ rpm and either manually or automatically load down the battery to _____ volts or _____ volts for a _____- volt system. Measure the alternator _____ output. This reading should be compared against the alternator's _____ output. Normally, the maximum output should be within _____% of the alternator's rated capacity. A _____ alternator may have slightly lower results.

2. Testing Charging Circuit Voltage Drop:

Step 1: Set the _____ up to measure _____, and select min/max if available. Connect the _____ probe of the _____ to the _____ terminal of the alternator and the _____ probe to the _____ post of the _____. The _____ probe goes on the _____ battery post because, in this case, the alternator output terminal is higher _____ than the positive battery terminal. For the meter to read correctly, the leads need to be connected as listed.

Step 2: Start the engine and _____ _____ as many electrical _____ as possible or use an external _____ _____ to load the battery. Read the maximum _____ _____ for the output circuit.

Step 3: Move the leads to measure the voltage drop on the _____ circuit by placing the _____ probe on the alternator _____ and the _____ probe on the _____ terminal of the battery. With the engine running and the circuit still _____, read the maximum _____ _____ for the ground circuit.

Step 4: If the measurements are _____, check each _____ of the circuit for excessive voltage drops by slowly bringing the _____ closer together on each _____ of the circuit. Determine any necessary actions.

3. Inspecting, Repairing, or Replacing Connectors and Wires of Charging Circuits:

Step 1: Locate and follow the appropriate _____ and _____ _____ in the service manual.

Step 2: Move the vehicle into the shop, apply the _____ _____, and _____ the vehicle wheels. Observe _____ and _____ procedures.

Step 3: If the vehicle has a _____ transmission, place it in "_____." If it has an _____ transmission, place it in "_____" or "_____."

Step 4: Trace the _____ _____ from the _____ to the _____ and around the _____ _____.

Step 5: Check the _____ and _____ for wear, damage, or _____.

Step 6: Disconnect the battery _____ cable if repairs are necessary.

Step 7: Repair damaged areas with replacement _____ or _____. Ensure all harnesses are _____ to prevent _____ or damage from _____.

Step 8: Reconnect all harness _____ and _____ all connections.

Step 9: Reconnect the battery _____ cable.

Step 10: Check repair by _____ _____ and running the vehicle.

Step 11: Clean the _____ _____ and return _____ and _____ to their proper storage.

4. Removing, Inspecting, and Replacing an Alternator:

Step 1:   Locate and follow the appropriate procedure in the _____ _____.

Step 2:   Move the vehicle into the _____, apply the _____ _____, and _____ the vehicle wheels. Observe _____ and _____ procedures.

Step 3:   If the vehicle has a _____ transmission, place it in "_____." If it has an _____ transmission, place it in "_____" or "_____."

Step 4:   Disconnect the _____ from the _____.

Step 5:   Disconnect _____ at the connector on the _____. Make a _____ of the location and any special insulating _____.

Step 6:   Loosen _____.

Step 7:   Slide the _____ off the _____.

Step 8:   Lift the _____ out of vehicle.

Step 9:   Place a new _____ onto the _____.

Step 10: Hand screw the _____ without tightening; connect _____ first if needed.

Step 11: After checking the condition of the _____ and _____ it if needed, slip the _____ on each _____ and _____ properly.

Step 12: If required, adjust belt _____ using belt _____ _____.

Step 13: Tighten the _____.

Step 14: Reconnect the _____.

Step 15: _____ the vehicle and _____ that the alternator is _____.

Step 16: _____ the work area and return _____ and _____ to their proper _____.

5. Overhauling an Alternator:

Step 1:   Locate and _____ the appropriate _____ in the service manual.

Step 2:   Check to see if the _____ need to be removed first. If so, remove the _____ _____ or _____.

Step 3:   Remove the through _____ holding the _____ together.

Step 4:   _____ the _____ apart.

Step 5:   Disassemble the component parts from the _____. Take note of the placement of _____ _____.

Step 6:   Clean, _____, and _____ all component parts. Use specialized _____ where necessary; for example, _____ tester, _____ tester, and _____.

Step 7:   Replace any _____ components. If the _____ _____ assembly requires replacement, ensure the new _____ _____ is machined on the _____.

Step 8:   Reassemble component parts into the _____.

Step 9:   Reassemble the alternator _____. Ensure the _____ are retained using a _____ _____ to prevent damage to them.

Step 10: Test the alternator in the alternator _____ _____. Ensure the _____ _____ circuit is working and test for maximum _____ output and _____ regulation.

Step 11: Clean the _____ _____ and return tools and materials to their proper _____.

Crossword Puzzle

Use the clues in the column to complete the puzzle.

Across

3. The small amount of magnetism left on the rotor after it is initially magnetized by the coil windings' magnetic field.

5. Making the alternator produce maximum amperage output.

Down

1. The practice of connecting alternators in parallel to provide higher charging voltage at idle with more available amperage.

2. A pattern produced by voltage fluctuations from the alternator that create differences between the peak voltage of an AC sine wave and the minimum voltage found in the trough between sine waves.

4. The voltage reference point the alternator uses for regulation of the output.

ASE-Type Questions

Read each item carefully, and then select the best response.

_____ 1. Technician A says that today, the average 12-volt electrical system for a late-model highway tractor add up to 150 amps at peak with an 84-amp average. Technician B says that both DC generators and alternators produce electricity by relative movement of conductors in a magnetic field. Who is correct?

    A. Technician A

    B. Technician B

    C. Both Technician A and Technician B

    D. Neither Technician A nor Technician B

_____ 2. Technician A says that alternators have more moving parts as compared to generators. Technician B says that alternators can produce power at engine idle speeds; generators cannot. Who is correct?

    A. Technician A

    B. Technician B

    C. Both Technician A and Technician B

    D. Neither Technician A nor Technician B

_____ 3. Technician A says that the two most important parts in an alternator used to produce electrical current are the rotor and stator winding. Technician B says that the rotor contains a spinning electromagnet that induces current flow in the stator winding, which is made up of numerous coils of wire. Who is correct?

    A. Technician A

    B. Technician B

    C. Both Technician A and Technician B

    D. Neither Technician A nor Technician B

_____ 4. Technician A says that the rotor is a rotating electromagnet that provides the magnetic field to induce voltage and current in the stator. Technician B says that the direct-gear drive mechanism is used in most cases but that a pulley drive may also be employed. Who is correct?

    A. Technician A

    B. Technician B

    C. Both Technician A and Technician B

    D. Neither Technician A nor Technician B

_____ 5. Technician A says that regulated current to the alternator rotor is supplied through a pair of graphite brushes sliding against slip rings on the rotor shaft. Technician B says that heavy-duty springs help the brushes maintain contact with the slip rings. Who is correct?

    A. Technician A

    B. Technician B

    C. Both Technician A and Technician B

    D. Neither Technician A nor Technician B

_____ 6. Technician A says that vehicles fitted with self-exciting alternators may require the engine rpm to be briefly increased after every start-up to initiate charging. Technician B says that using self-exciting alternators eliminates the need for a separate circuit from the key switch to the alternator and simplifies chassis wiring. Who is correct?

    A. Technician A

    B. Technician B

    C. Both Technician A and Technician B

    D. Neither Technician A nor Technician B

_____ 7. Technician A says that the stator is mounted between two end housings, and it holds the stator windings stationary so that the rotating magnetic field cuts through the stator windings, inducing an electric current in the windings. Technician B says that to smooth the pulsating current flow, there are three distinct layers of windings offset 60 degrees in each layer from one another. Who is correct?

    A. Technician A

    B. Technician B

    C. Both Technician A and Technician B

    D. Neither Technician A nor Technician B

_____ **8.** Technician A says that stators are normally serviced in a repair facility. Technician B says that stators can be visually checked during rebuilding for burnt, cut, or nicked winding laminations. Who is correct?
   A. Technician A
   B. Technician B
   C. Both Technician A and Technician B
   D. Neither Technician A nor Technician B

_____ **9.** Technician A says that alternators produce alternating current, which is acceptable for operating many electrical devices. Technician B says that converting the AC current to usable DC current is referred to as modulation. Who is correct?
   A. Technician A
   B. Technician B
   C. Both Technician A and Technician B
   D. Neither Technician A nor Technician B

_____ **10.** Technician A says that voltage regulators are first classified as either external or internal. Technician B says that the majority of late-model alternators have external regulators. Who is correct?
   A. Technician A
   B. Technician B
   C. Both Technician A and Technician B
   D. Neither Technician A nor Technician B

Electrical Wiring and Circuit Diagrams

Tire Tread:
© AbleStock

Chapter Review

The following activities have been designed to help you refresh your knowledge of this chapter. Your instructor may require you to complete some or all of these activities as a regular part of your training program. You are encouraged to complete any activity that your instructor does not assign as a way to enhance your learning.

Matching

Match the following terms with the correct description or example.

A. Deutsche Institute Norm (DIN) diagram
B. Isometric diagram
C. Map diagram

D. Schematic diagram
E. Valley Forge (VF) diagram

_____ **1.** A wiring diagram that shows the entire vehicle wiring circuit using pictorial symbols.
_____ **2.** A wiring diagram used to locate a component within a system and which shows the outline of a vehicle or piece of equipment where the component can be found.
_____ **3.** A schematic wiring diagram that uses SAE-type symbols.
_____ **4.** A line drawing that explains how a system works by using symbols and connecting lines.
_____ **5.** A schematic wiring diagram on which symbols, terminal connection numbers, line symbols, and operational status of items such as switches and relays are defined by a specific standard.

Multiple Choice

Read each item carefully, and then select the best response.

_____ **1.** Ohm's law predicts voltage drop using the formula _____.
  A. V_{drop} = Amperage ÷ Voltage
  B. V_{drop} = Resistance × Voltage
  C. V_{drop} = Amperage × Resistance
  D. V_{drop} = Resistance ÷ Amperage

_____ **2.** The _____ system is more than a hundred years old and measures wire gauge in numbers from 0000 to 50.
  A. American wire gage
  B. weights and measures
  C. metric gauge
  D. Both A and C

_____ **3.** Using the AWG system, a 60' length of wire used in a 24-volt system to carry 14.0 amps of current would need to be a size _____ wire.
  A. 10
  B. 12
  C. 14
  D. 16

_____ **4.** The _____ standard specifies the dimensions, test methods, and performance requirements for single-core primary wire intended for use in road vehicle applications.
  A. SAE J1128
  B. SAE J1926
  C. ISO 6722
  D. Both A and C

_____ **5.** Type _____ wire is an extra thin primary wire that has a cross-linked polyethylene jacket that is resistant to oil, grease, gasoline, and acids.
   A. GPT
   B. SXL
   C. TXL
   D. GXL

_____ **6.** Chassis wiring often uses numerical codes to identify _____.
   A. which circuit the wire belongs to
   B. which harness the wire belongs in
   C. the wire gauge and color
   D. All of the above

_____ **7.** The compact _____ connector is considered a premium connector and used when reliability of the connection is of utmost importance.
   A. Deutsch
   B. Weather Pack
   C. Metri-Pack
   D. Bosch/AMP

_____ **8.** Wires should be joined together by bending each into a double-J bend, then twisting to form a _____ splice.
   A. Brummel
   B. Western Union
   C. pigtail
   D. butt

_____ **9.** A(n) _____ shows the power source at the top of the page and the ground points at the bottom.
   A. pictorial diagram
   B. isometric diagram
   C. Deutsche Institute Norm (DIN) diagram
   D. All of the above

_____ **10.** In a DIN diagram, a wire identified using the abbreviation "ge" would be _____ in color.
   A. green
   B. yellow
   C. black
   D. red

True/False

If you believe the statement to be more true than false, write the letter "T" in the space provided. If you believe the statement to be more false than true, write the letter "F".

_____ **1.** Smaller wires become more resistant and heat up as amperage increases.

_____ **2.** Both wire classification systems measure both the wire and the insulator when determining the total diameter of a wire.

_____ **3.** The International Organization for Standardization has designed a color code system that is followed by all manufacturers.

_____ **4.** Multi-stranded wire is better at conducting higher amounts of current with less resistance because it has more surface area to conduct electron flow.

_____ **5.** Connector housings have male and female sides and are usually shaped so that they can be connected in only one way.

_____ **6.** The wires on Metri-Pack connectors must be soldered before being seated in the connector.

_____ **7.** One of the greatest enemies to wiring is water.

_____ **8.** Color codes are used to designate wire gauge to use for shrink crimp connectors.

_____ **9.** Schematic diagrams are used to show internal circuitry.

_____ **10.** Arrangement of the components and circuit paths on a current track diagram usually correspond to their physical locations on the vehicle.

Fill in the Blank

Read each item carefully, and then complete the statement by filling in the missing word(s).

1. Longer circuits and higher amperage require a larger _____ of wire.

2. In most wiring diagrams, metric-sized wire is specified in _____ rather than metric gauge diameter.

3. A(n) _____ wiring harness is often used for a rear taillight wiring harness that includes a separate wire for stop, turn, reverse, and tail lights.

4. The simplest wiring connector is a _____ _____ that uses small studs to which ring or spade type connectors are attached and secured with machine screws.

5. A(n) _____-_____-_____ terminal is inserted into the back of the connector cavity to seat after the terminal is crimped to the wire.

6. The male pin end of a Weather Pack connector is called the _____ while the female socket end is called the _____.

7. Once inside a wire, _____ will move into the smallest openings and spaces through adhesion.

8. If a connection is not _____, wiring can move within the connection, leading to arcing and resistance, which ultimately causes connection failure.

9. A(n) _____ diagram may start on one page and continue onto several more, mapping out individual circuits with a separate diagram.

10. Pin _____ are generally labeled on the plastic hard-shell connector housing and/or the corresponding component.

Labeling

Label the following diagrams with the correct terms.

1. Identify the components of a typical harness connector:

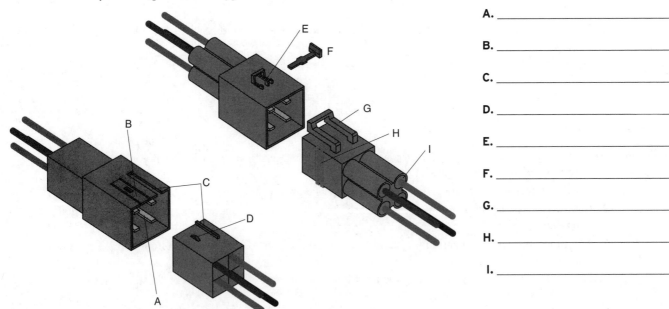

A. _____

B. _____

C. _____

D. _____

E. _____

F. _____

G. _____

H. _____

I. _____

2. Identify the components of a Weather Pack push-to-seat connector:

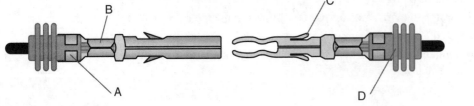

A. _____

B. _____

C. _____

D. _____

Deutsche Institute Norm (DIN) Symbols

Match the definitions to the correct DIN symbol.

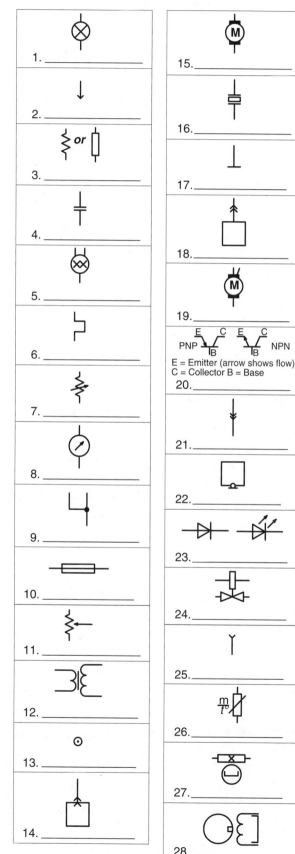

1. _____

2. _____

3. _____

4. _____

5. _____

6. _____

7. _____

8. _____

9. _____

10. _____

11. _____

12. _____

13. _____

14. _____

15. _____

16. _____

17. _____

18. _____

19. _____

20. _____

21. _____

22. _____

23. _____

24. _____

25. _____

26. _____

27. _____

28. _____

A. Ignition coil

B. Potentiometer (pressure or temp)

C. Transistors

D. Permanent magnet (one-speed motor)

E. Male connector

F. Diodes

G. Circuit breaker

H. Inductive sensor

I. Ground

J. Resistor to heating element

K. Female connector

L. Removable connection

M. Hall sensor

N. Component case directly grounded

O. Lamp

P. Distributed splice

Q. Bifilament lamp

R. Permanent magnet (two-speed motor)

S. Air mass sensor

T. Potentiometer (outside influence)

U. Connector attached to component

V. Connector attached to pigtail

W. Fuse

X. Solenoid valve, injector, cold start valve

Y. Piezoelectric sensor

Z. Capacitor

AA. Connector

BB. Gauge

Crossword Puzzle

Use the clues in the column to complete the puzzle.

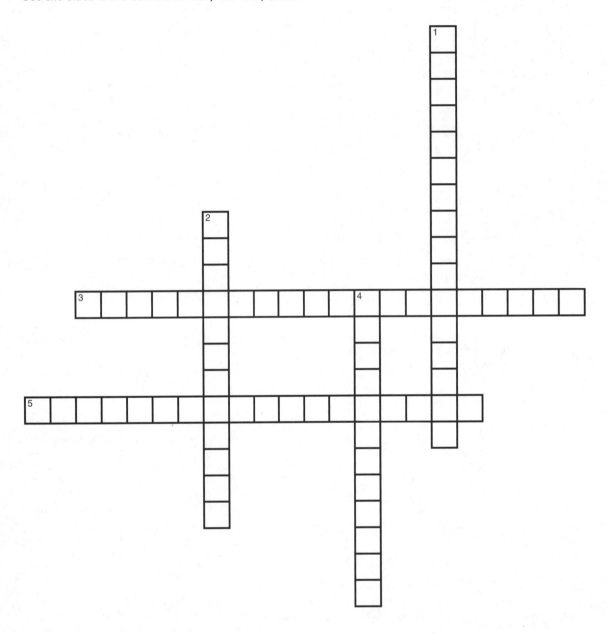

Across

3. An environmentally sealed push-to-seat electrical connection system supplied in one- to six-pin configurations.

5. A pull-to-seat electrical connector with flat terminals instead of round.

Down

1. A compact, environmentally sealed electrical connector that uses solid, round metal pins and hollow female sockets.

2. The movement of water through wiring due to its adhesive and cohesive properties.

4. Another name for a DIN diagram.

ASE-Type Questions

Read each item carefully, and then select the best response.

_____ 1. Technician A says that wires and wiring harnesses are the arteries of the vehicle's electrical system, and as such they need to be kept in good condition, free of any damage or corrosion. Technician B says that they carry the electrical power and signals through the vehicle to control virtually all of the systems on a vehicle. Who is correct?

    A. Technician A

    B. Technician B

    C. Both Technician A and Technician B

    D. Neither Technician A nor Technician B

_____ 2. Technician A says the insulation is designed to protect the wire and prevent leakage of the current flow so that it can get to its intended destination. Technician B says aluminum is typically used because it offers low electrical resistance and remains flexible even after years of use. Who is correct?

    A. Technician A

    B. Technician B

    C. Both Technician A and Technician B

    D. Neither Technician A nor Technician B

_____ 3. Technician A says selecting a wire gauge that is too large increases the amount of current flowing into the wiring harnesses. Technician B says the resistance of a wire affects how much current it can carry. Who is correct?

    A. Technician A

    B. Technician B

    C. Both Technician A and Technician B

    D. Neither Technician A nor Technician B

_____ 4. Technician A says that terminals installed to wire ends provide low-current termination to wires. Technician B says that terminals allow voltage to be conducted from the end of one wire to the end of another wire. Who is correct?

    A. Technician A

    B. Technician B

    C. Both Technician A and Technician B

    D. Neither Technician A nor Technician B

_____ 5. Technician A says a common mistake while soldering is trying to apply the solder directly to the tip of the soldering iron while the iron is heating up the wires. Technician B says it will not melt the solder leading to a cold joint. Who is correct?

    A. Technician A

    B. Technician B

    C. Both Technician A and Technician B

    D. Neither Technician A nor Technician B

_____ 6. Technician A says linear diagrams are a variation of the map diagram. Technician B says symbols for components are always pictorial. Who is correct?

    A. Technician A

    B. Technician B

    C. Both Technician A and Technician B

    D. Neither Technician A nor Technician B

_____ 7. Technician A says DIN schematic diagrams are also called power source track wiring diagrams because they show the power source at the top of the page and the ground points at the bottom. Technician B says newer DIN standards do indicate on which side of the vehicle a component may be located. Who is correct?

    A. Technician A

    B. Technician B

    C. Both Technician A and Technician B

    D. Neither Technician A nor Technician B

_____ **8.** Technician A says knowing the standards for wiring colors makes the job of reading and interpreting schematics easier. Technician B says some colors and terminal designations for wiring are used across a number of standards. Who is correct?

   A. Technician A

   B. Technician B

   C. Both Technician A and Technician B

   D. Neither Technician A nor Technician B

_____ **9.** Technician A says wiring diagrams also indicate the wire gauge used (shown in mm^2), designating the cross sectional area of the wire. Technician B says because standards exist for the maximum permissible voltage drop across a circuit, wire gauge is critical. Who is correct?

   A. Technician A

   B. Technician B

   C. Both Technician A and Technician B

   D. Neither Technician A nor Technician B

_____ **10.** Technician A says wiring diagrams tell the user where pin numbers for wires could terminate. Technician B says knowing where the wires terminate intensifies the diagnostic procedure. Who is correct?

   A. Technician A

   B. Technician B

   C. Both Technician A and Technician B

   D. Neither Technician A nor Technician B

Body Electrical Systems—Lighting Systems

Chapter Review

The following activities have been designed to help you refresh your knowledge of this chapter. Your instructor may require you to complete some or all of these activities as a regular part of your training program. You are encouraged to complete any activity that your instructor does not assign as a way to enhance your learning.

Matching

Match the following terms with the correct description or example.

A. Fluorescent bulb

B. Halogen bulb

C. Halogen infrared discharge (HID) bulb

D. High-intensity discharge (HID) lamps

E. Incandescent bulb

_____ 1. A light bulb that uses electrically heated filaments located at each end of a tube filled with a small amount of mercury or a noble gas, such as neon, argon, or xenon.

_____ 2. A conventional bulb that electrically heats a filament of metal to the temperature at which it produces light.

_____ 3. A light bulb produced by adding a small quantity of iodine or bromine gas.

_____ 4. Lamps that use an electric arc to produce higher light outputs of between 2,800 and 3,800 lumens.

_____ 5. A light bulb that has a special coating on an inside portion of the bulb wall, which reflects infrared heat back onto the filament, causing it to burn hotter.

Multiple Choice

Read each item carefully, and then select the best response.

_____ 1. Lamps facing sideways and all turn signals must emit _____ light.
   A. amber
   B. yellow
   C. red
   D. Either A or C

_____ 2. An incandescent bulb that is separated at the filament support was most likely damaged by _____.
   A. over-voltage failure
   B. vibration or shock
   C. leakage of air
   D. under-voltage failure

_____ 3. Some _____ type bulbs have no plastic base, and the wires turn up toward the sides of the bulb.
   A. Edison
   B. bayonet
   C. wedge
   D. Both A and C

_____ 4. What type of glass is used to withstand the higher temperatures and pressures inside a halogen bulb?
   A. Quartz silica glass
   B. Favrile glass
   C. Fused quartz
   D. Zerodur glass

_____ **5.** Another name for high-intensity discharge (HID) lamps is _____.
  A. tungsten oxyhalide lamps
  B. quartz lamps
  C. xenon lamps
  D. halogen lamps

_____ **6.** In high-intensity discharge bulbs, the light is produced by using a high-voltage electric arc of between _____.
  A. 120–240 V
  B. 240–480 V
  C. 1,200–1,500 V
  D. 2,000–2,500 V

_____ **7.** The life span of a light-emitting diode is roughly _____ hours.
  A. 5,000
  B. 10,000
  C. 100,000
  D. 500,000

_____ **8.** The _____ electrical connector is an SAE standard set for connecting the trailer cord to the tractor and trailer electrical system together.
  A. Metri-Pack
  B. J-560
  C. SAE J1128
  D. Weather Pack

_____ **9.** Trailer cords containing larger-gauge wire for the ABS circuit are _____ in color.
  A. green
  B. yellow
  C. red
  D. black

_____ **10.** The current for the directional signal switch in mechanical directional signal systems is supplied by the _____.
  A. turn signal flasher relay
  B. electronic control module
  C. service brake light switch
  D. Either A or C

True/False

If you believe the statement to be more true than false, write the letter "T" in the space provided. If you believe the statement to be more false than true, write the letter "F".

_____ **1.** Any light on the exterior of a vehicle must have photometric certification for FMVSS 105 standards.

_____ **2.** The metal filament on an incandescent bulb is essentially a resistor.

_____ **3.** An over-voltage failure in an incandescent bulb will leave a smoky residue inside the bulb.

_____ **4.** Conventional incandescent bulbs operate at approximately 50% efficiency.

_____ **5.** Any surface contamination, such as from greasy fingerprints, can damage a halogen bulb's glass after it is heated.

_____ **6.** A headlamp self-leveling system will sense the change in vehicle inclination produced by a cargo load or road grade to automatically adjust the headlamps' vertical aim.

_____ **7.** Daytime running lights are low- or high-beam lighting circuits powered at a reduced voltage of approximately 80% system voltage.

_____ **8.** LEDs have a significantly lower initial cost compared to other lighting types.

_____ **9.** Trailer cords connecting the trailer and tractor are between 60 inches and 100 inches in working length.

_____ **10.** In North America, the stop-turn signal is not integrated; the stop signals are red while the turn signals are amber.

Fill in the Blank

Read each item carefully, and then complete the statement by filling in the missing word(s).

1. In a(n) _____ electrical system, point-to-point wiring connects the dome light, horn, or power windows to a switch operated by the driver.

2. In a(n) _____ electrical system, a technician needs to know what conditions are necessary to activate a specific electrical circuit.

3. Light is produced by _____ whenever an electron moves from a higher orbital ring to a lower orbital requiring less energy.

4. A burnt out tungsten bulb has a(n) _____ bulb coating.

5. In a(n) _____ bulb a step-up voltage circuit or transformer causes some of the mercury to turn to a vapor, which in turn enables the gas inside the tube to become ionized.

6. Halogen _____ _____ bulbs are used only in headlight applications.

7. In general, small automotive lamps produce between 50 and 400 _____.

8. High-intensity discharge bulbs require the use of a(n) _____ to step up the battery voltage.

9. High beams reduce visibility due to light reflection when driving in fog, snow, or rain. This effect is called _____ - _____.

10. Flash to pass or _____ lights are integrated into most HD tractors.

Labeling

Label the following diagrams with the correct terms.

1. Identify the components of a bayonet type light bulb:

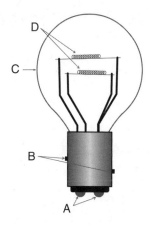

A. _____

B. _____

C. _____

D. _____

2. Identify the components of a headlight:

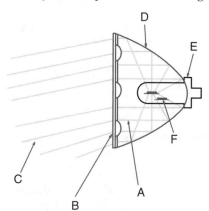

A. _____

B. _____

C. _____

D. _____

E. _____

F. _____

3. Identify the parts of an LED lamp:

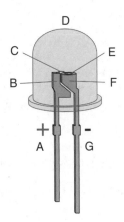

A. _____

B. _____

C. _____

D. _____

E. _____

F. _____

G. _____

Lamp and Reflector Locations

Match the lamp type or reflector to its correct location.

1. _____
2. _____
3. _____
4a. _____
4b. _____
5a. _____
5b. _____
6. _____
7. _____
8. _____
9. _____
10. _____
12a. _____
12b. _____
14. _____

A. Rear side reflex reflectors
B. Front side marker lamps
C. Rear identification lamps
D. Intermediate side reflex reflectors
E. Headlamps and parking lamps
F. License plate lamps
G. Rear marking
H. Rear side marker lamps
I. Tail/stop/turn lamps and reflex reflectors
J. Front clearance lamps
K. Backup lamps
L. Front side reflex reflectors
M. Intermediate side marker lamps
N. Front Identification lamps
O. Rear clearance lamp

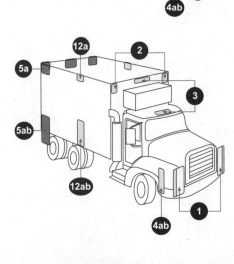

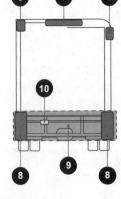

Crossword Puzzle

Use the clues in the column to complete the puzzle.

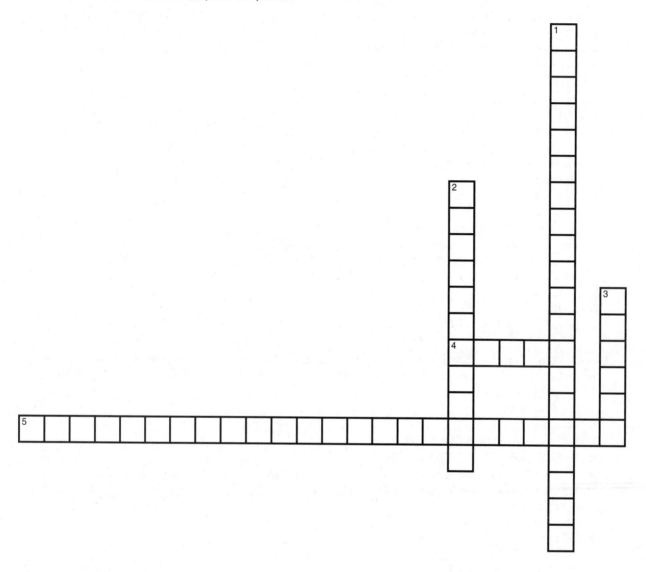

Across

4. The units used to measure light intensity.

5. A certification based on testing lamps to evaluate factors such as light color, brightness, and the angle at which the light is effectively observed.

Down

1. Lights designed to improve vehicle visibility in the daytime.

2. The designed-in logic of a circuit that determines what activates a specific circuit.

3. A particle of energy and the basic unit of light.

ASE-Type Questions

Read each item carefully, and then select the best response.

_____ 1. Technician A says that a traditional body electrical system consists of two parts. Technician B says that the first section is the standard electrical circuitry found in all vehicles and that optional accessories make up the other section of the body electrical system. Who is correct?
   A. Technician A
   B. Technician B
   C. Both Technician A and Technician B
   D. Neither Technician A nor Technician B

_____ 2. Technician A says that the designed-in logic of a circuit that determines what activates a specific circuit is referred to as ladder logic. Technician B says that it is not necessary to have the ability to access, read, and interpret electrical schematic diagrams to repair electrical circuits. Who is correct?
   A. Technician A
   B. Technician B
   C. Both Technician A and Technician B
   D. Neither Technician A nor Technician B

_____ 3. Technician A says that lighting standards are legislated by the Federal/Canadian Motor Vehicle Safety Standard 108 (FMVSS 105). Technician B says that it is not necessary for light lenses to carry SAE identification numbers indicating the standard they meet. Who is correct?
   A. Technician A
   B. Technician B
   C. Both Technician A and Technician B
   D. Neither Technician A nor Technician B

_____ 4. Technician A says that incandescent bulbs are the conventional bulb technology first invented by Thomas Edison. Technician B says that for every 1 volt above designed limits, the life expectancy of the bulb drops by 25%. Who is correct?
   A. Technician A
   B. Technician B
   C. Both Technician A and Technician B
   D. Neither Technician A nor Technician B

_____ 5. Technician A says that halogen bulbs are produced by adding small quantities of gases from the halogen family, such as iodine and bromine, which extends the efficiency and life of the bulb. Technician B says that because the filament can be operated at a higher temperature without burning up, more energy is converted to light, the light is whiter, and the bulb's life is extended. Who is correct?
   A. Technician A
   B. Technician B
   C. Both Technician A and Technician B
   D. Neither Technician A nor Technician B

_____ 6. Technician A says that high-intensity discharge (HID) lamps used for headlight systems employ an electric arc to produce the light. Technician B says that the intensity of light from high-intensity discharge bulbs is produced using close to half the current consumed by halogen bulbs, and the bulbs last half as long. Who is correct?
   A. Technician A
   B. Technician B
   C. Both Technician A and Technician B
   D. Neither Technician A nor Technician B

_____ 7. Technician A says that daytime running lights are designed to improve vehicle visibility in the daytime. Technician B says that either the low or high beam circuits are powered at a reduced voltage of approximately 50% system voltage. Who is correct?
   A. Technician A
   B. Technician B
   C. Both Technician A and Technician B
   D. Neither Technician A nor Technician B

_____ **8.** Technician A says that the J-560 electrical connector is an SAE standard set for connecting the trailer cord to the tractor and trailer electrical system together and has existed since the late 1950s. Technician B says that this five-pin connector bears the stamp SAE J560, indicating compliance with physical and performance standards of the SAE. Who is correct?
   A. Technician A
   B. Technician B
   C. Both Technician A and Technician B
   D. Neither Technician A nor Technician B

_____ **9.** Technician A says that plugs at the end of each cable may be molded and hard-wired with strain relief to prevent the weight of the cord from disconnecting from the plug. Technician B says that replacement plug leads are available and commonly used by technicians to repair cables. Who is correct?
   A. Technician A
   B. Technician B
   C. Both Technician A and Technician B
   D. Neither Technician A nor Technician B

_____ **10.** Technician A says that the directional signal switch in mechanical directional signal systems is supplied current from two sources. Technician B says that power is supplied by the service brake light switch; the other is through the turn signal flasher relay. Who is correct?
   A. Technician A
   B. Technician B
   C. Both Technician A and Technician B
   D. Neither Technician A nor Technician B

Body Electrical Systems— Instrumentation

Chapter Review

The following activities have been designed to help you refresh your knowledge of this chapter. Your instructor may require you to complete some or all of these activities as a regular part of your training program. You are encouraged to complete any activity that your instructor does not assign as a way to enhance your learning.

Matching

Match the following terms with the correct description or example.

A. Blink code

B. Capacitance touch screen

C. D'Arsonval gauge

D. Resistive touch screen

E. Tachograph

_____ **1.** A type of electromagnetic gauge that moves a pointing needle directly proportional to current flow through an electromagnet attached to the pointer.

_____ **2.** A method of providing fault code data for a specific system that involves counting the number of flashes from a warning lamp and observing longer pauses between the light blinks.

_____ **3.** A device fitted to a vehicle to record various pieces of information, such as time, speed, rest periods, and distance travelled by each of the vehicle's drivers.

_____ **4.** A display screen that uses two transparent plates, one of which is electrically charged.

_____ **5.** A display screen composed of two flexible, transparent sheets lightly coated with an electrically conductive yet slightly resistive material.

Multiple Choice

Read each item carefully, and then select the best response.

_____ **1.** A(n) _____ is used to indicate low fluid levels, low air pressure warning systems, or power divider engagement locks.

    A. mechanical ground switch

    B. electronic switch

    C. voltage drop circuit

    D. All of the above

_____ **2.** The malfunction indicator lamp and check engine lamp will _____ during engine start-up and then extinguish.

    A. blink two or three times

    B. cause a buzzing sound

    C. illuminate for three to five seconds

    D. Both A and C

_____ **3.** A voltmeter is an example of a type of gauge that uses _____ movement.

    A. bimetallic

    B. D'Arsonval

    C. mechanical

    D. bipolar

_____ 4. In a three-coil gauge design, a third coil called a _____ is placed between the minimum and maximum gauge reading.
   A. bucking coil
   B. sending unit
   C. moving coil
   D. balancing coil

_____ 5. The use of stepper motors to rotate pointers for analog bypasses the problem of inaccurate readings due to _____.
   A. voltage fluctuations
   B. temperature changes
   C. oil leaks from fluid dampened gauge clusters
   D. All of the above

_____ 6. Temperature sending units use a _____ similar to the design of a coolant thermostat.
   A. flexible bellow
   B. resistive wiper
   C. wax pellet
   D. magnetic sensor

_____ 7. A(n) _____ is a device used to record a vehicle's speed over time.
   A. odometer
   B. speed sensor
   C. tachograph
   D. speedometer

_____ 8. An electronic _____ is a microcontroller device constructed to sense and measure any source of magnetic fields.
   A. compass
   B. tachograph
   C. CAN gauge
   D. D'Arsonval gauge

_____ 9. A _____ uses a compact passive display technology and consumes little current to operate.
   A. resistive touch screen
   B. liquid crystal display
   C. plasma display
   D. capacitance touch screen

_____ 10. Erratic gauge readings may be caused by _____.
   A. a blown fuse
   B. missing terminating resistors
   C. short to ground
   D. poor, loose, or resistive grounds

True/False

If you believe the statement to be more true than false, write the letter "T" in the space provided. If you believe the statement to be more false than true, write the letter "F".

_____ 1. Electronic switches found in electronic control modules are the most common way warning lights are illuminated in today's vehicles.

_____ 2. In the absence of a readily available electronic service tool used to obtain fault codes, warning lights can often blink out fault codes.

_____ 3. Bimetallic gauges require a voltage regulator to maintain consistent readings.

_____ 4. One disadvantage of two- and three-coil gauge designs is that their movement is directly affected by variations in temperature.

_____ 5. Most stepper motor gauges have 360 possible steps of positions between zero and full-scale deflection.

_____ 6. Sending units are low-voltage electronic devices with no moving parts.

_____ 7. When a circuit is opened, circuit resistance becomes infinite and will move a gauge to either its minimum or maximum reading.

_____ **8.** DIP switches may need to be reset if the drive line components, such as tire size or rear axle ratios, have changed from those originally installed on the chassis.

_____ **9.** All touch screen devices digitize the input from finger contact using x, y, and z coordinates.

_____ **10.** A capacitance touch screen may be operated using either a finger or stylus.

Fill in the Blank

Read each item carefully, and then complete the statement by filling in the missing word(s).

1. The charging system indicator light is an example of a light operated through _____ _____.

2. Speedometers operated by cables and oil pressure read by bourdon tube gauges are examples of direct-reading _____ gauges.

3. By far, _____ _____ gauges are the most commonly used gauge technology in late-model instrument gauge clusters.

4. Two common types of stepper motors are used for instrument gauges: _____ and _____ motors.

5. Just two wires connecting the instrument panel gauge clusters to the _____ network are all that is necessary to display vehicle data and trip information, provide fault codes, and display warning lamps.

6. A(n) _____ _____ is an electromechanical device that converts pressure or fluid level into a variable voltage signal.

7. The engine _____ counts all of the pulses from both the speedometer and tachometer to track overall distance traveled by vehicle and engine.

8. _____ display means that LCDs do not emit light but instead use ambient light around the display to reflect images.

9. The _____ touch screen's advantages include its low cost, scratch resistance, durability, and capacity to operate in all climate conditions.

10. A(n) _____ touch screen permits the use of a dual-finger touch process.

Labeling

Label the following diagrams with the correct terms.

1. Identify the components of a bimetallic fuel gauge:

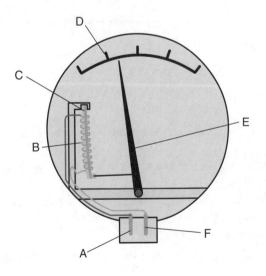

A. _____

B. _____

C. _____

D. _____

E. _____

F. _____

2. Identify the components of a D'Arsonval movement gauge:

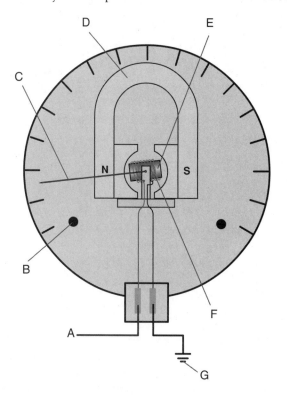

A. _____

B. _____

C. _____

D. _____

E. _____

F. _____

G. _____

3. Identify the layers of an LCD display:

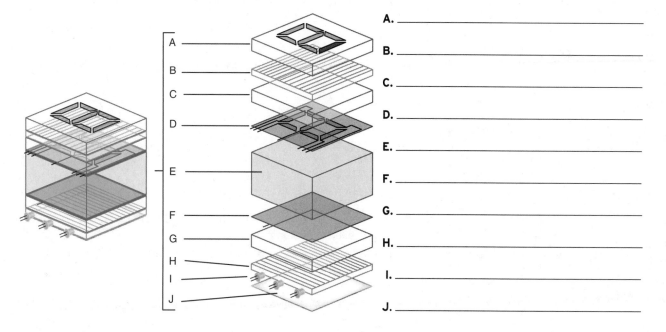

A. _____

B. _____

C. _____

D. _____

E. _____

F. _____

G. _____

H. _____

I. _____

J. _____

Crossword Puzzle

Use the clues in the column to complete the puzzle.

Across

3. Small slide switches located at the rear of the speedometer head placed in either an on or off (1 or 0) position.
4. A sequence in which the warning lights for several brief seconds with the key on and engine off or during key-on engine cranking.

Down

1. A gauge in which two dissimilar pieces of metal are bonded together and expand at different rates when heated, thereby converting the heating effect of electricity into mechanical movement.
2. A gauge in which three field coils are wound in series, with a coil at minimum reading, one at maximum reading, and one between the two.

ASE-Type Questions

Read each item carefully, and then select the best response.

_____ **1.** Technician A says warning lights can be built into gauges or mounted in a dedicated panel in the instrument. Technician B says warning lights require a power feed and ground for the light to illuminate. Who is correct?
  A. Technician A
  B. Technician B
  C. Both Technician A and Technician B
  D. Neither Technician A nor Technician B

_____ **2.** Technician A says normally closed pressure switches opened with air or oil pressure provide a path to ground to illuminate a bulb. Technician B says normally opened pressure switches opened with air or oil pressure provide a path to ground to illuminate a bulb. Who is correct?
  A. Technician A
  B. Technician B
  C. Both Technician A and Technician B
  D. Neither Technician A nor Technician B

_____ **3.** Technician A says after the engine starts and the alternator begins charging, charging system voltage is applied to both terminals of a bulb. Technician B says the charging system indicator light is an example of a light operated through voltage drop. Who is correct?
  A. Technician A
  B. Technician B
  C. Both Technician A and Technician B
  D. Neither Technician A nor Technician B

_____ **4.** Technician A says the malfunction indicator lamp (MIL) and check engine lamp (CEL) will illuminate for approximately 3 to 5 seconds during engine start-up and then extinguish. Technician B says if there are active fault codes, the lights will switch back on after start-up. Who is correct?
  A. Technician A
  B. Technician B
  C. Both Technician A and Technician B
  D. Neither Technician A nor Technician B

_____ **5.** Technician A says stepper motor gauges reduce the problems associated with inaccurate readings from bimetallic and electromagnetic coil gauges caused by voltage fluctuations. Technician B says stepper motors are brush-type DC electromechanical devices that generally use a permanent magnet shaft surrounded by more than two pair of electromagnetic coils. Who is correct?
  A. Technician A
  B. Technician B
  C. Both Technician A and Technician B
  D. Neither Technician A nor Technician B

_____ **6.** Technician A says speedometers electronically measure the driveshaft speed by counting a series of electrical pulses produced per mile or kilometer of distance traveled. Technician B says two wires connecting the instrument panel gauge clusters to the CAN network are all that is necessary to supply the data necessary to display vehicle data and trip information, provide fault codes, and display warning lamps. Who is correct?
  A. Technician A
  B. Technician B
  C. Both Technician A and Technician B
  D. Neither Technician A nor Technician B

_____ **7.** Technician A says gauge senders output an electronic signal based on an electrical input. Technician B says electronic modules are available to convert variable voltage values into digital signals for use by digital gauges. Who is correct?
  A. Technician A
  B. Technician B
  C. Both Technician A and Technician B
  D. Neither Technician A nor Technician B

_____ **8.** Technician A says gauge faults will range from not working at all, to erratic gauge operation or inaccurate readings must refer to the manufacturer's information for the correct test procedures. Technician B says gauge faults will range from not working at all, to erratic gauge operation or inaccurate readings can be repaired in-house. Who is correct?
- **A.** Technician A
- **B.** Technician B
- **C.** Both Technician A and Technician B
- **D.** Neither Technician A nor Technician B

_____ **9.** Technician A says digital tachographs are calibrated by accessing the tachograph's electronic memory. Technician B says calibration adjustments within the tachograph are located in a sealed area of the unit to prevent tampering by unauthorized personnel. Who is correct?
- **A.** Technician A
- **B.** Technician B
- **C.** Both Technician A and Technician B
- **D.** Neither Technician A nor Technician B

_____ **10.** Technician A says you should use a DVOM when checking for smooth operation of a fuel sender unit. Technician B says the fuel sender unit should be reconnected to the fuel gauge to check for full-range operation while it is out of the tank. Who is correct?
- **A.** Technician A
- **B.** Technician B
- **C.** Both Technician A and Technician B
- **D.** Neither Technician A nor Technician B

Electronic Signal Processing Principles

Chapter Review

The following activities have been designed to help you refresh your knowledge of this chapter. Your instructor may require you to complete some or all of these activities as a regular part of your training program. You are encouraged to complete any activity that your instructor does not assign as a way to enhance your learning.

Matching

Match the following terms with the correct description or example.

A. Electrically erasable programmable read-only memory (EEPROM)

B. Keep alive memory (KAM)

C. Programmable read-only memory (PROM)

D. Random access memory (RAM)

E. Read-only memory (ROM)

_____ **1.** Non-volatile memory technology that is used to store operating instructions or programming for an ECM.

_____ **2.** Memory used for permanent storage of instructions and fixed values used by the ECM that control the microprocessor.

_____ **3.** Memory that is retained by the ECM when the key is off.

_____ **4.** Memory that stores programming information and cannot be easily written over.

_____ **5.** A temporary storage place for information that needs to be quickly accessed.

Multiple Choice

Read each item carefully, and then select the best response.

_____ **1.** When engine operational problems leading to excess emissions occur, self-monitoring and self-diagnostic capabilities of electronic controls can _____.
   A. identify the problem
   B. alert the operator
   C. minimize noxious emission production
   D. All of the above

_____ **2.** A branch of information technology that uses specialized telecommunication applications for long-distance transmission of information to and from a vehicle is known as _____.
   A. tachography
   B. telematics
   C. reluctance
   D. pulse-width-modulation

_____ **3.** The control system element that collects sensor data and determines outputs based on a set of instructions or program software is known as _____.
   A. processing
   B. sensing
   C. input
   D. actuation

_____ **4.** A(n) _____ signal is electric current that is proportional to a continuously changing variable.
   A. digital
   B. analog
   C. binary
   D. pulse-width

_____ **5.** The smallest piece of digital or binary information is called a _____ and is represented by a single 0 or 1.
   A. speck
   B. byte
   C. dot
   D. bit

_____ **6.** When the voltage on a wire pair is a mirror opposite voltage when transmitting serial data it is called a
_____.
   A. binary translation
   B. pulse-width-modulation
   C. differential voltage
   D. baud signal

_____ **7.** A signal that varies in "ON" and "OFF" time is called a(n) _____ signal.
   A. analog
   B. pulse-width-modulation
   C. binary
   D. differential

_____ **8.** The percentage of time a pulse-width-modulation signal is high or on, in comparison to off time is referred
to as its _____.
   A. duty cycle
   B. frequency
   C. pulse width
   D. Either A or C

_____ **9.** The number of events or cycles that occur in a period, usually one second, is called _____.
   A. pulse width
   B. megahertz
   C. frequency
   D. duty cycle

_____ **10.** The CPU _____ is an oscillator inside the microprocessor that controls how fast instructions stored in
memory are processed.
   A. validation switch
   B. A-D converter
   C. modulator
   D. clock

True/False

If you believe the statement to be more true than false, write the letter "T" in the space provided. If you believe the
statement to be more false than true, write the letter "F".

_____ **1.** High-performance police cars were the first commercial vehicle systems transformed by electronic controls.

_____ **2.** In a few minutes with some keystrokes, a stock vehicle chassis can be reprogrammed to operate as an
ambulance, an on-highway tractor, dump truck, or bus.

_____ **3.** Sensing functions collect data about operational conditions or the state of a device by measuring some value
such as temperature, position, speed, or pressure.

_____ **4.** The alternating electrical current produced by a variable reluctance–type sensor would be considered a
digital signal.

_____ **5.** When serial digital data is transmitted using a pair of wires, each wire will transmit a voltage pulse
represented as a rectangular waveform.

_____ **6.** The term frequency refers to the number of data bits transmitted per second.

_____ **7.** The units for measuring pulse width are always expressed in units of time.

_____ **8.** Referred to as the electronic control module, a microprocessor or microcontroller is the heart of the control
unit.

_____ **9.** Non-volatile memory will be lost if power to the computer is interrupted.

_____ **10.** Random access memory is both readable and writable.

Fill in the Blank

Read each item carefully, and then complete the statement by filling in the missing word(s).

1. A(n) _____ report provides details such as diagnostic fault codes, fuel consumption, idle time, and emission system performance. The report can be extracted from a vehicle's electronic control module during scheduled maintenance.

2. The use of electronic engine and vehicle _____ provides for enhanced vehicle and occupant safety and security.

3. Programmable _____ provides flexibility to engines, transmissions, and body accessories for adaptation to specific job applications.

4. The presence of _____ is communicated through the malfunction indicator lamps.

5. The _____ of a system are functions performed by electrical signals produced by the processor.

6. The signal voltage from a throttle position sensor is a type of _____ data.

7. Every number from 0 to infinity and the letters of the alphabet letters can be represented by a combination of 0s and 1s using _____ code.

8. To convert analog signals to digital binary information, special circuits, known as _____ or analog to digital converters, are used.

9. A(n) _____-_____-_____ signal is commonly used as an output signal of an electronic control module.

10. ROM, RAM, and PROM are examples of different types of computer _____.

Elements of Electronic Signal Processing Systems

Identify which division each of the following system functions belongs to.

_____ 1. Fuel injector

_____ 2. Potentiometer

_____ 3. Switch

_____ 4. RAM

_____ 5. Voltage regulator

_____ 6. Relay

_____ 7. Thermistor

_____ 8. Actuator

_____ 9. Self-diagnosis

_____ 10. Check engine light

A. Sensing
B. Processing
C. Output

Crossword Puzzle

Use the clues in the column to complete the puzzle.

Across

2. A unit of 8 bits.

3. Reprogramming or recalibrating the ECM. Information is stored in the ECM's memory.

5. A special-purpose processor with limited capabilities, designed to perform a set of specific tasks.

Down

1. A type of data storage that is lost or erased when the ignition power is switched off.

4. A unit of measure for electrical frequency measurement, in cycles per second.

ASE-Type Questions

Read each item carefully, and then select the best response.

_____ 1. Technician A says that not a single vehicle system operates without at least some degree of electronic control. Technician B says that understanding the operating principles of electronic control systems is fundamental for choosing diagnostic strategies. Who is correct?
   A. Technician A
   B. Technician B
   C. Both Technician A and Technician B
   D. Neither Technician A nor Technician B

_____ 2. Technician A says that diesel engines were the first commercial vehicle systems transformed by electronic controls. Technician B says that smarter engines deliver ever-increasing power from smaller displacements. Who is correct?
   A. Technician A
   B. Technician B
   C. Both Technician A and Technician B
   D. Neither Technician A nor Technician B

_____ 3. Technician A says that telematics uses specialized telecommunication applications for long-distance transmission of information to and from a vehicle. Technician B says that telematics is not capable of transmitting information on fault codes. Who is correct?
   A. Technician A
   B. Technician B
   C. Both Technician A and Technician B
   D. Neither Technician A nor Technician B

_____ 4. Technician A says that technicians can take advantage of programmable electronic controls. Technician B says that power and torque rise profiles are easily altered electronically. Who is correct?
   A. Technician A
   B. Technician B
   C. Both Technician A and Technician B
   D. Neither Technician A nor Technician B

_____ 5. Technician A says that electronic control systems use a variety of sensors, wires, electrical actuators, and electronic modules moved with invisible electrical signals. Technician B says that the three major divisions of electronic control systems are sensing, processing, and output. Who is correct?
   A. Technician A
   B. Technician B
   C. Both Technician A and Technician B
   D. Neither Technician A nor Technician B

_____ 6. Technician A says that processing refers to the control system element that collects sensor data and determines outputs based on a set of instructions or program software. Technician B says that operational algorithms are included in the software that determines the steps taken when processing electrical data. Who is correct?
   A. Technician A
   B. Technician B
   C. Both Technician A and Technician B
   D. Neither Technician A nor Technician B

_____ 7. Technician A says that an analog signal is one type of electrical signal commonly used in electronic engine control applications. Technician B says that a tandem signal is one type of electrical signal commonly used in electronic engine control applications. Who is correct?
   A. Technician A
   B. Technician B
   C. Both Technician A and Technician B
   D. Neither Technician A nor Technician B

_____ **8.** Technician A says that, in contrast to analog signals, digital signals do not vary in voltage, frequency, or amplitude. Technician B says that the binary code does not lend itself to use in microprocessor circuits where processing large amounts of alphabetic or numerical data, represented in strings of 0s or 1s, is performed. Who is correct?

A. Technician A

B. Technician B

C. Both Technician A and Technician B

D. Neither Technician A nor Technician B

_____ **9.** Technician A says that serial data is used to transmit information from one electronic module to another. Technician B says that baud rate refers to the number of data bits transmitted per minute. Who is correct?

A. Technician A

B. Technician B

C. Both Technician A and Technician B

D. Neither Technician A nor Technician B

_____ **10.** Technician A says that a pulse-width-modulated (PWM) electrical signal is an electrical signal that shares similar characteristics with both a digital and analog signal. Technician B says that common examples of devices using PWM signals are solenoids, injectors, and light circuits. Who is correct?

A. Technician A

B. Technician B

C. Both Technician A and Technician B

D. Neither Technician A nor Technician B

Sensors

Chapter Review

The following activities have been designed to help you refresh your knowledge of this chapter. Your instructor may require you to complete some or all of these activities as a regular part of your training program. You are encouraged to complete any activity that your instructor does not assign as a way to enhance your learning.

Matching

Match the following terms with the correct description or example.

A. Hall effect sensor

B. Passive sensor

C. Potentiometer

D. Rheostat

E. Thermistor

_____ **1.** A sensor that does not use a current supplied by the ECM to operate.

_____ **2.** A variable resistor with three connections—one at each end of a resistive path, and a third sliding contact that moves along the resistive pathway.

_____ **3.** A temperature-sensitive variable resistor commonly used to measure coolant, oil, fuel, and air temperatures.

_____ **4.** A sensor commonly used to measure the rotational speed of a shaft.

_____ **5.** A variable resistor constructed of a fixed input terminal and a variable output terminal, which vary current flow by passing current through a long resistive tightly coiled wire.

Multiple Choice

Read each item carefully, and then select the best response.

_____ **1.** Oxygen sensors, NO_X sensors, and variable reluctance sensors are considered _____.

A. resistive sensors

B. variable capacitance sensors

C. voltage generators

D. switches

_____ **2.** When a switch is connected between the ECM and the battery positive, the switch is known as a(n) _____.

A. pull-up switch

B. single throw switch

C. pull-down switch

D. open switch

_____ **3.** A position sensor such as the throttle position sensor is usually a _____.

A. rheostat

B. potentiometer

C. thermistor

D. Hall effect sensor

_____ **4.** Knock sensors that measure abnormal combustion signals are a common application of _____.

A. variable capacitance pressure sensors

B. voltage generators

C. Wheatstone bridge sensors

D. piezoresistive sensors

_____ **5.** A _____ is an active sensor that uses the distance between two plates, or dielectric strength, inside the sensor to measure both dynamic and static pressure.
   A. variable reluctance sensor
   B. Wheatstone bridge sensor
   C. variable capacitance pressure sensor
   D. Hall effect sensor

_____ **6.** A _____ is a two-wire sensor commonly used to measure rotational speed, wheel speed, vehicle speed, and engine speed.
   A. variable reluctance sensor
   B. piezoresistive sensor
   C. variable capacitance sensor
   D. potentiometer

_____ **7.** What type of sensor is used to evaluate the operation of selective catalyst reduction (SCR) systems?
   A. CO_2 sensor
   B. Wide-range planar sensor
   C. Mass airflow sensor
   D. NO_X sensor

_____ **8.** The _____ constantly checks for malfunctions in any engine or emission-related electrical circuit or component providing input or output signals to an ECM.
   A. functionality monitor
   B. comprehensive component monitor
   C. input/output monitor
   D. All of the above

_____ **9.** To identify faults and measure signal voltage, _____ are often connected to internal pull-up resistors.
   A. thermistors
   B. planar sensors
   C. voltage generators
   D. variable reluctance sensors

_____ **10.** A _____ will produce waveforms or data that can be observed by using a graphing meter.
   A. Hall effect sensor
   B. variable reluctance sensor
   C. mass airflow sensor
   D. pressure sensor

True/False

If you believe the statement to be more true than false, write the letter "T" in the space provided. If you believe the statement to be more false than true, write the letter "F".

_____ **1.** A sensor will be considered active or passive depending on whether they use power supplied by the electronic control module to operate.

_____ **2.** The industry-standard reference voltage value used by all manufactures is 12 volts direct current.

_____ **3.** Switches are the simplest sensors of all, because they have no resistance in the closed position and infinite resistance in the open position.

_____ **4.** Rheostats are three-wire variable resistance sensors that are commonly used as input devices to an ECM.

_____ **5.** Three wire sensors, regardless of how they appear or what function they perform, have a common wiring configuration.

_____ **6.** Hall effect throttle position sensors are more reliable than dual-path throttle position sensors because they have no moving parts.

_____ **7.** The ability of a material to conduct or resist magnetic lines of force is known as capacitance.

_____ **8.** Wide-band oxygen sensors are commonly used on gasoline engines operating at stoichiometric air–fuel ratios.

_____ **9.** The potential for ammonia to be released to the atmosphere has led to the required use of an ammonia sensor for most engines produced since 2014.

_____ **10.** Output circuits, or output control devices, consist of display devices, serial data for network communication, and electromagnetic operator devices.

_____ **11.** Evenly spaced reluctor ring teeth are used to identify the cylinder stroke position.

_____ **12.** A functionality fault is triggered when the signal voltage of a sensor falls outside 85% of reference voltage.

_____ **13.** Rationality codes need careful pinpoint diagnostic tests to determine if a sensor is defective or some outside influence is affecting sensor data.

_____ **14.** When two resistors are connected in series, the greatest voltage drop takes place across the resistor with the lowest resistance.

_____ **15.** A broken magnet on a variable reluctance sensor will cause a low voltage reading.

Fill in the Blank

Read each item carefully, and then complete the statement by filling in the missing word(s).

1. Sensors are a type of _____ that convert physical conditions or states into electrical data.

2. The use of a(n) _____ voltage is important in processor operation, because the value of the variable resistor can be calculated by measuring voltage drop when another resistor with a known voltage input is connected in series with it.

3. In a(n) _____ temperature coefficient thermistor, the resistance decreases as the temperature increases.

4. For safety reasons, manufacturers will use an idle _____ switch to verify throttle position.

5. A(n) _____ _____ measures small changes in the resistance of tiny wires caused by stretching or contraction.

6. A(n) _____ bridge calculates the value of an unknown resistor using several other resistors of known fixed value.

7. The most common arrangement of a(n) _____ _____ sensor uses a metal interrupter ring or shutter and a permanent magnet positioned across from the sensor.

8. Diesel oxygen sensors are wide-range _____ sensors, which means they are flat rather than thimble-shaped.

9. A(n) _____ _____ sensor is a device that measures the weight of air entering the engine intake.

10. Electronic control systems have self-diagnostic capabilities to identify _____ in circuits and sensors.

11. Switch status can be determined by measuring the _____ _____ across a current-limiting resistor.

12. Three-wire circuits, whether digital or analog, passive or active, use a reference voltage, signal, and _____ wire, also referred to as ground return by some manufacturers.

13. When supplying a negative polarity or ground to a device, current is switched through a transistor called a(n) _____-_____ driver.

14. Several temperature and resistance values are supplied by the manufacturer to properly evaluate a(n) _____ when testing using an ohmmeter.

15. When performing pinpoint testing the signal voltage is always measured between the _____ return and signal wire for all sensors.

Labeling

Label the following diagrams with the correct terms.

1. Identify the parts of a Hall effect throttle position sensor:

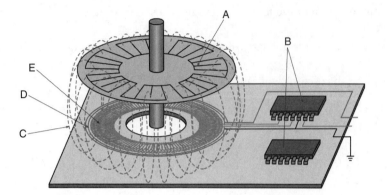

A. _____

B. _____

C. _____

D. _____

E. _____

2. Identify the parts of a silicon-based piezoresistive sensor:

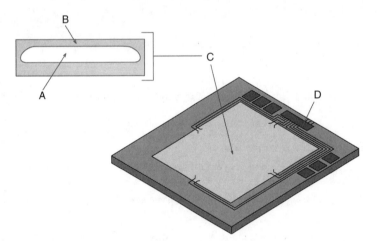

A. _____

B. _____

C. _____

D. _____

3. Identify the parts of a variable capacitance sensor:

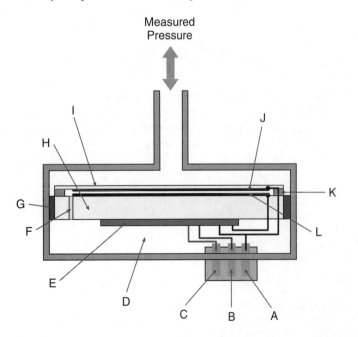

A. _____

B. _____

C. _____

D. _____

E. _____

F. _____

G. _____

H. _____

I. _____

J. _____

K. _____

L. _____

4. Identify the parts of an oxygen sensor:

A. _____

B. _____

C. _____

D. _____

E. _____

F. _____

G. _____

Society of Automotive Engineers (SAE) J1939 Failure Mode Identifiers (FMI)

Match the failure mode identifier code to the correct Society of Automotive Engineers text.

Failure mode identifier code:

0. _____
1. _____
2. _____
3. _____
4. _____
5. _____
6. _____
7. _____
8. _____
9. _____
10. _____
11. _____
12. _____
13. _____
14. _____
15. _____
16. _____
17. _____
18. _____
19. _____
20-30. _____
31. _____

A. Data valid but below normal operating range—moderately severe level
B. Current above normal or grounded circuit
C. Reserved for SAE assignment
D. Abnormal rate of change
E. Data valid but above normal operational range—most severe level
F. Data valid but above normal operating range—least severe level
G. Voltage above normal or shorted to high source
H. Condition exists
I. Abnormal frequency or pulse width or period
J. Special instructions
K. Data valid but below normal operational range—most severe level
L. Bad intelligent device or component
M. Received network data in error
N. Current below normal or open circuit
O. Data erratic, intermittent, or incorrect
P. Data valid but above normal operating range—moderately severe level
Q. Abnormal update rate
R. Mechanical system not responding or out of adjustment
S. Out of calibration
T. Voltage below normal or shorted to low source
U. Data valid but below normal operating range—least severe level
V. Root cause not known

Crossword Puzzle

Use the clues in the column to complete the puzzle.

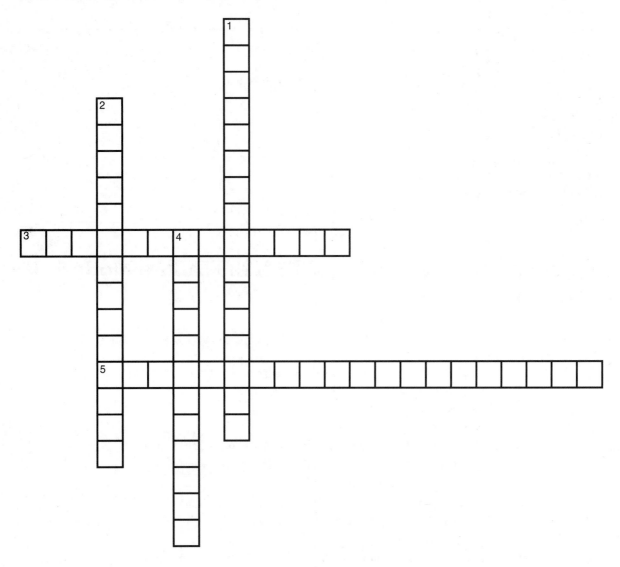

Across

3. A sensor used in selective catalyst reduction (SCR) that provides data to the ECM that is used to determine if ammonia values are out of anticipated range.

5. A circuit used for safety reasons that is used to verify throttle position.

Down

1. A precisely regulated voltage supplied by the ECM to sensors; the value is typically 5 VDC, but some manufacturers use 8 or 12 volts.

2. A switch connected between the ECM and a negative ground current potential.

4. A sensor that uses a current supplied by the ECM to operate.

ASE-Type Questions

Read each item carefully, and then select the best response.

_____ 1. All of following are examples of a terminal connector, *except*:
  A. split-bolt
  B. butt
  C. eye ring
  D. push-on spade

_____ 2. Two technicians are discussing engine management input sensors. Technician A says that switches are the simplest sensors of all, because they have no resistance in the closed position and infinite resistance in the open position. Technician B says that a zero-volt signal would present as a closed switch, while 12 volts would present as an open switch. Who is correct?
  A. Technician A
  B. Technician B
  C. Both Technician A and Technician B
  D. Neither Technician A nor Technician B

_____ 3. Technician A says that a knock sensor measuring abnormal combustion signals is a common application of piezoresistive sensors. Technician B says that silicon-based piezoresistive sensors are very sensitive to slight pressure changes. Who is correct?
  A. Technician A
  B. Technician B
  C. Both Technician A and Technician B
  D. Neither Technician A nor Technician B

_____ 4. A mass air flow (MAF) Hall effect sensor is being diagnosed using a graphing multimeter. Sometimes the circuit within the sensor can fail and produce a waveform unrecognizable to the ECM. Which of these is LEAST LIKELY resulting waveform?
  A. Technician A
  B. Technician B
  C. Both Technician A and Technician B
  D. Neither Technician A nor Technician B

_____ 5. If the problem is related to temperature, vibration, or moisture, the circuit or control module can be heated, lightly tapped, or even sprayed with water to simulate the failure conditions. What measuring tool with glitch testing capabilities can identify and record the circuit fault in microseconds?
  A. Technician A
  B. Technician B
  C. Both Technician A and Technician B
  D. Neither Technician A nor Technician B

_____ 6. Technician A says that switches are categorized as sensors whenever they provide information to an electronic control system. Technician B says that switch data may indicate a physical value such as open or closed, up or down, high or low, or it may indicate on and off. Who is correct?
  A. Technician A
  B. Technician B
  C. Both Technician A and Technician B
  D. Neither Technician A nor Technician B

_____ 7. All of these are examples of variable reluctance sensors, *except*:
  A. crankshaft position
  B. camshaft position
  C. vehicle speed signal
  D. engine coolant temperature

_____ 8. Technician A says that wide-band oxygen sensors produce a voltage proportional to a narrow oxygen level. Technician B says that oxygen sensors are used to measure air–fuel ratio in order to calibrate EGR flow rates and air–fuel ratios for exhaust after-treatment devices. Who is correct?
  A. Technician A
  B. Technician B
  C. Both Technician A and Technician B
  D. Neither Technician A nor Technician B

_____ **9.** At which of these locations is diesel exhaust fuel (DEF) added on a light-duty vehicle diesel equipped vehicle?

    A. Fitting near fuel door

    B. Fitting near the SCR (selective catalyst reduction)

    C. Directly into the fuel tank

    D. Special tank next to the fuel pump

_____ **10.** What type of engine fault checks sensor voltages and, in a few cases, current draw to determine whether the sensor or associated circuits are open or have shorts?

    A. Plausibility

    B. Out of range

    C. Functionality

    D. Rationality

On-Board Vehicle Networks

Chapter Review

The following activities have been designed to help you refresh your knowledge of this chapter. Your instructor may require you to complete some or all of these activities as a regular part of your training program. You are encouraged to complete any activity that your instructor does not assign as a way to enhance your learning.

Matching

Match the following terms with the correct description or example.

A. Controlled area networks (CAN)

B. Data bus

C. Differential mode transmission

D. Ladder logic

E. Multiplexing

_____ **1.** The typology forming the communication pathway of modules in a network.

_____ **2.** A software design system that replicates relay-based system operation into electronic software.

_____ **3.** A distributed network control system in which no single central control module is used.

_____ **4.** Transmission of more than one electrical signal or message takes place over a single wire or pair of wires.

_____ **5.** A situation in which network modules detect the voltage difference between two wires to determine if a signal is a 1 or a 0.

Multiple Choice

Read each item carefully, and then select the best response.

_____ **1.** The development of control module networks used to provide greater safety, efficiencies, and capabilities took place during the _____ of commercial vehicle electronics.
A. First Generation
B. Second Generation
C. Third Generation
D. Telematics Generation

_____ **2.** The rules or standards used to communicate over the networks are referred to as _____.
A. typology
B. network protocol
C. centralized control
D. ladder logic

_____ **3.** It is the job of the _____ to translate communication between different networks operating using different protocols or speeds.
A. gateway module
B. master module
C. data bus
D. slave module

_____ **4.** An electrical signal communication strategy called _____ requires the modules and other devices to take turns, sharing the data bus communication pathway.
A. master-slave networking
B. gateway protocol
C. time division multiplexing
D. distributed control

_____ **5.** GM claims that it realizes over a _____ reduction in wiring needed in some of its light-duty vehicles using network communication.
   A. 40%
   B. 50%
   C. 60%
   D. 70%

_____ **6.** Communicating self-diagnostic data to an electronic service tool from even a single module requires the use of _____.
   A. time division multiplexing
   B. bidirectional communication
   C. gateway protocols
   D. point-to-point communication

_____ **7.** Which of the following safety features was made possible by the use of network communication?
   A. Power door lock activation above 5 mph
   B. Virtual fusing of electrical circuits
   C. Dome lights that shut off after 10 minutes
   D. All of the above

_____ **8.** The most widely used type of network for integrating power train operation of all the latest vehicles is a _____.
   A. Bluetooth network
   B. serial communication network
   C. controlled area network
   D. centralized control network

_____ **9.** The SAE network standard J-1939 _____.
   A. requires terminating resistors
   B. communicates at 9,600 bps
   C. connects up to 20 modules or nodes
   D. All of the above

_____ **10.** Which CAN-bus message format would be something like, "Hello, everyone, can somebody please send the information labeled Y?"
   A. Error frame
   B. Data frame
   C. Remote frame
   D. Overload frame

True/False

If you believe the statement to be more true than false, write the letter "T" in the space provided. If you believe the statement to be more false than true, write the letter "F".

_____ **1.** Communication takes place between all the modules and devices connected to the network using an electrical signal-processing strategy called multiplexing.

_____ **2.** The word "bus," when used in network typology, describes a network connection that looks just like a bus route.

_____ **3.** The master module will make requests for information and sends commands to be executed by a distribution module.

_____ **4.** When paired together and connected in parallel to all modules in the network, the typology forming the communication pathway is called a ring.

_____ **5.** Multiplexed communication was originally designed to eliminate bulky wiring harnesses used on transit buses.

_____ **6.** Fault code reporting, the configuration of the DLC, communication language, and other network characteristics associated with emission control systems vary by manufacturer.

_____ **7.** Sensor data can be shared across a large number of devices connected into a network.

_____ **8.** The J-1708 data bus communicates at speeds up to 256,000 bps.

_____ **9.** On a controlled area network, the CAN-L (low) wire is yellow and carries positive voltage (CAN+).

_____ **10.** When the ignition key is turned on, the tractor bridge computer starts with J-560 outputs in smart mode.

Fill in the Blank

Read each item carefully, and then complete the statement by filling in the missing word(s).

1. On-board vehicle _____ are formed by connecting vehicle electronic control modules to one another to communicate and exchange information.

2. Master-slave networks are referred to as _____ network control.

3. A(n) _____ control network uses several to dozens of modules, all sharing information and sending output signals to electrical devices.

4. When using networks, electrical system complexity is absorbed by _____ instead of a huge array of hardwired components and circuit boards.

5. On-board _____ capabilities are built into electronic control systems to help technicians perform faster checks and repairs.

6. When a network-compatible _____ connects to a network, its presence is recognized and the network will provide access to information it needs to perform its job.

7. Modules containing _____ _____ transistors, which operate like a combined solid-state relay and a circuit breaker, also have virtual fusing for circuit protection.

8. _____ communication is like electronic Morse code. Instead of dots and dashes, however, 0s and 1s are transmitted in a series, one after another, using voltage pulses.

9. Wires are _____ to minimize electromagnetic interference caused by magnetic fields and radio waves.

10. Network signals are distorted and slowed if terminating _____ are missing or defective.

11. Messages sent and received over the network are constructed in _____ with a maximum message length of 130 bits.

12. If two or more modules start transmitting at once, the message _____ decides which message has access to the data bus.

13. Where wiring diagrams once depicted battery current flow through electrical connections and devices and showed relays switched open or closed, _____ _____ shows rules for software logic to control devices.

14. Cell phones are a common application for _____ technology, used to connect a phone with the audio system using the on-board network.

15. PLC is an acronym for _____-_____ _____ technology, which enables multiplex communication over constantly powered wires on the J-560 trailer plug.

Labeling

Label the following diagrams with the correct terms.

1. Identify the type of network topology:

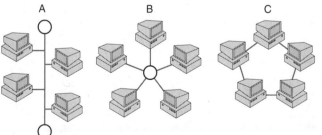

A. _____

B. _____

C. _____

2. Identify the pin configuration of a 9-pin DLC:

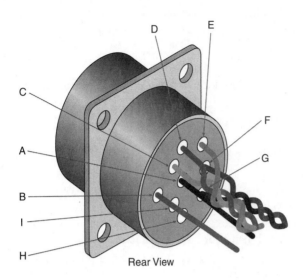

Rear View

Front View

A. _____

B. _____

C. _____

D. _____

E. _____

F. _____

G. _____

H. _____

I. _____

Skill Drills

Test your knowledge of skill drills by filling in the correct words in the photo captions.

1. Measuring Resistance of Terminating Resistors:

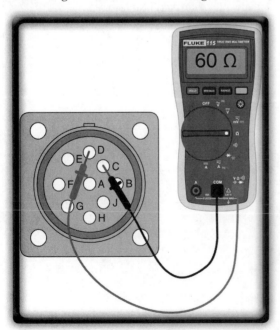

Step 1: With the ignition _____, disconnect the _____.

Step 2: Connect the leads of a digital _____ to pins _____ and _____ of the 9-pin diagnostic connector.

Step 3:   Set the multimeter to read in _____.

Step 4:   Measure and record the resistance. Normal resistance should be _____ ohms; _____ ohms indicates one _____ resistor; _____ ohms indicates an _____ resistor. With both resistors removed, there should be a high resistance of more than _____ ohms, but not _____ resistance.

2. Performing a DLC Voltage Check:

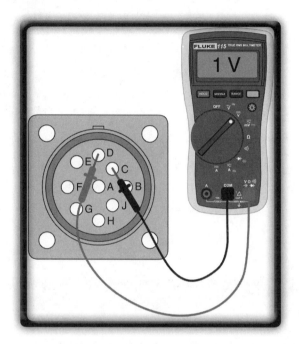

Step 1:   Set the DMM to read in _____.

Step 2:   With the ignition _____, connect the leads of a digital multimeter (DMM) to pins _____ and _____ of the 9-pin diagnostic connector.

Step 3:   Measure and record the _____. The voltage should be more than _____ volt. If not, there is no _____ _____ taking place.

3. Checking for Shorts in the CAN:

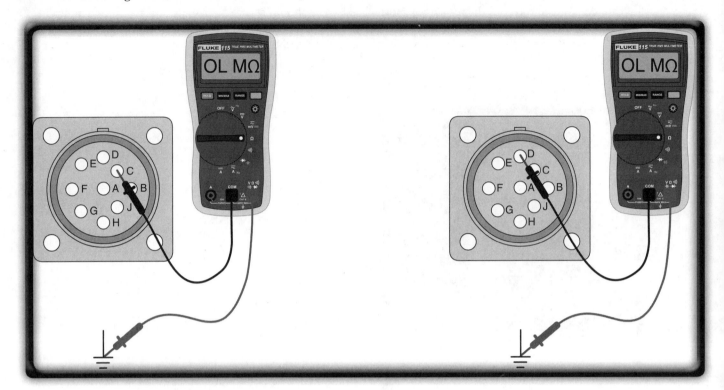

Step 1: With the ignition _____, disconnect the _____.

Step 2: Connect one lead of a _____ _____ to pin _____ of the 9-pin diagnostic connector.

Step 3: Connect the multimeter lead to _____ _____.

Step 4: Set the multimeter to read in _____.

Step 5: Measure and record the _____.

Step 6: Connect _____ lead of a _____ _____ to pin _____ of the 9-pin diagnostic connector.

Step 7: Connect the other multimeter lead to _____ _____.

Step 8: Measure and record the _____. The _____ between chassis ground and either pins C or D should be _____ or _____ of _____.

Crossword Puzzle

Use the clues in the column to complete the puzzle.

Across

2. Pieces of data sent by the master module.

3. The process of deciding which messages have priority to transmit over the network to prevent data collision between positive and negative signals canceling one another.

5. A short-range wireless technology that can automatically connect a device into a network.

Down

1. A point on a network.

4. The manner in which modules are connected to one another.

ASE-Type Questions

Read each item carefully, and then select the best response.

_____ 1. Two technicians are discussing checking the voltage at the 9-pin diagnostic connector or datalink connector (DLC). Technician A says that voltage is checked with the ignition on at terminals C and D. Technician B says that the voltage at terminals C and D should be 12.6 volts. Who is correct?

    A. Technician A

    B. Technician B

    C. Both Technician A and Technician B

    D. Neither Technician A nor Technician B

_____ 2. When checking for shorts on the CAN-bus, which of these voltage values is a technician MOST LIKELY to find?

    A. 1 volt

    B. 0.5 volts

    C. OL (out of limits)

    D. 0.2 volts

_____ 3. Which of the following connectors do technicians use in conjunction with electronic service tools—such as scan tools, scanners, PCs, and other devices—to communicate with modules connected to the vehicle networks on late-model trucks?

    A. 6-pin diagnostic connector

    B. 16-pin DLC

    C. 9-pin diagnostic connector

    D. 12-pin DLC

_____ 4. Two technicians are discussing truck serial data communication. Technician A says that trucks using the J-1939 SAE standard use a connection between the tractor and trailer, primarily to power the in-dash ABS trailer lamp called a power-line carrier (PLC). Technician B says that the PLC system can operate in conventional mode only when connected to a 2001 or later tractor or trailer is connected to one another. Who is correct?

    A. Technician A

    B. Technician B

    C. Both Technician A and Technician B

    D. Neither Technician A nor Technician B

_____ 5. Technician A says that network communication, when enabled, takes place over the brown and green (tail and right turn) wires of the J-560 trailer plug. Technician B says that the MOST LIKELY diagnostic routine to identify a network problem is to perform resistance and voltage checks of the CAN-bus at the DLC. Who is correct?

    A. Technician A

    B. Technician B

    C. Both Technician A and Technician B

    D. Neither Technician A nor Technician B

_____ 6. Two technicians are discussing truck serial data communication and networks. Technician A says that data carried on the CAN-bus has four distinct message formats: data frame, remote frame, error frame, and overload frame. Technician B says that cell phone and Bluetooth technology are two levels of customization realized using wireless network interface. Who is correct?

    A. Technician A

    B. Technician B

    C. Both Technician A and Technician B

    D. Neither Technician A nor Technician B

_____ 7. Technician A says that broken mechanical systems are often diagnosed visually or with mechanical tools such as pressure gauges and dial indicators. Technician B says that self-monitoring or self-diagnostic capabilities are, therefore, built into electronic control systems to help technicians perform faster. Who is correct?

    A. Technician A

    B. Technician B

    C. Both Technician A and Technician B

    D. Neither Technician A nor Technician B

_____ **8.** Which of the following safety features is LEAST LIKELY to be made possible by network communication?
  A. Headlights that are automatically switched on with wiper activation
  B. Interior bus lighting that dims to minimize windshield glare
  C. Automatic door opening when stopped for more than 5 minutes
  D. Dome or work light that shuts off after 10 minutes with door open and key off

_____ **9.** Two technicians are describing the use of electronic service tools. Technician A says that fault codes, communication language, and other features of the on-board network are standardized by EPA legislation. Technician B says that only the truck manufacturer's specific scan tool or software can read the legislated fault codes. Who is correct?
  A. Technician A
  B. Technician B
  C. Both Technician A and Technician B
  D. Neither Technician A nor Technician B

_____ **10.** Which of the following now come equipped with digital LCD displays that can serve as a numeric fault code reader?
  A. Scan tool
  B. Speedometer
  C. Odometer
  D. Clock

Chapter Review

The following activities have been designed to help you refresh your knowledge of this chapter. Your instructor may require you to complete some or all of these activities as a regular part of your training program. You are encouraged to complete any activity that your instructor does not assign as a way to enhance your learning.

Matching

Match the following terms with the correct description or example.

A. Active fault

B. Fault mode identifier (FMI)

C. Historical fault

D. Incipient fault

E. Intermittent fault

_____ **1.** A fault that took place at one time but that is now corrected and no longer active.

_____ **2.** A fault that is the result of system or component deterioration.

_____ **3.** A fault that is not ongoing and can be both active and historical.

_____ **4.** The type of failure detected in the SPN, PID, or SID.

_____ **5.** A fault that is currently taking place and uninterrupted in action.

Multiple Choice

Read each item carefully, and then select the best response.

_____ **1.** The simplest, most familiar definition of _____ is the diagnostic function of electronic control systems to identify or self-diagnose system faults and report fault codes.

    A. on-board diagnostics

    B. off-board diagnostics

    C. trouble code monitoring

    D. telematics

_____ **2.** The introduction of _____ in 2007 added a level of complexity to emissions systems that required monitoring to ensure they were properly functioning.

    A. particulate filters

    B. crankcase ventilation systems

    C. exhaust gas recirculation systems

    D. All of the above

_____ **3.** A _____ diagnostic strategy compares system and component behaviors to expected patterns of operation.

    A. traditional

    B. isolation-based

    C. model-based

    D. historical

_____ **4.** An unknown and uncontrolled input acting on the system such as electromagnetic interference, fluid or gas leakage from a hydraulic or pneumatic system, or excessive mechanical friction is known as a(n) _____.

    A. disturbance

    B. incipient fault

    C. preliminary incident

    D. intermittent fault

_____ 5. Directly measuring the level of emissions using a sensor to identify a noxious emission is called _____.
   A. continuity monitoring
   B. threshold monitoring
   C. rationality monitoring
   D. functionality monitoring

_____ 6. HD-OBD legislation for diesels includes _____.
   A. standardized names and abbreviations of components and systems
   B. reading of fault codes by aftermarket electronic test equipment
   C. standardized 9-pin DLC in the driver area
   D. All of the above

_____ 7. The threshold for diesel misfire detection is _____ per 1,000 crankshaft revolutions.
   A. 2%
   B. 4%
   C. 8%
   D. 10%

_____ 8. HD-OBD requirements for the diesel EGR monitor include detecting EGR _____ before emissions exceed HD-OBD thresholds.
   A. response rate
   B. flow rate
   C. cooling system performance
   D. All of the above

_____ 9. Two common _____ system monitors are diesel particulate filter (DPF) monitoring and selective catalyst reduction (SCR) monitoring.
   A. aftertreatment
   B. EGR
   C. fuel
   D. crankcase ventilation

_____ 10. Type _____ diagnostic trouble codes are emissions-causing faults that must occur at least once on two consecutive trips before the malfunction indicator light (MIL) will illuminate.
   A. A
   B. B
   C. C
   D. D

_____ 11. Both the J-1587/1708 and the J-1939 network connections are found in the _____ DLC.
   A. 6-pin
   B. 9-pin
   C. 12-pin
   D. None of the above

_____ 12. A _____ is the first byte or character of each message that identifies which control module on the J-1587 serial communication link originated the information.
   A. message identifier
   B. system identifier
   C. parameter identifier
   D. fault mode identifier

_____ 13. The _____ is the smallest identifiable fault.
   A. system identifier
   B. fault mode identifier
   C. suspect parameter number
   D. occurrence identifier

_____ 14. Suspect parameter number, source addresses, and failure mode indicator information are part of a larger J-1939 message called the _____.
   A. proprietary identification number
   B. fault identification number
   C. subsystem identification number
   D. parameter group number

_____ **15.** Priority fault codes _____ are reserved for messages that require prompt access to the bus in order to prevent severe mechanical damage.
  A. 1 and 2
  B. 3 and 4
  C. 5 and 6
  D. 7 and 8

True/False

If you believe the statement to be more true than false, write the letter "T" in the space provided. If you believe the statement to be more false than true, write the letter "F".

_____ **1.** The legislated standards for maximum vehicle emissions levels are called on-board diagnostic standards.

_____ **2.** The HD-OBD standards have fewer standardized legal requirements and are less comprehensive than the EMD standards.

_____ **3.** All OBD standards are developed by SAE International and adopted by the EPA.

_____ **4.** An illuminated malfunction indicator light or check engine light indicates a historical fault.

_____ **5.** An HD-OBD system executes, or runs, monitors once every 24 hours of engine operation.

_____ **6.** HD-OBD legislation requires 14 mandatory major system monitors for diesel engines.

_____ **7.** All emissions systems are monitored continuously.

_____ **8.** OBD crankcase ventilation system monitoring includes detecting closed-loop feedback control.

_____ **9.** A diesel exhaust fluid quality sensor can now determine the quality of DEF fluid by measuring its density.

_____ **10.** The higher the first number is in the message, the greater importance attached to the information.

Fill in the Blank

Read each item carefully, and then complete the statement by filling in the missing word(s).

1. A(n) _____ self-diagnostic strategy focuses on specific areas of commercial vehicle control, such as the engine, anti-lock braking, traction control, and transmissions.

2. A(n) _____ is a deviation of at least one characteristic property of the system from its standard behavior.

3. Fault _____ is best accomplished using a diagnostic fault tree supplied by the manufacturer.

4. Testing the operation of individual emissions system components using an organized procedure is known as a(n) _____.

5. The _____ _____ connector is the connection point for electronic service tools used to access fault code and other information provided by chassis electronic control modules.

6. OBD _____ software identifies fault codes, ensures emissions systems are operating correctly, and regularly evaluates malfunctions in the emissions systems unique to diesel engines.

7. The _____ _____ monitor tracks electrical circuits operating power train components that can cause a measurable emissions increase during any reasonable driving conditions.

8. During _____-_____ diagnostics, the technician may monitor system operation, perform actuator tests, pinpoint electrical tests, and inspect components.

9. After a repair has been made an HD-OBD service tool displays a(n) _____ code indicating that a monitor has completed its functionality test and no fault was found.

10. The _____ _____ represents the number of times a fault combination of SPN/FMI has taken place.

Message Identifier Numbers

Match the Message Identifier Number to its correct description.

MID number:

_____	**1.** 128	**A.**	Satellite
_____	**2.** 130	**B.**	Instrument cluster unit
_____	**3.** 136	**C.**	Collision avoidance
_____	**4.** 140	**D.**	ECM
_____	**5.** 180	**E.**	Off-board diagnostics
_____	**6.** 181	**F.**	Transmission control unit
_____	**7.** 190	**G.**	Cellular
_____	**8.** 229	**H.**	ABS
_____	**9.** 231	**I.**	Climate control module

Crossword Puzzle

Use the clues in the column to complete the puzzle.

Across

2. A branch of information technology that uses specialized applications for long-distance transmission of information to and from a vehicle.
4. A value or identifier of an item being reported with fault data.
5. A method of providing fault code data for a specific system that involves counting the number of flashes from a warning lamp and observing longer pauses between the light blinks.

Down

1. A fault code used by J-1587 protocols that identifies which subsystem has failed.
3. The field that designates which control module is sending the message.

ASE-Type Questions

Read each item carefully, and then select the best response.

_____ 1. Two technicians are discussing HD-OBD for trucks. Technician A says that the simplest, most familiar definition is the diagnostic function of electronic control systems to identify or self-diagnose system faults and report fault codes. Technician B says the automotive and light-duty truck version of OBD is called OBD II. Who is correct?
- **A.** Technician A
- **B.** Technician B
- **C.** Both Technician A and Technician B
- **D.** Neither Technician A nor Technician B

_____ 2. Technician A says that a fault is a deviation of at least one characteristic property of the system from its standard behavior. Technician B says that a historical fault took place at one time and can never be active again. Who is correct?
- **A.** Technician A
- **B.** Technician B
- **C.** Both Technician A and Technician B
- **D.** Neither Technician A nor Technician B

_____ 3. A(n) _____ fault is not ongoing and can be both active and historical.
- **A.** inactive
- **B.** incipient
- **C.** intermittent
- **D.** historical

_____ 4. All of following are part of the HD-OBD legislation for diesels, _except_:
- **A.** 9-pin diagnostic connector
- **B.** 6-pin diagnostic connector
- **C.** standardized emissions-related fault codes for all manufacturers
- **D.** reading of fault codes by aftermarket electronic test equipment

_____ 5. Which of these HD-OBD terms describes when the ECM stores a snapshot of the engine operating conditions present at the time the malfunction was detected?
- **A.** Freeze frame
- **B.** Diagnostic trouble code (DTC)
- **C.** C-type code
- **D.** D-type code

_____ 6. Technician A says that threshold monitoring directly measures the level of emissions using a sensor to identify a noxious emission. Technician B says that a historical fault took place at one time and can never be active again. Who is correct?
- **A.** Technician A
- **B.** Technician B
- **C.** Both Technician A and Technician B
- **D.** Neither Technician A nor Technician B

_____ 7. What kind of monitoring measures voltage drops and signal and ground return voltage from sensors or output devices to validate circuits are not open or shorted to ground and battery voltage?
- **A.** Intermittent
- **B.** Threshold
- **C.** Electrical circuit continuity
- **D.** Out of range

_____ 8. HD-OBD legislation for diesels includes all of the following features, _except_:
- **A.** standardized 6-pin DLC
- **B.** standardized emissions-related fault codes for all manufacturers
- **C.** reading of fault codes by aftermarket electronic test equipment
- **D.** standardized names and abbreviations of components and systems

_____ **9.** Which of these systems' faults is LEAST LIKELY to be detected before emissions exceed standards?

　　A. Oxidation catalyst

　　B. Lean NO_X (oxides of nitrogen) catalyst

　　C. SCR (selective catalyst reduction) catalyst

　　D. Glow plugs and intake air heaters

_____ **10.** Which part of the heavy-duty diesel HD-OBD management system stores diagnostic information?

　　A. Misfire

　　B. Vehicle-in vehicle-out information

　　C. Freeze frame

　　D. Trip

Commercial Vehicle Tires

Chapter Review

The following activities have been designed to help you refresh your knowledge of this chapter. Your instructor may require you to complete some or all of these activities as a regular part of your training program. You are encouraged to complete any activity that your instructor does not assign as a way to enhance your learning.

Matching

Match the following terms with the correct description or example.

A. Bias-ply tire
B. Nominal diameter
C. Overall diameter
D. Radial-ply tire
E. Section height

F. Section width
G. Static radius
H. Tire bead
I. Tire casing
J. Tread

_____ 1. The distance between the outside of the sidewalls on an inflated tire without any load on it.

_____ 2. A tire with two or more layers of casing plies and cord loops running radially from bead to bead.

_____ 3. Steel wire wound together to form a cable; when bundled together, they sit at the wheel rim to form an airtight seal between the tire and the rim.

_____ 4. A size code figure, for reference purposes only, as indicated in the tire and rim size designation.

_____ 5. The height of the sidewalls.

_____ 6. The distance from the tire center to ground level.

_____ 7. A tire constructed in a latticed, criss-crossing structure, with alternate plies crossing over each other and laid with the cord angles in opposite directions.

_____ 8. A cap of molded rubber compound attached to the top of a tire's belt system.

_____ 9. The diameter of an inflated tire at the outermost surface of the tread.

_____ 10. The foundational body of the tire, consisting of several layers of fabric cord, called plies, encased with a rubber compound.

Multiple Choice

Read each item carefully, and then select the best response.

_____ 1. Commercial vehicle tires contain larger air volume and produce a larger _____ with the road.
   A. section width
   B. contact patch
   C. weight ratio
   D. Both A and C

_____ 2. It is the function of a tire to _____.
   A. support the vehicle load
   B. absorb road shocks
   C. provide directional control of the vehicle
   D. All of the above

_____ **3.** Force from exploding tires is typically released at an angle of up to _____ degrees from the rupture.
   A. 15
   B. 30
   C. 45
   D. 90

_____ **4.** The most prevalent _____ in use today utilizes the wheel speed anti-lock braking system to measure the difference in the rotational speed of the four wheels.
   A. indirect TPMS
   B. inflation solenoid
   C. direct TPMS
   D. centrifugal sensor

_____ **5.** Tubeless tires use a single-piece, _____ wheel rim, which is a type of wheel rim that fits over the brake drum and is concave.
   A. lock ring
   B. drop-center
   C. offset
   D. deep-bead

_____ **6.** Tube-type tires require a piece of rubber that wraps around the rim to protect the inner tube from chafing, pinching, and cracking called a _____.
   A. chafing liner
   B. contact patch
   C. tire bead
   D. tire flap

_____ **7.** If a tire has a designation of 295/75 R 22.5, the number 75 represents the _____.
   A. tire width
   B. cross-sectional ratio in percent
   C. acceptable speed
   D. nominal rim diameter

_____ **8.** A tire with a section width of 12" and an aspect ratio of 75% would have a sidewall height of _____.
   A. 3"
   B. 4"
   C. 9"
   D. 12"

_____ **9.** What type of tires shift the bearing load centerline outwards to the axle end producing increased bearing wear?
   A. Super single tires
   B. Dual tires
   C. Wide-base single tires
   D. Both A and C

_____ **10.** The primary function of the _____ is to seal air inside a tire and keep moisture out.
   A. inner liner
   B. flipper
   C. chafer
   D. tread

_____ **11.** The hot curing process used for retreading commercial vehicle tires is also known as _____.
   A. precure
   B. tread cure
   C. mold cure
   D. regrooving

_____ **12.** The majority of tread separations are caused by _____.
   A. excessive heat
   B. road hazards
   C. manufacturing defects
   D. operational problems

_____ **13.** The process that uses a heated cutting tool to carve new tread or add stripes to a tire is called _____.
   A. tread curing
   B. regrooving
   C. gouging
   D. molding

_____ **14.** A 25% reduction in tire tread life and a significant loss of steering precision and cornering stability can be caused by _____.
   A. underinflation
   B. nitrogen inflation
   C. overinflation
   D. Both A and C

_____ **15.** Excessive loaded radial run-out on the tire, wheel, and hub assembly can be corrected by _____.
   A. balancing the tire
   B. adjusting the alignment
   C. replacing the tire
   D. adjusting the suspension components

True/False

If you believe the statement to be more true than false, write the letter "T" in the space provided. If you believe the statement to be more false than true, write the letter "F".

_____ **1.** One in 1,000 accidents involving a tire or wheel results in death.

_____ **2.** Tires for on-highway trucks carrying heavy loads will be different depending on whether they are used on a steering axle, drive axle, or trailer axle.

_____ **3.** An unrestrained wheel with a tire failure can fly as much as 66 feet (20 meters) through the air.

_____ **4.** Indirect TPMS sensors can only transmit to the receiver; they cannot receive any information.

_____ **5.** In a tube-type tire a liner of rubber is applied to the inside of the tire to create an airtight seal with the casing.

_____ **6.** Low profile tires have shorter, stiffer sidewalls, resulting in less heating and tread squirm.

_____ **7.** Bias-ply tires separate the mechanical action of the tread and sidewalls—which results in a better contact patch formed between the tire and road.

_____ **8.** Block style tread does not transmit torque and must roll with little resistance when the direction of the tire is changed.

_____ **9.** Retreaded truck tires represent a savings of over $3 billion US dollars annually in North America.

_____ **10.** Retreads cause most of the tire debris found on highways.

_____ **11.** The depth of the undertread is used to determine if a tire is suitable for regrooving.

_____ **12.** Vehicle weight is the primary determinant of tire inflation pressure.

_____ **13.** Filling tires with nitrogen eliminates the need for monthly tire pressure checks.

_____ **14.** Rib-type tread encounters less rolling resistance than block-type tread.

_____ **15.** A tire that is dynamically in balance is in balance when it is spinning as opposed to when it is stationary.

Fill in the Blank

Read each item carefully, and then complete the statement by filling in the missing word(s).

1. Together with hubs and rims, _____ have the job of safely supporting the vehicle weight over a wide range of speed, load, and road conditions.

2. The greatest _____ resistance is encountered by tires carrying the greater proportion of vehicle weight.

3. The tire _____ pressure is the level of air in the tire that provides it with load-carrying capacity and affects overall vehicle performance.

4. A(n) _____ TPMS directly measures the tire pressure via a sensor that is installed inside each wheel, which helps protect the TPMS from damage.

5. The use of a(n) _____ switch in the TPMS sensor allows the sensor to go to sleep when the vehicle stops, which extends battery life.

6. The tire _____ is the inner circumference of the tire and is the part of the tire that connects the tire onto the rim.

7. The _____ _____ is the distance covered by one revolution of the tire.

8. The _____ _____ refers to a comparison between the height of the sidewall (section height) to the section width expressed as a percentage.

9. Wide-base or _____ tires are large tires with a low aspect ratio that are often used to replace two single tires on a drive axle.

10. A specialized rubber compound called bead _____ is incorporated into the bead and extends into the sidewall area.

11. The retreading process known as _____ curing uses a molded, pre-cured tread strip or tread ring, which is glued to the casing.

12. Separated tire treads that litter the highway are often called road _____.

13. A _____ rupture is caused by impact with road debris at high speeds.

14. The three most popular types of pocket tire _____ _____ are the pencil type, the dial type, and the digital type.

15. A _____-filled tire can usually be identified by a fluorescent green cap on the valve stem.

Labeling

Label the following diagrams with the correct terms.

1. Identify the components of a tire:

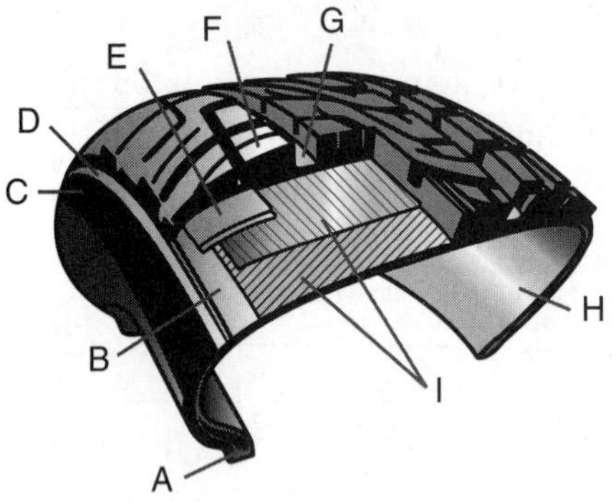

A. _____

B. _____

C. _____

D. _____

E. _____

F. _____

G. _____

H. _____

I. _____

2. Identify the features of a tire bead:

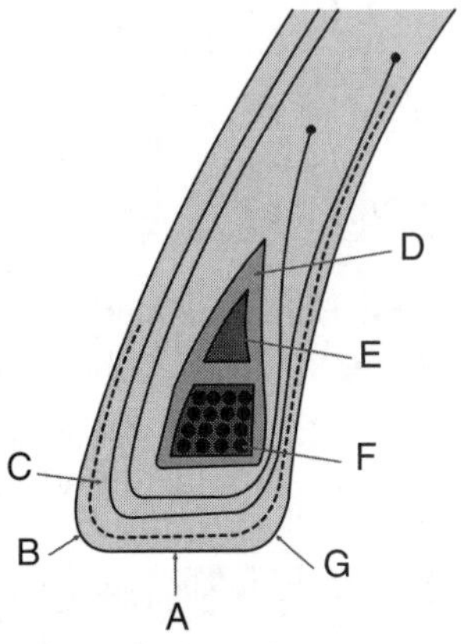

A. _____

B. _____

C. _____

D. _____

E. _____

F. _____

G. _____

Ride and Wear Problems and Incorrect Tire Pressures

Match the cause of the ride, wear, or tire pressure problem to its correct image.

A. Overinflation
B. Tandem rear axles not parallel
C. Excessive camber
D. Improperly centered trailer kingpin
E. Excessive toe
F. Underinflation
G. Dissymmetric kingpin offset

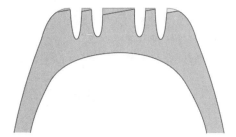

1. _____

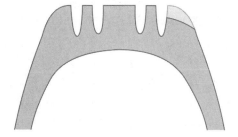

2. _____

3. _____

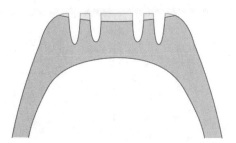

4. _____

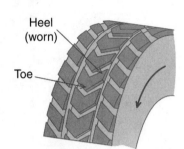

Heel
(worn)

Toe

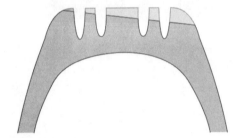

5. _____

6. _____

7. _____

Skill Drills

Test your knowledge of skill drills by filling in the correct words in the photo captions.

1. Checking and Adjusting the Tire Pressure:

Step 1: Park the vehicle so you can reach all _____ with the _____ _____.

Step 2: Check the recommended tire _____ and _____ on the tire _____, usually located on the driver's side door pillar or surrounding location.

Step 3:   Check the _____ markings on the tire for the maximum operating _____. At the same time, check the tire _____ and maximum load-carrying capacity of each tire, as customers sometimes install _____ tires. If the tire _____ do not meet the specifications of the vehicle, ask your supervisor for direction. Never allow a vehicle to be _____ with tires that do not meet the vehicle manufacturer's specifications. Doing so can have serious _____ repercussions.

Step 4:   Check the pressure when the tires are _____. Remove the _____ from the _____ _____ on the first tire. Use a reliable _____ _____ to check the air pressure in the tire. A pocket-type _____ gauge is ideal for this purpose. A gauge attached to the tire inflator is less likely to be _____ as it is more vulnerable to damage.

Step 5:   If you need to add air or _____, use short _____ so you do not overinflate the tire. Recheck the tire pressure after filling it and replace the _____ on the _____ _____. Repeat the process for the other tires. Check the pressure in the _____ tire. It may require a different amount of _____ _____ than the _____ tires.

2. Removing a Tire from a Wheel Rim (Tubeless):

Step 1:   Deflate the tire and _____ the _____ by hammering at points close to the _____ with a bead _____.

Step 2:   Apply _____ to the top of the bead on the _____ side and insert two _____ _____ at a distance of about _____ cm apart.

Step 3:   With one _____ _____ in position, pull the other one toward the _____ of the rim while _____ on the wheel.

Step 4:   Use the first tire iron to _____ the _____ over the _____ while holding the second tire iron in position by _____. Repeat this procedure until the _____ bead is completely _____.

Step 5:   Stand the tire _____ and apply tire _____ on the second _____.

Step 6:   Insert a tire iron between the _____ and rim at _____ degrees to the rim, and _____ the _____ right round until it is completely out.

3. Replacing a Screw-in Valve Stem:

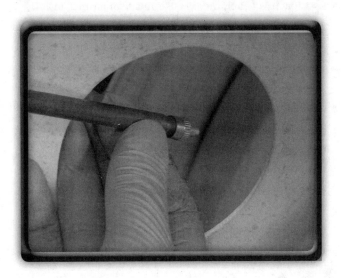

Step 1: If the valve stem is a _____-_____ valve stem, remove the _____ from the vehicle, _____ the tire, break the _____ _____ using the tire machine, and _____ the wheel on the tire machine.

Step 2: Unscrew the _____ that holds the _____ _____ to the _____. Remove the valve stem from the _____ of the rim.

Step 3: Discard the old _____ _____ and _____ them with new ones. Place the valve stem with _____ new sealing washer through the hole on the _____ of the _____.

Step 4: Place a new _____ _____ over the _____ _____ and thread the nut on by hand. Tighten the nut to the specified _____.

4. Inspecting the Wheel Assembly for Air Loss Using the Spray Bottle Method:

Step 1: Remove the tire from the vehicle and _____ it to its proper _____.

Step 2: Using a spray bottle of _____ _____, spray the _____ _____ and _____, tire _____, and tire _____ area.

Step 3: Inspect the tire, valve stem, and wheel assembly for _____, which would indicate a _____.

Step 4: Mark any _____ in the tire with a tire _____.

5. Measuring Tire Run-Out:

Step 1:   Research the procedure and specifications for measuring tire _____-_____ in the service information. Raise the vehicle on a _____ or place a _____ under the vehicle at a suitable _____ point and raise the vehicle. If using a jack, be sure to place _____ _____ under the _____ of the vehicle and slowly _____ the _____ onto the stand.

Step 2:   Select the run-out _____ or _____ _____, attachment, and _____ that fit the _____.

Step 3:   Mount the _____ _____ on a _____ surface to keep it _____.

Step 4:   Adjust the dial indicator so the _____ is _____ degrees to the _____ of the _____.

Step 5:   Press the dial indicator _____ against the tire and _____ the _____ one full turn. Keep pressing until the _____ settles about _____ into the _____.

Step 6:   Verify that the _____ is still _____ degrees to the _____ and _____ the indicator assembly into position.

Step 7:   Carefully _____ the tire a couple of times while observing the _____ readings. If the _____ hovers around a single _____ on the dial, the part has _____ run-out or surface _____ and the test is complete. If the _____ moves _____ left and right, note the variations.

Step 8:   Find the point of _____ movement to the _____ and _____ the dial so that _____ is over this point.

Step 9:   Continue to _____ the tire. Find the point of _____ movement to the _____ and note the reading. This measure indicates the run-out _____. Confirm this value by rotating the tire _____ more times to verify the _____ point and _____ point. The result will be the _____ _____-_____ measurement for the tire.

Step 10:   Compare these values with the manufacturer's _____. If the _____ is greater than the specifications, the _____ and/or _____ run-out must be _____.

Crossword Puzzle

Use the clues in the column to complete the puzzle.

Across

4. The process of matching up the tire's highest point with the rim's lowest point for the purpose of reducing the tire's radial run-out.

5. A tool used to break the tire bead seal from the rim.

Down

1. The depth of the area between the bottom of the original tread grooves and the top of the uppermost breaker.

2. A tire in which the air is not sealed in an inner tube.

3. A piece of rubber that wraps around the rim to protect the inner tube from chafing, pinching, and cracking caused by friction between the valve stem slot in the rim and the edges of the tire bead.

ASE-Type Questions

Read each item carefully, and then select the best response.

_____ **1.** Technician A says that tires are the leading cause of all roadside breakdowns. Technician B says that tires are the second most common source of mechanical defects leading to accidents. Who is correct?
  A. Technician A
  B. Technician B
  C. Both Technician A and Technician B
  D. Neither Technician A nor Technician B

_____ **2.** Technician A says "road alligators" are road debris that could be eliminated if retread tires were banned from use. Technician B says "road alligators" are not produced by the caps of a retread tire separating from the case, but are caused by underinflation of any tire. Who is correct?
  A. Technician A
  B. Technician B
  C. Both Technician A and Technician B
  D. Neither Technician A nor Technician B

_____ **3.** Consider one wheel of a dual wheel combination that has been removed from a trailer to repair a flat tire. Technician A says the tire should be inflated in a safety cage with a clip-on, remote inline air chuck. Technician B says the tire should be dismounted and inspected for damage before re-inflating. Who is correct?
  A. Technician A
  B. Technician B
  C. Both Technician A and Technician B
  D. Neither Technician A nor Technician B

_____ **4.** Technician A says that tires are marked with a date code indicating the date the tires must be discarded. Technician B says the date code is when the tires were manufactured. Who is correct?
  A. Technician A
  B. Technician B
  C. Both Technician A and Technician B
  D. Neither Technician A nor Technician B

_____ **5.** Technician A says that a TPMS system can save the owner fuel over a period of time. Technician B says that a TPMS helps prevents blowouts. Who is correct?
  A. Technician A
  B. Technician B
  C. Both Technician A and Technician B
  D. Neither Technician A nor Technician B

_____ **6.** Technician A says that using nitrogen to inflate a tire will prevent the tire from blowouts. Technician B says that when mounting and/or dismounting a tire from the rim fitted with a TPMS sensor, you must position the rim and tire properly on the tire machine or the TMPS can be damaged. Who is correct?
  A. Technician A
  B. Technician B
  C. Both Technician A and Technician B
  D. Neither Technician A nor Technician B

_____ **7.** Technician A says that the tires should be replaced when the indicator bars are visible in the tread. Technician B says that faulty shock absorbers cause cupping of the tread. Who is correct?
  A. Technician A
  B. Technician B
  C. Both Technician A and Technician B
  D. Neither Technician A nor Technician B

_____ **8.** Technician A says that it does not matter if you mix brands of tires on a common axle. Technician B says that the driver should check the tire pressures at least every three months. Who is correct?
  A. Technician A
  B. Technician B
  C. Both Technician A and Technician B
  D. Neither Technician A nor Technician B

_____ **9.** Technician A says that all tires are the same. Technician B says that the wheel nuts must be torqued after changing a wheel assembly. Who is correct?
   A. Technician A
   B. Technician B
   C. Both Technician A and Technician B
   D. Neither Technician A nor Technician B

_____ **10.** Technician A says that dynamic wheel unbalance can result in wheel shimmy. Technician B says that static wheel unbalance could cause wheel tramp to occur. Who is correct?
   A. Technician A
   B. Technician B
   C. Both Technician A and Technician B
   D. Neither Technician A nor Technician B

Wheel Rims and Hubs

Chapter Review

The following activities have been designed to help you refresh your knowledge of this chapter. Your instructor may require you to complete some or all of these activities as a regular part of your training program. You are encouraged to complete any activity that your instructor does not assign as a way to enhance your learning.

Matching

Match the following terms with the correct description or example.

A. Negative offset

B. Positive offset

C. Wheel end play

D. Wheel offset

E. Zero offset

_____ **1.** When the plane of the hub mounting surface is shifted from the centerline toward the outside or front side of the wheel.

_____ **2.** When the plane of the hub mounting surface is even with the centerline of the wheel.

_____ **3.** The distance from the hub mounting surface to the centerline of the wheel.

_____ **4.** The free movement of the wheel hub assembly along the axle spindle axis.

_____ **5.** When the hub mounting surface is toward the brake side or back of the wheel's centerline.

Multiple Choice

Read each item carefully, and then select the best response.

_____ **1.** The role of the _____ is to transfer the vehicle weight from the wheels to the axle ends and enable the wheel to rotate on the axle end.

A. wheel bearing

B. spindle

C. brake drum

D. hub

_____ **2.** The _____ is the distance across the rim flanges at the bead seat.

A. rim width

B. rim diameter

C. rim depth

D. rim offset

_____ **3.** The _____ are the threaded fasteners that attach the wheel to the vehicle.

A. flange bolts

B. wheel studs

C. cap bolts

D. wheel nuts

_____ **4.** Stretching a stud produces a spring-like force called _____.

A. preload

B. impact

C. counter torque

D. twist

_____ **5.** Heavy-duty commercial vehicles commonly use _____ type wheels.
   A. cast spoke
   B. alloy
   C. disc
   D. Both A and C

_____ **6.** If the wheel rim can be removed separately from the cast-iron spoke hub attached to the axle, the design is referred to as a(n) _____.
   A. demountable rim
   B. two-piece rim
   C. open-center rim
   D. Either A or C

_____ **7.** A _____ uses a series of machined pads on the hub to help center the wheel.
   A. demountable disc wheel
   B. hub-piloted disc wheel
   C. cast spoke wheel
   D. stud-piloted disc wheel

_____ **8.** In a _____ wheel bearing, configuration wheel bearings support the drive axle that transmits torque.
   A. full floating
   B. three-quarters floating
   C. semi-floating
   D. All of the above

_____ **9.** A _____ uses a precision spacer and close-tolerance bearings, eliminating the need to manually adjust bearings.
   A. preset hub
   B. floating hub
   C. standard hub
   D. Both A and C

_____ **10.** The established procedure for obtaining a wheel bearing end play of between 0.001" and 0.005" (0.025 mm and 0.127 mm) is called _____.
   A. J-1587
   B. TMC RP 618
   C. TPI 2219
   D. a preload chart

True/False

If you believe the statement to be more true than false, write the letter "T" in the space provided. If you believe the statement to be more false than true, write the letter "F".

_____ **1.** Wheel ends are one of the most crucial vehicle systems to competently maintain and service from both a safety and economic perspective.

_____ **2.** Alloy wheels are often called mag wheels because they are made of pure magnesium.

_____ **3.** Applying lubricant to the threads of a stud or nut can actually cause excessive tightening.

_____ **4.** Disc wheels are preferred in off-road or heavy-duty construction vehicle applications such as dump trucks, heavy equipment hauling, or logging.

_____ **5.** Dual tires cannot be used on cast spoke wheels.

_____ **6.** Stud-piloted disc wheels are the oldest type of wheel and are no longer used on new equipment.

_____ **7.** Different types of nuts and studs are used on steel and aluminum wheels.

_____ **8.** The hardware used to retain both hub-piloted and stud-piloted wheels is interchangeable.

_____ **9.** Full floating axles are used exclusively on heavy-duty commercial vehicles.

_____ **10.** Preset hubs are manufactured as a single piece unit and parts should never be interchanged.

Fill in the Blank

Read each item carefully, and then complete the statement by filling in the missing word(s).

1. Wheel rims, tires, and hubs are names given to major components making up part of what the trucking industry calls the _____ _____.

2. The wheel _____ is the outer circular lip of the metal on which the inside edge of the tire is mounted.

3. The _____ _____ refers to the number and spacing of the wheel nuts or wheel studs on the wheel hub on the wheel rim.

4. The measure of twisting force applied to wheel fasteners is called _____.

5. When rims are installed on spoke wheels, the lateral _____ _____ needs to be checked and adjusted.

6. A(n) _____ wheel is a simple, single, stamped steel or aluminum rim onto which the tire is mounted.

7. Lugs attached to the bearing hub to locate the wheel assembly correctly during assembly are called _____ _____.

8. Wheel hubs contain _____ used to reduce the friction between the stationary axle and rotating wheel.

9. When adjusting wheel bearings, technicians are actually setting a bearing load factor called _____.

10. Wheel _____ are an integral part of hubs used to keep oil or grease from leaking out between the wheel spindle and the rotating hub.

Labeling

Label the following diagrams with the correct terms.

1. Identify the components of a single wheel end:

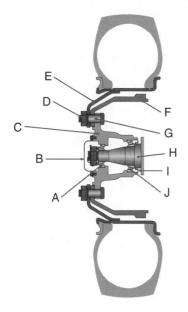

A. _____

B. _____

C. _____

D. _____

E. _____

F. _____

G. _____

H. _____

I. _____

J. _____

2. Identify the components of a dual demountable rim on a cast spoke hub:

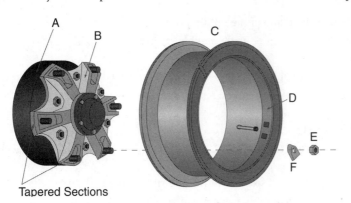

Tapered Sections

A. _____

B. _____

C. _____

D. _____

E. _____

F. _____

3. Identify the components of a hub-piloted disc wheel:

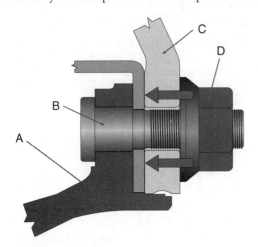

A. _____

B. _____

C. _____

D. _____

4. Identify the components of a stud-piloted disc wheel:

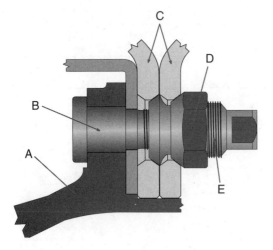

A. _____

B. _____

C. _____

D. _____

E. _____

Skill Drills

Test your knowledge of skill drills by filling in the correct words in the photo captions.

1. Preparing to Install a Wheel:

Step 1:   Remove _____ and foreign _____ from all _____ surfaces. When ready to install a wheel, note that the _____ should be already in place. If it is not, several more steps will be required to _____ the hub.

Step 2:   Inspect components for _____ or signs of severe _____. If installing a _____ _____, be certain that the _____ _____ openings are in _____ if applicable.

Step 3:   Snug the _____ _____ in a _____ pattern to _____ the _____ on the _____.

Step 4:   Torque the _____ _____ to specification using a calibrated _____ _____ tool.

Step 5:   Look for any _____ around the _____ _____ or the center _____ of the _____.

Step 6:   Inspect the _____ for damaged or _____ threads.

Step 7:   Inspect the _____ _____ for _____ or _____ _____ damage.

Step 8:   Make sure the _____, _____, and/or _____ are properly _____ and not damaged or _____.

Step 9:   Snug the _____ _____ fasteners to _____ the wheel and the _____ on the _____ evenly using _____ to _____ ft-lb (68 to 136 Nm) steps. Always start at the _____ o'clock position.

2. Manually Adjusting Wheel Bearings Using the TMC 618 Procedure:

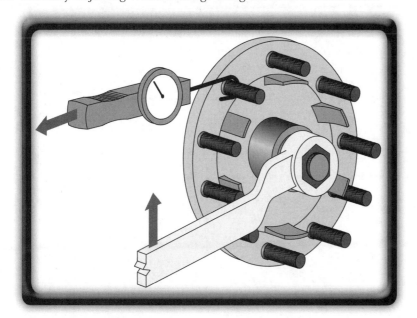

Step 1:   Lubricate the _____ with clean lubricant of the same type used in the _____ _____ or _____ _____.

Step 2:   Install the wheel _____ and _____ onto _____ and _____ the inner adjusting nut to _____ ft-lb (271 Nm) while _____ the hub assembly.

Step 3:   Back-off the _____ adjusting nut _____ full _____.

Step 4:   Re-torque the inner _____ _____ to _____ ft-lb (68 Nm) while _____ the _____ _____ assembly.

Step 5:   Back-off the _____ adjustment _____ following TMC RP 618 procedures.

Step 6:   Install the _____ _____.

Step 7:   Install and _____ the outer _____ _____ following TMC RP 618 procedures.

Step 8:   Verify hub _____ _____ with a _____ _____.

3. Measuring Wheel End Play:

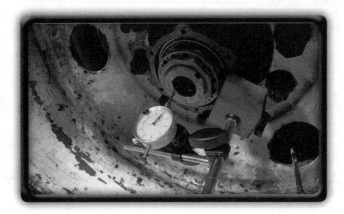

Step 1:   Attach a _____ _____ with its _____ base to the _____ _____ or brake _____.

Step 2:   Adjust the dial indicator so that its _____ or _____ is against the end of the _____ with its direction approximately _____ to the _____ of the spindle.

Step 3:   Grasp the wheel assembly at the _____ o'clock and _____ o'clock positions. Push the wheel assembly _____ and _____ while _____ it to _____ the bearings. The difference between the _____ and _____ values is _____ bearing _____ _____.

Crossword Puzzle

Use the clues in the column to complete the puzzle.

Across

3. A wheel hub that uses manually adjusted wheel bearing end play.

4. The edge of the rim that creates a seal between the tire bead and the wheel.

5. The exterior lip that holds the tire in place.

Down

1. The distance across the center of the rim, from bead seat to bead seat.

2. A steel or aluminum wheel rim that supports a tire and attaches to the hub using wheel studs and nuts.

ASE-Type Questions

Read each item carefully, and then select the best response.

_____ 1. Technician A says that you should always re-inflate a severely underinflated tire using the safety cage. Technician B says that you should use a clip-on air pressure chuck with an in-line remote mounted valve and pressure gauge. Who is correct?
   A. Technician A
   B. Technician B
   C. Both Technician A and Technician B
   D. Neither Technician A nor Technician B

_____ 2. Technician A says when tightening lug or wheel nuts a torque wrench must be used. Technician B says that an air wrench can be used but the final tightening should be done with a torque wrench. Who is correct?
   A. Technician A
   B. Technician B
   C. Both Technician A and Technician B
   D. Neither Technician A nor Technician B

_____ 3. Technician A says that tire markings now include load ratings on tires. Technician B says that they are only included on truck tires. Who is correct?
   A. Technician A
   B. Technician B
   C. Both Technician A and Technician B
   D. Neither Technician A nor Technician B

_____ 4. Technician A says that tire markings now include speed ratings on tires. Technician B says that they are only included on high performance tires. Who is correct?
   A. Technician A
   B. Technician B
   C. Both Technician A and Technician B
   D. Neither Technician A nor Technician B

_____ 5. Technician A says that tire markings now include temperature ratings on tires. Technician B says that they are only included on high performance tires. Who is correct?
   A. Technician A
   B. Technician B
   C. Both Technician A and Technician B
   D. Neither Technician A nor Technician B

_____ 6. Technician A says mismatching tires of the same size on a heavy vehicle will generally not affect ABS operation. Technician B says that on a heavy vehicle the ABS operation will be compromised by mismatched tires. Who is correct?
   A. Technician A
   B. Technician B
   C. Both Technician A and Technician B
   D. Neither Technician A nor Technician B

_____ 7. Technician A says that all cross-ply tires must be rotated at regular intervals. Technician B says that directional tires cannot be rotated from one side of the vehicle to the other. Who is correct?
   A. Technician A
   B. Technician B
   C. Both Technician A and Technician B
   D. Neither Technician A nor Technician B

_____ 8. Technician A says that wheel offset is the distance from the mounting surface centerline to the centerline of the wheel. Technician B says that wheel offset aligns with the inner wheel bearing. Who is correct?
   A. Technician A
   B. Technician B
   C. Both Technician A and Technician B
   D. Neither Technician A nor Technician B

_____ **9.** Technician A says that under-tightening wheel nuts can cause the wheels to loosen and become damaged. Technician B says that wheel nuts must be torqued in a set sequence. Who is correct?

   A. Technician A

   B. Technician B

   C. Both Technician A and Technician B

   D. Neither Technician A nor Technician B

_____ **10.** Technician A says that wheel bearing end play is between 0.001" and 0.005" (0.025 mm and 0.127 mm). Technician B says that wheel bearing end play is between 0.005" and 0.01" (0.127 mm and 0.25 mm). Who is correct?

   A. Technician A

   B. Technician B

   C. Both Technician A and Technician B

   D. Neither Technician A nor Technician B

Front Axles and Vehicle Alignment Factors

Tire Tread:
© AbleStock

Chapter Review

The following activities have been designed to help you refresh your knowledge of this chapter. Your instructor may require you to complete some or all of these activities as a regular part of your training program. You are encouraged to complete any activity that your instructor does not assign as a way to enhance your learning.

Matching

Match the following terms with the correct description or example.

A. Ackermann angle
B. Camber
C. Caster
D. Kingpin
E. Pitman arm

F. Steering knuckle
G. Thrust angle
H. Tie rod
I. Toe
J. Tracking

_____ 1. The relationship between the centerline of the vehicle and the angle of the rear tires.

_____ 2. A component that transfers the steering box output shaft motion to the steering linkage by converting rotational movement into liner motion.

_____ 3. A measurement of how much the front wheels are turned in or out from a straight-ahead position. The angle is referenced from a position directly above the tires and facing forward.

_____ 4. A device that connects the front wheel to the suspension; it pivots on the top and bottom, thus allowing the front wheels to turn.

_____ 5. The angle the steering arms make with the steering axis, projected toward the center of the rear axle.

_____ 6. The side-to-side vertical tilt of the wheel. It is viewed from the front of the vehicle and measured in degrees.

_____ 7. Connects each steering knuckle to the solid I-beam axle.

_____ 8. The positioning of the tires relative to the vehicle. Also called wheel alignment.

_____ 9. The angle formed through the wheel pivot points when viewed from the side in comparison to a vertical line through the wheel.

_____ 10. A steering component that transfers linear motion from the steering box to the steering arms at the front wheels.

Multiple Choice

Read each item carefully, and then select the best response.

_____ 1. A _____ includes the differential gearing and components used to transmit torque to the wheel ends.
A. live axle
B. dead axle
C. tag axle
D. pusher axle

_____ 2. A _____ is an example of a dead axle.
A. pusher axle
B. steering axle
C. lift axle
D. All of the above

_____ 3. The _____ is connected to the steering arm at one end and the pitman arm at the other in order to transfer steering gear force to the steering arm.
   A. drop arm
   B. kingpin
   C. drag link
   D. pinion

_____ 4. A _____ axle is mounted behind the drive axle.
   A. pusher
   B. tag
   C. drag
   D. Both A and C

_____ 5. The condition where the vehicle's rear is higher than the front is called _____.
   A. positive frame angle
   B. negative caster
   C. toe-out
   D. positive camber

_____ 6. Toe can be adjusted by changing the length of the _____.
   A. pitman arm
   B. drag link
   C. tie rod
   D. axle

_____ 7. The _____ is found by adding the kingpin inclination angle and the camber angle together.
   A. steering axis inclination angle
   B. included angle
   C. setback
   D. thrust angle

_____ 8. A _____ is produced when the kingpin inclination angle projects outside the tire's vertical centerline.
   A. positive scrub radius
   B. negative scrub radius
   C. positive thrust angle
   D. negative thrust angle

_____ 9. The difference in distance between any axle end and the perpendicular centerline is called _____.
   A. axle setback
   B. inclusion
   C. skew
   D. Either A or C

_____ 10. The alignment method where a vehicle's centerline is established by placing a line from the midpoint of the front axle and the midpoint of the rear-most axle is called _____.
   A. geometric centerline alignment
   B. frame centerline alignment
   C. thrust angle alignment
   D. Either A or C

True/False

If you believe the statement to be more true than false, write the letter "T" in the space provided. If you believe the statement to be more false than true, write the letter "F".

_____ 1. Non-drive axles are also called dead axles and do not have the capability to drive the vehicle.

_____ 2. Steering axles are used for the rear axle of most medium and heavy-duty vehicles.

_____ 3. Without correct wheel alignment, vehicles will experience premature suspension and steering component wear.

_____ 4. Most alignment specifications place a slightly more positive camber angle on the left wheel to correct the effects of road crown on directional stability.

_____ **5.** When the wheels are closer together in the rear than in the front, a toe-in condition exists.

_____ **6.** Steering axis inclination and kingpin inclination are industry terms used interchangeably since they refer to the same steering angle.

_____ **7.** The Ackerman angle is also called tire toe-out on turns.

_____ **8.** Trailer axles like most steering axles are categorized as live axles.

_____ **9.** The frame centerline alignment method uses the vehicle frame and not its axles as the reference point for making alignment adjustments.

_____ **10.** The term thrust line refers to the direction in which the rear wheels are pointing.

Fill in the Blank

Read each item carefully, and then complete the statement by filling in the missing word(s).

1. The most common configuration of the _____ axle is the solid I-beam.

2. Steering _____ are used to limit the turning angle of the steering knuckle.

3. The pitman arm is sometimes called the _____ arm.

4. What determines if an axle is a lift, tag, or pusher axle is the axle's _____ in relation to the drive axle.

5. Tag and pusher axles are also often _____ axles that can be mechanically raised and lowered to meet the regulated requirements for maximum weight loads per axle.

6. Wheel _____ refers to the positioning of the tires relative to the vehicle.

7. When the tires are closer together at the bottom and farther apart at the top, the condition is called positive _____.

8. Excess positive caster is responsible for a condition called caster _____ that can be dangerous to vehicle control and directional stability.

9. Tie-rod _____ are ball-and-socket joints attached to the steering knuckle steering arms.

10. The _____ radius is the difference between the intersection of a point on the tire contact patch between true vertical and the kingpin inclination angle.

Labeling

Label the following diagrams with the correct terms.

1. Identify the steering components:

A. _____

B. _____

C. _____

D. _____

E. _____

F. _____

2. Identify the components of the kingpin and steering knuckle:

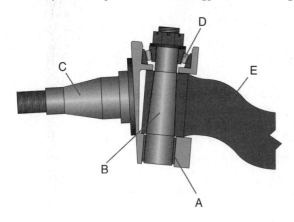

A. _____

B. _____

C. _____

D. _____

E. _____

3. Identify the drag link connections:

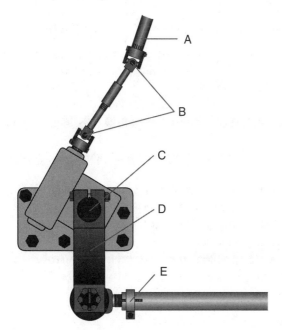

A. _____

B. _____

C. _____

D. _____

E. _____

Skill Drills

Test your knowledge of skill drills by filling in the correct words in the photo captions.

1. Performing a Pre-Alignment Inspection:

Step 1: Locate and follow the procedure in the _____ _____. Complete the job sheet or _____ _____.

Step 2: Remove any _____ items from the vehicle. Do not remove any item or equipment that is _____ with the vehicle and _____ kept in the vehicle.

Step 3: Check all tires for proper tire _____ and adjust tire _____ to specifications.

Step 4: Check the vehicle's _____ _____. It is impossible to carry out a successful wheel alignment when the vehicle's _____ _____ is incorrect.

Step 5: Check the play of the _____ _____. Excess play must be corrected before undertaking the wheel alignment.

Step 6: Inspect all _____ and _____ components according to service information, including the wheel _____. Repair or replace all damaged or worn suspension components prior to _____ the vehicle.

Step 7: Position the vehicle, making sure the _____ tires are positioned correctly on the _____.

Step 8: Attach the wheel end _____ of the alignment equipment to the _____.

Step 9: Perform manufacturer's set-up procedures such as _____ the sensors, correcting for wheel _____-_____, or wheel _____ compensation.

Step 10: Compare manufacturer _____ with _____ _____.

2. Measuring Toe-Out Using a Toe Tester or Trammel Bar:

Step 1: Locate and _____ the _____ in the service manual. Complete the _____ _____ or work order.

Step 2: Perform system _____-_____.

Step 3: Park the vehicle on a _____ surface in a _____-_____ position.

Step 4: Mark the _____ _____ at a position that is in line with the _____ of the wheel.

Step 5: Repeat step 3 on the other _____ _____.

Step 6: Set up the _____ tester or _____ _____ per the manufacturer's specifications with the measuring _____ on the marks that you have made on the rim flanges.

Step 7: Set the adjustable _____ on the equipment to _____.

Step 8: After _____ the measuring pins, move the vehicle _____ so the wheels rotate through _____ degrees, and replace the measuring pins.

Step 9: Take the measurement and _____ it with the manufacturer's specifications.

Step 10: Make any necessary adjustments and then _____ _____ the vehicle.

Step 11: Repeat the process to ensure that the _____ _____ is within specifications.

Step 12: List the test _____ and/or recommendations on the job _____ or work _____.

Step 13: Clean the _____ _____.

3. Checking KPI and Included Angle:

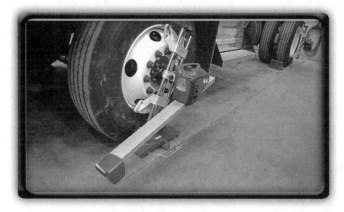

Step 1: Locate and follow the procedure in the _____ _____. Complete the _____ sheet or _____ order.

Step 2: Position the _____ on the alignment equipment _____ _____.

Step 3: Attach the wheel _____ on the vehicle to the locations specified by the alignment equipment manufacturer and compensate for tire and wheel rim _____-_____.

Step 4: _____ the alignment machine _____ for taking the KPI measurements and _____ them with the vehicle manufacturer's specifications. Typically, the KPI reading will require _____ the wheels to a specified _____ while on the turning plates.

Step 5: KPI is a _____-_____ angle; no changes can be made. The angle will help the technician to _____ that steering components are not _____.

Step 6: Calculate the _____ angle, if the alignment machine does not, by adding the _____ reading of each wheel to the _____ of each wheel and compare with specifications.

Step 7: _____ the test results and/or _____ on the job sheet or work order.

Step 8: _____ the work area.

4. Inspecting Axles for Parallelism and Tracking—Field Method:

Step 1:   Park the _____ _____ vehicle on a flat surface, and identify two points on the _____ and _____ axle. The two points on each axle must be equal distance from the _____ center. A good point is axle _____ seats.

Step 2:   Using a _____ bob, chalk _____ points onto the ground before the vehicle is moved away.

Step 3:   Measure the distances between the points using an "_____" pattern. No dimension should exceed a _____ to _____ variation of 0.125" (3.175 mm).

5. Lubricating Kingpins:

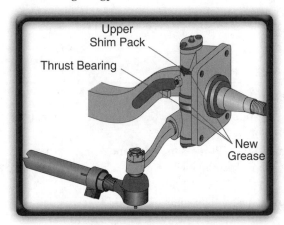

Step 1:   Relieve _____ on the _____ _____ by lifting the _____ from the ground and supporting the axle with _____ _____.

Step 2:   Perform an inspection of the _____ and _____ _____ assembly by measuring _____ and _____ movement.

Step 3:   Using a _____ _____, begin lubricating the kingpins by purging _____ and _____ from the pin with a couple of _____ of grease.

Step 4:   Stop greasing when only _____ grease begins to flow from the _____ _____ at the lower and upper end of the _____ _____. Do not over lubricate the assembly. Excess grease attracts abrasive _____, which can wear out the _____.

Crossword Puzzle

Use the clues in the column to complete the puzzle.

Across

2. The difference in distance between any axle end and the perpendicular centerline. Also called axle setback or setback.
5. A measure of how small a circle the vehicle can turn in when the steering wheel is turned to the limit.
6. An arm that extends from the steering knuckle. The tie rods connect to these arms in order to steer the wheels.
7. The shaft of the suspension system to which the tires and wheels are attached; used to transmit driving torque to the wheels.

Down

1. When the top of the tire is closer to the center of the vehicle than the bottom of the tire.
2. A geometric arrangement of linkages in the steering of a vehicle designed to solve the problem of keeping the wheels properly oriented through various positions of the steering and suspension systems.
3. The direction in which the rear wheels are pointing.
4. A rear, non-drive rear-mounted axle, ahead of the drive axle.

ASE-Type Questions

Read each item carefully, and then select the best response.

_____ 1. Technician A says a key function of axles is to maintain the position of the wheels relative to each other and the vehicle body. Technician B says there are two main categories of axles, which are drive and non-drive. Who is correct?
   A. Technician A
   B. Technician B
   C. Both Technician A and Technician B
   D. Neither Technician A nor Technician B

_____ 2. Technician A says the steering knuckle enables the articulation of the wheel end. Technician B says the steering knuckle is connected to the I-beam through the master pin. Who is correct?
   A. Technician A
   B. Technician B
   C. Both Technician A and Technician B
   D. Neither Technician A nor Technician B

_____ 3. Technician A says a snug fit is required between the pin and bushings. Technician B says if the pin cannot be installed into the bushings by hand, or the pin is too tight, the kingpin should be machined slightly smaller. Who is correct?
   A. Technician A
   B. Technician B
   C. Both Technician A and Technician B
   D. Neither Technician A nor Technician B

_____ 4. Technician A says steering stops are used to limit the turning angle of the steering knuckle. Technician B says stops are adjusted to cut power assist with zero clearance remaining between the spindle stop and the axle. Who is correct?
   A. Technician A
   B. Technician B
   C. Both Technician A and Technician B
   D. Neither Technician A nor Technician B

_____ 5. Technician A says when installing an adjustable drag link, the front tires must be squared with the chassis frame. Technician B says the steering wheel spokes must be correctly oriented in a straight-ahead position, and the steering box must be centered. Who is correct?
   A. Technician A
   B. Technician B
   C. Both Technician A and Technician B
   D. Neither Technician A nor Technician B

_____ 6. Technician A says wheel alignment refers to the positioning of the tires relative to the vehicle. Technician B says rolling resistance and correct wheel alignment is not an issue with regard to fuel consumption. Who is correct?
   A. Technician A
   B. Technician B
   C. Both Technician A and Technician B
   D. Neither Technician A nor Technician B

_____ 7. Technician A says caster can be adjusted by heating and slightly bending the axle. Technician B says caster can be adjusted by using tapered shims placed between the suspension springs and the axle. Who is correct?
   A. Technician A
   B. Technician B
   C. Both Technician A and Technician B
   D. Neither Technician A nor Technician B

_____ **8.** Technician A says when travelling forward, toe should be zero degrees to prevent tire wear. Technician B says too much toe-in will wear the inside edges of tires. Who is correct?

    A. Technician A

    B. Technician B

    C. Both Technician A and Technician B

    D. Neither Technician A nor Technician B

_____ **9.** Technician A says the Ackerman angle refers to a steering principle that states the inner wheel should have a smaller turning angle than the outside wheel because it has a smaller turning radius. Technician B says the Ackermann angle producing toe-out on turns is an adjustable angle. Who is correct?

    A. Technician A

    B. Technician B

    C. Both Technician A and Technician B

    D. Neither Technician A nor Technician B

_____ **10.** Technician A says the geometric centerline (thrust angle) has the advantage of eliminating error due to a bent or damaged frame. Technician B says vehicles with solid, adjustable rear axles cannot use this method. Who is correct?

    A. Technician A

    B. Technician B

    C. Both Technician A and Technician B

    D. Neither Technician A nor Technician B

Truck Frames

Chapter Review

The following activities have been designed to help you refresh your knowledge of this chapter. Your instructor may require you to complete some or all of these activities as a regular part of your training program. You are encouraged to complete any activity that your instructor does not assign as a way to enhance your learning.

Matching

Match the following terms with the correct description or example.

A. Compression

B. Galvanic corrosion

C. Maximum bending moment

D. Neutral axis

E. Resilient mounts

F. Section change

G. Stress concentration

H. Swaged

I. Tensile strength

J. Yield strength

_____ **1.** Attachments that are spring loaded or made with rubber or polyurethane elements that accommodate movement.

_____ **2.** The amount of force required before a material deforms or breaks.

_____ **3.** Anything that reduces or changes the integrity or strength of the material.

_____ **4.** An engineering term used to describe the amount of force required to permanently deform a material.

_____ **5.** A point where a component becomes thicker/thinner or more or less rigid forming a weak point where breakage can begin.

_____ **6.** A force that pushes down on the top flange of a frame rail between two support points and that tends to squeeze the flange of the frame rail together.

_____ **7.** The area in the middle of a frame rail web where the tension and compression forces cancel each other out.

_____ **8.** The point on the frame at which the load force is concentrated.

_____ **9.** When two metal components are fitted together by deforming the metal of one to fit the other precisely.

_____ **10.** Condition caused by the electrolytic effect that can occur when two dissimilar metals are in contact.

Multiple Choice

Read each item carefully, and then select the best response.

_____ **1.** Found only in very heavy off-road equipment and in some heavy hauler flatbed trailers the strongest type of frame rail is the _____.

   A. C-channel

   B. full-box rail

   C. I-beam

   D. L-plate

_____ **2.** No matter how much force is placed on the frame rails, the forces will be the lowest at the _____.

   A. neutral axis

   B. cross members

   C. neutral fiber

   D. Either A or C

_____ **3.** The _____ is the ability of the frame to support the force trying to bend it at the point where this bending force is greatest.
  A. resist bending moment
  B. section modulus
  C. yield strength
  D. tension

_____ **4.** Steel alloyed with carbon at levels of 0.9–2.5% is known as _____.
  A. low-carbon steel
  B. medium-carbon steel
  C. high-carbon steel
  D. cast iron

_____ **5.** The point at which force is concentrated on the frame is called the _____.
  A. tensile strength
  B. maximum bending moment
  C. yield point
  D. Either A or C

_____ **6.** Frame rails can be reinforced by installing _____.
  A. extra C-channel rails
  B. L-plates, or inverted L-plates
  C. fishplates
  D. All of the above

_____ **7.** The recommended and most secure mounting system for attaching a vehicle body to a ladder-type frame are _____.
  A. U-bolt mounts
  B. outrigger mounts
  C. fishplate mounts
  D. spring-loaded mounts

_____ **8.** The condition where one frame rail is further forward than the other is called _____.
  A. twist
  B. sideway
  C. diamond
  D. Either A or C

_____ **9.** When the vehicle frame is bowed outward when viewed from the top the condition is called _____.
  A. sideway
  B. twist
  C. sag
  D. bow

_____ **10.** Which type of welding process is used to repair cracked frame rails?
  A. Shielded metal arc welding
  B. Gas metal arc welding
  C. Gas tungsten arc welding
  D. All of the above

True/False

If you believe the statement to be more true than false, write the letter "T" in the space provided. If you believe the statement to be more false than true, write the letter "F".

_____ **1.** The most common frame design for heavy-duty trucks is the full-box frame.

_____ **2.** Forces cancel each other at the center of the frame rail web, which is the upright section of the frame rail.

_____ **3.** Holes are commonly drilled in the flanges to bolt the cross-members to the frame rails.

_____ **4.** Stress risers can lead to a crack in the rail, which is a serious safety risk.

_____ **5.** Section modulus has a direct relationship to the material of which the component is made.

_____ **6.** Making the flange wider will allow the frame to carry a bigger load than making the web taller.

_____ **7.** Both drop-front and drop-forward designs allow a lower mounting position for the engine and drive train, which in turn lowers the vehicle's center of gravity.

_____ **8.** Huck® brand fasteners work in the same way as nuts and bolts but are tightened with a special torque wrench.

_____ **9.** Corrosion of a frame does not greatly affect the integrity of the frame metal.

_____ **10.** Most manufacturers prohibit the heating or welding of any frames unless specifically authorized by their engineering department.

Fill in the Blank

Read each item carefully, and then complete the statement by filling in the missing word(s).

1. The vehicle _____ is the backbone of the vehicle; it provides the structure to which all other vehicle components can be attached.

2. The load pushing down on the frame creates _____ on the top flange of the frame rail and _____ on the bottom flange.

3. Until a material reaches its _____ strength, the material can deform but will return to its original shape when the load is removed.

4. In order to determine the actual strength of a particular frame, the _____ _____ _____ must be calculated and then compared to the total force acting on the frame.

5. Aluminum _____ is aluminum mixed with other metals to increase its strength.

6. Resilient mounting systems allow the vehicle frame to _____ as necessary.

7. The Commercial Vehicle Safety Alliance sets _____-_____-_____ criteria for commercial vehicles.

8. During _____ corrosion, one metal becomes the anode and the other becomes the cathode.

9. In order to determine if a frame has had damage due to impact or collision, it is necessary to check frame _____.

10. A fatigue _____ is usually caused by chronic overload or a section change in the frame rail, which causes a weak point.

Labeling

Label the following diagrams with the correct terms.

1. Identify the following types of frame rail design:

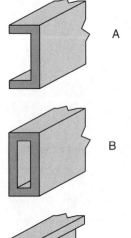

A

B

C

A. _____

B. _____

C. _____

2. Identify the components of a C-channel frame rail:

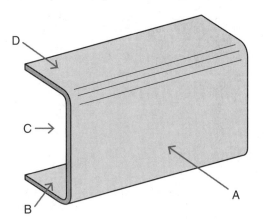

A. _____

B. _____

C. _____

D. _____

3. Identify the components of a fishplate mounting system:

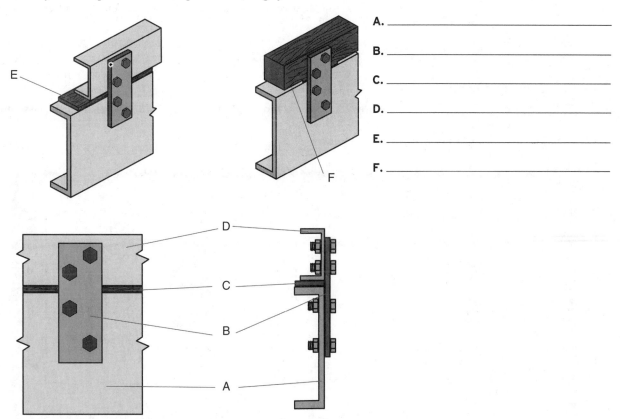

A. _____

B. _____

C. _____

D. _____

E. _____

F. _____

Skill Drills

Test your knowledge of skill drills by filling in the correct words in the photo captions.

1. Conducting Exterior Inspections of Frame:

Step 1: Check the vehicle frame and the frame members for _____ or other types of deformities and for any _____ and excessive _____ or scale.

Step 2: Check _____ _____ for cracks, _____, looseness, or _____. In addition, inspect them for any _____ or _____ fasteners, including fasteners attaching functional components, such as the _____, transmission, _____ _____, suspension, body parts, and _____-_____ components.

Step 3: Check for any condition that causes the _____ or _____ to be in contact with a _____ or any part of the _____ _____ and for _____ or unengaged locking _____ in adjustable axle assemblies.

2. Repairing a Crack in a Frame Between Bolt Holes:

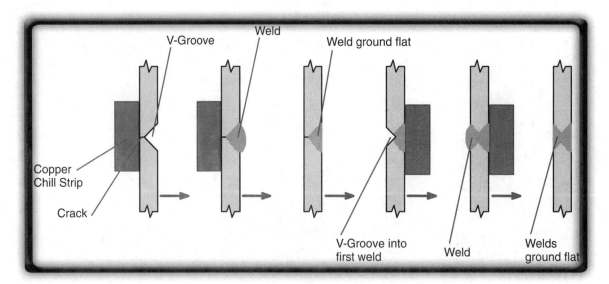

Step 1: _____ the entire area around the crack of all _____, _____, _____, or _____.

Step 2: Grind a 'v' groove into the _____ _____ to a depth 1/8" (3.175 mm) less than the rail metal thickness. Clamp a _____ _____ made of aluminum or copper to the _____ of the rail from the groove.

Step 3: Grind the finished weld _____ with the frame rail. Leaving a weld 'cap' protruding on either side of the rail produces a _____ _____ because of the frame thickness. As a result, its _____ _____ would be increased at that point, so the weld cap must be ground flat. Grind the weld in the direction of the frame rail _____ to minimize stress risers at the weld.

Step 4: Repeat steps 1 through step 3 for the _____ _____ of the crack. Start by _____ the 'v' _____ deep enough to reach the first weld material.

Step 5:   Weld the groove with the appropriate _____ _____ and again grind the weld flush. When welding _____ _____ frames with tensile strengths of 110,000 to 120,000 psi, use a low-hydrogen _____ with higher-than-average crack resistance, such as AWS-E-11018.

Step 6:   After welding to repair a frame, reinforce the rail with _____ or _____ to re-establish the frame strength. (Follow the guidelines outlined in the Frame Reinforcement section found earlier in the chapter.) Remember that _____ and _____ the frame reinforcement plates is essential. Otherwise, they will create a _____ _____ and lead to failure due to increased stiffness at the reinforcement.

3. Repairing a Crack in the Web or Flange:

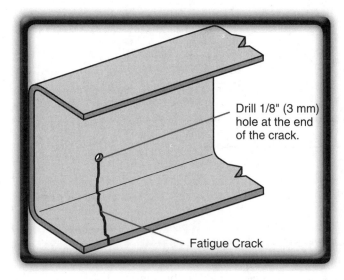

Drill 1/8" (3 mm) hole at the end of the crack.

Fatigue Crack

Step 1:   Follow the steps in SKILL DRILL 26-3 for repairing a _____ in a frame with _____ _____.

Step 2:   After _____ and _____ the first _____ in the crack determine the exact end of the crack and _____ a small 1/8" (3.175 mm) hole. This will stop the crack from proceeding past the _____ _____, then continue the above outlined repair procedure.

Step 3:   Crack repairs that extend to the _____ _____ should be reinforced with _____ or _____ that reinforces the flange area as well as the _____ of the frame rail.

Crossword Puzzle

Use the clues in the column to complete the puzzle.

Across

1. The flat surface at the top and bottom of a frame rail.
3. A type of frame damage characterized by a sideways bending or deformation of the frame.
4. A frame-body attachment consisting of brackets welded to the vehicle and then bolted to the frame web.

Down

1. Flat plate used to re-enforce the frame rail or a plate bolted to the frame rail web to attach components to the frame.
2. A type of frame damage that occurs when one rail bends up and the other rail bends down.
5. A type of frame damage characterized by the upward bending of the frame rails that can be caused by uneven loading of the frame.

ASE-Type Questions

Read each item carefully, and then select the best response.

_____ 1. Technician A says that actual frame rail strength can be calculated by multiplying the section modulus by the yield strength. Technician B says that to determine actual rail strength the RBM is multiplied by the section modulus. Who is correct?

  A. Technician A

  B. Technician B

  C. Both Technician A and Technician B

  D. Neither Technician A nor Technician B

_____ 2. Technician A says that most frame fatigue cracks are caused by overloading of the frame. Technician B says that cracks often occur at a section change, where the frame becomes less flexible. Who is correct?

  A. Technician A

  B. Technician B

  C. Both Technician A and Technician B

  D. Neither Technician A nor Technician B

_____ 3. Technician A says that welding heat-treated frames changes the frame strength and is not sanctioned by the manufacturer. Technician B says that damaged heat-treated frame rails should be replaced not repaired. Who is correct?

  A. Technician A

  B. Technician B

  C. Both Technician A and Technician B

  D. Neither Technician A nor Technician B

_____ 4. Technician A says that the frame rail top flange is under compression when a load is placed on it. Technician B says that the frame rail's bottom flange is under tension where the suspension mounts to the frame. Who is correct?

  A. Technician A

  B. Technician B

  C. Both Technician A and Technician B

  D. Neither Technician A nor Technician B

_____ 5. Technician A says that the neutral fiber refers to the center of the frame web. Technician B says the neutral fiber is where most of a frame rail stress is concentrated. Who is correct?

  A. Technician A

  B. Technician B

  C. Both Technician A and Technician B

  D. Neither Technician A nor Technician B

_____ 6. Technician A says I-channel frames are the most common configuration for heavy vehicles. Technician B says connecting cross-members tie the rails together both to maintain their alignment and to stop them from twisting under the heavy loads the rails have to carry. Who is correct?

  A. Technician A

  B. Technician B

  C. Both Technician A and Technician B

  D. Neither Technician A nor Technician B

_____ 7. Technician A says Huck® fasteners are a type of nuts and bolts. Technician B says Huck® fasteners are one of the most secure attaching systems available and should last for the life of the vehicle. Who is correct?

  A. Technician A

  B. Technician B

  C. Both Technician A and Technician B

  D. Neither Technician A nor Technician B

_____ 8. Technician A says U-bolts are the most secure mounting system for attaching a truck body to a frame. Technician B says U-bolts and their ease of installation makes them popular with builders of truck bodies. Who is correct?

  A. Technician A

  B. Technician B

  C. Both Technician A and Technician B

  D. Neither Technician A nor Technician B

_____ **9.** Technician A says outrigger mounting is the recommended method of attaching flexible bodies to ladder-type frames. Technician B says outrigger brackets are welded to the vehicle body and also welded to the frame web. Who is correct?
   A. Technician A
   B. Technician B
   C. Both Technician A and Technician B
   D. Neither Technician A nor Technician B

_____ **10.** Technician A says fishplates are flat plates used to reinforce the frame rail. Technician B says fishplate does not require holes to be drilled in the frameweb and the body sub-frame. Who is correct?
   A. Technician A
   B. Technician B
   C. Both Technician A and Technician B
   D. Neither Technician A nor Technician B

Suspension Systems

Chapter Review

The following activities have been designed to help you refresh your knowledge of this chapter. Your instructor may require you to complete some or all of these activities as a regular part of your training program. You are encouraged to complete any activity that your instructor does not assign as a way to enhance your learning.

Matching

Match the following terms with the correct description or example.

A. Auxiliary spring
B. Contact patch
C. Equalizer
D. Hysteresis
E. Oscillation

F. Overslung
G. Parallelogram
H. Self-dampening
I. Shock absorber
J. Torsion bar

_____ 1. The support for a tandem drive axle, using a standard leaf spring suspension system; it supports the rear of the front spring and the front of the rear spring.

_____ 2. A (usually) hydraulic piston and cylinder arrangement designed to minimize spring oscillation.

_____ 3. The rhythmic up-and-down motion of the suspension caused by road shock.

_____ 4. A design element in suspension systems used to keep the wheels or the axles in alignment throughout suspension articulation.

_____ 5. Part of a vehicle's suspension system that twists in response to the movement of the wheels and absorbs their vertical movement.

_____ 6. The area of the tire in contact with the road.

_____ 7. This occurs when something is deflected but does not rebound with the same force, usually due to the internal friction inherent in the material as it deflects.

_____ 8. A second leaf spring in a leaf spring suspension that does not take any of the weight until the vehicle is close to fully loaded.

_____ 9. The interleaf friction in a leaf spring pack that helps to stop spring oscillation.

_____ 10. A suspension where the leaf spring sits on top of the axle.

Multiple Choice

Read each item carefully, and then select the best response.

_____ 1. The condition caused by excessive suspension oscillation that can lead to loss of control and extreme tire wear is called _____.
A. torsion
B. wheel hop
C. axle torque
D. jounce

_____ 2. The _____ weight is the portion of the vehicle that is not supported by the suspension system springs.
A. overslung
B. underslung
C. unsprung
D. sprung

_____ 3. The movement of the spring when it is loaded is referred to as _____.
   A. rebound
   B. spring rate
   C. torsion
   D. oscillation

_____ 4. A _____ consists of a semi-elliptically curved spring steel plate clamped to an axle at its middle and that supports the body of the vehicle at both ends.
   A. leaf spring
   B. coil spring
   C. torsion bar
   D. torque rod

_____ 5. When mounted transversely, torque rods are called _____.
   A. leaf springs
   B. axle rods
   C. track rods
   D. torsion bars

_____ 6. All suspensions limit axle movement with a rubber or a solid stop mounted between the frame and the axle called a _____.
   A. axle stop
   B. bellows
   C. jounce block
   D. Either A or C

_____ 7. Made from fiberglass, carbon fiber, and epoxy formed into one large semi-elliptical leaf with steel re-enforced contact points, _____ weigh up to 75% less than a comparable steel leaf spring.
   A. constant-rate springs
   B. parabolic leaf springs
   C. composite leaf springs
   D. taper leaf springs

_____ 8. Rubber spring equalizer beam suspensions will usually have four vertical _____ attached to frame hangers.
   A. saddles
   B. drive pins
   C. shock absorbers
   D. track rods

_____ 9. The _____ consists of at least a pressure protection valve, height-control valve, and the connecting lines.
   A. air-control system
   B. equalizer system
   C. Kenworth stabilizer
   D. electronically controlled air suspension system

_____ 10. A dangerous phenomenon that can occur particularly with air spring suspension trailers or straight trucks as the vehicle is being unloaded is called _____.
   A. articulation
   B. hysteresis
   C. dock walk
   D. jounce

True/False

If you believe the statement to be more true than false, write the letter "T" in the space provided. If you believe the statement to be more false than true, write the letter "F".

_____ 1. Elasticity is the property of a material that causes it to be restored to its original shape after distortion.

_____ 2. Heavier unsprung weights allow the tires to follow the road contour more easily without bouncing.

_____ 3. One of the major functions of a suspension system is to minimize suspension oscillation.

_____ 4. Light-duty commercial vehicles usually use heavy coil springs or torsion bars at the front and leaf springs at the rear.

_____ **5.** Air spring suspensions are completely self-dampening and do not require shock absorbers or any additional dampers to stop spring oscillation.

_____ **6.** The taper leaf and parabolic leaf springs produce less interleaf friction, leading to a softer ride.

_____ **7.** Constant-rate springs are thinner at the outer ends of the leaf and get progressively thicker toward the center of the leaf.

_____ **8.** The spring center bolt locates the spring in the lower shock bracket, which is the bracket to which the shock absorber bolts.

_____ **9.** Air spring suspension systems provide better shock isolation than any of the other types of suspension systems.

_____ **10.** In an air spring equalizing beam suspension system, the air spring is mounted on a specially modified leaf spring that takes the place of the trailing arm.

Fill in the Blank

Read each item carefully, and then complete the statement by filling in the missing word(s).

1. The _____ weight is the weight of the vehicle components supported by the springs.

2. The suspension system must maintain a vehicle's _____ stability, which is the vehicle's ability to be stable from side to side.

3. Interleaf _____, caused by the springs in a multileaf spring pack rubbing together, can dissipate unwanted oscillation.

4. The load _____ of a spring refers to the load the spring can carry.

5. When more than one steel plate or leaf is stacked together and used for a spring, it is called a multileaf spring or a spring _____.

6. The _____ shock absorber system uses sensors that monitor vehicle acceleration, brake pressure, speed, and the pressure in the air spring bellows.

7. The swing _____ allows for the lengthening and shortening of the spring as it cycles through jounce and rebound.

8. The lever principle employed by _____ _____ suspension systems reduces the road shocks to the frame by 50%.

9. The _____ system uses equalizing beams that are not solidly attached to the axles. Instead, they ride in brackets called saddles that are welded to the axles.

10. Bellows come in two basic configurations—reversing sleeve (rolling lobe) and _____ air spring.

Labeling

Label the following diagrams with the correct terms.

1. Identify the different shock absorber valves:

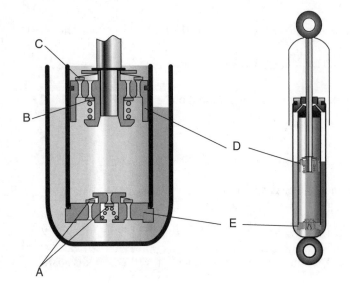

A. _____

B. _____

C. _____

D. _____

E. _____

2. Identify the components of a front leaf spring suspension:

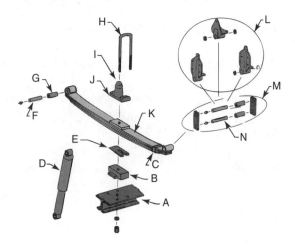

A. _____

B. _____

C. _____

D. _____

E. _____

F. _____

G. _____

H. _____

I. _____

J. _____

K. _____

L. _____

M. _____

N. _____

3. Identify the components of an air spring system:

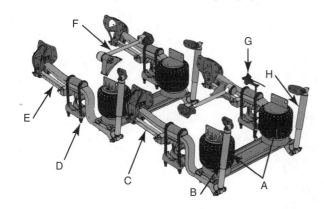

A. _____

B. _____

C. _____

D. _____

E. _____

F. _____

G. _____

H. _____

4. Identify the components of air springs:

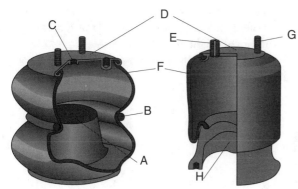

A. _____

B. _____

C. _____

D. _____

E. _____

F. _____

G. _____

H. _____

5. Identify the components of a height control valve:

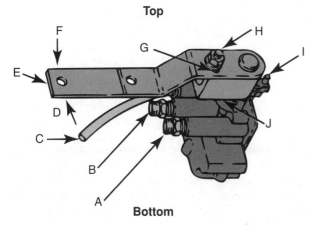

Top

Bottom

A. _____

B. _____

C. _____

D. _____

E. _____

F. _____

G. _____

H. _____

I. _____

J. _____

Skill Drills

Test your knowledge of skill drills by filling in the correct words in the photo captions.

1. Inspecting a Leaf Spring System:

Step 1: Inspect the entire system for _____ or _____ components such as fasteners, _____, spring clamps, or clips.

Step 2: Inspect for proper spring _____ in the hangers and for suspension _____ with the vehicle frame, attachments, or brake components.

Step 3: Check and re-torque frame _____, _____, and shock absorber _____ hardware. Most late model frames are using "Huck" brand fasteners at the frame hangers. Inspect Huck bolt fasteners for _____. (Huck bolt fasteners cannot be re-torqued by traditional methods.)

Step 4: Check for rust streaking from the frame hanger. Streaks can indicate movement between the _____ and _____. If rust streaking is found, investigate further to find the _____ fasteners.

2. Performing an In-Service Inspection of a Suspension System:

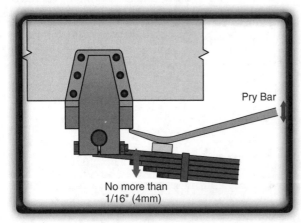

Pry Bar

No more than
1/16" (4mm)

Step 1: Check the leaf _____ for missing or _____ leaves.

Step 2: Check for deep _____ or _____ in the leaves, particularly in monoleaf springs.

Step 3: Inspect _____ leaf springs for missing interleaf _____ and/or anti-friction pads.

Step 4: Check the spring leaves for _____ _____. Replace any spring that shows excessive abrasive wear. Replace the individual leaves or the entire _____ _____ per manufacturer's recommendations.

Step 5: Check the spring _____ _____, top plates, axle _____, and axle _____ for cracks and/or looseness.

Step 6: Re-torque mounting U-bolts and hardware to _____ following the _____ shown. (Most suspension manufacturers recommend that leaf spring mounting U-bolts and hardware torque be re-checked every _____ miles [32,000 km].) Springs should be _____ _____ while U-bolts are torqued. Failure to tighten in this order can lead to _____ of the U-bolt.

Step 7: Check spring hangers for spring _____ and signs of _____ _____ in the hangers; this could indicate worn mounting _____.

Step 8: Use a _____ _____ to check _____ pin and _____ spring mounting bushings for wear and movement. Excessive movement (greater than 1/16" or 4 mm) usually requires _____ replacement, but check manufacturer's specification.

Step 9: Determine if bronze and steel _____ _____ require lubrication. They should be lubricated as part of the vehicle's regular _____ _____ and _____ schedule. Check for _____ before lubricating the bushing.

Step 10: Check rubber _____ mounting bushings for any free _____. Bushings are made of rubber encased by inner and outer _____ _____. The spring will move slightly when a pry bar is used. Any bushing that allows the spring to move _____ at all should be _____.

Step 11: Check that the _____ and _____ metal _____ of the bushing are not in _____ with each other. If they are, replace the bushing.

Step 12: Check the _____ of the bushings for end _____, which results from excessive movement.

Step 13: Replace _____ bushings. Push the bushing out using a _____. Remove the _____. Press a new bushing into place. Special tools are available to remove and insert bushings while the spring is still attached to the _____.

Step 14: Check the rear spring _____ on front suspensions for any _____ movement or _____ of the spring or shackle at the _____ points on the frame and at the spring. There should be no perceptible _____.

Step 15: Check unusual _____ _____ on the vehicle. River wear and/or _____ can indicate _____ problems (wandering and wheel hop). If the tire _____ is correct, carefully examine the suspension system to determine the cause.

Step 16: Check spring hanger _____ _____ for excessive wear. Wear at the slipper pads is _____. Replace only when wear is _____.

Step 17: Check the _____ of the spring hanger _____. Abrasive wear indicates the spring is not _____ properly or is loose in its mounting bushing. The _____ should not _____ the inside of the hanger legs in normal operation.

Step 18: Visually inspect _____ _____ for oil leaks, damaged rubber bushings, and broken _____. Drive the vehicle _____ miles (80 km) or more. The shock absorber should be _____ to the touch. A _____ shock absorber is not working properly.

3. Inspecting and Maintaining Shock Absorbers:

Step 1: Check the _____ mounting fasteners for correct _____. Check mounting brackets for _____ welds and metal-to-metal contact caused by worn _____. Replace the shock if the bushing allows _____ _____.

Step 2: Check the shocks for _____ or _____ caused by _____ _____. Damage to the shock _____ can cause internal or external _____, or it may stop the shock from working altogether. _____ shocks displaying this kind of damage.

Step 3:   Check shocks for _____ _____. Misting of oil on the inside of the _____ _____ and the _____ _____ is normal and necessary for seal and rod lubrication. Any _____ fluid, however, indicates a _____ shock that should be replaced. Suspect shocks can be checked using the _____ method after a 15-minute road test. If the shock is working correctly, the action of the shock will cause the fluid to _____ _____. A weak or defective shock will stay relatively cool. If the shock on the same axle is _____ than its mate, the pair should be _____.

4. Adjusting the Ride Height:

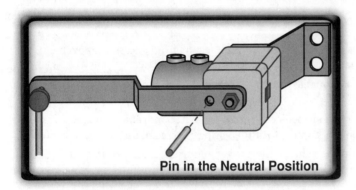

Pin in the Neutral Position

Step 1:   Loosen the height-control _____ and disconnect it at the _____ or the _____ as required.

Step 2:   Manually _____ or _____ the valve lever until the ride _____ is _____.

Step 3:   When the ride height is correct, _____ the valve in the _____ position.

Step 4:   Center the _____ control lever on the height-control valve in the _____ position and pin it into place with a 1/8" (3 mm) pin or _____ _____.

Step 5:   Adjust the _____ _____ so it can be connected with the valve in the center position and then _____.

Step 6:   Re-connect the _____ _____.

Step 7:   Remove the _____ or drill bit and ensure that the _____ _____ has remained within specification.

Step 8:   Road test the vehicle for _____ or _____ minutes and _____ the ride height using the above procedure. If the ride height is not within specification, _____ the procedure.

CAUTION: Remember to _____ the _____ when the job is complete! Failure to remove the pin will result in a _____ _____ and _____ _____ to the height-control valve.

5. Aligning Axles:

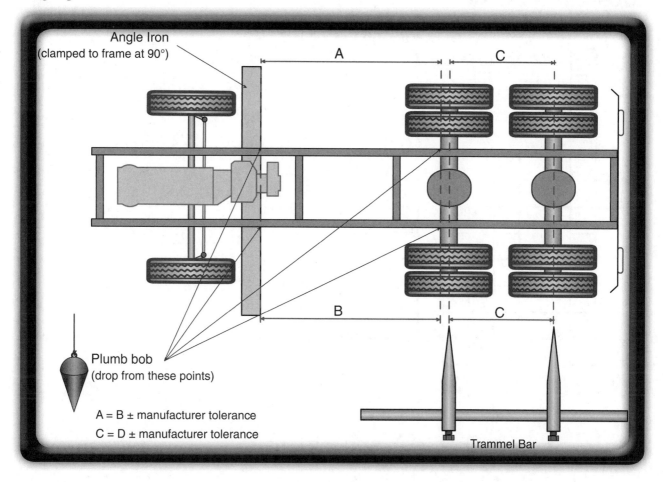

Step 1:   Park the vehicle on a _____ _____. Do not apply the parking brakes. Roll the vehicle _____ and _____ by hand to relieve _____ on the suspension. _____ the front wheels to keep minimal _____ on the rear axle(s). Check and adjust _____ pressures to the recommended level.

Step 2:   Lift the rear wheels with a _____ and check for _____-_____ and correct as necessary. Ensure the front wheels are in the _____-_____ position.

Step 3:   Using a _____ _____, clamp a long straight edge to the vehicle frame in front of the rear _____. Ensure that the straight edge is exactly _____ degrees to the frame _____.

Step 4:   Suspend a _____ _____ from the outer edge of the frame at the straight edge on both sides of the vehicle. Measure the _____ from the plum bob to the _____ _____ axle on both sides (measurements A and B on the diagram). The distances should be _____ to within 1/16" (1.5 mm). Compare the readings with the manufacturer's _____ for the particular vehicle.

Step 5:   If the axle is a _____, then measure the distance between the _____ of the front rear axle wheel and the _____ wheel on the rear _____ (measurements C and D in the diagram).

Step 6:   Use an adjustable _____ _____ to take these measurements. This dimension should be _____ to within 1/16" (1.5 mm). This specification is _____. Check the manufacturer's specification for the particular axle.

Crossword Puzzle

Use the clues in the column to complete the puzzle.

Across

3. The upward motion of the wheels and axles in reaction to road bumps or terrain.

6. A helical metal spring.

Down

1. Movement of axles.

2. The spring component of an air spring suspension; a tough rubber bag filled with air.

4. The downward motion of the wheel and axle after a road bump or shock has occurred.

5. A suspension system where the leaf spring is mounted under the axle.

ASE-Type Questions

Read each item carefully, and then select the best response.

_____ 1. Technician A says that all multileaf spring packs are variable rate. Technician B says that auxiliary springs are usually variable rate. Who is correct?
   A. Technician A
   B. Technician B
   C. Both Technician A and Technician B
   D. Neither Technician A nor Technician B

_____ 2. Technician A says that higher spring rate aids in lateral stability. Technician B says that higher spring rates lead to a much softer ride. Who is correct?
   A. Technician A
   B. Technician B
   C. Both Technician A and Technician B
   D. Neither Technician A nor Technician B

_____ 3. Technician A says that variable-rate multileaf springs change rate because the contact point between the springs and the cams changes as load is added. Technician B says that some monoleaf springs can be variable rate. Who is correct?
   A. Technician A
   B. Technician B
   C. Both Technician A and Technician B
   D. Neither Technician A nor Technician B

_____ 4. Technician A says that all torque rods are adjustable to control axle alignment. Technician B says that usually torque rods are only adjustable on one side. Who is correct?
   A. Technician A
   B. Technician B
   C. Both Technician A and Technician B
   D. Neither Technician A nor Technician B

_____ 5. Technician A says suspension systems must tolerate a huge number of forces when a vehicle is being driven down the road. Technician B says vehicle suspension systems generally use the elastic properties of special metals or air springs to provide the springing medium that a suspension system requires. Who is correct?
   A. Technician A
   B. Technician B
   C. Both Technician A and Technician B
   D. Neither Technician A nor Technician B

_____ 6. Technician A says the suspension system must ensure the vehicle's tires stay in contact with the road surface. Technician B says wheel hop caused by excessive suspension oscillation can lead to loss of control and extreme tire wear. Who is correct?
   A. Technician A
   B. Technician B
   C. Both Technician A and Technician B
   D. Neither Technician A nor Technician B

_____ 7. Technician A says a basic function of the suspension system is to securely connect the axles to the frame of the vehicle. Technician B says the suspension system must maintain the axle spacing and alignment as the axles articulate over uneven road surfaces and bumps. Who is correct?
   A. Technician A
   B. Technician B
   C. Both Technician A and Technician B
   D. Neither Technician A nor Technician B

_____ 8. Technician A says a shock absorber is effective in minimizing suspension oscillation. Technician B says interleaf friction in leaf springs is not effective in minimizing suspension oscillation. Who is correct?
   A. Technician A
   B. Technician B
   C. Both Technician A and Technician B
   D. Neither Technician A nor Technician B

_____ **9.** Technician A says torque rods are used to keep the axles in alignment with each other and with the frame. Technician B says torque rods are usually not adjustable. Who is correct?

A. Technician A

B. Technician B

C. Both Technician A and Technician B

D. Neither Technician A nor Technician B

_____ **10.** Technician A says most hydraulic shock absorbers are designed with an inner and an outer tube. Technician B says the outer tube is also known as the primary tube, and it does not hold a supply of hydraulic fluid. Who is correct?

A. Technician A

B. Technician B

C. Both Technician A and Technician B

D. Neither Technician A nor Technician B

Steering Systems and Integral Steering Gears

Chapter Review

The following activities have been designed to help you refresh your knowledge of this chapter. Your instructor may require you to complete some or all of these activities as a regular part of your training program. You are encouraged to complete any activity that your instructor does not assign as a way to enhance your learning.

Matching

Match the following terms with the correct description or example.

A. Clock spring
B. Pitman arm
C. Road feel

D. Steering ratio
E. Tie rod

_____ **1.** The force transmitted from the tires back through the steering system to the driver.

_____ **2.** A steering component that transfers linear motion from the steering box to the steering arms at the front wheels.

_____ **3.** The mechanical advantage produced by the steering gear that converts large turns of the steering wheel into smaller turns of the tire to ease steering for the driver.

_____ **4.** A steering component that converts the steering gear sector shaft movement to a sweeping arc resembling linear movement.

_____ **5.** A special rotary electrical connector located between the steering wheel and the steering column that maintains a constant electrical connection with the wiring system while the vehicle's steering wheel is being turned.

Multiple Choice

Read each item carefully, and then select the best response.

_____ **1.** Steering systems are typically classified by _____.
   A. arrangement of the steering linkage
   B. type of suspension system
   C. type of steering gear or power-assist mechanism
   D. Either A or C

_____ **2.** The _____ steering system uses a conventional worm-gear steering box as its base then adds an air or hydraulic cylinder attached to the steering linkage.
   A. integral piston
   B. external power-assist
   C. rack-and-pinion
   D. All of the above

_____ **3.** Multi-shaft steering columns using shafts connected on sliding splines, called _____, enable the column to change in length.
   A. universal joints
   B. pinions
   C. slip yokes
   D. worm gears

_____ 4. A 16:1 steering ratio means that a steering wheel turned 360 degrees would turn the wheels _____ degrees.
- **A.** 12
- **B.** 18
- **C.** 22.5
- **D.** 24

_____ 5. Recirculating-ball steering systems consist of a steering box with a worm gear inside a metal block called a _____ with a threaded hole in it.
- **A.** ball-nut rack
- **B.** pinion
- **C.** jack screw
- **D.** steering knuckle

_____ 6. The _____ senses the change in force applied to the steering wheel at the beginning of a turn and directs pressurized fluid to either side of the power piston when turning is initiated.
- **A.** rotary valve
- **B.** kingpin
- **C.** spool valve
- **D.** Either A or C

_____ 7. A condition called _____ can occur when a wheel hits a bump and the axle lifts or drops on the side where the steering gear is located.
- **A.** bump steer
- **B.** axle drag
- **C.** drop arm
- **D.** pitman hop

_____ 8. The ball-and-socket joints attached to both the left and right steering knuckle's lower steering arms are called _____.
- **A.** pitman joints
- **B.** tie-rod ends
- **C.** drag links
- **D.** ball-nut racks

_____ 9. Engine-driven power steering pumps use _____ as hydraulic fluid.
- **A.** power steering gear fluid
- **B.** automatic transmission fluid
- **C.** engine oil
- **D.** Any of the above

_____ 10. The _____ is a combination flow meter, shutoff valve, and pressure gauge that enables a technician to measure hydraulic flow pressure in the steering system and to apply a load to the pump using the system's hydraulic lines.
- **A.** power steering leak detector
- **B.** power steering micron gauge set
- **C.** power steering fluid anemometer
- **D.** power steering system analyzer

True/False

If you believe the statement to be more true than false, write the letter "T" in the space provided. If you believe the statement to be more false than true, write the letter "F'.

_____ 1. The purpose of the steering gear is to convert and multiply the rotational force from the steering wheel to operate the steering linkage.

_____ 2. A sharper turning radius is the major advantage of the integral piston steering system.

_____ 3. Manual steering capabilities are built into every steering system in the event of a loss of power steering assist.

_____ 4. Trucks and buses have significantly larger steering wheels than automobiles or light-duty vehicles.

_____ 5. Manual steering gears provide assistance to the driver's effort and fewer turns of the steering wheel are required to move steer tires.

_____ **6.** A lower steering ratio reduces shocks from the road and reduces the driver's steering effort.

_____ **7.** Two critical components of the hydraulic control mechanism of all power steering gears are the rotary valve and the torsion bar.

_____ **8.** Rack-and-pinion steering systems incorporate a pitman arm and a drag link to minimize the problem of bump steer.

_____ **9.** An aligning mark is often used on the sector shaft and pitman arm to correctly center the wheels with the steering gear.

_____ **10.** A good power steering system reduces the effort required to steer the vehicle and provides good steering feedback to the driver.

Fill in the Blank

Read each item carefully, and then complete the statement by filling in the missing word(s).

1. The _____ _____ includes the steering wheel, column, steering gear, its power-assist mechanism, and steering linkage connecting the steering gear to the steer axle wheels.

2. The three major power steering _____ systems are the integral piston system, the external power-assist system, and the rack-and-pinion system.

3. Steering force is transmitted through the drag link to the steering _____ by the upper steering arm.

4. Steering shafts make up the steering _____, which is typically a combination of two or more steering shafts.

5. A(n) _____ box is used to sharply change steering column angles.

6. A(n) _____-_____ steering gear uses sector shafts with both long and short lengths of teeth.

7. The _____ rod is a thin, spring-like metal rod that connects to the outside section of the rotary valve.

8. The parts that make up the steering _____ are the pitman (drop) arm, drag link, tie-rod ends, and the upper and lower steering arms.

9. Steering knuckles use a _____, which permits knuckle rotation during steering.

10. The most common type of power steering has an engine-driven hydraulic pump that delivers hydraulic fluid to the _____ _____ at the steering gear through connecting hoses and pipes.

Labeling

Label the following diagrams with the correct terms.

1. Identify the components of a conventional steering system:

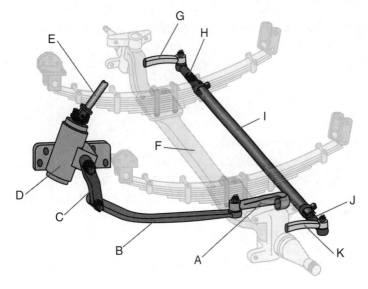

A. _____

B. _____

C. _____

D. _____

E. _____

F. _____

G. _____

H. _____

I. _____

J. _____

K. _____

2. Identify the components of a steering column with flexible joint:

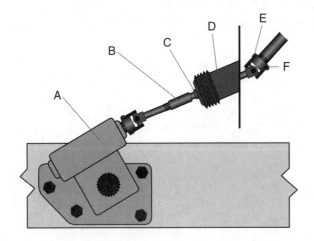

A. _____

B. _____

C. _____

D. _____

E. _____

F. _____

3. Identify the components of a basic worm type steering gear:

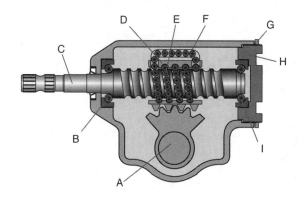

A. _____

B. _____

C. _____

D. _____

E. _____

F. _____

G. _____

H. _____

I. _____

4. Identify the components of a hydraulic circuit for a power steering system using an integral steering gear:

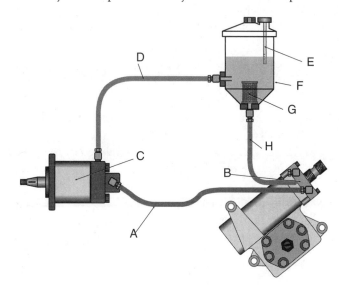

A. _____

B. _____

C. _____

D. _____

E. _____

F. _____

G. _____

H. _____

5. Identify the components of a kingpin assembly:

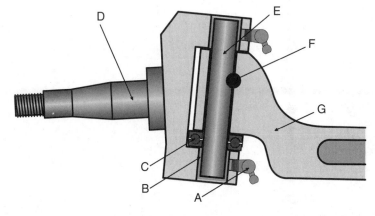

A. _____

B. _____

C. _____

D. _____

E. _____

F. _____

G. _____

Skill Drills

Test your knowledge of skill drills by filling in the correct words in the photo captions.

1. Centering the Steering Linkage:

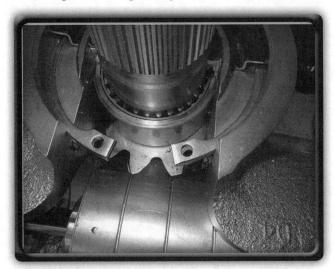

Step 1: Square the tires with the _____ so the tires are tracking in a dead _____-_____ position. This can be done by _____ the distance of the front and rear of the tire to adjust for the same distance from the _____ _____.

Step 2: Disconnect the _____ _____ at both ends.

Step 3: Disconnect the steering gear _____ _____.

Step 4: Check the _____ _____on the _____ _____ and _____ _____ to verify that they line up.

Step 5: Turn the _____ _____ with a 12-point socket, and count the number of turns. Precisely find and mark the _____ point between the _____ _____ of the input shaft.

Step 6: Measure the distance between the hole of the _____ arm and the _____ arm used by the _____ _____. It must be exactly the same length as the drag link. If not, the correct drag link or an _____ drag link must be _____ and adjusted.

Step 7: Reconnect the steering _____ _____, ensuring that the steering wheel _____ are _____ for a straight-ahead position.

Step 8: If the steering wheel is not centered, _____ the steering wheel and _____it with the _____ properly _____ to a straight-ahead position.

2. Using a Power Steering System Analyzer:

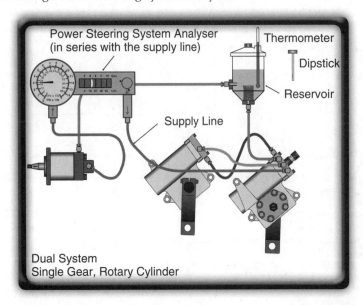

Step 1:   Connect the PSSA gauge in _____ with the output _____ _____ of the power steering _____.

Step 2:   Start and _____ the engine and check the system reservoir oil level. Also, observe whether the oil is flowing in the _____ _____ through the gauge using the _____ on the flow meter.

Step 3:   Place a thermometer in the _____. A digital type thermometer with a _____ _____ is ideal.

Step 4:   While the engine is at idle speed, warm the _____ _____. This is performed by slowly closing the _____ _____ until a pressure reading of approximately _____ psi (6,900 kPa) is reached. Hold this pressure until system temperature reaches _____°F (82°C). Fluid should never reach _____°F (121°C). If it does, testing must be suspended until the fluid cools.

Step 5:   Completely re-open the _____ _____ when the temperature is _____°F (82°C).

Step 6:   Measure and record _____ pressure, also referred to as _____ pressure. Normal system _____ pressure is between 0 and _____ psi (0 and 690 kPa) with the engine idling and no _____ input. Dual steering gear systems should have slightly _____ back pressure.

3. Measuring Pump Maximum Relief Pressure:

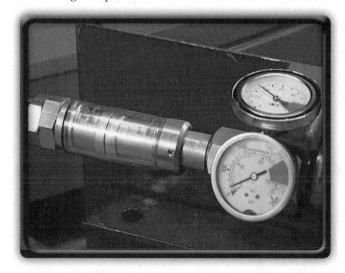

Step 1:   With the engine at _____, slowly turn the PSSA _____ valve until it is _____.

Step 2:   Measure and record the _____ pressure. This reading corresponds to the pressure at which the _____ valve opens. Be sure to open the _____ _____ as quickly (within 15 seconds) as possible to avoid _____ the oil or damaging lines or the steering pump.

Step 3:   Compare _____ with manufacturer's _____.

4. Testing Flow Volume:

Step 1: Connect the PSSA gauge in _____ with the _____ pressure line of the _____ _____ pump.

Step 2: Start and idle the engine and check system reservoir _____ _____. Also, observe whether the oil is flowing in the correct _____ through the gauge using the arrow on the _____ _____.

Step 3: While the engine is at idle speed warm the _____ _____. This is performed by slowly closing the _____ _____ until a pressure reading of approximately _____ psi (6,900 kPA) is reached. Hold this pressure until the system temperature reaches _____°F (121°C). Fluid should never reach _____°F (121°C). If it does, testing must be suspended until the fluid _____.

Step 4: Completely re-open the _____ _____ when the temperature is _____°F (121°C).

Step 5: Read the _____ _____, which measures _____ _____ of the pump. Flow is measured in _____ or _____ per minute.

Step 6: Raise the engine speed to _____ rpm and record the _____ observed on the flow gauge.

Step 7: Compare observations with _____ specifications.

5. Testing for Internal Leakage:

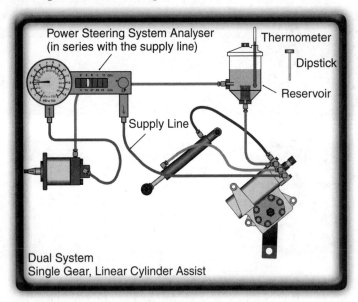

Step 1: Place a 1" (2.5 cm) thick _____ spacer or other suitable spacer between the _____ _____ and _____ contact point to prevent _____ with the _____ and relieving steering pressure.

Step 2: With the engine at _____, turn the _____ _____ with approximately _____ lb (9.1 kg) of _____ effort against the spacer between the stops.

Step 3: Observe and record _____ and _____ _____ for each left and right turn. Pressures should be very near the pressures achieved during the steering _____ _____ pressure checks.

Step 4: If flow volumes exceed _____ gallon (3.8 liters) per _____ at the steering stops, the gear is _____ oil _____ and should be _____.

Crossword Puzzle

Use the clues in the column to complete the puzzle.

Across

3. A gear with a helical, threaded shaft that is attached to the steering column and meshes with a wheel that transfers motion from the steering wheel to the steering linkage.

4. A connecting linkage that transfers movement of the pitman arm to the upper steering arm.

5. A column affixed between the steering wheel and the steering box, usually made to collapse during a crash.

Down

1. A cross-shaped joint with bearings on each leg where one set of parallel legs is connected to the end of one shaft and the other set of parallel legs is connected to the end of a second shaft.

2. A thin, spring-like metal rod that connects to one end of the rotary valve to change its position.

ASE-Type Questions

Read each item carefully, and then select the best response.

_____ 1. Technician A says if the steering column input shaft is not aligned correctly it will have tight spots or bind when turned. Technician B says if the power steering fluid level is low there will be a noise when turning the steering wheel. Who is right?
  A. Technician A
  B. Technician B
  C. Both Technician A and Technician B
  D. Neither Technician A nor Technician B

_____ 2. Technician A says if the kingpins are not lubricated, the vehicle will be hard to steer. Technician B says clunking noises when turning the steering wheel are acceptable. Who is right?
  A. Technician A
  B. Technician B
  C. Both Technician A and Technician B
  D. Neither Technician A nor Technician B

_____ 3. Technician A says if the steering effort is high whenever the steering wheel is turned, one of the power steering pressure relief valves in the steering gear is defective. Technician B says if the power flow control valve in the power steering pump is defective, the vehicle will be hard to steer. Who is right?
  A. Technician A
  B. Technician B
  C. Both Technician A and Technician B
  D. Neither Technician A nor Technician B

_____ 4. Technician A says using recirculating ball bearings reduces friction between the worm gear and block. Technician B says another advantage of recirculating ball bearings is to allow almost zero clearance between the worm gear and block. Who is correct?
  A. Technician A
  B. Technician B
  C. Both Technician A and Technician B
  D. Neither Technician A nor Technician B

_____ 5. Technician A says the rotary valve (also called the spool valve) senses the change in force applied to the steering wheel at the beginning of a turn. Technician B says that essentially, this valve directs pressurized fluid to either side of the power piston when turning is initiated. Who is correct?
  A. Technician A
  B. Technician B
  C. Both Technician A and Technician B
  D. Neither Technician A nor Technician B

_____ 6. Technician A says rack-and-pinion steering systems do not include tie rods. Technician B says rack-and-pinion steering systems do not include a pitman arm or a drag link. Who is correct?
  A. Technician A
  B. Technician B
  C. Both Technician A and Technician B
  D. Neither Technician A nor Technician B

_____ 7. Technician A says the drag link is a steering linkage rod connecting the pitman arm at one end to the upper steering arm at the other. Technician B says, in addition to that basic bridging function, the drag link performs a leveling function. Who is correct?
  A. Technician A
  B. Technician B
  C. Both Technician A and Technician B
  D. Neither Technician A nor Technician B

_____ **8.** Technician A says the kingpin passes through the knuckle's upper arm, through the end of the I-beam, and then through the knuckle yoke's lower arm. Technician B says a snap ring keeps the kingpin in place and locks the pin into position through the center of the I-beam axle. Who is correct?

A. Technician A

B. Technician B

C. Both Technician A and Technician B

D. Neither Technician A nor Technician B

_____ **9.** Technician A says for safety reasons, castellated nuts using cotter pins to lock the ball stud and nut together are used on all steering linkage components. Technician B says it is satisfactory to use heat on rusted steering components in order to take them apart. Who is correct?

A. Technician A

B. Technician B

C. Both Technician A and Technician B

D. Neither Technician A nor Technician B

_____ **10.** Technician A says pressurizing the power steering oil produces heat that can damage the oil. Technician B says on heavy vehicles an oil cooler is used to prevent overheating. Who is correct?

A. Technician A

B. Technician B

C. Both Technician A and Technician B

D. Neither Technician A nor Technician B

Chapter Review

The following activities have been designed to help you refresh your knowledge of this chapter. Your instructor may require you to complete some or all of these activities as a regular part of your training program. You are encouraged to complete any activity that your instructor does not assign as a way to enhance your learning.

Matching

Match the following terms with the correct description or example.

A. Chemical fade

B. Glazing

C. Heat fade

D. Mechanical fade

E. Water fade

_____ **1.** A type of brake fade that takes place when steam or gases from vaporized lining materials form between hot lining and the drum reducing the coefficient of friction.

_____ **2.** A type of brake fade that occurs when water gets between the friction surfaces and the drum and acts as a lubricant reducing braking efficiency.

_____ **3.** Loss of brake effectiveness that occurs when drums expand due to heat.

_____ **4.** The loss or reduction in the coefficient of friction as brake temperature increases.

_____ **5.** A cause of brake fade characterized by a hard, glassy burnt appearance to the lining surface diminishing its CoF.

Multiple Choice

Read each item carefully, and then select the best response.

_____ **1.** Deceleration during braking produces an effect called _____ that moves weight from the rear axles and transfers it forward.
   A. brake fade
   B. fulcrum shift
   C. inertia shift
   D. torque balance

_____ **2.** Force multiplication in a braking system is achieved by forcing friction material against drums and discs using _____.
   A. hydraulic fluid
   B. electrical pressure
   C. air pressure
   D. Either A or C

_____ **3.** One advantage that hydraulic braking systems have over air systems is _____.
   A. fewer and simpler brake components
   B. faster force transmission through smaller lines
   C. connecting the tractor and trailer braking systems is easier
   D. hydraulics are not sensitive to altitude changes

_____ **4.** What type of air brake foundation system is most commonly used on heavy-duty commercial vehicles today?
   A. Cam brakes
   B. Air disc systems
   C. Wedge brakes
   D. Hydraulic drum brakes

_____ **5.** With a primary-secondary shoe design, an action called _____ causes shoe-drum friction to rotate the brake shoe into the drum with more force.
- **A.** hydraulic force
- **B.** wedge pressure
- **C.** self-energization
- **D.** cam pressure

_____ **6.** Brake block and lining are _____ to the brake shoe table.
- **A.** riveted
- **B.** bolted
- **C.** glued
- **D.** Any of the above

_____ **7.** The _____ refers to the size or surface area of a brake chamber multiplied by the length of the slack adjuster in inches.
- **A.** coefficient of friction
- **B.** AL factor
- **C.** edge code
- **D.** brake block

_____ **8.** Long stroke chambers have a _____ stroke travel.
- **A.** 2"
- **B.** 2.5"
- **C.** 3"
- **D.** 4"

_____ **9.** Actuators with a unique diaphragm construction that delivers consistent output force regardless of the pushrod position are called _____.
- **A.** roto-chambers
- **B.** stroke chambers
- **C.** service chambers
- **D.** power springs

_____ **10.** A _____ automatic slack adjuster reduces pushrod travel based on torque input.
- **A.** stroke sensing
- **B.** power sensing
- **C.** clearance sensing
- **D.** rotation sensing

True/False

If you believe the statement to be more true than false, write the letter "T" in the space provided. If you believe the statement to be more false than true, write the letter "F".

_____ **1.** The braking system now has a large element of electronic control operating the braking system with virtually no driver input.

_____ **2.** Increasing vehicle speed has a greater effect than vehicle weight on the braking system power.

_____ **3.** Too much braking performed by the front axle can cause the trailer or rear axles to swing out.

_____ **4.** The control of air pressure through brake circuits requires fewer valves and components than hydraulic systems.

_____ **5.** The name *cam brake* is given because of an "S"-shaped camshaft, or S-cam, used to force brake shoes onto the brake drum.

_____ **6.** Left-hand cams rotate clockwise, while right-hand cams turn counterclockwise.

_____ **7.** Changes to the coefficient of friction take place when the condition of the surfaces between the objects varies.

_____ **8.** Anti-fade is an opposite condition of heat fade, where the coefficient of friction increases as the brakes get hotter.

_____ **9.** When inboard mounted drums are used it is only necessary to remove the wheels to replace the drum; the hub seal and bearings are left undisturbed.

_____ **10.** Before the most recent shorter stopping requirements were introduced, wedge brakes comprised 95% of all heavy-duty North American air brake systems.

Fill in the Blank

Read each item carefully, and then complete the statement by filling in the missing word(s).

1. Brakes convert the vehicle's kinetic energy into heat energy using _____.

2. Braking power can be measured in _____ used to decelerate a vehicle rather than accelerate a vehicle.

3. Another term for brake application force is _____ pressure.

4. Brake _____ are the braking components found at the wheel ends.

5. Higher application force by brake pads against the rotors makes _____ brake systems more efficient than other types of foundation brakes.

6. A(n) _____-_____ camshaft rotates in the same direction as the drum to energize the brakes.

7. Two broad categories of _____ material are non-asbestos organic (NAO) lining and semi-metallic linings.

8. All brake block friction material is identified by a stenciled-on _____ _____.

9. A(n) _____ brake drum is made with a cast iron core surrounded by a steel band.

10. Actuators are like brake chambers except they have additional components such as power _____ used to apply park brakes or internal pushrod lock mechanisms.

11. When a brake chamber uses only a single chamber, it is called a(n) _____ chamber.

12. The _____ _____ is a mechanical lever between the brake chamber and the foundation brake assembly.

13. Disc brakes use _____ instead of drums.

14. The disc brake adjustment mechanism consists of threaded spindles, also called _____, which are used to set the air gap between the pads and rotor.

15. A(n) _____ brake system uses a ramp-and-roller design inside a wheel cylinder to multiply force supplied by an air chamber.

Labeling

Label the following diagrams with the correct terms.

1. Identify the components of a typical S-cam brake foundation system:

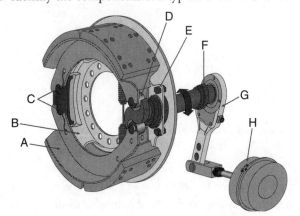

A. _____

B. _____

C. _____

D. _____

E. _____

F. _____

G. _____

H. _____

2. Identify the brake drum terminology:

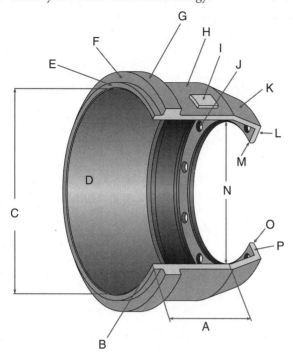

A. _____

B. _____

C. _____

D. _____

E. _____

F. _____

G. _____

H. _____

I. _____

J. _____

K. _____

L. _____

M. _____

N. _____

O. _____

P. _____

3. Identify the components of a combination or dual spring brake and service brake actuator:

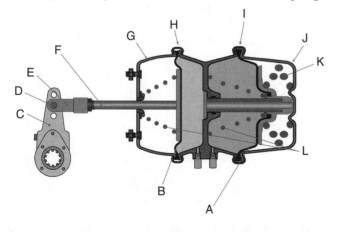

A. _____

B. _____

C. _____

D. _____

E. _____

F. _____

G. _____

H. _____

I. _____

J. _____

K. _____

L. _____

4. Identify the components of a Bendix clearance sensing slack adjuster:

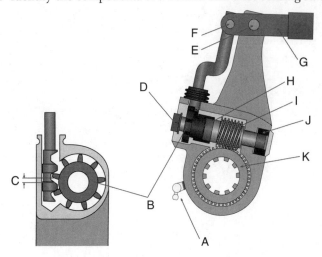

A. _____

B. _____

C. _____

D. _____

E. _____

F. _____

G. _____

H. _____

I. _____

J. _____

K. _____

5. Identify the components of a floating caliper system:

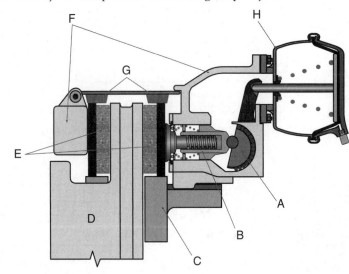

A. _____

B. _____

C. _____

D. _____

E. _____

F. _____

G. _____

H. _____

Crossword Puzzle

Use the clues in the column to complete the puzzle.

Across

4. A disc brake caliper that floats on two pins.

5. The inability of the brakes to maintain its effectiveness.

Down

1. The energy of a body in motion.

2. Brake drums made with a cast iron core surrounded by a steel band.

3. The force applied to the foundation brakes during braking.

ASE-Type Questions

Read each item carefully, and then select the best response.

_____ 1. Technician A says that vehicles require more power to stop than they do to accelerate. Technician B says that all new trucks must be equipped with anti-lock brakes. Who is correct?
   A. Technician A
   B. Technician B
   C. Both Technician A and Technician B
   D. Neither Technician A nor Technician B

_____ 2. Technician A says that the latest legislative requirements for truck brake systems demand shorter stopping distances. Technician B says that, to achieve shorter stopping distances, all drum brakes are legally required to be replaced by disc brakes. Who is correct?
   A. Technician A
   B. Technician B
   C. Both Technician A and Technician B
   D. Neither Technician A nor Technician B

_____ 3. Technician A says that brake systems convert potential energy to heat. Technician B says that brakes use friction to stop a vehicle. Who is correct?
   A. Technician A
   B. Technician B
   C. Both Technician A and Technician B
   D. Neither Technician A nor Technician B

_____ 4. Technician A says that more heat helps the brakes to work better. Technician B says that a vehicle must be able to stop in less than 1/10th of the time it takes to accelerate a given speed. Who is correct?
   A. Technician A
   B. Technician B
   C. Both Technician A and Technician B
   D. Neither Technician A nor Technician B

_____ 5. Technician A says that if the vehicle weight is doubled, the stopping force must be doubled. Technician B says that if the vehicle speed is doubled the stopping force required is increased eight times. Who is correct?
   A. Technician A
   B. Technician B
   C. Both Technician A and Technician B
   D. Neither Technician A nor Technician B

_____ 6. Technician A says that air brake systems transmit pressures much more quickly than hydraulic systems. Technician B says that compressed air stores potential energy. Who is correct?
   A. Technician A
   B. Technician B
   C. Both Technician A and Technician B
   D. Neither Technician A nor Technician B

_____ 7. Technician A says that air brake systems are better than hydraulics in tractor trailer applications because it is easier to connect and disconnect components. Technician B says that air brake systems use more engine power to operate. Who is correct?
   A. Technician A
   B. Technician B
   C. Both Technician A and Technician B
   D. Neither Technician A nor Technician B

_____ 8. Technician A says that air brake systems are regulated under FMVSS 135. Technician B says that hydraulic brake systems have lower initial cost when compared to air brake systems. Who is correct?
   A. Technician A
   B. Technician B
   C. Both Technician A and Technician B
   D. Neither Technician A nor Technician B

_____ **9.** Technician A says that wedge brakes are the most common foundation brake used on air brake systems. Technician B says that disc brakes are becoming more popular in air brake systems. Who is correct?
- **A.** Technician A
- **B.** Technician B
- **C.** Both Technician A and Technician B
- **D.** Neither Technician A nor Technician B

_____ **10.** Technician A says that S-cams can be left or right handed. Technician B says that S-cam foundation brakes can have one or two anchors. Who is correct?
- **A.** Technician A
- **B.** Technician B
- **C.** Both Technician A and Technician B
- **D.** Neither Technician A nor Technician B

Air Brake Foundation Systems and Air Brake Circuits

Chapter Review

The following activities have been designed to help you refresh your knowledge of this chapter. Your instructor may require you to complete some or all of these activities as a regular part of your training program. You are encouraged to complete any activity that your instructor does not assign as a way to enhance your learning.

Matching

Match the following terms with the correct description or example.

A. Anti-compounding valve

B. Double check valves

C. Foot valve

D. Inversion valve

E. Limiter valve

F. One-way check valve

G. Pressure-compensating balance valve

H. Pressure protection valve

I. Proportioning valve

J. Push-pull park/emergency control valve

_____ **1.** A normally closed valve that opens after a preset pressure is reached that is used to control the charging of air system reservoirs or circuits draining out of the reservoir.

_____ **2.** An air pressure proportioning valve used to increase brake application pressure to the front brakes when a trailer is not towed by a tractor.

_____ **3.** Hand-operated dash valve used to control the operation of the spring brakes for a straight truck, tractor, and/or trailer.

_____ **4.** The center of the brake delivery system.

_____ **5.** A feature of air brake valves that ensures a consistent delivery of air pressure is maintained in spite of leaks in the delivery system lines or air chambers.

_____ **6.** An air control system design feature that prevents simultaneous application of the service and spring brakes.

_____ **7.** A normally open valve that requires air pressure to close.

_____ **8.** A valve that functions to change service brake application pressure by reducing service brake application relative to signal pressure from the foot valve.

_____ **9.** A brake valve with two air inlets and one air outlet. Only the higher inlet pressure will leave the single valve outlet.

_____ **10.** A valve with the purpose to protect the air reservoirs and other air system storage units from completely draining if a leak occurs downstream of one reservoir.

Multiple Choice

Read each item carefully, and then select the best response.

_____ **1.** The _____ supplies pressure to the rear brakes and the trailer air brakes.
   A. primary circuit
   B. hydraulic circuit
   C. secondary circuit
   D. Synflex system

_____ **2.** Primary brake circuits commonly use _____ color coded air lines.
   A. green
   B. yellow
   C. red
   D. blue

_____ **3.** The _____ holds the truck/trailer or tractor stationary when parked.
   A. park brake circuit
   B. secondary circuit
   C. emergency brake circuit
   D. Either A or C

_____ **4.** High air temperatures from the air compressor discharge port are lowered by using _____ tubing to connect the compressor with an air dryer or air reservoir.
   A. anodized aluminum
   B. Synflex
   C. annealed copper
   D. brass

_____ **5.** The supply tank, also called the _____, is the first reservoir receiving air from the compressor.
   A. service reservoir
   B. uploader tank
   C. wet tank
   D. Either A or C

_____ **6.** A(n) _____ located in the compressor intake port will limit air pressure to approximately 10 psi (69 kPa) if supplied with turbocharged air.
   A. inlet pressure regulating valve
   B. unloader valve
   C. turbocharger cut-off valve
   D. governor

_____ **7.** When the compressor unloads, the dryer _____ opens and causes the trapped air volume in the dryer to blast out the bottom of the dryer.
   A. exhaust valve
   B. purge valve
   C. drain valve
   D. pressure protection valve

_____ **8.** The Bendix _____ integrates the spin-on desiccant cartridge, turbocharger cut-off valve, governor, and four pressure-protection valves together into a single component.
   A. dryer integrated module
   B. electronic air control system
   C. air dryer integrated system
   D. purge pack module

_____ **9.** An air _____ uses the small volume of air from the foot valve delivery port to switch a larger volume of air supplied by the reservoir tanks.
   A. solenoid
   B. relay valve
   C. condenser
   D. booster

_____ **10.** The term _____ refers to the signal pressure required by the relay valve to begin supplying air to the brake chambers.
   A. crack pressure
   B. treadle pressure
   C. release pressure
   D. snub pressure

True/False

If you believe the statement to be more true than false, write the letter "T" in the space provided. If you believe the statement to be more false than true, write the letter "F".

_____ **1.** Air pressure is a more efficient method for braking a loaded heavy-duty vehicle than using hydraulic fluid.

_____ **2.** Air systems operate at higher pressures than hydraulic systems.

_____ **3.** The limiting factor to a compressor's size is its expected duty cycle.

_____ **4.** Any abnormal change to system cut-in or cut-out pressure can be corrected by adjusting the set screw settings on the governor.

_____ **5.** Turbocharger cut-off valves are located in either the air compressor or internal to the air dryer.

_____ **6.** Air dryers are like an in-line filtration system used to remove air contaminants passed by the air compressor.

_____ **7.** The PBS injection booster distributes air to the brake chambers and controls the air pressure supplied for braking.

_____ **8.** Foot valves are self-balancing or pressure-balanced devices.

_____ **9.** The pressure-compensating relay valves ensure air pressure from the delivery ports is proportional only to pedal travel.

_____ **10.** Trailer swing-out occurs when the tractor's drive axle brakes have higher braking force than the trailer axles.

_____ **11.** If a pneumatic imbalance exists, the brake linings on some axles will wear faster than others.

_____ **12.** The bobtailing proportioning relay valve is a type of double check valve that has two supply ports and one delivery port.

_____ **13.** Without a quick-release valve or a quick-release function built into the relay valves, air would need to flow back to the foot valve or park brake valve to vent from the brake chambers.

_____ **14.** The label "inversion valve" is given to any normally closed valve that requires air pressure to open.

_____ **15.** The trailer control valve is primarily used for parking.

Fill in the Blank

Read each item carefully, and then complete the statement by filling in the missing word(s).

1. In heavy-duty combination vehicles, _____ is used to transmit pressure and multiply the force of a driver's leg during brake application.

2. Brake _____ creates a delay between driver application and brake actuation because the speed of air pressure transmission is much slower.

3. An engine-driven air _____ is the source of power for the air brake system.

4. The _____ controls air system pressure by stopping and starting compressor loading.

5. Pistons that control intake valve operations are called _____ valves.

6. Each reservoir must be equipped with a _____ valve to remove water and oil that may contaminate supply system air.

7. The dryer _____ is made up of tiny silica beads that are a tough granular material capable of adsorbing water and oil into their surface.

8. The _____ _____ _____ system is designed to help manufacturers meet the 2016 Greenhouse Gas Emission Standards by optimizing when the air compressor engages and disengages.

9. The treadle valve, commonly known as the _____ valve, can be either floor mounted or suspended to the firewall or bulkhead of the cab.

10. Without _____ _____, some brakes will work harder than others and brakes on an axle can lock up, leading to vehicle instability during braking, brake fade, and brake fires.

11. Testing done by University of Michigan Transportation Research Institute recommends that _____ braking should be the braking technique used when downhill braking.

12. The air couplers attached to the trailer hoses connecting the tractor and trailer air systems are called _____ because they resemble a pair of hands during a handshake when coupled.

13. The red octagonal-shaped _____ _____ valve is used to control the tractor protection system and route air from the secondary brake reservoir to the trailer brake reservoir.

14. The primary function of tractor _____ valves is to prevent a rapid loss of air from the tractor during a trailer breakaway condition or when either the tractor or trailer develops a severe air leak.

15. Trailers with _____ brake priority fill the trailer air reservoir before filling the separate spring brake chambers.

Labeling

Label the following diagrams with the correct terms.

1. Identify the components of the air supply charging system:

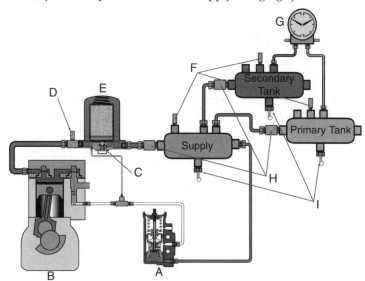

A. _____

B. _____

C. _____

D. _____

E. _____

F. _____

G. _____

H. _____

I. _____

2. Identify the components of a reservoir safety valve:

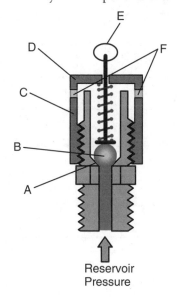

A. _____

B. _____

C. _____

D. _____

E. _____

F. _____

3. Identify the components of an air dryer:

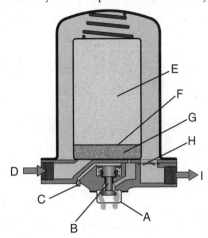

A. _____

B. _____

C. _____

D. _____

E. _____

F. _____

G. _____

H. _____

I. _____

4. Identify the components of a foot (treadle) valve:

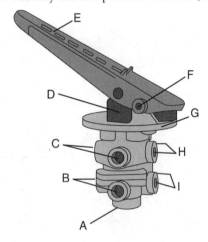

A. _____

B. _____

C. _____

D. _____

E. _____

F. _____

G. _____

H. _____

I. _____

Crossword Puzzle

Use the clues in the column to complete the puzzle.

Across

3. A tractor traveling without a trailer.

5. A process in which material collects on the surface and the air dryer adsorbs moisture from the air and then discharges it in the purge cycle.

6. An air control valve that regulates the air system cut-in and cut-out pressure.

Down

1. A reinforced nylon material used to make flexible airlines.

2. A condition caused by incorrect pneumatic balance between a tractor and trailer.

4. The state of the air compressor when it is building system air pressure.

ASE-Type Questions

Read each item carefully, and then select the best response.

_____ 1. Technician A says that an air brake system consists of a supply system, a delivery system, and an emergency park brake system. Technician B says that air brake systems have been used on road vehicles for more than 100 years. Who is correct?
   A. Technician A
   B. Technician B
   C. Both Technician A and Technician B
   D. Neither Technician A nor Technician B

_____ 2. Technician A says that today's truck air brake systems will usually have two reservoirs: a primary and a secondary. Technician B says that all truck air brake systems today will use an air dryer to remove moisture. Who is correct?
   A. Technician A
   B. Technician B
   C. Both Technician A and Technician B
   D. Neither Technician A nor Technician B

_____ 3. Technician A says that the primary and secondary reservoirs are used so the system can be divided into two brake circuits: one supplying the front brakes and the other supplying the rear brake. Technician B says the primary reservoir normally delivers to the front brakes and the secondary reservoir delivers to the rear brakes. Who is correct?
   A. Technician A
   B. Technician B
   C. Both Technician A and Technician B
   D. Neither Technician A nor Technician B

_____ 4. Technician A says that the primary reservoir provides the air pressure to apply the parking brakes on an air brake system. Technician B says that a trailer can be supplied with air by either the primary or secondary reservoir. Who is correct?
   A. Technician A
   B. Technician B
   C. Both Technician A and Technician B
   D. Neither Technician A nor Technician B

_____ 5. Technician A says that air from the treadle valve is used to apply the rear brake chambers. Technician B says air from the treadle valve is used to apply the front brake chambers.
   A. Technician A
   B. Technician B
   C. Both Technician A and Technician B
   D. Neither Technician A nor Technician B

_____ 6. Technician A says that double check valves are used in the air brake system so that the reservoir with the higher pressure will supply a circuit. Technician B says that the tractor protection valve will close if there is a sudden full air loss in the trailer supply line. Who is correct?
   A. Technician A
   B. Technician B
   C. Both Technician A and Technician B
   D. Neither Technician A nor Technician B

_____ 7. Technician A says that air dryer desiccant absorbs water from the air. Technician B says when the air dryer purges, extremely dry air rushes over the desiccant to flush the water from its surface. Who is correct?
   A. Technician A
   B. Technician B
   C. Both Technician A and Technician B
   D. Neither Technician A nor Technician B

_____ **8.** Technician A says that the air dryer purge cycle can last up to 30 seconds. Technician B says that most of the air expelled during the dryer purge exits the dryer in a couple of seconds. Who is correct?

    A. Technician A

    B. Technician B

    C. Both Technician A and Technician B

    D. Neither Technician A nor Technician B

_____ **9.** Technician A says that two dash gauges are used to indicate system air pressure. Technician B says that the low air warning system usually activates at approximately 65 psi (448 kPa). Who is correct?

    A. Technician A

    B. Technician B

    C. Both Technician A and Technician B

    D. Neither Technician A nor Technician B

_____ **10.** Technician A says that quick release valves are used on the front and rear brakes to speed up the exhaust of actuation air from the chambers. Technician B says that relay valves are used on the rear brake system to speed up brake application. Who is correct?

    A. Technician A

    B. Technician B

    C. Both Technician A and Technician B

    D. Neither Technician A nor Technician B

Servicing Air Brake Systems

Tire Tread:
© AbleStock

Chapter Review

The following activities have been designed to help you refresh your knowledge of this chapter. Your instructor may require you to complete some or all of these activities as a regular part of your training program. You are encouraged to complete any activity that your instructor does not assign as a way to enhance your learning.

Matching

Match the following terms with the correct description or example.

A. Brake balance

B. Brake pull (brake steer)

C. Brake timing imbalance

D. Pneumatic balance

E. Soft (slack) brakes

_____ **1.** An unintended left or right direction change by a vehicle during a brake application.

_____ **2.** The ability of the braking system to apply the correct amount of braking torque to each wheel end at the correct time.

_____ **3.** The correct timing of brake application air pressure to each vehicle axle at the correct pressure.

_____ **4.** A situation in which the brakes are applied but the vehicle is not slowing or stopping effectively.

_____ **5.** A situation in which some brakes receive air faster than others.

Multiple Choice

Read each item carefully, and then select the best response.

_____ **1.** The latest types of brake lining may be manufactured using any of the following ingredients, *except*:

    A. mineral wool

    B. asbestos fibers

    C. aramid fibers

    D. brass

_____ **2.** Which of the following conditions causes soft braking?

    A. Worn foundation components

    B. Glazing

    C. Incorrect slack adjuster length

    D. All of the above

_____ **3.** A squealing noise heard when applying brake pressure would be caused by _____.

    A. glazing

    B. dislocated brake parts

    C. foreign material embedded in friction material

    D. Any of the above

_____ **4.** The acceptable level of air leakage in 2 minutes from either the primary or secondary supply reservoir of a tractor/trailer combination vehicle is _____.

    A. 2 psi

    B. 4 psi

    C. 6 psi

    D. 8 psi

_____ **5.** If more than one oil unit of water or a cloudy oil water emulsion is drained from the reservoir tanks during a Bendix Air System Inspection Cup test you should _____.
   A. replace the air drier desiccant
   B. replace the air compressor
   C. perform an air leakage test of the entire air system
   D. Both A and C

_____ **6.** The recommended procedure to check for proper brake stroke adjustment is _____.
   A. slack stroke measurement
   B. applied stroke measurement
   C. the use of stroke indicators
   D. free stroke measurement

_____ **7.** To test for the proper operation of the automatic emergency brake system you would perform a _____.
   A. chuff test
   B. dual circuit integrity test
   C. air brake pressure balance test
   D. gladhand test

_____ **8.** A common cause of torque imbalance is _____.
   A. oversized drums and thin rotors
   B. glazed friction material
   C. improperly installed automatic slacks
   D. All of the above

_____ **9.** Unbalanced brake pressures are typically caused by _____.
   A. malfunctioning relay valves
   B. improper brake adjustment
   C. a broken brake shoe
   D. All of the above

_____ **10.** Frequent dryer purging accompanied by compressor unloading could be caused by _____.
   A. worn or malfunctioning air compressor
   B. cracked cylinder head
   C. excessive air system leakage
   D. governor malfunction

_____ **11.** Yellow nylon tubing would indicate that the air line is part of the _____ air circuit.
   A. primary
   B. parking brake
   C. secondary
   D. suspension

_____ **12.** Drum wear is measured using a(n) _____.
   A. inside bore gauge
   B. steel ruler
   C. drum micrometer
   D. Either A or C

_____ **13.** A blue tint on the inside of the brake drum is usually caused by _____.
   A. dirt or contaminants in the brake system
   B. eccentric drum wear
   C. extremely high temperatures
   D. linings worn down to the rivets

_____ **14.** Camshafts and bushings should be inspected for _____ free play.
   A. axial
   B. linear
   C. radial
   D. Both A and C

_____ **15.** When the slack allows _____ of brake stroke, the brakes must be adjusted.
   A. ¼" (0.64 cm)
   B. ½" (1.27 cm)
   C. 1" (2.54 cm)
   D. 2" (5.08 cm)

True/False

If you believe the statement to be more true than false, write the letter "T" in the space provided. If you believe the statement to be more false than true, write the letter "F".

_____ **1.** Spring brakes contain power (a spring) that can easily maim or kill someone if released from a brake chamber.

_____ **2.** Before beginning an FMVSS 121 Dual Air Brake System Test, you must first fill the air supply reservoirs to 120 psi.

_____ **3.** All air leaks can be detected using soapy water or easily listening for telltale hissing.

_____ **4.** The air dryer is responsible for removing oil passed into the air supply by the compressor.

_____ **5.** Stroke travel indicates whether the brakes are properly adjusted to obtain optimal drum-shoe clearance.

_____ **6.** When replacing a spring brake actuator, the pushrod should protrude into the clevis yoke at least ½" (1.27 cm).

_____ **7.** Identification of a defective modulator valve can easily be pinpointed by the absence of a sound or an unusual noise made by the valve.

_____ **8.** A duplex gauge can measure air pressure supplied to the trailer as well as the time it takes to build and release air pressure in the service line.

_____ **9.** A tractor valve may have a crack pressure as high as 15 psi while trailers typically use valves between 1 and 4 psi.

_____ **10.** If the governor is malfunctioning, the cut-out pressure should be adjusted based on the manufacturer's specifications.

_____ **11.** Purging is identified by the sudden exhaust of air draining from the dryer.

_____ **12.** Complaints such as slow brake application or slow brake release can indicate an air line is kinked, restricted, or clogged.

_____ **13.** Brake drum corrosion, scoring, or cracking is best removed by machining the drum to its maximum diameter.

_____ **14.** Replacement or relining of brake shoes is required when lining thickness at the center of the shoe has reached 5/16" (0.79 cm).

_____ **15.** Electronic pad wear indicators measure brake pad wear electronically and send CAN signals to the driver when wear occurs.

Fill in the Blank

Read each item carefully, and then complete the statement by filling in the missing word(s).

1. The National Institute of Occupational Safety and Health recommends technicians wear an N-95 disposable _____ _____ when working around brake dust.

2. Complaints about smell are typically related to _____ brake lining.

3. Conducting _____ tests will help eliminate potential problem areas and help the technician arrive at an accurate diagnosis of the problem.

4. Measuring the pushrod stroke length using a lever to move the slack adjuster is called _____ stroke measurement.

5. Removing the spring brake actuator will require _____ the power spring.

6. The purpose of measuring air brake pressure between different axles is to verify correct pneumatic brake _____ of the brake system.

7. If a _____ imbalance exists, the linings at some of the wheel ends will wear faster than others.

8. Pneumatic imbalance is measured with a _____ gauge.

9. The copper line at the compressor end is _____ to prevent cracking due to vibration and thermal cycling.

10. The pressure at which the governor loads is called the governor _____-_____ pressure.

11. The _____ injection system sends methanol into the air system to prevent moisture from freezing in the system.

12. When the linings and/or brake camshafts are worn enough to allow the cam to rotate past the rollers a _____-_____ condition may occur.

13. New or "green" brakes require a break-in procedure called _____ .

14. Automatic _____ adjusters have an internal adjusting mechanism to monitor and maintain the proper clearance between the brake linings and drum.

15. Maintaining air _____ brakes involves inspecting brake pads, rotor surfaces, and running clearance.

Skill Drills

Test your knowledge of skill drills by filling in the correct words in the photo captions.

1. Measuring Brake Stroke Length with Applied Stroke Measurement:

Step 1:   Using the _____ _____ as a guide, adjust the air system pressure to between _____ and _____ psi.

Step 2:   Make a full _____ _____ application. While holding the applied brake pressure, _____ and _____ the distance from the brake chamber _____ to the center of the pushrod _____ _____.

Step 3:   Subtract the measured _____ _____ stroke distance from the _____ stroke and record. _____ your findings to the actuator stroke table (Table 31-2, page 985). _____ at all wheel locations. On trailers, use the _____ or _____ valve to apply the service brakes to measure _____ angle.

2. Inspecting and Testing the Brake Application (Foot) Valve, Fittings and Mounts; Adjusting or Replacing as Needed:

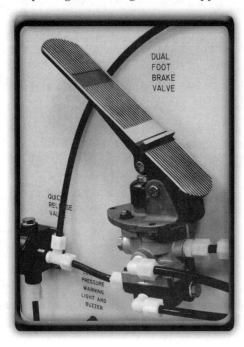

Step 1: Locate and follow the appropriate procedure in the _____ _____.

Step 2: Complete the accompanying _____ _____ or _____ _____ with all pertinent information.

Step 3: Move vehicle into the shop, apply the _____ _____, and _____ the vehicle wheels.

Step 4: Check and inspect _____ _____ operation as follows.
   • Connect test gauges to the _____ and _____ delivery ports on the _____ _____.
   • Release _____ _____ and start the _____ and build air pressure to _____ psi (830 kPa).
   • Depress the _____ to several different positions; check the _____ on the test gauges to ensure that it _____ equally and proportionately with the movement of the _____ _____.
   • Fully depress the brake pedal, then _____ it. The reading on the test gauges should promptly fall to _____.
   • Make and _____ a pressure application of _____ psi (550 kPa) and check the valve for _____.
   • Coat the _____ _____ and _____ of the valve with a _____ solution, and check for leakage. The leakage permitted is a _____ every _____ seconds.

Step 5: If the _____ _____ does not function as described above, or if _____ is excessive, _____ as follows.
   • Drain all of the _____ _____.
   • Mark the brake valve air _____ and _____ lines for assembly _____.
   • Disconnect the air lines from the _____ _____, and _____ them to keep out _____.
   • Remove _____ from the mounting bracket.
   • Remove the _____ _____ from mounting bracket.
   • Note the locations and positions of the _____ _____ valves and _____, then remove them from the brake valve. Clean _____ and old _____ from the _____.
   • Make sure to _____ the old valve with the _____ new one.
   • Apply a small quantity of _____ _____ to the male _____ of each of the double check valves and the _____.
   • Install the _____ _____ valves and _____ in the _____ of the brake valves. Attach the brake valve and mounting bracket to the _____ _____.
   • Clean _____, _____, and other foreign material from the _____ of the _____ _____.
   • Using a light oil, _____ the _____ _____ roller and roller _____.
   • Install brake pedal; _____ the pedal as needed to _____ the _____ in the brake pedal and the _____ _____.
   • Connect the _____ _____ as previously marked. Tighten the nuts _____-tight. Using a _____, further tighten the nuts.

Step 6:   Start engine, _____ up the _____ system, inspect for air _____ and check brake _____.

Step 7:   List the test _____ and/or recommendations on the _____ _____ or work order and _____ work area and return _____ and _____ to proper storage.

3. Inspecting and Testing the Trailer Brake Control Valve (Hand Valve); Replacing as Needed:

Step 1:   Locate and _____ the appropriate _____ in the service manual.

Step 2:   Complete the accompanying _____ _____ or _____ _____ with all pertinent information.

Step 3:   Move vehicle into the shop, apply the _____ _____, _____ the vehicle wheels, and release the _____ _____.

Step 4:   Connect the test gauge to the _____ port of the _____ _____, or connect the gauge to the _____ _____ coupling located behind the _____. When the gauge is connected to the service hose coupling, install a _____ hose coupling on the _____ (emergency) hose coupling, and place the _____ _____ in the _____ charging position.

Step 5:   Move the _____ of the _____ valve to the fully _____ position. The test gauge should register _____ reservoir pressure.

Step 6:   Upon _____ release, the gauge should immediately register _____.

Step 7:   Locate the exhaust _____ or exhaust _____ and apply a _____ solution.

Step 8:   With the valve in the _____ position, _____ leakage should not exceed _____ bubble in _____ seconds.

Step 9:   With the valve _____ _____, leakage at the _____ should not exceed one _____ in 5 _____.

Step 10: If the _____ does not function properly or if leakage is _____, replace the _____ _____. Caution: Open the air reservoir _____ _____ to _____ air from the system _____ removing any lines.

Step 11: To replace the _____, remove _____ _____ if needed.

Step 12: Mark the _____ air lines and _____ the air lines from the _____.

Step 13: Loosen the _____ that holds the hand valve _____ _____ to the steering column and remove _____ from the steering column by _____ the bracket out of the clamp.

Step 14: Remove the _____ _____ from the _____ by removing the _____ Phillips _____.

Step 15: Remove _____ fitting from _____ valve and install in _____ valve.

Step 16: Install the mounting bracket on the new _____ _____ and securely tighten the three _____.

Step 17: Slide the mounting bracket through the _____ on the _____ _____. Position the _____ on the steering column and _____ the clamp firmly.

Step 18: Using the reference _____ made during removal, attach the _____ _____ to the _____ _____ and tighten the lines firmly using two _____.

Step 19: Install _____ _____ if removed.

Step 20: Retest new _____ _____ using the _____ _____.

Step 21: Set parking _____ and remove _____ _____.

Step 22: List the _____ _____ and/or recommendations on the _____ _____ or _____ and _____ work area and return _____ and _____ to proper storage.

4. Installing Brake Shoes:

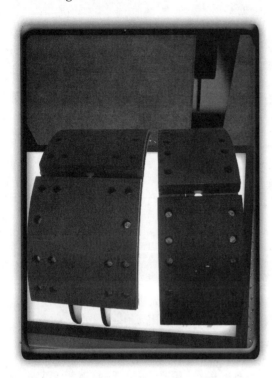

Step 1: Install the _____ _____ into the _____ centering the _____ in the _____. Use never-seize _____ when installing the _____ _____.

Step 2: Install _____ new brake shoe retaining _____ in the _____ _____ end of the _____.

Step 3: Place the _____ shoe onto the _____ _____. The opposite end of the shoe rests against the _____-_____. Swing the _____ shoe, with _____ _____ attached onto the anchor pin then continue swinging the shoe toward the S-cam. Return spring _____ should hold the shoes in this position.

Step 4: Connect the _____ of the larger brake shoe return spring onto the _____ spring pin at the _____ end of the _____ shoe. While _____ the shoes against the S-cam, connect the other end of the _____ to the return spring _____ of the other _____.

Step 5: Using a _____ _____ inserted between the _____ end of one of the _____ _____ and the _____, pry the shoe from the cam until the brake shoe _____ and _____ can be installed between the S-cam and the _____ in the _____ of the brake shoe. Duplicate the procedure on the other _____. The _____ ends connecting with the _____ require never-seize lubricant.

Step 6: Turn the _____ adjuster adjusting screw until the brake chamber pushrod yoke _____ _____ aligns with the correct _____ in the slack's _____. The clevis pin should be _____ with never-seize compound and a new _____ pin installed. The cam rollers should be in _____ position on the S-cam.

Step 7: The brake _____ and _____ can now be installed and _____ to manufacturer's specifications.

Step 8: While slowly _____ the wheel, the _____ adjuster can be adjusted until a slight amount of _____ is sensed as the shoe and drum _____ becomes smaller. When the _____ _____ are applied, both slack adjusters should move in _____, stopping at identical _____ with the same pushrod _____ _____. The brakes should apply and release simultaneously.

5. Replacing Automatic Slack Adjusters:

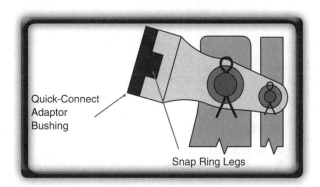

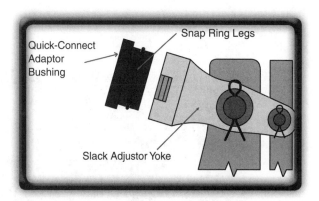

Step 1:   Release the spring brakes. If the brakes are left _____, the spring brake will need to be _____ before removing the _____ _____.

Step 2:   Disconnect the _____ _____ attaching hardware. Most slack adjusters are locked onto the S-camshaft using a removable _____-_____. Disconnect the clevis yoke clevis _____ and the _____ from the chamber _____. If the slack used a quick-connect type _____, it should ideally be replaced with a standard _____ type since quick-connect clevises _____ over time, contribute to longer brake stroke _____ or over stroking.

Step 3:   Remove the slack adjuster from the _____-_____. Slack adjusters that have been on a long time or left unlubricated may be _____ and require a purpose made _____ to remove. Otherwise the slack may require the use of a large _____ or _____ _____ to coax the slack from the _____ on the S-cam.

Step 4:   Inspect other brake _____ components. Remove the _____ _____ if equipped to check the _____ of the brake foundation assembly. There should be adequate brake _____. The S-cam should not have excessive _____ due to worn _____. The brake _____ should also be inspected for cracks, leaks, proper _____, and _____ pushrods.

Slack Adjuster Arm Length	"A" Std Quick Connector or Easy-ON Adaptor	"A" Extended Easy-ON Adaptor
5"	1 15/16" – 3 1/32"	2 7/16" – 3 17/32"
5 1/2"	1 15/16" – 3 3/16"	2 7/16" – 3 11/16"
6"	1 3/16" – 3 1/16"	2 11/16" – 3 11/16"

Step 5: Choose the _____ parts. Models, types, and brands of slack adjusters should never be _____ on the same _____ since it can lead to variations in brake _____ travel and brake _____ imbalance. Replace _____ slack adjusters on an axle if the matching _____ slack cannot be found. Some slack adjusters are made specifically for _____ or _____ side of vehicle applications, provide _____ for axle parts.

Step 6: Before mounting the slack adjuster on the _____, confirm that the brake chamber _____ length allows a _____-degree angle between the slack adjuster and _____ or whether pushrod _____ or _____ is required. To perform this check, follow one of the following two methods:

Method 1:
- Place carpenter's _____ so that one edge is _____ to the _____ pushrod and the other edge of the _____ passes through the centerline of the _____.
- The hole of the _____ and the _____ leg of square must pass through the _____ of the S-cam. If not, the brake chamber _____ needs _____ or replacement depending on whether it's too _____ or _____.

Method 2:
- Measure the distance from the end of the _____ without the _____ to the edge of the _____ that passes though the camshaft centerline. Determine the distance needed to _____ the yoke. That distance depends on the slack adjuster _____ length—between _____" (12.7 cm) and _____" (15.2 cm)—and requires comparison between the _____ length and the manufacturer's service information for the type of _____ _____ used.

Step 7:   Install the _____ after _____ and _____ the
S-cam with anti-seize compound. Install the
large flat _____ and _____ the slack adjusters
to enable approximately _____" (1.27 mm)
movement of the slack along the _____-_____.

Crossword Puzzle

Use the clues in the column to complete the puzzle.

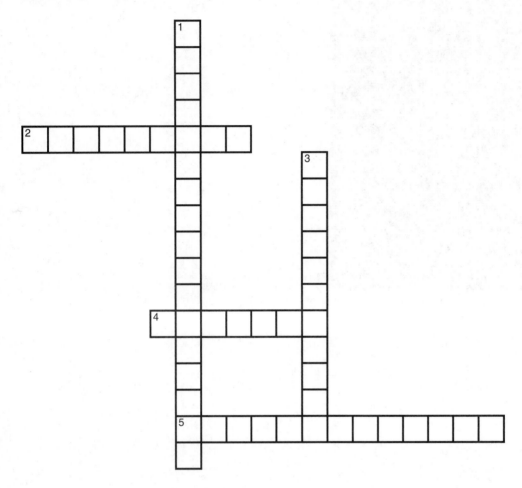

Across

2. A test performed on the anti-lock braking systems that results in air pressure being exhausted from the modulator and making a short chuffing sound.

4. A mirror-like finish produced through continuous braking pressure and pressure between lining and brake drums.

5. A situation in which braking torque is uniform for all wheels.

Down

1. The distance travelled by the brake chamber pushrod.

3. Two air gauges in a single housing.

ASE-Type Questions

Read each item carefully, and then select the best response.

_____ 1. Technician A says that brake balance can be upset by replacing brakes on one wheel end only. Technician B says that brake balance can be upset by replacing the air line with one of a larger size. Who is correct?
   A. Technician A
   B. Technician B
   C. Both Technician A and Technician B
   D. Neither Technician A nor Technician B

_____ 2. Technician A says that brake dust no longer contains asbestos, so we don't have to worry about it as much as in the past. Technician B says that brake dust should be vacuumed off the wheel end with a HEPA filter equipped vacuum cleaner. Who is correct?
   A. Technician A
   B. Technician B
   C. Both Technician A and Technician B
   D. Neither Technician A nor Technician B

_____ 3. Technician A says that a cam-over condition can be caused by a failed automatic slack adjuster. Technician B says that a cam-over condition can cause a seized brake condition where the brakes won't release. Who is correct?
   A. Technician A
   B. Technician B
   C. Both Technician A and Technician B
   D. Neither Technician A nor Technician B

_____ 4. Technician A says that when testing for brake leakage, a single axle vehicle with brakes applied should leak no more than 4 psi (28 kPa) in 2 minutes. Technician B says that the acceptable leakage for a tractor and one trailer combination is no more than 6 psi (41 kPa) in 2 minutes. Who is correct?
   A. Technician A
   B. Technician B
   C. Both Technician A and Technician B
   D. Neither Technician A nor Technician B

_____ 5. Technician A says that all compressors pass some oil to the vehicle air system. Technician B says that oil passing is nothing to worry about, as it helps lubricate the air brake valves. Who is correct?
   A. Technician A
   B. Technician B
   C. Both Technician A and Technician B
   D. Neither Technician A nor Technician B

_____ 6. Technician A says that brake chamber stroke length varies widely and can be as much as 3" (7.6 cm) on some brake chambers. Technician B says chamber stroke length is unimportant as long as the angle between the slack adjuster and the push rod is 90 degrees or more with the brakes applied. Who is correct?
   A. Technician A
   B. Technician B
   C. Both Technician A and Technician B
   D. Neither Technician A nor Technician B

_____ 7. Technician A says that, when looking at the head of an installed S-cam camshaft, if one of the lobes points up on the left-hand side, it is a left-hand camshaft. Technician B says that, when looking at the head of an installed S-cam camshaft, if one of the lobes points down on the right-hand side, then it is a right-hand camshaft. Who is correct?
   A. Technician A
   B. Technician B
   C. Both Technician A and Technician B
   D. Neither Technician A nor Technician B

_____ **8.** Technician A says that, when replacing a spring brake chamber system, air can be used to cage the brake, and then the caging bolt should be installed hand tight. Technician B says that, for safety, the entire system air should be drained before removing the chamber. Who is correct?
  A. Technician A
  B. Technician B
  C. Both Technician A and Technician B
  D. Neither Technician A nor Technician B

_____ **9.** Technician A says that tractor and straight truck relay valves can be interchanged on a vehicle without affecting braking. Technician B says that an elbow installed on a relay valve control port can affect brake timing. Who is correct?
  A. Technician A
  B. Technician B
  C. Both Technician A and Technician B
  D. Neither Technician A nor Technician B

_____ **10.** Technician A says that air system reservoirs should be drained weekly unless they are equipped with automatic drain valves. Technician B says that, if oil drains from the primary or secondary drain valve, it indicates the dryer cartridge needs to be replaced or the compressor is defective. Who is correct?
  A. Technician A
  B. Technician B
  C. Both Technician A and Technician B
  D. Neither Technician A nor Technician B

Anti-Lock Braking, Vehicle Stability, and Collision Avoidance Systems

Chapter Review

The following activities have been designed to help you refresh your knowledge of this chapter. Your instructor may require you to complete some or all of these activities as a regular part of your training program. You are encouraged to complete any activity that your instructor does not assign as a way to enhance your learning.

Matching

Match the following terms with the correct description or example.

A. Differential braking

B. Directional stability control systems

C. Torque limiting

D. Traction control

E. Wheel lock-up

_____ 1. A stability control system that assists the driver in maintaining a vehicle's intended driving path by controlling yaw.

_____ 2. An enhancement to the ABS system that is used to improve vehicle stability when accelerating.

_____ 3. A condition where the drive or steer tires have stopped rotating when braking.

_____ 4. Applying the brakes on an individual slipping wheel to transfer torque to a stationary or slowly turning wheel with traction.

_____ 5. A reduction in engine power out; used as strategy to reduce wheel slip or loss of directional control.

Multiple Choice

Read each item carefully, and then select the best response.

_____ 1. Anti-lock braking systems _____.

A. decrease stopping distances on slippery surfaces

B. enhance steering control during hard braking

C. extend tire life

D. All of the above

_____ 2. According to FMVSS 121, tractors and trailers currently need to remain within a _____ lane under hard braking conditions.

A. 8-foot-wide

B. 10-foot-wide

C. 12-foot-wide

D. 15-foot-wide

_____ 3. The vehicle's _____ collects information from the sensor inputs and processes the information using specialized algorithms.

A. ABS modulator

B. electronic control unit

C. telematics system

D. power line carrier

_____ **4.** Power line carrier technology changes both the frequency and amplitude of the _____ power wire between the trailer and tractor.
   A. #2 black
   B. #4 red
   C. #6 brown
   D. #7 blue

_____ **5.** Wheel speed calculations using an exciter ring with 100 teeth are typically based on a default tire size of _____ revolutions per mile.
   A. 375
   B. 430
   C. 510
   D. 750

_____ **6.** When activated on air brake systems, modulators adjust braking force by taking the air pressure supplied by the foot valve and _____.
   A. holding the supplied brake pressure in the service chambers
   B. releasing or dumping brake pressure supplied to the service chambers
   C. reapplying brake pressure to service chambers after it has been dumped
   D. All of the above

_____ **7.** Since additional auxiliary electrical devices and the current demands of the ABS have increased the total trailer power consumption, the minimum diameter of the ground white wire conductor has increased to _____.
   A. 14 AWG
   B. 12 AWG
   C. 8 AWG
   D. 6 AWG

_____ **8.** ABS configuration is defined by the location and number of _____ used.
   A. wheel sensors
   B. trailer connectors
   C. modulator valves
   D. Both A and C

_____ **9.** A traction control enhancement to the ABS, called _____, uses the ABS system components to improve vehicle stability in situations when excessive drive torque is transmitted to the wheels, causing the tires to slip or lose traction.
   A. electronic stability regulation (ESR)
   B. torque limitation control (TLC)
   C. automatic traction control (ATC)
   D. Either A or C

_____ **10.** A vehicle control system that measures lateral acceleration of a vehicle to minimize the likelihood of a vehicle rollover is called _____.
   A. adaptive yaw control
   B. roll stability control
   C. directional stability control
   D. Either A or C

True/False

If you believe the statement to be more true than false, write the letter "T" in the space provided. If you believe the statement to be more false than true, write the letter "F".

_____ **1.** Anti-lock braking systems (ABS) minimize the loss of control that takes place when tires stop rotating.

_____ **2.** To enhance the effectiveness of the ABS system, drivers should still pump the brake pedal during slippery road conditions.

_____ **3.** The black J-560 trailer connector is used to connect trailers with ABS systems since it supplies a constant power source to the ABS module.

_____ **4.** The wheel speed sensor is a variable reluctance sensor consisting of a permanent magnet wrapped with hundreds of coils of very fine wire.

_____ **5.** When referencing a speed sensor or modulator valve position, the driver's seat is the vehicle's reference point.

_____ **6.** Modulator valves are typically constructed from cast iron and contain two normally closed solenoids.

_____ **7.** After the introduction of ABS, legislation required the #7 blue auxiliary power circuit be dedicated to supply continuous current to the trailer ABS system.

_____ **8.** A blue-colored trailer cord identifies a cord meeting SAE standards for ABS trailer cords with larger diameter conductors and ground pins.

_____ **9.** Adaptive cruise control allows the collision avoidance system to steer a vehicle through a curve without driver input.

_____ **10.** ABS/ATC control modules require a precise rolling circumference ratio between steer axle and drive axle tires in order for ABS and ATC to perform properly.

Fill in the Blank

Read each item carefully, and then complete the statement by filling in the missing word(s).

1. An anti-lock braking system (ABS) can "_____" the brakes on individual wheels (or pairs of wheels) independently, and with greater speed and accuracy than a driver.

2. By opening and closing the supply of air to the brakes, the _____ valves enable independent control of brake pressure at each end of the axle.

3. ABS-equipped vehicles must have a dedicated _____ ABS malfunction indicator lamp.

4. Blink codes, also called _____ codes, are a fault reporting strategy in which a fault indicator light will blink on and off to report a fault code number.

5. The reluctor wheel, also known as the _____ ring, is pressed onto the inner wheel hub or cast into a brake drum.

6. ABS _____ valves are high capacity, on/off air valves that contain a pair of electric solenoids used to control air brake application pressure.

7. The ISO 3731 connector is commonly used in _____ but only occasionally in North America.

8. Automatic _____ regulation improves traction by minimizing wheel spin.

9. Reducing drive torque by reducing engine power, or _____-_____, helps prevent both oversteer and understeer conditions.

10. Collision _____ systems are vehicle stability control systems that detect objects beside and in front of a vehicle that have the potential to collide with the vehicle.

Labeling

Label the following diagrams with the correct terms.

1. Identify the components of a wheel sensor assembly:

A. _____

B. _____

C. _____

D. _____

2. Identify the components of a typical directional stability control system:

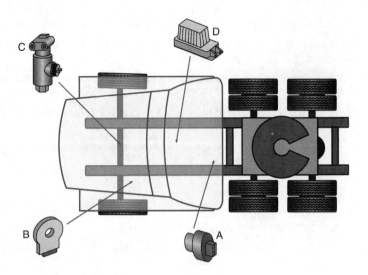

A. _____

B. _____

C. _____

D. _____

SAE J-560 Standards for 7-Pin Tractor/Trailer Electrical Connectors

Match the wire color, gauge, and function to each pin of the SAE J-560 trailer plug.

Color:

A. Yellow

B. Brown

C. White

D. Red

E. Black

F. Blue

G. Green

1. _____ Pin #1

2. _____ Pin #2

3. _____ Pin #3

4. _____ Pin #4

5. _____ Pin #5

6. _____ Pin #6

7. _____ Pin #7

Wire gauge:

A. 12 AWG

B. 10 AWG

C. 8 AWG

8. _____ Pin #1

9. _____ Pin #2

10. _____ Pin #3

11. _____ Pin #4

12. _____ Pin #5

13. _____ Pin #6

14. _____ Pin #7

Function:

A. Clearance, marker, and ID

B. Stop

C. Ground

D. Auxiliary and ABS

E. Tail

F. Left turn

G. Right turn

15. _____ Pin #1

16. _____ Pin #2

17. _____ Pin #3

18. _____ Pin #4

19. _____ Pin #5

20. _____ Pin #6

21. _____ Pin #7

Crossword Puzzle

Use the clues in the column to complete the puzzle.

Across

3. A condition when the drive axles of a vehicle push the rear of a vehicle and steering control is lost. Also called power jackknifing.

5. The toothed wheel mounted on the wheel hub, which is used by the wheel speed sensor to generate wheel speed data. Also called the exciter ring.

Down

1. An electrically operated ABS air control valve used to modulate the air pressure supplied to service brake chambers.

2. A vehicle rollover condition occurring when a truck strikes a curb and then rolls down an embankment.

4. The rotation of a vehicle around its vertical axis; the difference between the vehicle's intended direction and the actual direction of travel.

ASE-Type Questions

Read each item carefully, and then select the best response.

_____ 1. Technician A says that the ABS system only exhausts air pressure from a selected brake chamber when the wheel is about to lock-up or has locked-up. Technician B says that the modulator valve can exhaust, hold, and rebuild air pressure in a service chamber when the wheels are approaching lock-up or have locked-up. Who is correct?

 A. Technician A
 B. Technician B
 C. Both Technician A and Technician B
 D. Neither Technician A nor Technician B

_____ 2. Technician A says that a modulator code fault could be caused by a defective solenoid inside the valve. Technician B says a modulator fault code can be caused by a misadjusted slack adjuster. Who is correct?

 A. Technician A
 B. Technician B
 C. Both Technician A and Technician B
 D. Neither Technician A nor Technician B

_____ 3. Technician A says that an ABS trailer electrical cord is color coded green. Technician B says that trailer electrical cords are different only as to the wire size of the conductors. Who is correct?

 A. Technician A
 B. Technician B
 C. Both Technician A and Technician B
 D. Neither Technician A nor Technician B

_____ 4. Technician A says that anti-lock braking systems improve vehicle control even though they increase stopping distance. Technician B says that, in today's vehicles, anti-lock braking systems usually incorporate some kind of traction control. Who is correct?

 A. Technician A
 B. Technician B
 C. Both Technician A and Technician B
 D. Neither Technician A nor Technician B

_____ 5. Technician A says that wheel speed sensors are usually Hall-effect sensors. Technician B says that wheel speed sensors create a digital signal. Who is correct?

 A. Technician A
 B. Technician B
 C. Both Technician A and Technician B
 D. Neither Technician A nor Technician B

_____ 6. Technician A says that ABS systems are regulated under FMVSS 121. Technician B says that every axle of a tractor trailer system must have ABS. Who is correct?

 A. Technician A
 B. Technician B
 C. Both Technician A and Technician B
 D. Neither Technician A nor Technician B

_____ 7. Technician A says that ABS systems must have a red warning lamp on the dash that lights up when an ABS system malfunction occurs. Technician B says the ABS warning lamp must come on for a few seconds when the key is switched on and then go out if the system is functioning correctly. Who is correct?

 A. Technician A
 B. Technician B
 C. Both Technician A and Technician B
 D. Neither Technician A nor Technician B

_____ 8. Technician A says that, since March 2001, vehicles that tow ABS equipped trailers must show a trailer ABS malfunction on a dash indicator light. Technician B says that trailer ABS systems communicate with the tractor by using power line carrier technology. Who is correct?

 A. Technician A
 B. Technician B
 C. Both Technician A and Technician B
 D. Neither Technician A nor Technician B

_____ **9.** Technician A says that tractor ABS modulator valve solenoids are cycled when the ignition is first turned on. Technician B says that applying the brake pedal and then switching the ignition on allows the operator to check that the solenoids are exhausting air as they should. Who is correct?
  A. Technician A
  B. Technician B
  C. Both Technician A and Technician B
  D. Neither Technician A nor Technician B

_____ **10.** Technician A says that blink codes must always be used to check for ABS system malfunctions. Technician B says that ABS wheel sensor air gap is set by loosening a lock nut and then adjusting the gap. Who is correct?
  A. Technician A
  B. Technician B
  C. Both Technician A and Technician B
  D. Neither Technician A nor Technician B

Fundamentals of Hydraulic and Air-Over-Hydraulic Braking Systems

Chapter Review

The following activities have been designed to help you refresh your knowledge of this chapter. Your instructor may require you to complete some or all of these activities as a regular part of your training program. You are encouraged to complete any activity that your instructor does not assign as a way to enhance your learning.

Matching

Match the following terms with the correct description or example.

A. Backing plate
B. Brake drum
C. Caliper
D. Rotor
E. Servo action

_____ **1.** A drum brake design where one brake shoe, when activated, applies an increased activating force to the other brake shoe, in proportion to the initial activating force.

_____ **2.** A hydraulic device that uses pressure from the master cylinder to apply the brake pads against the rotor.

_____ **3.** The main rotating part of a disc brake system.

_____ **4.** A short, wide, hollow cylinder that is capped on one end and bolted to a vehicle's wheel; it has an inner friction surface that the brake shoe is forced against.

_____ **5.** A metal plate to which the brake lining is fixed.

Multiple Choice

Read each item carefully, and then select the best response.

_____ **1.** The basic hydraulic braking system is augmented by a _____ system.
   A. vacuum booster
   B. hydroelectric booster
   C. hydroboost
   D. Either A or C

_____ **2.** A _____ system uses one master cylinder section to pressurize the front caliper pistons and the other section to pressurize the rear caliper pistons.
   A. front/rear split
   B. leading/trailing split
   C. left/right split
   D. Either A or C

_____ **3.** Disc brakes stop the wheel by _____ forcing friction material against both sides of the brake disc.
   A. mechanically
   B. pneumatically
   C. electromagnetically
   D. Any of the above

_____ **4.** The _____ converts non-hydraulic pressure from a driver's application of the brake pedal into hydraulic pressure.
- **A.** caliper
- **B.** wheel cylinder
- **C.** master cylinder
- **D.** power booster

_____ **5.** In a _____ split brake configuration, one circuit controls the right front brake and the left rear brake, and the other circuit controls the left front brake and the right rear brake.
- **A.** longitudinal
- **B.** diagonal
- **C.** horizontally
- **D.** crosswise

_____ **6.** Located in each wheel usually at the top, above the shoes, the _____ exerts force onto the shoes so they can contact the drum and stop the vehicle with friction.
- **A.** slave cylinder
- **B.** secondary piston
- **C.** wheel cylinder
- **D.** proportioning valve

_____ **7.** The _____ is used to hold off the application of the front brakes on vehicles with disc brakes on the front wheels and drum brakes on the rear wheels.
- **A.** metering valve
- **B.** proportioning valve
- **C.** pressure differential valve
- **D.** servo

_____ **8.** The _____ uses a differential in pressure principle to assist the driver by increasing the braking force applied to the brake master cylinder.
- **A.** hydroboost
- **B.** air booster
- **C.** vacuum booster
- **D.** pressure differential valve

_____ **9.** A(n) _____ converts the control line air pressure from the foot brake valve into hydraulic pressure to operate the wheel cylinders or calipers and apply the brakes.
- **A.** combination booster
- **B.** air booster
- **C.** diaphragm booster
- **D.** vacuum booster

_____ **10.** Of the different types of hydraulic ABS formats, the _____ ABS is the most commonly found today.
- **A.** single-channel
- **B.** two-channel
- **C.** three-channel
- **D.** four-channel

True/False

If you believe the statement to be more true than false, write the letter "T" in the space provided. If you believe the statement to be more false than true, write the letter "F".

_____ **1.** Air-over-hydraulic braking systems use an air compressor to provide power assistance over the hydraulic components to the braking system.

_____ **2.** A leading/trailing shoe drum brake arrangement is more powerful than a twin-leading-shoe drum brake configuration.

_____ **3.** The self-servo effect arises in the two-leading brake shoe arrangement because the leading shoes are effectively dragged into the brake drum's friction surface and achieve maximum braking force.

_____ **4.** The wedge-type brake shoe adjuster has become the industry standard and is currently used by most manufacturers.

_____ **5.** Drum brakes are less prone to "brake fade," and recover more quickly from immersion than disc brakes.

_____ **6.** The primary piston is moved directly by the pushrod or the power booster; it generates hydraulic pressure to move the secondary piston.

_____ **7.** If there is a moderate leak anywhere in the system the pressure differential valve will sense the pressure difference between the two separate hydraulic brake circuits and illuminate the brake warning light.

_____ **8.** Air brake systems require some kind of power assist—be it vacuum, hydraulic, or air—to achieve the needed braking force.

_____ **9.** The direct-acting type of air booster is used primarily on heavier trucks.

_____ **10.** Most modern trucks that are equipped with hydraulic braking systems are also equipped with anti-lock braking systems.

Fill in the Blank

Read each item carefully, and then complete the statement by filling in the missing word(s).

1. The hydraulic brake system is usually filled with a glycol-ether-based _____ _____.

2. The leading shoe when the vehicle is traveling forward becomes the _____ shoe when the vehicle is moving in reverse.

3. The _____ adjusting screw consists of a threaded bolt and two nuts marked either "L" or "R."

4. A disc brake slows rotation of the wheel by the friction caused by pushing brake pads against a brake disc with a set of _____.

5. The mechanically operated _____ brake's primary function is to hold the vehicle in a stationary position when parked.

6. The _____ valve can include the pressure differential valve, metering valve, and proportioning valve(s) in one unit.

7. The _____ system uses pressurized hydraulic fluid to provide brake power assist.

8. All types of boosters have a piston _____ detector to warn the driver if the brakes should be too far out of adjustment or a fault occurs in the hydraulic circuit.

9. All vehicles are required to have a park brake system that can also act as a(n) _____ brake should there be a failure of the service brakes.

10. The ABS electronic _____ _____ contains a powerful computer that controls all the functions of the ABS system.

Labeling

Label the following diagrams with the correct terms.

1. Identify the components of a leading/trailing brake shoe configuration:

A. _____

B. _____

C. _____

D. _____

E. _____

F. _____

2. Identify the components of a tandem master cylinder:

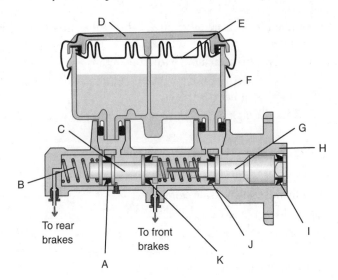

A. _____

B. _____

C. _____

D. _____

E. _____

F. _____

G. _____

H. _____

I. _____

J. _____

K. _____

3. Identify the components of a double-action wheel cylinder:

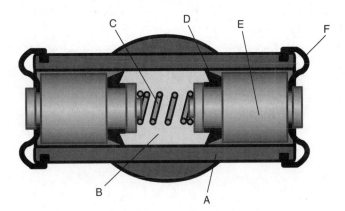

A. _____

B. _____

C. _____

D. _____

E. _____

F. _____

4. Identify the components of a typical vacuum brake booster:

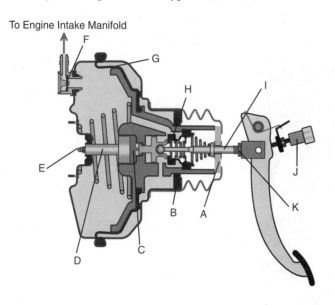

A. _____

B. _____

C. _____

D. _____

E. _____

F. _____

G. _____

H. _____

I. _____

J. _____

K. _____

5. Identify the components of a park brake in the off position:

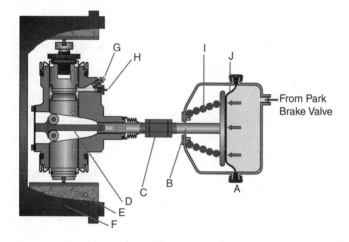

A. _____

B. _____

C. _____

D. _____

E. _____

F. _____

G. _____

H. _____

I. _____

J. _____

Skill Drills

Test your knowledge of skill drills by filling in the correct words in the photo captions.

1. Inspecting Hydraulic and Air-Over-Hydraulic Brake Systems for Fluid Leaks:

Step 1: Two _____ are required to perform these tests: one to _____ the system, the other to _____ the inspection. First, _____ the system for signs of a _____ at the brake component _____ and the brake _____ and see if there is any evidence of a _____ leak.

Step 2: If you find no evidence of a _____, have your co-worker put his or her _____ on the _____ _____ and, with foot pressure applied on the brake pedal, inspect the system and _____ for obvious _____ in and around the _____ _____.

Step 3: With _____ still applied, check the _____ lines and connections at the _____.

Step 4: Inspect all brake _____ and line _____ connections in the hydraulic _____ system for evidence of a _____ or brake _____.

Step 5: If there is _____ _____ near a connection point, perform the following activities:

a. _____ and _____ the entire area.

b. Determine the _____ of the _____.

c. Relieve system _____ (refer to the appropriate maintenance manual for complete instructions).

1. Make the necessary _____.

2. Inspect any _____ for damage and, if no damage is evident, _____ the fittings by referring to the appropriate maintenance manual for _____ specifications.

3. If a _____ has been damaged, _____ the fitting; again, refer to the appropriate maintenance manual for _____ specifications.

4. If any hydraulic system fittings were found _____ or _____ (brake circuit open), _____ the closed circuit after repair; refer to the brake _____ instructions given in the appropriate maintenance manual.

Step 6: After all necessary _____ have been made and the system _____, verify that the _____ circuits are _____ properly.

2. Removing and Replacing a Drum Brake Assembly:

Step 1: Before raising the _____, _____ the other wheels that are not being removed. Loosen the wheel _____/_____ from the wheel end being _____. If the wheel assembly being removed is a _____ _____ assembly, release the _____ (parking) brake and place the transmission into _____.

Step 2: Raise the vehicle and place _____ _____ in the correct location to _____ the vehicle. Remove the already loosened _____ nuts/bolts, and, if necessary, as in the case of _____ _____ arrangements, get help from a co-worker to remove the _____ assembly from the vehicle.

Step 3: With reference to the appropriate manufacturer's workshop _____, remove any _____ nut and/or _____ nuts (if applicable) and remove the _____ _____.

Step 4: Remove the brake _____ and return springs following the _____ outlined in the workshop manual. You need to be _____ removing _____ _____ to ensure the _____ do not come off prematurely, as this could cause both _____ and _____.

Step 5: With the springs _____ from their _____ _____, remove the brake _____ from their location points. Then carry out a _____ _____ of all the components.

Step 6: Reinstall the brake _____ as outlined in the _____ _____, observing all _____ precautions. Make sure that the _____ _____ are correctly _____ and installed.

Step 7: Reinstall the _____ _____ as outlined in the workshop manual. Install the bearing hub and _____ _____. Get a co-worker to assist you in the _____ of the hub assembly and brake drum into its _____ position.

Step 8: Replace the _____ _____ adjusting nut and tighten the _____ bearing to the correct _____ specification. If fitted, fit and torque the _____ nut and securing _____.

Step 9: With a co-worker's help, _____ the _____ assembly and _____ on the nuts/bolts. Torque the wheel _____/_____ to the specified _____ setting as listed in the workshop manual.

Step 10: Follow that correct _____ outlined in the _____ _____ for adjusting the _____.

Step 11: Carry out the _____ adjustment as per the manufacturer's specifications. Make sure that the _____ _____ rotates freely and does not _____ on the _____.

Step 12: Jack up the vehicle and remove the _____ _____. Make sure that there are no _____ left behind, and _____ the vehicle to the _____. Recheck the wheel nuts/bolts _____.

3. Bleeding the Air Out of a Hydraulic Braking System:

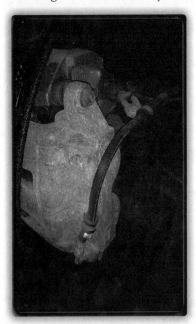

Step 1: Clear communication between _____ and the _____ is required for successful _____.

Step 2: Ask an assistant to slowly _____ the _____ _____ down.

Step 3: Starting with the _____ _____ that is the farthest from the _____ _____, attach a clear bleeder _____ to the bleeder screw and insert the _____ into a clear plastic _____, then open the bleeder screw _____-_____ to _____-_____ turn.

Step 4: Observe any old _____ _____ and _____ _____ coming out of the _____ _____.

Step 5: When the brake fluid stream _____, close the bleeder screw _____ and have the assistant slowly _____ the pedal. This allows the _____ _____ to pull a fresh charge of _____ _____ from the _____.

Step 6: Repeat the previous _____ steps until there are no more _____ _____ coming out of the _____ _____.

Step 7: Close off the bleeder screw and _____ it to the manufacturer's specifications. Be sure that you DO NOT _____ the system so much that the _____ runs dry and admits _____ into the hydraulic braking system.

Step 8: Check the _____ in the master cylinder _____, top it off, and reinstall the reservoir _____.

Step 9: Repeat this procedure for each of the _____ _____ units, moving _____ to the master cylinder, one wheel at a time, until all of the _____ has been removed and the _____ _____ is not _____.

Step 10: Start the _____ and ensure the proper functioning of the _____ with the _____ _____ operational.

4. Testing the Metering or the Proportioning Valves:

Step 1:   Research the testing _____ and _____ in the appropriate service information.

Step 2:   Disconnect the _____ line and _____ line from the _____ valve or _____ valve. Use a _____ _____ wrench to accomplish this.

Step 3:   Connect the valve _____ tester to the _____ port and outlet _____ of the _____ valve or the proportioning _____. Reconnect the inlet _____ to the valve, with the _____ _____ teed into it.

Step 4:   Operate the brake pedal and _____ both pressure gauge _____; _____ the findings to _____.

5. Inspecting, Measuring, Removing, and Reinstalling a Rotor Assembly:

Step 1:   Locate and _____ the appropriate procedure in the _____ _____, and refer to it for steps 2, 11, 13, and 15 if assistance is needed.

Step 2:   Remove _____.

Step 3:   Use a _____-_____ to force the _____ piston(s) back, and inspect the caliper _____ and _____ for _____.

Step 4:   Inspect and measure _____ on vehicle.

Step 5:   Check brake rotor lateral _____ with _____ _____.

Note: Tighten the wheel _____ to zero _____ _____.

Step 6:   Record findings on _____ _____ or _____ _____.

Step 7:   Check _____ _____ to see if _____ specifications are _____.

Step 8:   Loosen wheel _____ nut, and remove _____ _____ assembly.

Step 9:   Clean _____ _____ assembly and _____.

Step 10: Remove _____ from wheel _____. Note: _____ and _____ may be made as _____ unit.

Step 11: Clean and _____ wheel bearings with _____.

Step 12: Install new rotor _____ on _____.

Step 13: Install _____ wheel bearing _____ into hub.

Step 14: Reinstall _____ and _____ assembly back on _____.

Step 15: Adjust _____ _____.

Step 16: Check to make sure hub _____ freely.

Step 17: List the _____ _____ and/or recommendations on the _____ _____ or work order. Clean work area, and return _____ and _____ to proper storage.

Crossword Puzzle

Use the clues in the column to complete the puzzle.

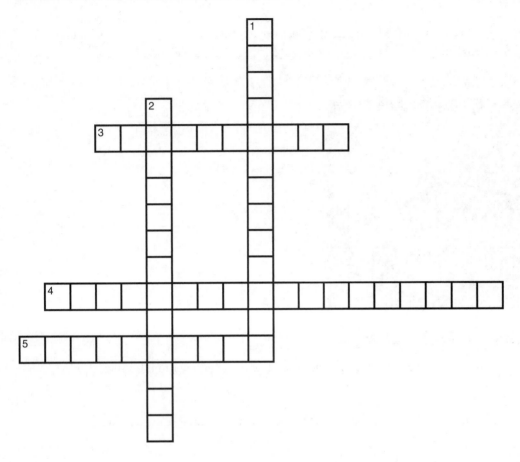

Across

3. Hydraulic fluid that transfers forces under pressure through the hydraulic lines to the wheel braking units.

4. A valve that limits brake application pressure to the rear brakes when the vehicle is not heavily loaded.

5. A steel shoe and brake lining friction material that applies force to the brake drum during braking.

Down

1. Brake shoes installed so that they are applied in the opposite direction to the forward rotation of the brake drum; not self-energizing and less efficient at developing braking force.

2. A vacuum-operated boost system for hydraulic brakes.

ASE-Type Questions

Read each item carefully, and then select the best response.

_____ 1. Technician A says that the drum-to-lining clearance must be maintained at all times. Technician B says that there would be a delay in the brakes applying if there were an excessively large drum-to-lining clearance. Who is correct?
  - **A.** Technician A
  - **B.** Technician B
  - **C.** Both Technician A and Technician B
  - **D.** Neither Technician A nor Technician B

_____ 2. Technician A says that if the drum-to-lining clearance is too tight, the result would be dragging brakes. Technician B says if the drum-to-lining clearance is too tight, the result would be overheated brakes. Who is correct?
  - **A.** Technician A
  - **B.** Technician B
  - **C.** Both Technician A and Technician B
  - **D.** Neither Technician A nor Technician B

_____ 3. Technician A says that when a driver applies the brake—and the primary piston moves forward and covers the compensating port—that this completes the primary circuit. Technician B says that when a driver applies the brake—and the primary piston moves forward and covers the compensating port—that this creates a pressure chamber for the trapped fluid. Who is correct?
  - **A.** Technician A
  - **B.** Technician B
  - **C.** Both Technician A and Technician B
  - **D.** Neither Technician A nor Technician B

_____ 4. Technician A says that the reservoir serves as a storage tank of compressed air for the air brake system. Technician B says that reservoirs may provide a location where air, heated by compression, can be cooled and the water vapor condensed. Who is correct?
  - **A.** Technician A
  - **B.** Technician B
  - **C.** Both Technician A and Technician B
  - **D.** Neither Technician A nor Technician B

_____ 5. Technician A says that brake shoes in a medium- to heavy-duty vehicle can be in a leading and trailing brake shoe configuration. Technician B says that the brake shoes can be in a screw cam operating brake configuration. Who is correct?
  - **A.** Technician A
  - **B.** Technician B
  - **C.** Both Technician A and Technician B
  - **D.** Neither Technician A nor Technician B

_____ 6. Technician A says that you would usually find a cam-operated brake on a light- or medium-duty vehicle. Technician B says that you would usually find a cam-operated brake on a large, heavy vehicle. Who is correct?
  - **A.** Technician A
  - **B.** Technician B
  - **C.** Both Technician A and Technician B
  - **D.** Neither Technician A nor Technician B

_____ 7. Technician A says that compared with drum brakes, disc brakes offer better stopping performance because the disc is more readily cooled. Technician B says that compared with disc brakes, drum brakes offer better stopping performance because the drum is more readily cooled. Who is correct?
  - **A.** Technician A
  - **B.** Technician B
  - **C.** Both Technician A and Technician B
  - **D.** Neither Technician A nor Technician B

_____ **8.** Technician A says that tandem brake systems can be split from front to rear. Technician B says that tandem brake systems can be split diagonally. Who is correct?
  A. Technician A
  B. Technician B
  C. Both Technician A and Technician B
  D. Neither Technician A nor Technician B

_____ **9.** Technician A says that in air-over-hydraulic systems, the primary components are the compressor, brake master cylinder, wheel cylinders, and air actuated brake chambers. Technician B says that the system should be inspected in two ways: foot-pressure applied and by conducting a system test. Who is correct?
  A. Technician A
  B. Technician B
  C. Both Technician A and Technician B
  D. Neither Technician A nor Technician B

_____ **10.** Technician A says that hydraulic brake wheel cylinders are always dual acting. Technician B says that a disc brake caliper must have at least two pistons. Who is correct?
  A. Technician A
  B. Technician B
  C. Both Technician A and Technician B
  D. Neither Technician A nor Technician B

Fifth Wheels and Hitching Devices

Chapter Review

The following activities have been designed to help you refresh your knowledge of this chapter. Your instructor may require you to complete some or all of these activities as a regular part of your training program. You are encouraged to complete any activity that your instructor does not assign as a way to enhance your learning.

Matching

Match the following terms with the correct description or example.

A. Fifth wheel
B. Full trailer
C. Gross combined weight rating
D. Gross trailer weight
E. Gross vehicle weight

F. Gross weight limit
G. Pintle hook
H. Semi-trailer
I. Trailer
J. Vertical load

_____ 1. The maximum carrying capacity of a trailer calculated by measuring the trailer weight and load.

_____ 2. The cargo carrying portion of a combination vehicle.

_____ 3. The maximum legal weight of a vehicle that can travel on roads and bridges.

_____ 4. The maximum design weight of a vehicle including a full tank of fuel, fully loaded to its capacity, and with all passengers.

_____ 5. A specific maximum weight limit determined by the vehicle manufacturer.

_____ 6. The weight supported by a hitching device, which is applied downwards by the weight of the trailer.

_____ 7. A trailer that is supported at both ends with an axle and does not rest on a fifth wheel.

_____ 8. Trailer hitching device that uses a fixed towing horn, which connects with a draw bar eye, attached to the towed vehicle.

_____ 9. A plate-type coupling device designed to support the weight of a semi-trailer.

_____ 10. A trailer that has some of its load carried by the tractor through a hitching device.

Multiple Choice

Read each item carefully, and then select the best response.

_____ 1. The vehicle formed by connecting a truck with a trailer is called a(n) _____.
A. semi
B. A-train
C. combination vehicle
D. tandem vehicle

_____ 2. The _____ design is less commonly used in North America but is used almost exclusively in Europe because the tractors are shorter and more maneuverable.
A. cab forward
B. cab over engine
C. shunt truck
D. full trailer

_____ **3.** A _____ is used to move semi-trailers around a warehouse yard or intermodal facility.
   A. shunt truck
   B. terminal tractor
   C. yard tractor
   D. All of the above

_____ **4.** The _____ is a set of retractable legs attached to the trailer, which support a semi-trailer when it is not resting on a fifth wheel.
   A. landing gear
   B. converter dolly
   C. bipod
   D. draw bar

_____ **5.** A(n) _____ is a three-unit combination of tractor plus two trailers.
   A. shunt truck
   B. camel train
   C. A-train
   D. tandem vehicle

_____ **6.** The formula that established the maximum weights for a commercial motor vehicle based on the number of axles the vehicle had and the spacing between those axles is known as _____.
   A. Bridge Formula B
   B. the Federal Bridge Gross Weight Formula
   C. the Federal Bridge Formula
   D. All of the above

_____ **7.** The load the draw bar places on the pintle hook, coupler, or ball hitch is called the _____.
   A. gross trailer weight
   B. draw bar rating
   C. tongue weight
   D. gross combined vehicle weight

_____ **8.** The fifth wheel should be able to flex _____ degrees around a horizontal axis.
   A. 3–6
   B. 15–30
   C. 45–50
   D. 90

_____ **9.** The standard type of fifth wheel used in on-highway applications is the _____.
   A. fully oscillating fifth wheel
   B. semi-oscillating fifth wheel
   C. rigid fifth wheel
   D. two-height fifth wheel

_____ **10.** Fifth wheels have maximum operating limits and capacities. These limits are expressed in terms of _____.
   A. vertical load
   B. "D" capacity
   C. draw bar capacity
   D. All of the above

True/False

If you believe the statement to be more true than false, write the letter "T" in the space provided. If you believe the statement to be more false than true, write the letter "F".

_____ **1.** The weight of a vehicle supported by a single axle should never exceed more than 10,000 lb (4,536 kg).

_____ **2.** The B-train configuration is the most stable of the three combination vehicle types.

_____ **3.** The longer the axle spread better weight distribution is achieved to prevent road and bridge damage.

_____ **4.** Pintle hooks are used on light- and medium-duty vehicles having a 12,000 lb (5,443 kg) towing weight capacity.

_____ **5.** Rigid fifth wheels are a specialty stationary fifth wheel that can be either air or hydraulically operated.

_____ **6.** Every fifth wheel assembly uses a locking mechanism to securely hold the trailer kingpin to the fifth wheel.

_____ **7.** A no-slack lock mechanism uses two swinging jaws and a yoke to lock the jaws securely around the kingpin.

_____ **8.** Flitch plates are pieces of angle iron that attach the mounting plate to the tractor frame.

_____ **9.** The location of the fifth wheel can be moved using a slider mechanism to enable even distribution of weight over the drive axles and front steer axle.

_____ **10.** The swing radius is determined by the distance between the kingpin and the front of the trailer.

Fill in the Blank

Read each item carefully, and then complete the statement by filling in the missing word(s).

1. The front of a trailer is supported by the tractor and articulates on the _____ wheel.

2. A(n) _____ is a commercial motor vehicle chassis designed to exclusively tow trailers.

3. A(n) _____-_____ uses one, two, or even three axles depending on their length and load carrying capacity.

4. Full trailers are most often semi-trailers, which are converted to full trailers using a converter _____, which is a fifth wheel supported by one or two axles.

5. C-dollies have two separate _____ _____ used to tow each side of the dolly.

6. Goose neck trailers such as those hauling large motor homes under 10,000 lb (4,536 kg), can use _____ hitches mounted to the bed of a pick-up truck.

7. A _____ fifth wheel does not oscillate about either axis of the vehicle.

8. The steel plate, load-bearing surface on the underside of the front of a semi-trailer is called the _____ _____, it is often referred to as the upper half of the fifth wheel.

9. The three basic styles of _____ are mushroom, bolted, and cruciform.

10. Manual release mechanisms often use a _____ safety latch to minimize the likelihood of an unintended jaw release.

Labeling

Label the following diagrams with the correct terms.

1. Identify the various coupling device components:

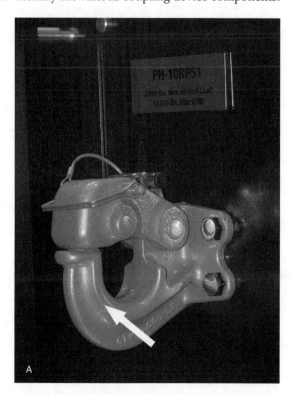

A. _____

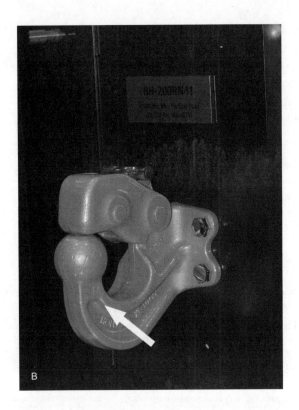

B. _____

C. _____

D. _____

E. _____

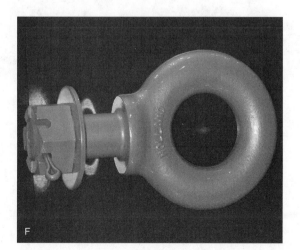

F. _____

2. Identify the components of a fifth wheel:

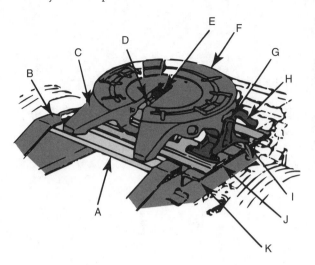

A. _____

B. _____

C. _____

D. _____

E. _____

F. _____

G. _____

H. _____

I. _____

J. _____

K. _____

Skill Drills

Test your knowledge of skill drills by filling in the missing words in the photo captions.

1. Lubricating a Fifth Wheel:

Step 1: Grease the top plate _____ _____ using water-resistant lithium-based _____. Note that the _____ _____ is on the side or under the front of the top plate. Grease the _____ _____ through the fittings.

Step 2: Fill the _____ with _____ _____ if applicable.

Step 3:   Lubricate the _____ _____ (indicated) and _____ with a light _____.

Step 4:   On _____ fifth wheels, _____ a light oil on the _____ and _____ _____.

2. Inspecting the Slider Mechanism on a Fifth Wheel:

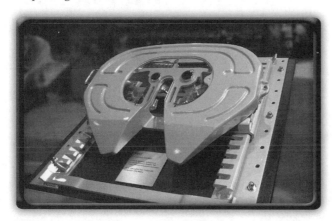

Step 1:   With trailer attached, check for excessive _____ at the _____ _____ by moving the trailer _____ and _____.

Step 2:   If excessive movement is present, _____ the trailer and conduct the following inspections.
  • Inspect all the slider _____ _____ for _____ or missing or damaged parts.
  • Inspect the locking _____ for full _____.
  • Check the _____ _____ for proper operation—both _____ and _____.

Step 3:   Adjust the _____ or replace the parts as required. In some cases, the _____ _____ can be adjusted, in others, _____ is the only solution.

Crossword Puzzle

Use the clues in the column to complete the puzzle.

Across

2. A single point connection configuration for a hitch that uses a tongue-shaped draw bar, which loops over a ball connected to the tow vehicle.

5. The pin attached to a trailer's upper couple, which is used to lock the fifth wheel to the trailer.

6. Bars used to connect tow vehicles to a tractor or lead towing unit.

Down

1. The distance between the centerline of two axles.

3. Trailer hitching device, similar to pintle hooks, but in which the towing horn pivots and is not fixed.

4. A shock absorbing insulator used to absorb shock loads transmitted by the trailer when the tow vehicle is accelerating or decelerating.

ASE-Type Questions

Read each item carefully, and then select the best response.

_____ **1.** Technician A says that the position of the fifth wheel has to move farther forward than a conventional cab forward tractor to distribute trailer weight evenly over the axles. Technician B says that a conventional cab forward tractor needs to move the fifth wheel farther ahead than a cab over engine. Who is correct?
  A. Technician A
  B. Technician B
  C. Both Technician A and Technician B
  D. Neither Technician A nor Technician B

_____ **2.** Technician A says that a fully oscillating fifth wheel is the best fifth wheel to use for a frameless dump trailer with an articulating upper coupler. Technician B says that a rigid type fifth wheel is safer. Who is correct?
  A. Technician A
  B. Technician B
  C. Both Technician A and Technician B
  D. Neither Technician A nor Technician B

_____ **3.** Technician A says that a semi-oscillating fifth wheel is the most commonly used fifth wheel on tractors towing semi-trailers. Technician B says that a fully oscillating fifth wheel helps prevent liquid tanker barrels from cracking. Who is correct?
  A. Technician A
  B. Technician B
  C. Both Technician A and Technician B
  D. Neither Technician A nor Technician B

_____ **4.** A fifth wheel kingpin is checked with a go–no go gauge. The 2" (5.1 cm) pin slipped into both the wider and narrower slots of the gauge. Technician A recommends replacing the kingpin. Technician B says all fifth wheel lock jaws are designed to safely accommodate variations in sizes of kingpins. Who is correct?
  A. Technician A
  B. Technician B
  C. Both Technician A and Technician B
  D. Neither Technician A nor Technician B

_____ **5.** Technician A says the A-train configuration uses a fifth wheel connection between trailers. Technician B says the B-train configuration is the least stable of the three combination vehicle types. Who is correct?
  A. Technician A
  B. Technician B
  C. Both Technician A and Technician B
  D. Neither Technician A nor Technician B

_____ **6.** Technician A says that, in North America, one of the most common ways trucks are categorized is by gross vehicle weight (GVW). Technician B says that GVW refers to the maximum design weight of a vehicle including a full tank of fuel, fully loaded to its capacity, and with all passengers. Who is correct?
  A. Technician A
  B. Technician B
  C. Both Technician A and Technician B
  D. Neither Technician A nor Technician B

_____ **7.** Technician A says pintle hooks are coupled by raising the draw bar eye over the pintle horn and locking it closed with a pivoting latch. Technician B says a snubber or load dampener was used in the past to minimize shock loads but is no longer being used. Who is correct?
  A. Technician A
  B. Technician B
  C. Both Technician A and Technician B
  D. Neither Technician A nor Technician B

_____ **8.** Technician A says that ball hitches are used on light- and medium-duty vehicles having a 14,000 lb (6,350 kg) towing weight capacity. Technician B says that ball hitches have the advantage of providing a positive no-slack fit because the draw bar has a spring-loaded tensioner at the connection point with the ball. Who is correct?
  A. Technician A
  B. Technician B
  C. Both Technician A and Technician B
  D. Neither Technician A nor Technician B

_____ **9.** Technician A says that tongue weight (TW) is the load the draw bar places on the pintle hook, coupler, or ball hitch. Technician B says that, as a general rule, the vertical load on the trailer tongue should be at least 30% of the gross trailer weight. Who is correct?
  A. Technician A
  B. Technician B
  C. Both Technician A and Technician B
  D. Neither Technician A nor Technician B

_____ **10.** Technician A says that, to prevent damage to roadways and bridges, the vehicle weight supported by tires and axles is limited by legislation. Technician B says that generally, tires should apply no more than 800 lb (363 kg) per square inch of road contact patch. Who is correct?
  A. Technician A
  B. Technician B
  C. Both Technician A and Technician B
  D. Neither Technician A nor Technician B

Heavy-Duty Clutches

Chapter Review

The following activities have been designed to help you refresh your knowledge of this chapter. Your instructor may require you to complete some or all of these activities as a regular part of your training program. You are encouraged to complete any activity that your instructor does not assign as a way to enhance your learning.

Matching

Match the following terms with the correct description or example.

A. Flywheel
B. Friction
C. Input shaft
D. Release fork
E. Resonance

_____ 1. The relative resistance to motion between any two bodies in contact with one another.

_____ 2. The frequency at which the driveline's vibrations are the most damaging.

_____ 3. The actuator that moves the release bearing.

_____ 4. A heavy round metal disc attached to the end of the crankshaft to smooth out vibrations from the crankshaft assembly and provide one of the friction surfaces for a clutch disc used on manual transmission/transaxle applications.

_____ 5. The component to which the clutch discs are splined.

Multiple Choice

Read each item carefully, and then select the best response.

_____ 1. The _____ is the outside part of the clutch bolted to the flywheel and holds all of the clutch components except the clutch disc.
   A. pressure plate
   B. clutch cover
   C. diaphragm
   D. bell housing

_____ 2. Calculated slippage that prevents driveline shock is known as _____.
   A. kinetic friction
   B. coefficient of friction
   C. resonance
   D. input pressure

_____ 3. The amount of torque a clutch can transmit before it starts to slip is known as the _____.
   A. friction limit
   B. clamp load
   C. clutch capacity
   D. fail point

_____ 4. The _____ style clutch cover is available in both push and pull types.
   A. diaphragm spring
   B. angle spring
   C. coil spring
   D. Both A and C

_____ **5.** The law that states that the force delivered by a spring to an object is directly related to its compression or extension is known as _____.
   A. Boyle's law
   B. Hooke's law
   C. Newton's law
   D. Bernoulli's principle

_____ **6.** The _____ pull-style clutch manufactured by Eaton is by far the most popular in heavy-duty on-highway trucks today.
   A. angle spring
   B. coil spring
   C. diaphragm spring
   D. dual spring

_____ **7.** The point at which all of the driveline components start to oscillate in unison is known as the _____ frequency.
   A. harmonic
   B. dissonant
   C. resonant
   D. dynamic

_____ **8.** The most common type of flywheel in use today is the _____.
   A. flat-type flywheel
   B. pot-type flywheel
   C. disc-type flywheel
   D. dual mass flywheel

_____ **9.** Most clutches in heavy-duty vehicles are actuated by _____ linkage systems.
   A. mechanical
   B. hydraulic
   C. electronic
   D. air-assisted

_____ **10.** In a _____ linkage system the master cylinder controls a reaction plunger and a pilot valve, which allows pressure to act on a servo piston to move the cross-shaft lever.
   A. two-pedal centrifugal
   B. air-assisted hydraulic
   C. automatically actuated
   D. electronic

True/False

If you believe the statement to be more true than false, write the letter "T" in the space provided. If you believe the statement to be more false than true, write the letter "F".

_____ **1.** Prior to the invention of the clutch, machinery was typically directly connected to the engine.

_____ **2.** Torsional vibrations are powerful vibrations caused by the engine firing impulses twisting and accelerating the crankshaft.

_____ **3.** In a push-type angle spring clutch, the springs act directly against the back of the pressure plate to supply clamping force.

_____ **4.** Self-adjusting clutches have an automatic adjusting system that relies on pressure plate movement to cause an adjustment.

_____ **5.** Asbestos is still the material of choice in the production of organic friction discs.

_____ **6.** Both ceramic and organic discs are available in both rigid and or dampened disc styles.

_____ **7.** Soft-dampened clutches control torsional vibration by placing friction material between the spring cage plates of the clutch disc and the friction driven plate.

_____ **8.** Dual mass flywheels are commonly used for heavy-duty applications.

_____ **9.** The damper springs used to absorb torsional vibrations also absorb the vibrations associated with gear rattle.

_____ **10.** The torque-limiting clutch brake is designed to slip if the torque applied exceeds its setting.

Fill in the Blank

Read each item carefully, and then complete the statement by filling in the missing word(s).

1. The _____ of friction is a measure of the friction that exists between two particular bodies in contact.

2. The _____ _____ is the friction surface of the clutch cover and squeezes the clutch disc against the flywheel.

3. The _____ bearing is a hollow bearing through which the shaft passes and allows the pushing or pulling of clutch release levers to release the clutch.

4. The _____ spring is a single cone-shaped spring. Its outer edge rests against the pressure plate, and the inner part of the spring is cut into segments called fingers.

5. In most medium-to-heavy applications, organic clutch discs have been replaced by discs with _____ facings.

6. The _____ plate is the plate that contacts the back of the forward clutch friction disc and the front of the rear friction disc on dual disc clutches.

7. The _____ bearing may be as simple as a brass bushing or needle bearing mounted in a pocket formed in the rear of the crankshaft.

8. A(n) _____ _____ is usually mounted on the transmission input shaft and designed to slow down or stop the transmission rotation when the driver wishes to engage first or reverse from a neutral position.

9. In a hydraulically actuated clutch, a(n) _____ cylinder will be mounted at the transmission to actuate the cross-shaft.

10. Vehicles equipped with automated transmissions usually require _____ actuated clutches.

Labeling

Label the following diagrams with the correct terms.

1. Identify the components of a standard vehicle clutch:

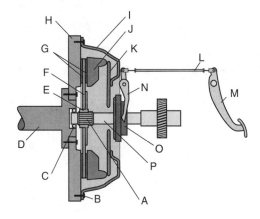

A. _____

B. _____

C. _____

D. _____

E. _____

F. _____

G. _____

H. _____

I. _____

J. _____

K. _____

L. _____

M. _____

N. _____

O. _____

P. _____

2. Identify the components of a coil spring pressure plate:

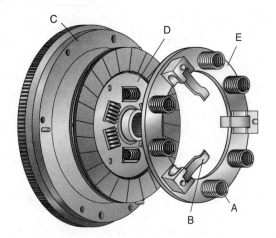

A. _____

B. _____

C. _____

D. _____

E. _____

3. Identify the components of a cable linkage clutch actuation system:

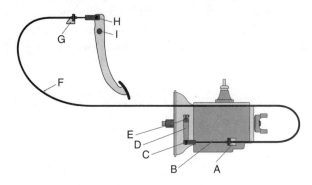

A. _____

B. _____

C. _____

D. _____

E. _____

F. _____

G. _____

H. _____

I. _____

Crossword Puzzle

Use the clues in the column to complete the puzzle.

Across

4. A disc with a ring of torsional dampening springs around its hub designed to absorb engine torsional vibrations.

5. A bearing that supports the front of the transmission input shaft; mounted in the flywheel or the rear of the crankshaft.

Down

1. A type of transmission shaft brake geared to one countershaft, which controls gearing rotational speed while shifting.

2. Pin used in a pot-type flywheel to drive the intermediate plate.

3. The force squeezing the clutch disc(s) between the pressure plate and the flywheel.

ASE-Type Questions

Read each item carefully, and then select the best response.

_____ 1. Technician A says that a pilot bearing should always be replaced when a clutch is replaced. Technician B says that soft-dampened clutches are better at absorbing torsional vibrations. Who is correct?
  A. Technician A
  B. Technician B
  C. Both Technician A and Technician B
  D. Neither Technician A nor Technician B

_____ 2. Technician A says that since North American clutch manufacturers no longer use asbestos there is no need to be concerned by clutch dust. Technician B says that compressed air is the best way to clean the clutch housing when performing a clutch replacement. Who is correct?
  A. Technician A
  B. Technician B
  C. Both Technician A and Technician B
  D. Neither Technician A nor Technician B

_____ 3. Technician A says that coil spring clutches are the best because the heavy coil springs provide exceptional clamp load. Technician B says that diaphragm spring style clutches are a better choice because they do not lose clamp load. Who is correct?
  A. Technician A
  B. Technician B
  C. Both Technician A and Technician B
  D. Neither Technician A nor Technician B

_____ 4. Technician A says that the release bearing in pull-type clutches only rotates when disengaging the clutch. Technician B says that the release bearing in pull-type clutches is replaced whenever the clutch is replaced. Who is correct?
  A. Technician A
  B. Technician B
  C. Both Technician A and Technician B
  D. Neither Technician A nor Technician B

_____ 5. Technician A says that using dual discs in a clutch doubles the clutch capacity. Technician B says that increasing clamp load can increase clutch capacity. Who is correct?
  A. Technician A
  B. Technician B
  C. Both Technician A and Technician B
  D. Neither Technician A nor Technician B

_____ 6. Technician A says that most heavy-duty truck clutches will use organic linings. Technician B says that the most common clutch type used in heavy trucks is the angle spring clutch. Who is correct?
  A. Technician A
  B. Technician B
  C. Both Technician A and Technician B
  D. Neither Technician A nor Technician B

_____ 7. Technician A says that clutch brakes help the driver up shift. Technician B says that brakes can be replaced without removing the transmission. Who is correct?
  A. Technician A
  B. Technician B
  C. Both Technician A and Technician B
  D. Neither Technician A nor Technician B

_____ 8. Technician A says that a diaphragm spring clutch is a better choice than a coil spring style clutch because it doesn't lose clamp load as the disc wears. Technician B says that diaphragm spring clutches are only found in light-duty vehicles. Who is correct?
  A. Technician A
  B. Technician B
  C. Both Technician A and Technician B
  D. Neither Technician A nor Technician B

_____ **9.** Technician A says that the clutch should be adjusted when the pedal free play is reduced by half. Technician B says that some clutches with hydraulic actuation systems do not require adjustment. Who is correct?

    A. Technician A

    B. Technician B

    C. Both Technician A and Technician B

    D. Neither Technician A nor Technician B

_____ **10.** Technician A says that clutch wear is non-existent when the clutch is engaged. Technician B says that clutch wear will be increased on a clutch with mechanical linkage if there is no pedal free play in the cab. Who is correct?

    A. Technician A

    B. Technician B

    C. Both Technician A and Technician B

    D. Neither Technician A nor Technician B

Servicing Heavy-Duty Clutches

Chapter Review

The following activities have been designed to help you refresh your knowledge of this chapter. Your instructor may require you to complete some or all of these activities as a regular part of your training program. You are encouraged to complete any activity that your instructor does not assign as a way to enhance your learning.

Matching

Match the following terms with the correct description or example.

A. Clutch chatter **D.** Slip yoke

B. Clutch linkage **E.** Vocation

C. Free play

_____ **1.** Clearance between two components.

_____ **2.** The type of service a vehicle is involved in.

_____ **3.** The condition of the clutch alternately engaging and slipping quite rapidly when the driver engages the clutch.

_____ **4.** A splined tube that allows for driveshaft length changes.

_____ **5.** The mechanical connection between the driver's clutch pedal and the clutch cross shaft.

Multiple Choice

Read each item carefully, and then select the best response.

_____ **1.** Excessive dust buildup from friction material, worn clutch brakes on pull-type clutches, and signs of overheating or burning of clutch components may indicate _____.
  A. driver error or abuse
  B. poor maintenance
  C. equipment failure
  D. adjustment issues

_____ **2.** The angle spring clutch is adjusted using a(n) _____.
  A. quick-adjust device
  B. adjusting ring
  C. locking tang
  D. Either A or C

_____ **3.** Self-adjusting clutches replaced the large internal adjusting ring with a set of _____.
  A. spur gears
  B. movable cam rings
  C. release forks
  D. locking tangs

_____ **4.** The primary cause of clutch failure is _____.
  A. excess heat
  B. release fork free play
  C. clutch chatter
  D. linkage binding

_____ **5.** A warped or damaged pressure plate, flywheel, or clutch disc can cause _____.
  A. gear clash
  B. slippage
  C. clutch chatter
  D. pilot bearing failure

_____ **6.** A hard-to-depress clutch pedal can be caused by _____.
  A. worn or damaged release bearings
  B. linkage binding
  C. worn or damaged input shaft splines
  D. too much free play

_____ **7.** If the clutch pedal has _____, it may not have enough travel to fully release the pressure plate, causing the gears to clash or grind when shifting.
  A. too much free-play
  B. a loose jamb nut
  C. too little free-play
  D. linkage binding

_____ **8.** If you are removing an Eaton Solo or other self-adjusting clutch, four _____ will be required to cage the clutch pressure plate for removal.
  A. shipping blocks
  B. removable cam rings
  C. guide studs
  D. shipping bolts

_____ **9.** When replacing any type of clutch, the _____ should be checked with a dial indicator to ensure proper clutch operation and service life.
  A. flywheel friction surface
  B. pilot bearing bore
  C. flywheel housing face
  D. All of the above

_____ **10.** Fourteen inches (36.6 cm) clutch pot-style flywheels are unique in that the _____ is driven by six drive pins installed in the flywheel.
  A. diaphragm spring
  B. intermediate plate
  C. throw out bearing
  D. crankshaft

True/False

If you believe the statement to be more true than false, write the letter "T" in the space provided. If you believe the statement to be more false than true, write the letter "F".

_____ **1.** Clutch friction material contains dust and fibers that can be very harmful and even carcinogenic.

_____ **2.** Sealed release bearings require periodic lubrication.

_____ **3.** Clutch linkage adjustment should be performed regularly to compensate for clutch disc wear on a pull-type clutch.

_____ **4.** Improper or old fluid in the hydraulic system can cause master cylinder and slave cylinder damage.

_____ **5.** All hydraulic systems are fitted with a bleeder screw to remove air from the system.

_____ **6.** A clutch alignment tool or an old input shaft can be used to hold the friction discs in alignment for clutch reassembly.

_____ **7.** The clutch bell housing pilot is the small protrusion that fits inside a mating recess in the flywheel housing known as the flywheel housing pilot.

_____ **8.** Thoroughly grease or oil the splines of the transmission input shaft before installing a new clutch to prevent chatter.

_____ **9.** A 15.5" (39.4 cm) clutch is extremely heavy and serious injury could result from trying to install this clutch alone without the use of a clutch jack.

_____ **10.** When a self-adjusting clutch is removed, the shipping bolts must be installed after the cover attaching bolts are loosened.

Fill in the Blank

Read each item carefully, and then complete the statement by filling in the missing word(s).

1. During a vehicle service, all moving components of the clutch actuation system should be _____, as should the release bearing, clutch release fork, and cross-shaft.

2. Clutch brake _____, or squeeze, is affected by total pedal travel and is adjusted by adjusting the clutch linkage.

3. The most common form of internal adjustment involves turning a large adjusting _____ inside the clutch cover.

4. Readjustment of the release fork clearance should be performed when in-cab pedal _____ _____ drops to half of the normal amount achieved after a correct adjustment.

5. The _____ bleeding method uses the master cylinder to push fluid and air from the system.

6. The driver's shift lever and the _____ _____ bolted to the top of the transmission must be removed in order to remove the clutch.

7. To safely and correctly install a new clutch requires _____ studs, which are long threaded studs that support the clutch while the bolts are removed.

8. Heavier clutch installations may require the use of a clutch _____.

9. The clutch _____ housing surrounds the clutch assembly and attaches to the flywheel housing.

10. Certain heavy-duty 14" (36.6 cm) intermediate plates require the installation of three anti-rattle _____.

Skill Drills

Test your knowledge of skill drills by filling in the correct words in the photo captions.

1. Checking and Adjusting a Push-Type Clutch:

Step 1: Research the procedure and specifications for _____ and _____ the _____ _____ in the appropriate service information. You are looking specifically for the proper clutch pedal _____, the proper clutch pedal _____ _____, and the procedure for making adjustments.

Step 2: Following the specified procedure, _____ the clutch _____ parts for _____, _____, or bent or missing components. Look for signs of _____, _____, and excessive _____.

Step 3: Start with the clutch _____ assembly and inspect all components inside the _____. It is good practice to operate the _____ _____ while you are inspecting the components to _____ any looseness or _____.

Step 4: Check the _____ _____ components _____ the cab for the same signs as the components _____ the cab.

Step 5: Measure the clutch pedal height. Clutch pedal height is normally measured from the _____ _____ to the top of the clutch pedal _____ with the clutch pedal _____. Make sure there are no _____ _____ or other obstructions that will affect the operation of the pedal. Compare your reading with the specifications and determine any necessary actions to _____ any _____.

Step 6:   Measure the clutch pedal free play. Pedal free play is normally measured from the _____ of the pedal at _____ to where all play is taken up between the pedal and the _____ _____. This can be felt by _____ or _____. Perform any adjustments as necessary, following the manufacturer's procedure.

Step 7:   Start the vehicle and _____ the clutch. The clutch should engage at the proper _____ and have the proper _____ _____. Make a gear selection to ensure the gears do not _____ going into _____. While in gear, slowly _____ the clutch and see how far the clutch pedal must travel before the clutch starts to _____ in forward motion. If it is not within the manufacturer's specifications, discuss this with your supervisor.

2. Checking and Adjusting a Hydraulic Clutch:

Step 1:   Research the _____ and specifications for _____ and _____ the hydraulic clutch components in the appropriate service information.

Step 2:   Inspect the clutch _____ _____ for correct fluid _____ and test the _____ of the fluid.

Step 3:   Inspect all line _____ to the master cylinder. If a _____ at the rear of the master cylinder is suspected, it may be necessary to _____ the master cylinder from the _____ to inspect behind it for leaks if no other visible external leaks are present.

Step 4:   Make sure no hydraulic lines are _____ or _____ at their connections. This will require that the system be repaired and _____ of any _____.

Step 5:   Check all rubber hoses for _____ _____, _____, or _____. Make sure all hydraulic components are _____ in their mountings.

Step 6:   Check the _____ on the _____ cylinder for _____, which may indicate a leaking slave cylinder _____ _____.

Step 7:   Check clutch pedal height. Clutch pedal height is normally measured from the _____ _____ to the top of the clutch pedal _____ with the clutch pedal _____. Compare your reading with the specifications and determine any necessary actions to _____ any _____.

Step 8:   Measure clutch pedal free play using a _____ _____. Pedal free play is normally measured from the top of the pedal at rest to where all play is taken up between the _____ and the _____ _____. Compare your reading with the factory specifications and determine any necessary actions to correct.

Step 9:   Note that newer _____ actuated clutches run with no _____ _____ in the cab. Always check manufacturers' specifications for the vehicle you are working on before undertaking any _____.

3. Bleeding/Flushing a Hydraulic Clutch System Using the Gravity Method:

Step 1: If the fluid needs to be _____, use a _____ _____ or old anti-freeze _____ to suck the fluid out of the clutch master cylinder _____. Fill it with the specified _____.

Step 2: Open the _____ _____ on the _____ cylinder.

Step 3: Allow _____ and _____ to drain from the system into a _____.

Step 4: Keep the _____ _____ filled.

Step 5: Once all _____ and _____ _____ are removed, close the _____ _____ and operate the _____ _____ to check for normal operation.

4. Bleeding/Flushing a Hydraulic Clutch System Using the Manual Method:

Step 1: If the fluid needs to be _____, use a suction gun or old _____-_____ _____ to suck the fluid out of the clutch _____ _____ reservoir. Fill it with the specified fluid.

Step 2: Have an _____ depress the _____ _____ slowly. Open the _____ _____ on the _____ _____ and let fluid run out into a container.

Step 3: When all of the _____ stops flowing, _____ the bleeder valve and slowly _____ the pedal.

Step 4: Repeat this process until all _____ and _____ _____ are _____ from the system.

Step 5: After _____ the clutch _____ system, check for correct _____ _____, and fill the _____ cylinder to the correct level with the specified type of _____ _____.

5. Bleeding/Flushing a Hydraulic Clutch System Using the Pressure Method:

Step 1: Hook up the _____ or vacuum _____ _____ to the vehicle with the correct _____.

Step 2: Apply _____ or _____ to the system.

Step 3: Open the _____ _____ and allow the fluid and air to be _____ from the system. Capture the fluid in the _____ or use a _____ to direct it into a _____ _____. Repeat this process as necessary.

Step 4: After _____ the hydraulic _____ _____, check for correct _____ _____, and fill the _____ _____ to the correct level with the specified type of _____ _____.

Crossword Puzzle

Use the clues in the column to complete the puzzle.

Across

3. Wooden blocks that support the release bearing and cage the pressure plate on pull-type clutches.
4. The round housing bolted to the rear of the engine to which the clutch bell housing is bolted.

Down

1. A tool with a clutch alignment tool that fits into the clutch, used to carry the weight of the clutch for installation or removal.
2. Long threaded studs that stop a component from falling while the attaching bolts are removed.
3. The point of clutch pedal actuation on a pull-type clutch when the clutch brake is being actuated.

ASE-Type Questions

Read each item carefully, and then select the best response.

_____ 1. Technician A says that the primary cause of premature clutch failure is excessive heat. Technician B says that driver skill can greatly affect clutch life. Who is correct?
   A. Technician A
   B. Technician B
   C. Both Technician A and Technician B
   D. Neither Technician A nor Technician B

_____ 2. Technician A says that angle spring pull-type clutches are adjusted by turning the large adjustment ring in the clutch cover. Technician B says that the adjustment will change the clutch brake squeeze dimension. Who is correct?
   A. Technician A
   B. Technician B
   C. Both Technician A and Technician B
   D. Neither Technician A nor Technician B

_____ 3. Technician A says that clutch brake squeeze should occur in the last inch (25.4 mm) of clutch pedal travel near the floor. Technician B says that clutch can be altered by a linkage adjustment. Who is correct?
   A. Technician A
   B. Technician B
   C. Both Technician A and Technician B
   D. Neither Technician A nor Technician B

_____ 4. Technician A says that a pull-type clutch with mechanical linkage should have 0.125" (3.2 mm) free play between the release fork and the release bearing. Technician B says that a pull-type clutch release bearing free travel dimension should be at least 0.5" (1.27 cm). Who is correct?
   A. Technician A
   B. Technician B
   C. Both Technician A and Technician B
   D. Neither Technician A nor Technician B

_____ 5. Technician A says that if there is no free play at the fork on a pull-type clutch with mechanical linkage, premature clutch wear out is possible. Technician B says that some hydraulically actuated clutches are designed to operate with no fork to release bearing clearance. Who is correct?
   A. Technician A
   B. Technician B
   C. Both Technician A and Technician B
   D. Neither Technician A nor Technician B

_____ 6. Technician A says that, when installing clutch discs, heavy grease should be used on the input shaft splines so the discs don't "hang up." Technician B says that doing so can cause grease contamination of the discs, so it is not recommended. Who is correct?
   A. Technician A
   B. Technician B
   C. Both Technician A and Technician B
   D. Neither Technician A nor Technician B

_____ 7. Technician A sees significant wear on the clutch bell housing face and recommends its replacement. Technician B states that wear in this location is normal and does not require replacement. Who is correct?
   A. Technician A
   B. Technician B
   C. Both Technician A and Technician B
   D. Neither Technician A nor Technician B

_____ 8. Technician A says that riding the clutch pedal can cause bent drive straps. Technician B says that bent or warped drive straps are caused by shock loading the driveline. Who is correct?
   A. Technician A
   B. Technician B
   C. Both Technician A and Technician B
   D. Neither Technician A nor Technician B

_____ **9.** Technician A says that coasting with the clutch disengaged is a bad driving practice. Technician B says that using clutch brake to hold a vehicle on a hill is safe practice. Who is correct?

    A. Technician A

    B. Technician B

    C. Both Technician A and Technician B

    D. Neither Technician A nor Technician B

_____ **10.** Technician A says that Eaton Solo clutches can be adjusted manually when required. Technician B says that Eaton Solo clutches are self-adjusting. Who is correct?

    A. Technician A

    B. Technician B

    C. Both Technician A and Technician B

    D. Neither Technician A nor Technician B

Basic Gearing Concepts

Tire Tread:
© AbleStock

Chapter Review

The following activities have been designed to help you refresh your knowledge of this chapter. Your instructor may require you to complete some or all of these activities as a regular part of your training program. You are encouraged to complete any activity that your instructor does not assign as a way to enhance your learning.

Matching

Match the following terms with the correct description or example.

A. Bevel gear

B. Helical gear

C. Idler gear

D. Pinion gear

E. Spur gear

_____ **1.** Gear used in transmissions to drive a vehicle backward.

_____ **2.** A small driving gear.

_____ **3.** A gear with teeth cut parallel to its axis of rotation.

_____ **4.** Gear cut on an angle allowing a power flow to turn a corner.

_____ **5.** A gear with teeth cut on an angle or spirally to its axis of rotation.

Multiple Choice

Read each item carefully, and then select the best response.

_____ **1.** The _____ is the area of a gear that actually comes into contact with a mating gear.

    A. root

    B. addendum

    C. tooth face

    D. top land

_____ **2.** The _____ of a gear is the bottom of the valley formed between two teeth.

    A. fillet radius

    B. dedendum

    C. root

    D. Either A or C

_____ **3.** The average contact point of a given tooth is its _____.

    A. pitch circle

    B. root diameter

    C. pitch diameter

    D. Either A or C

_____ **4.** The center of the gear, or shaft, is the _____.

    A. load

    B. effort

    C. fulcrum

    D. pitch

_____ **5.** If the driving gear has 30 teeth and the driven gear has 5 teeth each complete turn of the driving gear will turn the driven gear _____ complete revolutions.
   A. 6
   B. 15
   C. 60
   D. 150

_____ **6.** Any ratio with a first number greater than one is known as a(n) _____.
   A. gear reduction
   B. overdrive ratio
   C. underdrive ratio
   D. Either A or C

_____ **7.** If the driving gear has 45 teeth and the driven gear has 15 teeth the gear ratio would be expressed as _____.
   A. 1:3
   B. 3:1
   C. 4.5:1.5
   D. 9:3

_____ **8.** The dual-cut helices on _____ gears cause all axial thrust to be cancelled out.
   A. spur
   B. spiral bevel
   C. herringbone
   D. pinion

_____ **9.** The main disadvantage of helical gears is that they cause _____.
   A. axial thrust
   B. a high-pitched whine
   C. radial thrust
   D. tooth chatter

_____ **10.** Until recently _____ gears have been predominantly used in the steering mechanism of front-wheel-drive, light-duty vehicles.
   A. worm
   B. rack-and-pinion
   C. spiral bevel
   D. herringbone

True/False

If you believe the statement to be more true than false, write the letter "T" in the space provided. If you believe the statement to be more false than true, write the letter "F".

_____ **1.** Mechanical advantage is anything that allows us to move greater distances or weight with less effort.

_____ **2.** The upper portion of the tooth contact area is called the dedendum and the lower portion of this area is called the addendum.

_____ **3.** Clockwise rotation is usually referred to as forward rotation and counterclockwise rotation as reverse rotation.

_____ **4.** Too little backlash will not allow lubricant in between teeth, too much backlash can allow the gears to climb out of mesh and slip.

_____ **5.** A compound gear ratio is the relationship between one driving and one driven gear.

_____ **6.** Any ratio in which the first number is less than one is known as an underdrive ratio.

_____ **7.** To calculate ratios with multiple gears divide the product of all of the driven gears by the product of all of the drive gears.

_____ **8.** All gears are classified as either overdrive or underdrive.

_____ **9.** When two externally toothed gears are in mesh, the driven gear will turn in the reverse direction to the drive gear.

_____ **10.** Idler gears do not need to be included when calculating gear ratios.

Fill in the Blank

Read each item carefully, and then complete the statement by filling in the missing word(s).

1. In medium and heavy-duty vehicles, gears are typically made from _____ _____ _____.

2. The _____ _____ of a gear is the smallest circle of the gear measured at the fillet radius, or root, of the teeth.

3. Modern gears are designed with a special tooth shape called a(n) _____ that compensates for the changing point of contact between gears as they rotate through mesh.

4. The simplest form of a gear is the _____.

5. The sizing of the gears and the relationship between them is known as the _____ _____.

6. The _____ advantage is the effort applied by the driving gear multiplied by the ratio.

7. When we have a ratio with more than one pair of gears involved it is called a(n) _____ ratio.

8. The purpose of _____ gears is to act as a bridge between two gears and reverse the direction of rotation without changing the ratio.

9. Spur gears in mesh produce _____ thrust they tend to want to push away from each other perpendicular to their axis.

10. The helical tooth configuration of the _____ bevel gear imparts the advantages of helical gearing to the bevel gear set, making them stronger and quieter.

Labeling

Label the following diagrams with the correct terms.

1. Identify the parts of the anatomy of gears:

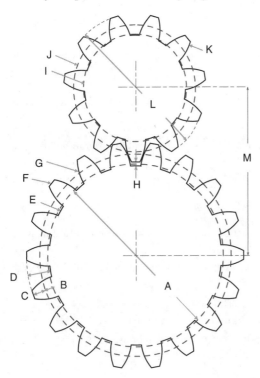

A. _____

B. _____

C. _____

D. _____

E. _____

F. _____

G. _____

H. _____

I. _____

J. _____

K. _____

L. _____

M. _____

Crossword Puzzle

Use the clues in the column to complete the puzzle.

Across

2. The apex of a tooth.

5. The clearance between teeth in mesh with each other.

6. A simple machine that can allow a large object to be moved with less force.

Down

1. The simplest mechanism that allows us to gain mechanical advantage.

3. The number of teeth per unit of pitch diameter on a gear.

4. A manufacturing process that makes the surface of a gear much harder than its core.

ASE-Type Questions

Read each item carefully, and then select the best response.

_____ 1. Technician A says that the gear attached to the input shaft on a countershaft transmission is a drive gear and the gear it meshes with on the countershaft is a driven gear. Technician B says that all the countershaft speed gears are drive gears and all the main shaft speed gears are driven gears. Who is correct?
  A. Technician A
  B. Technician B
  C. Both Technician A and Technician B
  D. Neither Technician A nor Technician B

_____ 2. Technician A says a ratio that involves more than one set of gears is known as a compound ratio. Technician B says that the formula to calculate ratio is drive over driven. Who is correct?
  A. Technician A
  B. Technician B
  C. Both Technician A and Technician B
  D. Neither Technician A nor Technician B

_____ 3. Technician A says that all modern gearing uses an involute tooth shape. Technician B says the involute compensates for differing points of contact as a gear goes through mesh. Who is correct?
  A. Technician A
  B. Technician B
  C. Both Technician A and Technician B
  D. Neither Technician A nor Technician B

_____ 4. Technician A says that to calculate gear compound ratios you add all the driven gears together and divide by all the drive gears added together. Technician B says that idler gears are not used in gear ratio calculations. Who is correct?
  A. Technician A
  B. Technician B
  C. Both Technician A and Technician B
  D. Neither Technician A nor Technician B

_____ 5. Technician A says that externally toothed gears in mesh turn in opposite directions. Technician B says that idler gears are used to change the direction of rotation. Who is correct?
  A. Technician A
  B. Technician B
  C. Both Technician A and Technician B
  D. Neither Technician A nor Technician B

_____ 6. Technician A says that the meshing of peg gears causes an uneven speed in the driven gear. Technician B says that the distance between the contact point and the center of peg gears in mesh is constantly changing. Who is correct?
  A. Technician A
  B. Technician B
  C. Both Technician A and Technician B
  D. Neither Technician A nor Technician B

_____ 7. Technician A says that an underdrive ratio increases torque. Technician B says that an underdrive ratio creates a speed increase at the output. Who is correct?
  A. Technician A
  B. Technician B
  C. Both Technician A and Technician B
  D. Neither Technician A nor Technician B

_____ 8. Technician A says that overdrive ratio increases torque available at the output shaft. Technician B says that an overdrive ratio is always less than 1:1. Who is correct?
  A. Technician A
  B. Technician B
  C. Both Technician A and Technician B
  D. Neither Technician A nor Technician B

_____ **9.** Technician A says that bevel gears are used to make a power flow turn a corner. Technician B says that bevel gears are usually found in the drive axle. Who is correct?
   A. Technician A
   B. Technician B
   C. Both Technician A and Technician B
   D. Neither Technician A nor Technician B

_____ **10.** Technician A says that rack-and-pinion gears are never found on heavy-duty trucks. Technician B says that herringbone gears are not normally used in heavy-duty trucks. Who is correct?
   A. Technician A
   B. Technician B
   C. Both Technician A and Technician B
   D. Neither Technician A nor Technician B

CHAPTER 38

Standard Transmissions

Tire Tread:
© AbleStock

Chapter Review

The following activities have been designed to help you refresh your knowledge of this chapter. Your instructor may require you to complete some or all of these activities as a regular part of your training program. You are encouraged to complete any activity that your instructor does not assign as a way to enhance your learning.

Matching

Match the following terms with the correct description or example.

A. Double clutch

B. Shift forks

C. Sliding clutch

D. Synchronizer

E. Transfer case

_____ **1.** Device used to move the sliding clutches or collars in a transmission.

_____ **2.** A component that is bolted to the back of the transmission or connected to it by a short driveshaft; allows the output of a transmission to flow to both the rear and the front axles.

_____ **3.** A technique drivers use to synchronize gear and shaft speed.

_____ **4.** A device to match shaft and gear speeds for clash-free engagement.

_____ **5.** A device with splines on the inside and outside used as a gear selection method for manual transmissions.

Multiple Choice

Read each item carefully, and then select the best response.

_____ **1.** The transmission's _____ is driven by the clutch friction disc.
  A. input shaft
  B. main shaft
  C. countershaft
  D. output shaft

_____ **2.** The main shaft is also called the _____.
  A. input shaft
  B. output shaft
  C. idler shaft
  D. countershaft

_____ **3.** In _____ transmissions, a main shaft gear that is splined to the main shaft is slid into and out of mesh with a corresponding countershaft gear to create the ratio.
  A. sliding clutch
  B. synchronized
  C. sliding-gear
  D. All of the above

_____ **4.** The shift _____ are rectangular notches either formed into or attached to the shift rails.
  A. fingers
  B. forks
  C. gates
  D. levers

_____ **5.** The _____ synchronizer is positioned between a pair of main shaft gears and has two cone-shaped synchronizer friction rings.
   A. disc-and-plate-type
   B. pin-type
   C. block-type
   D. insert-type

_____ **6.** Most of today's single countershaft transmissions are _____.
   A. synchronized
   B. sliding clutch
   C. constant mesh
   D. Either A or C

_____ **7.** The _____ is basically another transmission attached to the main transmission.
   A. bellcrank
   B. auxiliary section
   C. overdrive module
   D. main box

_____ **8.** There are two types of _____ auxiliary sections: an original and a low-inertia type.
   A. two-speed
   B. three-speed
   C. four-speed
   D. five-speed

_____ **9.** The _____ auxiliary design allows the auxiliary to momentarily disengage from the main box during compound shifts, making it easier to move the shift lever.
   A. low-inertia
   B. split-shift
   C. deep reduction
   D. Both A and C

_____ **10.** The _____ colored splitter shift control button is used only for deep reduction transmissions.
   A. red
   B. green
   C. blue
   D. yellow

True/False

If you believe the statement to be more true than false, write the letter "T" in the space provided. If you believe the statement to be more false than true, write the letter "F".

_____ **1.** A basic transmission will have two shafts running parallel to each other and installed in a housing known as the transmission case.

_____ **2.** When the input gear turns the countershaft driven gear, all of the countershaft gears turn with it.

_____ **3.** The main shaft gears on a collar shift transmission are splined directly to the main shaft.

_____ **4.** The synchronized transmission is a constant-mesh transmission.

_____ **5.** The reverse idler shaft supports the speed gears.

_____ **6.** The shift lever is the only part of the transmission shift mechanism that the driver sees on a daily basis.

_____ **7.** A majority of North American vehicles are equipped with sliding-gear transmissions.

_____ **8.** Synchronization eliminates the need for double clutching techniques.

_____ **9.** Single countershaft transmissions are the unit of choice for most light- and medium-duty vehicles manufactured in North America.

_____ **10.** The two-speed auxiliary arrangement requires two shift levers in the cab to coordinate the shifting of both transmissions at once.

_____ **11.** The deep-reduction transmission has 15 available speeds and is engaged for off-road operation.

_____ **12.** The Roadranger valve is designed to allow a splitter shift while in low range.

_____ **13.** The job of the splitter shift cylinder is to control the splitter sliding clutch.

_____ **14.** Transfer cases only have two shafts, an input shaft and an output shaft.

_____ **15.** A power take-off device is a device attached to the transmission that is gear-driven and can be used to run accessories.

Fill in the Blank

Read each item carefully, and then complete the statement by filling in the missing word(s).

1. The transmission allows us to move extremely heavy loads by using _____ multiplication.

2. The ratio difference between each gear, or range, to the next available gear is known as the ratio _____.

3. The _____ gears on the countershaft and the main shaft create the transmission's ratios.

4. Below the pivot point the end of the shift lever forms the shift _____, a flat-sided piece that sits into the shift gates.

5. Shift rails have a(n) _____ system that prevents two rails from being moved from the neutral position at once.

6. The plain-type _____ has a central hub that is splined to the main shaft and a sliding collar that is splined to the hub.

7. A(n) _____ is a shaft or lever used in a mechanical linkage with a pivot in the center that reverses the normal direction of motion.

8. The _____ _____ located on the transmission's information plate indicates whether the transmission is an overdrive model or not, how many forward ranges it has, its torque capacity, and its ratio set.

9. A(n) _____ countershaft transmission splits the input torque between two or three countershafts spaced 180 or 120 degrees apart.

10. In _____-_____ gearing, the main shaft and countershaft gears have finer cut teeth—meaning more teeth are in mesh for increased strength.

11. The simplest auxiliary is the _____-_____ auxiliary.

12. A(n) _____ shift occurs when two parts of the transmission are being shifted at once.

13. The slave air valve is mounted on the side of the transmission and controls air flow to the _____ _____ cylinder.

14. The _____ _____ allows air to flow to both sides of the splitter cylinder piston in low split and drains the air from the rear side of the cylinder piston in high split.

15. A transfer case is sometimes called a(n) _____ _____, as the design allows the front driveshaft to clear the bottom of the transmission in order to go to the front axle.

Labeling

Label the following diagrams with the correct terms.

1. Identify the transmission shafts:

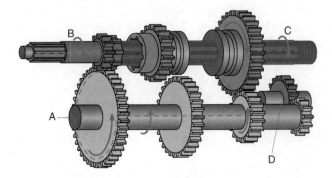

A. _____

B. _____

C. _____

D. _____

2. Identify the air control system components:

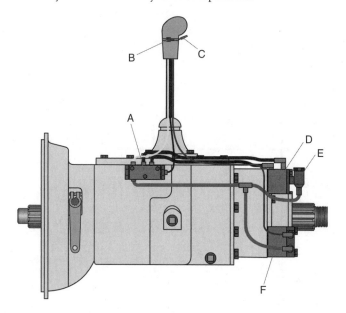

A. _____

B. _____

C. _____

D. _____

E. _____

F. _____

Crossword Puzzle

Use the clues in the column to complete the puzzle.

Across

2. A device with splines on the inside only, used as a gear selection method in manual transmissions.

4. Spring-loaded steel balls that hold the shift rails in position.

5. The cover on the transmission that holds the shift rails and forks.

Down

1. The shaft inside a transmission driven by the input gear.

2. A raised section with a pivot into which the shift lever fits.

3. The path it takes from the beginning of an assembly to the end. In a transmission, it changes as different gears are selected by the driver.

ASE-Type Questions

Read each item carefully, and then select the best response.

_____ 1. Technician A says that in order to make a range shift in a Fuller Roadranger transmission, you move the range selector valve lever first and then shift the transmission to the correct gear. Technician B says that you shift the transmission to neutral first and then move the range selector valve lever. You only shift to the correct gear once you hear the range shift complete. Who is shifting the transmission correctly?
  A. Technician A
  B. Technician B
  C. Both Technician A and Technician B
  D. Neither Technician A nor Technician B

_____ 2. Technician A says that the splitter control button on a Fuller 13-speed manual transmission can be operated in both low and high ranges. Technician B says that the splitter control button on a Fuller 18-speed manual transmission can be operated in both high and low range. Who is correct?
  A. Technician A
  B. Technician B
  C. Both Technician A and Technician B
  D. Neither Technician A nor Technician B

_____ 3. Technician A says that the splitter piston in a Fuller 18-speed transmission moves forward for high split. Technician B says that the splitter piston in the 13-speed Fuller is rearward during low range. Who is correct?
  A. Technician A
  B. Technician B
  C. Both Technician A and Technician B
  D. Neither Technician A nor Technician B

_____ 4. Technician A says that the air shift system in a Fuller 13-speed RTLO series transmission operates at 57–63 psi (393–434 kPa). Technician B says that the Fuller FR series transmission's air system also operates at 57–63 psi (393–434 kPa). Who is correct?
  A. Technician A
  B. Technician B
  C. Both Technician A and Technician B
  D. Neither Technician A nor Technician B

_____ 5. Technician A says that the slave air valve in a Fuller 13-speed RTLO series transmission is moved by air for both the low- and high-range positions. Technician B says that in the Fuller FR series transmissions the spool valve in the shift control air module moves to the high-range position by spring pressure. Who is correct?
  A. Technician A
  B. Technician B
  C. Both Technician A and Technician B
  D. Neither Technician A nor Technician B

_____ 6. Technician A says that a standard transmission noise that occurs in all gears except fifth in a five-speed non-overdrive transmission could indicate a failed output shaft pilot bearing. Technician B says that the rear output shaft support bearing could be the cause. Who is correct?
  A. Technician A
  B. Technician B
  C. Both Technician A and Technician B
  D. Neither Technician A nor Technician B

_____ 7. Technician A says that the Fuller deep reduction transmission has the deep reduction gear at the rear of the auxiliary section. Technician B says that the auxiliary section main shaft in a Fuller deep-reduction transmissions is in two pieces. Who is correct?
  A. Technician A
  B. Technician B
  C. Both Technician A and Technician B
  D. Neither Technician A nor Technician B

_____ **8.** Technician A says that in a low split position the splitter sliding clutch is forward in the 13-speed Fuller transmission. Technician B says that the range synchronizer is rearward when the 13-speed transmission is in low range. Who is correct?
  A. Technician A
  B. Technician B
  C. Both Technician A and Technician B
  D. Neither Technician A nor Technician B

_____ **9.** Technician A says that, when a 13-speed fuller transmission auxiliary section is in low split, air is present at both sides of the splitter cylinder piston. Technician B says that, when the 13-speed Fuller transmission auxiliary section is in high split, air is present at the back of the splitter cylinder piston only. Who is correct?
  A. Technician A
  B. Technician B
  C. Both Technician A and Technician B
  D. Neither Technician A nor Technician B

_____ **10.** Technician A says that air is present at both sides of the range cylinder piston in a Fuller 13-speed transmission auxiliary section when it is in low range. Technician B says that air is present at the back of the range cylinder piston only in a Fuller 13-speed transmission auxiliary section when it is in high range. Who is correct?
  A. Technician A
  B. Technician B
  C. Both Technician A and Technician B
  D. Neither Technician A nor Technician B

Servicing Standard Transmissions

Chapter Review

The following activities have been designed to help you refresh your knowledge of this chapter. Your instructor may require you to complete some or all of these activities as a regular part of your training program. You are encouraged to complete any activity that your instructor does not assign as a way to enhance your learning.

Matching

Match the following terms with the correct description or example.

A. Line haul

B. Nomenclature

C. Pre-dampening

D. Reluctor

E. Vocational

_____ **1.** A toothed wheel used with magnetic sensors, usually to measure shaft speed.

_____ **2.** A truck that spends most of its time in on-highway operations under medium to heavy loading.

_____ **3.** A truck that is subject to primarily off-road operation and typically is heavily loaded.

_____ **4.** The meaning of the letters and digits in truck transmission's model numbers.

_____ **5.** A clutch system that absorbs minor torsional vibrations to prevent gear rattle at idle.

Multiple Choice

Read each item carefully, and then select the best response.

_____ **1.** The most common petroleum or synthetic-based lubricant recommended for medium-/heavy-duty transmissions is _____ weight engine oil.
   A. SAE 30
   B. SAE 40
   C. SAE 50
   D. SAE 60

_____ **2.** Transmissions that are filled at the factory with petroleum-based oils will usually require an initial drain and fill after _____ of operation.
   A. 1,000 miles (1,610 km)
   B. 3,000 miles (4,830 km)
   C. 5,000 miles (8,050 km)
   D. 10,000 miles (16,100 km)

_____ **3.** Which of the following conditions may result in operating temperatures consistently over 250°F (121°C)?
   A. Engine retarder use
   B. Use of cabin heater
   C. Restricted transmission air flow
   D. Either A or C

_____ **4.** A _____ service vehicle operates under extreme (maximum) loading most of the time, or is operated on heavy grades.
   A. severe-duty
   B. line-haul
   C. vocational
   D. heavy-duty

_____ **5.** On a line-haul vehicle used for high-mileage operation you should check fluid levels and inspect for leaks at regular preventive maintenance intervals, not to exceed _____.
  A. 10,000 miles (16,100 km)
  B. 12,000 miles (19,312 km)
  C. 15,000 miles (24,140 km)
  D. 18,000 miles (29,000 km)

_____ **6.** A vocational vehicle used for heavy-duty, off-road, or specialized applications should have its fluid levels checked and be inspected for leaks every _____.
  A. 50 hours
  B. 100 hours
  C. 3 months
  D. 10,000 miles (16,100 km)

_____ **7.** According to Eaton Fuller's recommendations for lube change intervals a medium-duty transmission using Dextron III ATF should be changed every _____.
  A. 50,000 miles (80,470 km) or 1 year
  B. 100,000 miles (161,000 km) or 1 year
  C. 150,000 miles (241,500 km) or every 2 years
  D. 180,000 miles (289,700 km) or every 2 years

_____ **8.** The oil filter should be replaced every _____.
  A. 100,000 miles (161,000 km)
  B. 150,000 miles (241,500 km)
  C. transmission fluid change
  D. Both A and C

_____ **9.** Knocking or thudding sounds as the gears go through mesh may be caused by _____.
  A. damaged gears
  B. worn or damaged bearings
  C. spur-type gears
  D. driveshaft imbalance

_____ **10.** Hard shifting may be caused by a sliding clutch that is binding due to a _____.
  A. twisted main shaft
  B. distorted main shaft key
  C. bent shift yoke
  D. All of the above

True/False

If you believe the statement to be more true than false, write the letter "T" in the space provided. If you believe the statement to be more false than true, write the letter "F".

_____ **1.** These days, manufacturers are warranting their products up to and including 750,000 miles depending on vocation and load factors.

_____ **2.** Vocational transmissions should only be filled using gear oils with extreme pressure additives.

_____ **3.** The air tanks should be drained and checked for contamination on a monthly basis.

_____ **4.** The correct lubricant fill level is even with the edge of the check hole.

_____ **5.** An oil weep is usually an indication of a more serious problem.

_____ **6.** Noises that appear to be coming from the transmission may actually be originating elsewhere in the driveline.

_____ **7.** Gear slip out can occur in the main box and in the auxiliary section.

_____ **8.** Most repair shops can perform a transmission overhaul.

_____ **9.** Unless a snap ring is distorted or broken it may be reused.

_____ **10.** Eaton Fuller twin countershaft transmission input shafts are replaceable without dismantling the transmission.

Fill in the Blank

Read each item carefully, and then complete the statement by filling in the missing word(s).

1. The most common _____ recommended for medium-/heavy-duty transmissions is SAE 50 weight engine oil—either petroleum based or synthetic.

2. If operating temperatures are at or above 250°F (121°C), the use of an external transmission _____ _____ is required.

3. Severe-duty service requires more frequent oil changes; most manufacturers recommend that change frequency be based on oil _____.

4. The key to keeping any transmission in working order is following regular _____ procedures.

5. The first step in any maintenance activity is to _____ the problem.

6. A growling noise can be caused by _____ that are worn and badly damaged.

7. If the air lines are _____, a constant leak of air will be heard at the Roadranger valve while it is in high range.

8. A fin _____ may be required to assist in straightening an oil cooler's fins.

9. Drive train systems are frequently the subject of premature _____ caused by overloading, driver error or abuse, or poor maintenance practices.

10. Driver _____ or inexperience is commonly a cause of shock load failures.

Labeling

Label the following diagrams with the correct terms.

1. Identify the components of a range cylinder:

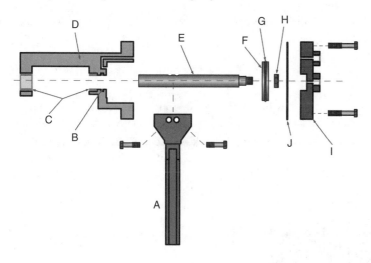

A. _____

B. _____

C. _____

D. _____

E. _____

F. _____

G. _____

H. _____

I. _____

J. _____

Skill Drills

Test your knowledge of skill drills by filling in the correct words in the photo captions.

1. Changing the Transmission Fluid:

Step 1: Raise the vehicle using an approved lift and make sure it is _____. Check all lift specifications and _____ _____, including _____, before the vehicle is elevated. Obtain a clean _____ _____ to put the used fluid in.

Step 2: Inspect the transmission for any leaks.

Step 3: Remove the _____ _____ from the bottom of the _____, being careful of the hot transmission fluid. Let gearbox fluid _____ until it has _____ _____. If necessary, remove the drain plug for the _____ _____ and drain the fluid.

Step 4: Replace the drain plug(s), _____ to the manufacturer's specification, and remove the _____ _____(s).

Step 5: Refill the transmission to the _____ _____ using manufacturer-approved _____ fluid. Replace the _____ _____ and tighten to the manufacturer's specification. Use a shop towel to wipe away any _____.

Step 6: _____ _____ the vehicle. If necessary, put the vehicle back on the _____ and check for any _____ that may have resulted from the service. Always _____ _____ your work before returning the vehicle to the _____.

2. Inspecting the Transmission Oil Filter and Cooler:

Step 1: Locate and _____ the appropriate _____ in the service manual.

Step 2: Complete the accompanying _____ _____ or _____ _____ with all pertinent information.

Step 3: Move the vehicle into the shop, apply the _____ _____, and _____ the vehicle's _____. Observe _____/_____ procedures.

Step 4: If the vehicle has a _____ transmission, place it in "_____"; if it has an _____ transmission, place it in "_____" or "_____." (Note: Some vehicles with automatic transmissions do not have "_____.")

Step 5: Inspect and replace the transmission oil filter:

    a. Check transmission _____ _____ for leaks. If a leak is found, _____ the filter. (Note: If a filter is _____ for any reason, a _____ _____ must be installed.)

    b. Place a _____ _____ under the filter if _____ is necessary.

    c. Remove the oil filter using an oil filter _____ _____ and make sure the _____ _____ from the _____ filter has not been left on the transmission filter _____.

    d. Wipe the _____ _____ on the transmission clean.

    e. Apply a thin coat of transmission _____ to the new filter's _____ _____.

    f. Screw on the _____ filter. (Note: It may be necessary to _____ the transmission _____ _____ prior to removing the filter.)

Step 6: Inspect and replace transmission oil cooler:

    a. Check the _____ for signs of _____. (Note: If there are _____ from the _____, it may have to be _____.)

    b. Check all _____ and _____ for any signs of _____.

    c. Check that the _____ on the cooler's _____ are _____. Use a _____ _____ to straighten the _____, if necessary.

    d. Refer to the _____ _____ for removal and replacement _____ if it is determined that a new _____ must be installed.

Step 7: List the _____ _____ and/or recommendations on the job sheet or work order, _____ the work area, and return _____ and _____ to their proper storage.

3. Replacing the Input Shaft:

Step 1: Remove the _____ according to the procedure in the Heavy-Duty Clutch Servicing chapter. Remember not to let the transmission _____ on the _____ _____ as it is removed. With the transmission suitably _____ on a transmission _____ or a _____, remove the six _____ and four _____ that secure the clutch _____ _____ and remove the housing. Remove the six bolts securing the front _____ _____ and remove the cover and _____. Remove and discard the rubber _____ _____ if present. This _____ is merely for _____ purposes and is not required further.

Step 2: Using _____ _____ pliers, remove the front bearing snap ring from the _____ _____. Use a soft iron _____ to drive the _____ _____ to the rear as far as it will go (approximately 0.25" or 6.35 mm). A _____ is a large 2" (5 cm) diameter _____ approximately 8" (20 cm) long.

Step 3: Grasp the _____ _____ and _____ it. Try to move it forward as far as it will go. If it is difficult to move forward, _____ the transmission housing _____ _____ with the _____ as it is pulled forward. This will expose the large _____ _____ on the outside of the _____ bearing; do not remove this _____ _____.

Step 4: Install the _____ _____ #7070A kit (Owatonna tool company) or equivalent. This tool pulls on the large external _____ _____ on the _____. Remove the _____ bearing.

Step 5: Remove the bearing _____ from the _____ _____. Remove the internal snap ring from the input drive gear using a small _____. Remove the input shaft. The _____ _____ will remain in place in the transmission case.

Step 6: Check and replace (as needed) the input shaft _____ _____. This bushing supports the forward end of the main shaft. Because the _____ _____ "floats," the bushing _____ needs replacing. The input shaft has a _____ _____ just in front of the bearing. The grooves are the _____ _____ "threads." It is critical that they are _____ and _____ or the transmission may _____. Clean or replace as necessary.

Step 7:   To reinstall the input shaft, _____ the removal _____. Insert the input shaft into the _____ _____ and reinstall the _____ snap ring in the gear. Install the _____ on the input shaft _____ the snap ring.

Step 8:   Carefully _____ the input bearing. Slide it over the input shaft and install it using bearing _____ _____ #5066 (Owatonna tool company) or equivalent. This driver has a large _____ that contacts both bearing _____ and is recommended by Eaton Fuller. Drive the bearing until the bearing contacts the _____ _____. Reinstall the input shaft snap ring to _____ the _____. Do not _____ the rubber _____ _____ if present—it is for shipping purposes only.

Step 9:   Reinstall the front bearing _____ with a new _____. Be careful to _____ _____ the oil drain _____ _____ in the _____ and in the _____ to the oil return hole in the transmission case. Apply _____ 242 to the _____ _____ and _____ to 40 to 45 ft-lb (54 to 61 Nm). Reinstall the clutch _____ _____ and torque to specification. Reinstall the _____ as described in the clutch chapter.

4. Replacing Rear Seals:

Step 1: Disconnect the _____ at the output _____ of the transmission. Place the transmission in _____ _____ low range. This will prevent the yoke from _____. Remove the yoke nut using a 2.75" (70 mm) _____. Remove the yoke using a yoke _____ tool.

Step 2: Remove the vehicle _____ _____ (VSS). Remove the speedometer _____ (rotor) and the O-ring from the _____. Carefully pry the seal out with a _____ or _____ _____ inserted into the seal _____. Do not pry against the seal _____.

Step 3: Remove the _____ _____ from the speedometer reluctor (rotor) using a suitable _____ _____ if necessary. Check the sealing surface of the reluctor for _____, _____, or _____. Do not try to _____ the surface. If damaged, _____ it.

Step 4: Install the seal into the housing using a suitable _____ _____. The Eaton P/N 5564501 driver is for the 7 series transmission; the 9 series transmission uses a _____ _____. Check the OEM manual for the correct _____. Then, install the _____ _____ onto the _____ reluctor using the proper _____. The Eaton P/N 71223 driver is for the 7 series transmission; the 9 series uses a _____ driver. Check the _____ _____ for the _____ driver.

Step 5: Install the O-ring and the speedometer reluctor. Install the speedometer _____. If the sensor is the _____-_____ type, adjust it by _____ the sensor in until it contacts a _____ on the reluctor. Then _____ _____ _____ ½ to 1 turn.

Step 6: Install the _____ _____ and _____ the _____ to 450–500 ft-lb (9,610–9,677 Nm). If the _____ lock on the nut is _____ or _____ significantly, replace the nut. Reinstall the _____ _____ and top up the transmission with the correct _____ until the level is _____ with the _____ _____.

5. Disassembling the Auxiliary Section:

Step 1: Remove the _____ section _____ _____. Use a yoke _____ as needed. Place a clean shop towel into the _____ _____ to stop the _____ _____ from turning. With yoke removed, remove the speedometer _____ and the O-ring from the _____ _____.

Step 2: Use a _____ and a _____ _____ to drive the _____ output shaft _____ slightly (0.5" or 13 mm) to facilitate _____ of the auxiliary countershafts. Remove the countershaft _____ _____ one at a time while _____ the countershafts. Remove each countershaft and its bearing _____. _____ the countershafts so they can be re-installed on the _____ _____.

Step 3: Remove the _____ _____, the yoke, and the range _____ _____ together from the front of the _____ and set aside. Drive the auxiliary _____ _____ forward with the maul and _____ it. Do not misplace the large, steel bearing _____. If _____ replacing the output _____ _____, leave the _____ output shaft bearing in place as shown.

Step 4: If _____ the output shaft bearings, place the output shaft in a _____ with the _____ _____ supported by _____. Press the output shaft _____ the range gear and the _____ to remove it. Note that the front and rear support bearings are _____, so do not _____ _____ _____. The front rear support bearing inner _____ is slightly larger. Remove the rear bearing _____ from the auxiliary section _____.

Step 5: Remove the _____ output shaft support _____ and _____. Some models have a _____-_____ outer and inner bearing race as shown.

Crossword Puzzle

Use the clues in the column to complete the puzzle.

Across

2. The condition in which a transmission jumps out of gear and to neutral when under load, caused by worn components such as sliding clutches and shift forks. Also called gear slip out.

3. A lubricant that is manufactured rather than refined and so has much longer service life; it can be a blend of natural and synthetic materials.

5. Very minor oil seepage usually caused by a wicking effect and not usually a reason for a repair.

Down

1. A transmission shift linkage that is not mounted directly above the shift cover and that must be properly maintained and lubricated to prevent hard shifting.

4. The tapered profile of the teeth on a sliding clutch such that the outer edge is thicker than the inner; the profile helps keep the clutch engaged under load.

ASE-Type Questions

Read each item carefully, and then select the best response.

_____ 1. Technician A says that normal non-synthetic lubricant can be used to top up a transmission that is equipped with synthetic oil. Technician B says that a transmission shipped from the factory with synthetic oil will have a much longer service interval than one with mineral-based oil. Who is correct?
   A. Technician A
   B. Technician B
   C. Both Technician A and Technician B
   D. Neither Technician A nor Technician B

_____ 2. Technician A says that the correct lubricant level in a transmission should reach the bottom of the fill plug hole. Technician B says that as long as you can feel the fluid with the first digit of your hand the level is OK. Who is correct?
   A. Technician A
   B. Technician B
   C. Both Technician A and Technician B
   D. Neither Technician A nor Technician B

_____ 3. Technician A says that transmission rattling at idle can be caused by engine torsional vibrations. Technician B says that a clutch with pre-dampening can eliminate gear rattle at idle. Who is correct?
   A. Technician A
   B. Technician B
   C. Both Technician A and Technician B
   D. Neither Technician A nor Technician B

_____ 4. Technician A says that if an Eaton Fuller Roadranger transmission is an overdrive model it will have an O in the first four letters of its model number. Technician B says that an F in the third or fourth letter position of the model number means it is a five-speed model. Who is correct?
   A. Technician A
   B. Technician B
   C. Both Technician A and Technician B
   D. Neither Technician A nor Technician B

_____ 5. Technician A says that, for today's transmissions with synthetic lube, preventative maintenance is basically a visual inspection of all the transmission systems. Technician B says that transmissions equipped with straight mineral oil have oil change intervals of 500,000 miles (805,000 kilometers). Who is correct?
   A. Technician A
   B. Technician B
   C. Both Technician A and Technician B
   D. Neither Technician A nor Technician B

_____ 6. Technician A says that when overhauling a Fuller 10-speed auxiliary section, the auxiliary drive ear must be timed to the auxiliary countershafts. Technician B says that auxiliary section countershaft support straps are necessary to reinstall the auxiliary section. Who is correct?
   A. Technician A
   B. Technician B
   C. Both Technician A and Technician B
   D. Neither Technician A nor Technician B

_____ 7. Technician A says that the air filter regulator is the first place to check if a Fuller 13-speed transmission air shift system is not working correctly. Technician B says that the air supply to the air filter regulator passes through a pressure protection valve. Who is correct?
   A. Technician A
   B. Technician B
   C. Both Technician A and Technician B
   D. Neither Technician A nor Technician B

_____ **8.** Technician A says that you must line up the range cylinder shift bar in the shift cover with the range cylinder shift fork while installing the shift cover on a 13-speed Fuller transmission. Technician B says that the Fuller 13-speed transmission range shift cylinder is located at the back of the auxiliary section. Who is correct?

A. Technician A

B. Technician B

C. Both Technician A and Technician B

D. Neither Technician A nor Technician B

_____ **9.** Technician A says that auxiliary countershaft end play must be checked and adjusted if the auxiliary countershaft bearings are replaced. Technician B says that the main shaft end play should be checked before reinstalling the auxiliary section. Who is correct?

A. Technician A

B. Technician B

C. Both Technician A and Technician B

D. Neither Technician A nor Technician B

_____ **10.** Technician A says that worn clutching teeth on the range synchronizer sliding clutch are normal and the clutch does not need to be replaced. Technician B says that worn range synchronizer clutching teeth are a sign of driver abuse. Who is correct?

A. Technician A

B. Technician B

C. Both Technician A and Technician B

D. Neither Technician A nor Technician B

Automated Manual Transmissions

Tire Tread:
© AbleStock

Chapter Review

The following activities have been designed to help you refresh your knowledge of this chapter. Your instructor may require you to complete some or all of these activities as a regular part of your training program. You are encouraged to complete any activity that your instructor does not assign as a way to enhance your learning.

Matching

Match the following terms with the correct description or example.

A. AS-Tronic
B. AutoSelect
C. DT-12
D. Engine Synchro Shift (ESS)
E. I-Shift

F. Procision
G. SureShift
H. TC-Tronic
I. Traxon
J. UltraShift

_____ 1. Meritor's first AMT; limited to synchronizing engine speeds to assist the shifting process.

_____ 2. Meritor's first line of fully automated transmissions.

_____ 3. Eaton's two-pedal AMT; completely shift by wire with no clutch pedal.

_____ 4. Eaton's first AMT; very limited electronic control.

_____ 5. The Volvo AMT; Mack trucks use the same transmission.

_____ 6. A ZF AMT that uses a torque converter for input; for heavy applications.

_____ 7. ZF's AMT for medium- and heavy-duty trucks and buses.

_____ 8. ZF's latest AMT with five different input modules available.

_____ 9. A 12-speed AMT manufactured by Detroit Diesel.

_____ 10. Eaton's dual-clutch seven-speed AMT; introduced in 2014.

Multiple Choice

Read each item carefully, and then select the best response.

_____ 1. The shifting process for an electronically automated transmission is controlled by the _____.
   A. transmission control unit
   B. engine shift control module
   C. transmission electronic control module
   D. Either A or C

_____ 2. Unloading the gear train as a shift is being made is known as _____.
   A. downshifting
   B. break torque
   C. gear jamming
   D. double clutching

_____ 3. The technique of shifting a truck transmission without using the clutch pedal except for starting from a stop is referred to as _____.
   A. gear jamming
   B. syncro shifting
   C. double clutching
   D. Either A or C

_____ **4.** The original SAE communication protocol for commercial vehicles was known as _____; it was quite slow in terms of data transmission at 9,600 bits per second.
   A. CAN
   B. ISO 9141
   C. J-1587
   D. IDB-1394

_____ **5.** The first fully automated standard transmission to hit the North American market was the Eaton _____.
   A. AutoShift
   B. Synchro Shift
   C. SureShift
   D. I-Shift

_____ **6.** The _____ automated transmission series is Volvo's 12-speed, two-pedal design with electric-over-air actuation that is controlled by the transmission TCU.
   A. I-Shift
   B. AS-Tronic
   C. Traxon
   D. DT-12

_____ **7.** In 2004, Mercedes Benz introduced the _____ two-pedal, six-speed automated transmission designed for medium-duty trucks with up to a 60,000 lb (27,216 kg) gross vehicle weight.
   A. UltraShift
   B. TC-Tronic
   C. automatic gear shift
   D. I-Shift

_____ **8.** The SAE _____ communication protocol features data transmission at a rate of at least 250,000 bits per second and up to 500,000 bits per second.
   A. J-1587
   B. Snapshot
   C. J-1939
   D. IDB-1394

_____ **9.** For clash-free shifts to occur, the transmission control software must know the precise speed of the _____.
   A. input shaft
   B. countershaft
   C. main shaft
   D. All of the above

_____ **10.** Using Eaton Fuller's new transmission nomenclature the letter _____ would indicate a wet shifting clutch configuration.
   A. D
   B. S
   C. E
   D. W

True/False

If you believe the statement to be more true than false, write the letter "T" in the space provided. If you believe the statement to be more false than true, write the letter "F".

_____ **1.** The only way a vehicle can reduce its output of carbon dioxide is by supplementing the engine's power output with another energy source, such as hybrid electric technology.

_____ **2.** Automated manual transmissions allow the driver to keep both hands on the steering wheel.

_____ **3.** The Super Ten Top Two transmission is an electronics-over-air-actuated, three-pedal, fully automated transmission.

_____ **4.** The Meritor Engine Synchro Shift was the first automated transmission that did not require manual shifting.

_____ **5.** The DT-12 system does not use a clutch pedal.

_____ **6.** Data mechanical clutches are operated centrifugally.

_____ **7.** In the first generation of AutoShift transmissions, the system manager and the shift lever were combined into a single electronic module.

_____ **8.** AutoShift and UltraShift transmissions use six different speed sensors to calculate the relationship between the various shaft speeds.

_____ **9.** The momentary engine ignition interrupt relay is only supplied if the vehicle has an UltraShift transmission with a data mechanical (or DM) clutch.

_____ **10.** The SOLO self-adjusting clutch is the only clutch used by Eaton Fuller in its line of electronically automated transmissions.

Fill in the Blank

Read each item carefully, and then complete the statement by filling in the missing word(s).

1. The only way a vehicle can reduce its output of _____ _____ is by supplementing the engine's power output with another energy source, such as hybrid electric technology.

2. New technologies and strategies from engine advancements to truck body shapes designed to reduce drag are being used to achieve higher _____ _____.

3. Two-pedal model electronically automated transmissions have no clutch pedal, the transmission's operation is entirely shifted by _____.

4. The _____-_____ capability of the transmission control unit allows it to troubleshoot and analyze its own functions.

5. A _____-_____ transmission has two separate input shafts controlled by two separate clutches.

6. A data _____ records all the relevant TCU data before and after a diagnostic code is set to ease diagnoses.

7. The _____ _____ relay interrupts the circuit to the starter solenoid when it is not activated, preventing the vehicle from starting.

8. The _____ _____ _____ used on Eaton AutoShift and UltraShift transmissions consists of two shift motors: the shift finger and the shift finger position sensors.

9. Eaton claims that the _____ transmission can achieve an 8 to 10% improvement in fuel economy over an automatic transmission when installed in a vehicle used for around-town deliveries.

10. The fault code _____ _____ is a step-by-step method of diagnosing and repairing a fault.

Labeling

Label the following diagrams with the correct terms.

1. Identify the components of an inertia brake assembly:

Released
(Coil off)

A. _____

B. _____

C. _____

D. _____

2. Identify the components of the Eaton Procision transmission:

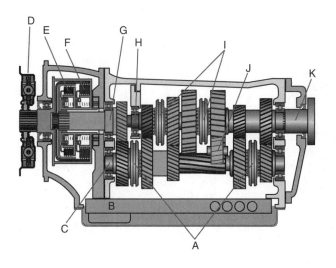

A. _____

B. _____

C. _____

D. _____

E. _____

F. _____

G. _____

H. _____

I. _____

J. _____

K. _____

3. Identify the components of the four solenoid-controlled air actuators in a ZF transmission:

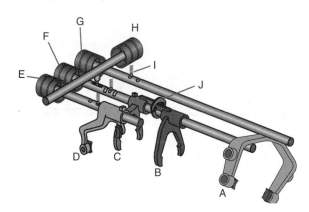

A. _____

B. _____

C. _____

D. _____

E. _____

F. _____

G. _____

H. _____

I. _____

J. _____

Skill Drills

Test your knowledge of skill drills by filling in the correct words in the photo captions.

1. Enabling the Self-Diagnostic Mode and Retrieving Codes:

Step 1: Place the transmission in _____.

Step 2: Set the _____ _____.

Step 3: To retrieve active codes: Start with the key in the _____ position. Turn the key off and on _____ times within _____ _____. End with the key in the ON position. After 5 seconds, the _____ _____ should begin _____ two-digit _____ _____. If no faults are active, the service light will flash code _____ (no codes). Note: A code _____ may show up in the dash at key ON. That is a _____ power-up _____ of the display.

Step 4: To retrieve _____ codes: Start with the _____ in the ON position. Turn the key off and on _____ times within _____ seconds. End with the key in the ON position. After 5 seconds, the _____ _____ should begin flashing _____-_____ fault codes. If there are no inactive _____, the service light will flash code _____ (no codes).

Step 5: Two-digit fault codes may be read directly from the _____ _____ or by observing the flashing service transmission _____, if equipped. Observe the _____ of flashes on the _____ _____, and record the _____. The flash codes are displayed as follows: _____ flash, a short _____, and then _____ flashes equals code _____. There is a _____ _____ of 3 to 4 seconds _____ codes. Then the next code will be flashed. For example _____ flashes, a _____ pause, and then _____ flashes equals code _____. Another _____ _____ would follow and the two codes would _____ once more.

2. Clearing Inactive Codes:

Step 1: Place the _____ _____ in neutral.

Step 2: Set the _____ _____.

Step 3: Turn the _____ _____ on but do not _____ the engine.

Step 4: Start with the key in the _____ position. Turn the key off and on _____ times within _____ _____. End with the key in the ON position. Note: If the _____ have been successfully _____, the service lamp will come on and stay on for _____ seconds. The _____ _____ will show code _____ (no codes).

Step 5: Turn the key _____ and allow the system to _____ _____.

3. Using a Scan Tool to Diagnose Transmissions:

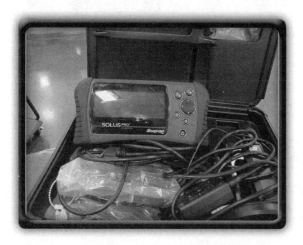

Step 1:   Locate and _____ the appropriate procedure in the _____ _____.

Step 2:   Complete the accompanying _____ _____ or _____ _____ with all pertinent information.

Step 3:   Move the _____ into the shop and _____ it on _____ _____.

Step 4:   Apply parking brakes, _____ the vehicle _____, and observe _____/_____ procedures.

Step 5:   If the vehicle has a _____ transmission, place it in _____; if it has an _____ or _____ transmission, place it in _____ or _____. Note: Some vehicles with automatic transmissions do not have _____.

Step 6:   Check for active and inactive _____ _____ using the appropriate service manual procedure and _____ _____.

Step 7:   Record any _____ trouble codes on the _____ _____ or _____ _____.

Step 8:   Use a _____ to _____ the problem(s) associated with the trouble code(s).

Step 9:   Record all diagnostic _____.

Step 10: Repair or _____ the affected systems or _____.

Step 11: Clear all _____ and _____ trouble codes.

Step 12: List the _____ _____ and/or recommendations on the job sheet or work order, _____ the _____ _____, and return _____ and _____ to their proper _____.

Crossword Puzzle

Use the clues in the column to complete the puzzle.

Across

1. This records all the relevant TCU data before and after a diagnostic code is set to ease diagnoses.
4. Twelve- and 16-speed ZF AMTs released in partnership with Meritor.
5. A measurement of how much of the fuel used is actually turned into power to drive the vehicle.

Down

2. A transmission control module used with older Gen 1 and Gen 2 Eaton AutoShift transmissions.
3. A component used to control the speed of the transmission countershaft and main shaft gears.

ASE-Type Questions

Read each item carefully, and then select the best response.

_____ 1. Technician A says that two-pedal AMTs still require a clutch. Technician B says that in three-pedal AMTs the driver uses the clutch only for starting off and stopping the vehicle. Who is correct?
  A. Technician A
  B. Technician B
  C. Both Technician A and Technician B
  D. Neither Technician A nor Technician B

_____ 2. Technician A says that all AMTs use a standard dry disc clutch. Technician B says that the Volvo I-Shift uses a large organic dry disc clutch. Who is correct?
  A. Technician A
  B. Technician B
  C. Both Technician A and Technician B
  D. Neither Technician A nor Technician B

_____ 3. Technician A says that the new Eaton Procision uses two multi-plate wet clutches as inputs. Technician B says that the Procision transmission has two input shafts. Who is correct?
  A. Technician A
  B. Technician B
  C. Both Technician A and Technician B
  D. Neither Technician A nor Technician B

_____ 4. Technician A says that the AS-Tronic transmission from ZF uses a splitter gear at the input to double the ratios in the front box section. Technician B says that the rearward split in the splitter section of the ZF AS-Tronic is always the high split position. Who is correct?
  A. Technician A
  B. Technician B
  C. Both Technician A and Technician B
  D. Neither Technician A nor Technician B

_____ 5. Technician A says that the 12-speed Volvo I-Shift transmission has the same basic power flows as the 12-speed AS-Tronic from ZF. Technician B says the 12-speed Volvo I-Shift has only one countershaft. Who is correct?
  A. Technician A
  B. Technician B
  C. Both Technician A and Technician B
  D. Neither Technician A nor Technician B

_____ 6. Technician A says that the sliding clutches in a Fuller UltraShift transmission have wider tooth spacing than non-automated transmission models. Technician B says that the main shaft gears in a Fuller UltraShift transmission have wider tooth spacing than non-automated transmission models. Who is correct?
  A. Technician A
  B. Technician B
  C. Both Technician A and Technician B
  D. Neither Technician A nor Technician B

_____ 7. Technician A says that a Fuller 18-speed UltraShift transmission uses two air solenoids to control splitter shift in the auxiliary section. Technician B says that a Fuller 18-speed UltraShift transmission uses two air solenoids to control the range shift in the auxiliary section. Who is correct?
  A. Technician A
  B. Technician B
  C. Both Technician A and Technician B
  D. Neither Technician A nor Technician B

_____ 8. Technician A says the MEIIR relay is controlled by the engine ECM. Technician B says that the MEIIR relay is only actuated when there is catastrophic clutch failure. Who is correct?
  A. Technician A
  B. Technician B
  C. Both Technician A and Technician B
  D. Neither Technician A nor Technician B

_____ **9.** Technician A says that the Eaton Procision seven-speed transmission does not need to break torque while shifting though gears 1 to 7. Technician B says that the Eaton Procision transmission preselects seventh gear while still in sixth to make the shift quicker. Who is correct?

    A. Technician A

    B. Technician B

    C. Both Technician A and Technician B

    D. Neither Technician A nor Technician B

_____ **10.** Technician A says that the ZF AS-Tronic transmission has an overdrive gear in the range section. Technician B says that the AS-Tronic can have either two or three main shaft gears. Who is correct?

    A. Technician A

    B. Technician B

    C. Both Technician A and Technician B

    D. Neither Technician A nor Technician B

Torque Converters

Chapter Review

The following activities have been designed to help you refresh your knowledge of this chapter. Your instructor may require you to complete some or all of these activities as a regular part of your training program. You are encouraged to complete any activity that your instructor does not assign as a way to enhance your learning.

Matching

Match the following terms with the correct description or example.

A. Impeller

B. Stator

C. Torque converter

D. Torus

E. Turbine

_____ **1.** The torque converter element that is splined to the transmission input shaft.

_____ **2.** The hollowed-out donut shape of the rear of the converter housing and the turbine.

_____ **3.** The element inside a torque converter most responsible for torque multiplication.

_____ **4.** A type of fluid coupling that is also capable of multiplying torque.

_____ **5.** The bladed element in a torque converter or fluid coupling that is fixed to the housing and therefore rotates with it.

Multiple Choice

Read each item carefully, and then select the best response.

_____ **1.** When conditions are correct, the _____ connects the turbine to the converter shell, and the engine power is transmitted one to one to the driveline, eliminating any loss in efficiency.

A. torus

B. lock-up clutch

C. impeller

D. stator

_____ **2.** The _____ is the driving "fan."

A. impeller

B. turbine

C. stator

D. torus

_____ **3.** One half of the _____ is attached to the middle of the impeller's blades to provide strength and create a circular passage for fluid flow.

A. split guide ring

B. lock-up clutch

C. pump drive hub

D. stator

_____ **4.** The _____ has a series of curved blades that are designed to catch the oil being thrown forward by the rotating impeller.

A. stator

B. impeller

C. turbine

D. torus

_____ **5.** The inner hub of the stator is splined to the _____, which surrounds and supports the transmission input shaft.
   A. stator support
   B. split guide ring
   C. ground shaft
   D. Either A or C

_____ **6.** During _____, the fluid being thrown outward by the centrifugal force is thrown forward by the torus shape of the rear half of the shell.
   A. rotary flow
   B. centrifugal flow
   C. vortex flow
   D. torus flow

_____ **7.** The amount of torque produced by the torque converter is based on _____.
   A. the angle of the turbine blades
   B. the speed differential between the impeller and the turbine
   C. the angle of the stator blades
   D. All of the above

_____ **8.** The stator is mounted on a _____ one-way clutch.
   A. sprag-type
   B. pin-type
   C. roller-type
   D. Either A or C

_____ **9.** With the _____ lock-up strategy, the transmission controller engages lock-up every time the transmission reaches a certain gear range.
   A. programmed
   B. centrifugal
   C. modulated
   D. Either a or C

_____ **10.** The lock-up clutch piston squeezes the _____ between the piston and the backing plate.
   A. flywheel
   B. lock-up clutch disc
   C. one-way clutch
   D. flex plate

True/False

If you believe the statement to be more true than false, write the letter "T" in the space provided. If you believe the statement to be more false than true, write the letter "F".

_____ **1.** Just as a gear ratio multiplies the output torque in a transmission, the torque converter multiplies the input torque.

_____ **2.** The turbine and the impeller touch each other.

_____ **3.** The impeller is capable of driving the turbine at full engine speed.

_____ **4.** Any air inside the torque converter will cause aeration, excess heat, and very poor torque transmission.

_____ **5.** During the coupling phase, the impeller, the turbine, the stator, and the fluid are all turning together at essentially the same speed.

_____ **6.** The torque converter is coupled directly to the engine crankshaft and the flywheel.

_____ **7.** Lock-up clutches are essential in today's automatic transmissions as a way to minimize wasted energy in the driveline.

_____ **8.** The first place the fluid goes on exiting the torque converter is usually the transmission oil cooler.

_____ **9.** Pressure testing is the first test a technician should perform when diagnosing transmission or converter complaints.

_____ **10.** A high stall speed is almost always caused by a slipping clutch.

Fill in the Blank

Read each item carefully, and then complete the statement by filling in the missing word(s).

1. The torque converter is a sophisticated type of fluid _____ that allows the vehicle to slow down and stop without any disconnection of components.

2. The rear half of the shell has a hollow stub attached to its center called the _____ _____ hub that drives the transmission oil pump gears.

3. The forward end of the input shaft or the front of the turbine is usually supported by a(n) _____ inside the torque converter housing that serves to locate the turbine radially.

4. The _____ is shaped like a wheel with curved blades for spokes.

5. The _____-_____ (one-way) clutch sits on the stator inner hub and supports the stator wheel.

6. The most popular type of lock-up clutch in the truck market is the _____ type.

7. The torque _____ phase occurs any time the torque converter is increasing the engine's torque output to the transmission's input shaft.

8. Converters with _____ _____ stators allow the angle of the stator blades to be changed hydraulically to benefit both starting off and high-speed operation.

9. In light-duty vehicles, the _____ _____ is usually a single plate of flexible steel bolted directly to the crankshaft.

10. The fluid pathway features anti-drain-back _____ _____ that ensure the fluid does not drain back out of the torque converter when the vehicle is shut off.

Skill Drills

Test your knowledge of skill drills by filling in the correct words in the photo captions.

1. Performing a Stall Test on Engines with Smoke Controls:

Step 1: Install an accurate _____ and a method to monitor transmission _____.

Step 2: With the engine and transmission at _____ temperature, _____ _____ the vehicle in a location where it can be _____ at a speed necessary to conduct the test.

Step 3: Drive the vehicle in a low enough gear that the _____ can be held _____ _____ without exceeding the speed limit. (Do not operate the vehicle in _____ _____ as the _____ could be placed under excessive stress.)

Step 4: Holding the _____ in the wide open position, apply the _____ _____ until the vehicle comes to a complete stop. Immediately record the engine _____ and then release the throttle. This will be the _____ _____.

2. Performing a Lock-Up Converter Test:

Step 1: Scan the vehicle to identify any _____ the transmission _____ has identified related to the _____ circuit; record your findings.

Step 2: Look up the _____ procedure for the _____ in the service information and _____ the step-by-step diagnostic _____.

Step 3: Test-drive the vehicle and _____ the operation of the _____ _____. When the TCC is applied, the TCC _____ should be less than the _____ slippage specified. (Some manufacturers specify maximum TCC slippage of _____ rpm.) If TCC slippage is _____ than specifications, the TCC is not functioning correctly. First suspect an _____ failure and check for loose _____ or _____.

Step 4: Check the TCC circuit for _____ at the transmission. The system's _____ may be blown. If it is blown, _____ _____ it blew.

Step 5: If full power and _____ are not available at the _____ _____, locate the open or high _____ using a _____ to measure _____ _____.

Step 6: If power and ground are available at the TCC connector on the transmission, measure the _____ of the _____ through the TCC connector. If out of specifications, the transmission will need to be _____ and the _____ removed to test the wires and solenoid. If the _____ is not within specifications, _____ the solenoid.

Step 7: If _____ and _____ are available to the TCC connector, and the TCC resistance is within specifications, the _____ solenoid will need to be removed and checked to see if the _____ is actually opening and closing. Apply power and ground to the solenoid while attempting to _____ _____ through the solenoid. If the solenoid operates properly, the problem is likely in the TCC itself. If the _____ does not allow _____ to flow, place the solenoid in a clean container of automatic transmission fluid and electrically _____ the solenoid to see if you can remove any _____ from the solenoid. If this does not work, it will be necessary to _____ the solenoid.

3. Performing Pressure Tests:

Step 1:   Refer to the appropriate _____ information to find the _____ to test the transmission's _____ pressures. Verify the correct transmission fluid _____ in the transmission.

Step 2:   Place a _____ _____ under the transmission and remove the correct pressure _____ _____ plug(s). Place the test port _____(s) off to the side where they will not be lost.

Step 3:   Install a transmission _____ _____(s) capable of measuring the _____ pressure into the _____ _____(s) on the transmission.

Step 4:   Start the vehicle and place the vehicle in the correct _____ conditions to monitor the _____ according to the manufacturer (for example, transmission at operating temperature, in _____, engine _____). Record the pressure(s).

Step 5:   Shut off the engine, _____ the transmission pressure tester(s), _____ the _____, and _____the test port plug(s).

Step 6:   Clean off any transmission _____ that dripped onto the transmission, restart the vehicle to check for _____, and _____ _____ the fluid if necessary.

4. Inspecting for Leakage and Replacing Seals, Gaskets, and Bushings:

Step 1:   Place the vehicle in a _____ condition for the inspection. Carefully _____ the _____ _____, output _____, and _____ shaft seals for _____.

Step 2:   Inspect the transmission _____ _____, side pan gasket (if equipped), and _____ _____ gasket.

Step 3:   Inspect the extension housing _____ by moving the _____ up and down. If there is excessive _____ in the driveshaft, the extension housing bushing must be _____. Place a _____ _____ under the extension housing and remove the _____ from the vehicle.

Step 4:   Remove the _____ _____ from the vehicle. On some older vehicles, the _____ and _____ can be replaced while it is still in the vehicle using a specially designed _____. Remove the extension housing _____ using the correct _____.

Step 5:   Use the correct-sized _____ _____ to _____ the extension housing bushing.

Step 6:   Use the correct-sized bushing driver to carefully _____ the bushing into place. Take note of any _____ holes that need to be _____ _____ before installation.

Step 7:   Use the correct seal _____ _____ to install the new _____ in the _____.

Step 8:   Lubricate the _____ of the seal with clean _____ _____.

Step 9:   Reinstall the _____ _____ and the _____.

5. Disassembling a Torque Converter:

Step 1: Place the _____ _____ on a bench with a _____ system. When the converter is _____ there will be a significant amount of transmission _____ inside, so be prepared.

Step 2: Before removing the bolts, _____ the two _____ of the _____ so that it can be reassembled in the exact same location. The converter _____ are usually individually _____, but it always makes sense to reinstall the _____ the way they came apart.

Step 3: Check the turbine _____ _____ dimension before disassembly. This will allow you to _____ any _____ when you have it apart. This is accomplished by _____ a special tool that grabs the _____ and allows you to _____ it. Measure the total _____ and calculate the _____ required to bring it to specification.

Step 4: Remove the converter _____ (there may be as many as 50). Remove the _____ half from the rest of the converter. Although it is the _____ half, it is still quite _____, so be careful. You may need to _____ the _____ with a _____ _____ hammer to separate the halves. When they are apart, discard the sealing _____. Remove the _____ and the thrust washers/bearings that support it, and then remove the _____.

Step 5: Next, remove the _____ backing plate. It may be sandwiched between the front and the rear half of the _____, or it may be _____ into the front half of the converter _____. Remove the lock-up _____ _____, and finally remove the lock-up clutch _____. It should be _____ in terms of its position in the converter shell. To remove the piston, apply a small amount of _____ _____ to the piston apply side.

Crossword Puzzle

Use the clues in the column to complete the puzzle.

Across

2. Fluid flow inside the torque converter that follows the rotation of the housing.
4. A flexible plate used to connect the torque converter to the engine.
5. The maximum speed the engine can drive the torque converter impeller with the turbine held stationary.

Down

1. Apparent force by which a rotating mass tries to move outward away from its axis of rotation.
3. A power transfer device that uses fluid to transmit power to the driveline.

ASE-Type Questions

Read each item carefully, and then select the best response.

_____ 1. Technician A says that a fluid coupler is capable of transmitting torque to a driveline as long as the load is not too great. Technician B says that a fluid coupling can multiply torque up to four to one. Who is correct?
   A. Technician A
   B. Technician B
   C. Both Technician A and Technician B
   D. Neither Technician A nor Technician B

_____ 2. Technician A says that the primary key to torque multiplication in a torque converter is the stator. Technician B says that the angle of the blades in the turbine affects torque multiplication. Who is correct?
   A. Technician A
   B. Technician B
   C. Both Technician A and Technician B
   D. Neither Technician A nor Technician B

_____ 3. Technician A says that the stator locks up during the torque converter coupling phase. Technician B says that the stator freewheels during the torque multiplication phase. Who is correct?
   A. Technician A
   B. Technician B
   C. Both Technician A and Technician B
   D. Neither Technician A nor Technician B

_____ 4. Technician A says that vortex flow in the torque converter is highest during full stall. Technician B says that vortex flow follows the rotation of the converter housing or shell. Who is correct?
   A. Technician A
   B. Technician B
   C. Both Technician A and Technician B
   D. Neither Technician A nor Technician B

_____ 5. Technician A says that the torque multiplication factor of a torque converter is affected by the angle of the stator blades. Technician B says that the turbine end play can affect the torque converter's multiplication factor. Who is correct?
   A. Technician A
   B. Technician B
   C. Both Technician A and Technician B
   D. Neither Technician A nor Technician B

_____ 6. Technician A says that selecting drive in an automatic transmission while the rpm is very high can damage the stator one-way clutch. Technician B says that the stator one-way clutch is usually a roller-type clutch. Who is correct?
   A. Technician A
   B. Technician B
   C. Both Technician A and Technician B
   D. Neither Technician A nor Technician B

_____ 7. Technician A says that the split guide ring in the torque converter helps to direct the flow of fluid during torque multiplication phase. Technician B says that the split guide ring in the torque converter helps to direct the flow of fluid during the coupling phase. Who is correct?
   A. Technician A
   B. Technician B
   C. Both Technician A and Technician B
   D. Neither Technician A nor Technician B

_____ 8. Technician A says that light-duty torque converters should be replaced at transmission overhaul. Technician B says that light-duty torque converters are not designed to be rebuilt. Who is correct?
   A. Technician A
   B. Technician B
   C. Both Technician A and Technician B
   D. Neither Technician A nor Technician B

_____ **9.** Technician A says that turbine end play is an important check when rebuilding a heavy-duty torque converter. Technician B says that stator end play is checked after the torque converter is reassembled. Who is correct?
   A. Technician A
   B. Technician B
   C. Both Technician A and Technician B
   D. Neither Technician A nor Technician B

_____ **10.** Technician A says that, during the torque multiplication phase in the torque convertor, the oil exiting the stator is flowing opposite to impeller rotation. Technician B says that, during the torque multiplication phase in the torque converter, the oil exiting the turbine is flowing is flowing opposite to impeller rotation. Who is correct?
   A. Technician A
   B. Technician B
   C. Both Technician A and Technician B
   D. Neither Technician A nor Technician B

Planetary Gear Concepts

Tire Tread:
© AbleStock

Chapter Review

The following activities have been designed to help you refresh your knowledge of this chapter. Your instructor may require you to complete some or all of these activities as a regular part of your training program. You are encouraged to complete any activity that your instructor does not assign as a way to enhance your learning.

Matching

Match the following terms with the correct description or example.

A. Carrier

B. Pinion gear

C. Reaction member

D. Ring gear

E. Sun gear

_____ 1. A small gear housed in the planetary carrier.

_____ 2. The housing that holds the pinion gears of a planetary gear set and their shafts.

_____ 3. The small, externally toothed gear at the center of the planetary gear set.

_____ 4. The element of the planetary gear set that is held stationary.

_____ 5. An internally toothed gear that surrounds the pinion gears.

Multiple Choice

Read each item carefully, and then select the best response.

_____ 1. One simple planetary gear set can be arranged to produce _____.

A. two different forward overdrives

B. two different forward reduction ratios

C. one reverse reduction ratio and one reverse overdrive ratio

D. All of the above

_____ 2. To obtain a _____ ratio, two members of the planetary gear set are inputted at the same speed.

A. direct drive

B. overdrive

C. reverse

D. neutral

_____ 3. If the carrier is the _____ member of the gear set, the resulting power flow will always be a forward reduction or underdrive ratio.

A. input

B. output

C. reaction

D. reduction

_____ 4. When the sun gear is the output component and the ring gear is the held component the result is _____.

A. minimum forward overdrive

B. minimum forward reduction

C. maximum forward overdrive

D. maximum forward reduction

_____ **5.** If the ring gear is the input component, the sun gear is the output component, and the carrier is the held member, the result would be _____.

  A. reverse overdrive

  B. underdrive

  C. neutral

  D. minimum forward overdrive

_____ **6.** If the carrier is the output member of the planetary gear set, the ring gear is the input, and the sun gear is the held member, the ratio can be calculated using the formula _____.

  A. Ratio = R × S ÷ S

  B. Ratio = S + R ÷ R

  C. Ratio = S ÷ S + R

  D. Ratio = R ÷ S + R

_____ **7.** The formula, Ratio = S ÷ S + R is used to calculate the _____.

  A. minimum forward underdrive

  B. minimum forward overdrive

  C. maximum forward overdrive

  D. reverse underdrive

_____ **8.** The formula Ratio = S ÷ R is used to calculate _____.

  A. reverse underdrive

  B. reverse overdrive

  C. minimum forward underdrive

  D. minimum forward overdrive

_____ **9.** The _____ gear set consists of an interconnected planetary gear train with two separate and different-sized sun gears.

  A. Simpson

  B. Ravigneaux

  C. Lepelletier

  D. Wilson

_____ **10.** The _____ gear set, patented in 1990, produces six forward speeds, including two overdrives and one reverse.

  A. Lepelletier

  B. Wilson

  C. Simpson

  D. Ravigneaux

True/False

If you believe the statement to be more true than false, write the letter "T" in the space provided. If you believe the statement to be more false than true, write the letter "F".

_____ **1.** All automatic transmissions rely on a combination of planetary gears and power train control devices to create their power flows.

_____ **2.** The ring gears revolve around the sun gear like planets in our solar system.

_____ **3.** Planetary gears create a serious amount of axial thrust under load.

_____ **4.** If the three rules of planetary gears are not met and any of the planetary gear components are free to turn, the result will be neutral and no torque or rotational output can be transmitted.

_____ **5.** Minimum forward reduction is obtained with the sun gear as input, the ring gear held, and the carrier as output.

_____ **6.** The hydraulic clutch can be used either to input rotational power to a planetary gear component or to hold a component stationary.

_____ **7.** The reaction plates of the rotating clutch are sandwiched between the friction plates.

_____ **8.** The friction material on a brake band is extremely thin and wears off very quickly in cases when the transmission slips.

_____ **9.** The Simpson compound planetary gear arrangement is capable of producing five forward gear ratios and one reverse.

_____ **10.** Knowing which devices are operational during which range is essential to the correct diagnoses of transmission failure.

Fill in the Blank

Read each item carefully, and then complete the statement by filling in the missing word(s).

1. Planetary gears are also known as _____ gears.

2. If the carrier is the held or reaction member of the gear set, then the result will always be a(n) _____ gear.

3. The actual reductions and overdrives will vary based on the number of _____ on the three components.

4. If the ring gear is the input component and the sun gear is the held component the result is the _____ forward reduction.

5. When used to input the gear set, the hydraulic clutch is called a(n) _____ clutch and consists of a hub or drum that is splined or attached directly (or indirectly) to the transmission input shaft.

6. When the clutch reaction plates are splined directly to the inside of the transmission case and the friction plates are splined to the component we want to hold it is called a(n) _____ clutch.

7. One end of the _____ band is anchored to the transmission case and the other is attached to a hydraulic piston known as a servo piston.

8. Planetary gear power flows that utilize more than one gear set to produce the ratios are known as _____ planetary gear sets.

9. The _____ gear set consists of three interconnected planetary gears that can produce five forward speeds including one overdrive.

10. A power train control device _____ _____ helps us to understand which control devices are in use during which power flow.

Labeling

Label the following diagrams with the correct terms.

1. Identify the components of a simple planetary gear set:

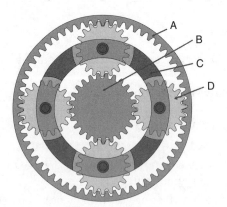

A. _____

B. _____

C. _____

D. _____

2. Identify the components of a brake band:

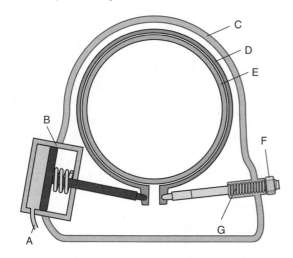

A. _____

B. _____

C. _____

D. _____

E. _____

F. _____

G. _____

Crossword Puzzle

Use the clues in the column to complete the puzzle.

Across

4. A hydraulic clutch used to hold a planetary gear component stationary and usually splined to the transmission case.

5. A friction faced metal band that surrounds a planetary component; when applied hydraulically, it holds the component stationary.

Down

1. A gear arrangement consisting of a ring gear with internal teeth, a carrier with two or more small pinion gears in constant mesh with the ring gear, and an externally toothed sun gear in the center in constant mesh with the planetary pinions.

2. The element of the planetary gear set that receives input from the power source.

3. Gears that revolve around a common centerline.

ASE-Type Questions

Read each item carefully, and then select the best response.

_____ 1. Technician A says that a simple planetary gear set can produce seven different ratios. Technician B says that planetary gears are epicyclical. Who is correct?
   A. Technician A
   B. Technician B
   C. Both Technician A and Technician B
   D. Neither Technician A nor Technician B

_____ 2. Technician A says that if the planetary carrier is the output member, a reverse will be the outcome if the rules of planetary gears are satisfied. Technician B says that if the carrier is input, a forward overdrive will be the result if the rules of planetary gears are satisfied. Who is correct?
   A. Technician A
   B. Technician B
   C. Both Technician A and Technician B
   D. Neither Technician A nor Technician B

_____ 3. Technician A says that helical planetary gears do not produce any thrust. Technician B says that planetary gears do not produce radial thrust. Who is correct?
   A. Technician A
   B. Technician B
   C. Both Technician A and Technician B
   D. Neither Technician A nor Technician B

_____ 4. Technician A says that holding the sun gear stationary and inputting the ring gear of a planetary gear set will produce the maximum forward reduction at the carrier. Technician B says that holding the carrier stationary and inputting the sun gear of a planetary gear set will produce a reverse reduction at the ring gear. Who is correct?
   A. Technician A
   B. Technician B
   C. Both Technician A and Technician B
   D. Neither Technician A nor Technician B

_____ 5. Technician A says that hydraulic clutches can be used to hold or input planetary gear components. Technician B says that one-way clutches are used to provide engine braking. Who is correct?
   A. Technician A
   B. Technician B
   C. Both Technician A and Technician B
   D. Neither Technician A nor Technician B

_____ 6. Technician A says that one-way clutches can be sprag or roller type. Technician B says that a one-way clutch is used in manual low in the Simpson gear train. Who is correct?
   A. Technician A
   B. Technician B
   C. Both Technician A and Technician B
   D. Neither Technician A nor Technician B

_____ 7. Technician A says that hydraulic clutches are used to drive or input a planetary gear component. Technician B says that hydraulic clutches can sometimes be adjusted from the outside of the transmission case. Who is correct?
   A. Technician A
   B. Technician B
   C. Both Technician A and Technician B
   D. Neither Technician A nor Technician B

_____ 8. Technician A says that two hydraulic clutches are used to input to the Simpson gear set. Technician B says the Simpson gear set shares a common sun gear. Who is correct?
   A. Technician A
   B. Technician B
   C. Both Technician A and Technician B
   D. Neither Technician A nor Technician B

_____ **9.** Technician A says that, to achieve direct in the Simpson gear, the front ring gear and the front sun gear are inputted and the front carrier is the output. Technician B says that reverse is a compound power flow in the Simpson gear set. Who is correct?

  A. Technician A
  B. Technician B
  C. Both Technician A and Technician B
  D. Neither Technician A nor Technician B

_____ **10.** Technician A says that second gear in a Simpson gear set is a compound power flow. Technician B says that the Simpson gear set only has one compound power flow. Who is correct?

  A. Technician A
  B. Technician B
  C. Both Technician A and Technician B
  D. Neither Technician A nor Technician B

Hydraulically Controlled Automatic Transmissions

Chapter Review

The following activities have been designed to help you refresh your knowledge of this chapter. Your instructor may require you to complete some or all of these activities as a regular part of your training program. You are encouraged to complete any activity that your instructor does not assign as a way to enhance your learning.

Matching

Match the following terms with the correct description or example.

A. Governor valve

B. Modulator valve

C. Priority valve

D. Shift relay valve

E. Trimmer valve

_____ **1.** The spool valve that directs clutch apply pressure to the correct clutch.

_____ **2.** A check valve that protects the hydraulic controls.

_____ **3.** A valve that creates a pressure based on road speed.

_____ **4.** A valve used to soften a clutch application.

_____ **5.** A valve that produces a pressure based on throttle position.

Multiple Choice

Read each item carefully, and then select the best response.

_____ **1.** The front planetary ring gear, the center planetary carrier, and the rear planetary carrier of the Allison transmission are all connected together by the _____.

A. sun gear shaft

B. connecting drum

C. main shaft

D. carrier shaft

_____ **2.** According to the Allison transmission application chart, if only the first clutch is applied, the transmission must be in the _____ range.

A. neutral

B. first

C. second

D. third

_____ **3.** When the reverse gear of the Alison transmission is selected, the _____ clutch is applied.

A. first

B. third

C. fourth

D. Both A and C

_____ **4.** An unnecessary load on the engine that decreases fuel economy is called a _____.

A. restriction

B. parasitic loss

C. reduction loss

D. diminution

_____ **5.** The main pressure regulator valve is a _____ valve that sets the main or working pressure of the transmission.
   A. butterfly
   B. ball
   C. spool
   D. check

_____ **6.** Transmission fluid exits the torque converter through the converter out circuit and is directed to the _____.
   A. control valve body
   B. transmission oil cooler
   C. rear lube circuit
   D. sump

_____ **7.** The _____ is responsible for creating modulator pressure and can be controlled by mechanical throttle cable on diesel engines, by vacuum on gasoline engines, or electrically using an electric solenoid.
   A. modulator valve
   B. priority valve
   C. throttle valve
   D. Either A or C

_____ **8.** The _____ valves control the movement of the shift relay valves.
   A. priority
   B. trimmer
   C. shift signal
   D. modulator

_____ **9.** Allison's _____ valves consist of a bore with a spring-loaded plug at its base, a pin that limits the plug's movement down in the bore, and a cup that sits on top of the plug.
   A. shift signal
   B. trimmer
   C. priority
   D. hold regulator

_____ **10.** The main pressure is highest in the _____ gear.
   A. neutral
   B. first
   C. fourth
   D. reverse

True/False

If you believe the statement to be more true than false, write the letter "T" in the space provided. If you believe the statement to be more false than true, write the letter "F".

_____ **1.** Caterpillar is by far the largest supplier of automatic transmissions to the North American truck and coach market.

_____ **2.** All automatic transmissions used in the truck and coach market today are fully electronically controlled.

_____ **3.** When the driver selects any forward range of an Allison four-speed transmission, the transmission will always start in first range and then automatically shift sequentially to the highest selected range as road speed increases.

_____ **4.** Most heavy-duty transmissions use an external vane pump that is driven by the engine's timing chain.

_____ **5.** When the vehicle is not running and there is no hydraulic pressure, the main pressure regulator valve is held in the seated position by a spring at its base.

_____ **6.** The positioning of the governor valve controls the operation of the neutral safety switch.

_____ **7.** Governor pressure is predicated on road speed.

_____ **8.** All of the main pressure used to apply the clutches in the transmission flows through the priority valve.

_____ **9.** In a modulated lock-up, as soon as the transmission shifts into a certain range or has attained a predetermined road speed, the lock-up clutch will be applied.

_____ **10.** Forced full throttle downshifts allow the driver to make the transmission downshift in order to gain torque multiplication when needed, such as when trying to overtake a slower moving vehicle.

Fill in the Blank

Read each item carefully, and then complete the statement by filling in the missing word(s).

1. The Voith _____ bus transmission uses the torque converter as an integrated retarder to augment the vehicle brakes.

2. The front and the center sun gears of the Allison transmission are splined to the sun gear _____ and are connected together.

3. It is important for the technician to read and understand a clutch _____ chart when diagnosing a transmission issue.

4. A(n) _____ pump is similar to a gear pump, but it uses a rotor operating inside a matching chamber instead of a gear.

5. The _____ is designed to hold sufficient fluid for operation when the fluid is fully deployed throughout the transmission's hydraulic circuits.

6. The control valve _____ is a casting that holds the many spool valves needed to operate the transmission.

7. The _____ selector valve is a spool valve in the control valve body that is mechanically positioned when the driver moves the shift selector.

8. The top shift signal valve is called the shift _____ valve and the lower shift signal valve is the _____ shift signal valve.

9. The fluid from the _____ _____ valve is directed between the shift modulator and the shift signal, ensuring that the shift signal valve cannot move to the upshifted position.

10. The _____ plate has precisely sized and positioned orifices and/or openings that then coincide with various openings cast or cut into the transmission case.

Labeling

Label the following diagrams with the correct terms.

1. Identify the components of an Allison AT 500 series transmission:

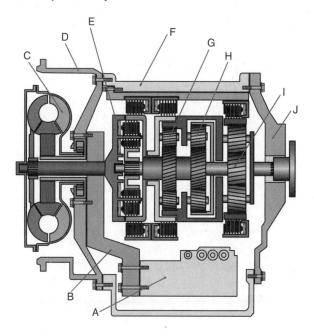

A. _____

B. _____

C. _____

D. _____

E. _____

F. _____

G. _____

H. _____

I. _____

J. _____

2. Identify the components of an Allison four-speed gear train:

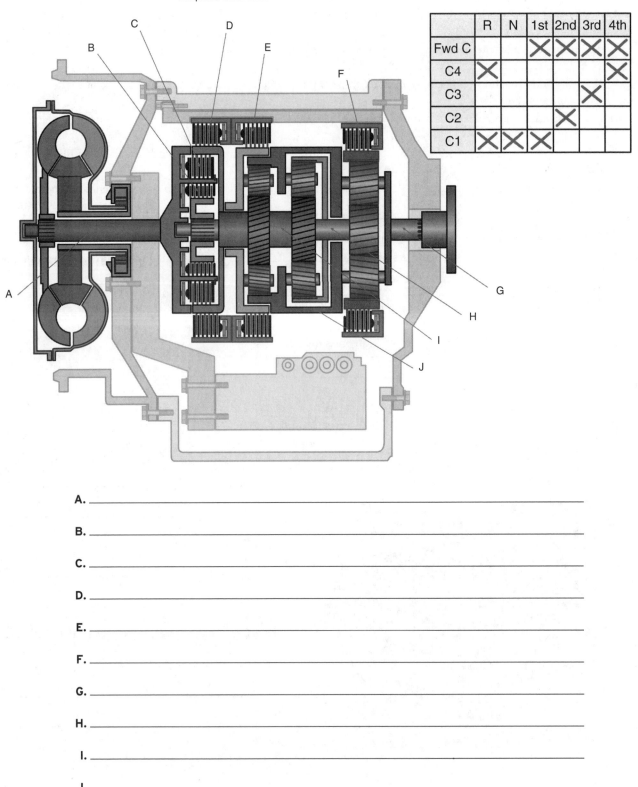

Simplifed Gear train

	R	N	1st	2nd	3rd	4th
Fwd C			✕	✕	✕	✕
C4	✕					✕
C3					✕	
C2				✕		
C1	✕	✕	✕			

A. _____

B. _____

C. _____

D. _____

E. _____

F. _____

G. _____

H. _____

I. _____

J. _____

3. Identify the components of a governor valve:

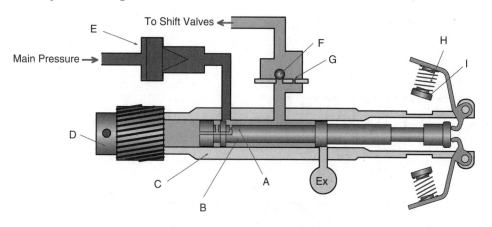

A. _____

B. _____

C. _____

D. _____

E. _____

F. _____

G. _____

H. _____

I. _____

Crossword Puzzle

Use the clues in the column to complete the puzzle.

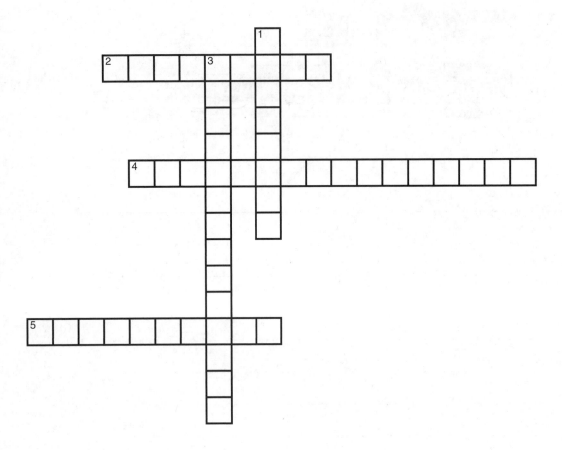

Across

2. The shaft that is driven by the countershaft and provides output for the transmission. Also called output shaft.

4. A pathway connecting one part of the transmission's hydraulic control with another part.

5. A valve that has a series of lands and cutaways in a precise fitting bore.

Down

1. A hydraulic pump that uses sliding vanes to move the fluid.

3. A plate that separates the control valve body and the transmission case.

ASE-Type Questions

Read each item carefully, and then select the best response.

_____ 1. Technician A says that most commercial vehicles will have scheduled torque converter lock-up. Technician B says that modulated torque converter lock-up saves fuel. Who is correct?
   A. Technician A
   B. Technician B
   C. Both Technician A and Technician B
   D. Neither Technician A nor Technician B

_____ 2. Technician A says that the trimmer regulator valve is used to modify shift harshness based on throttle position. Technician B says that trimmer valves are used to let clutches slip a bit before they are fully applied. Who is correct?
   A. Technician A
   B. Technician B
   C. Both Technician A and Technician B
   D. Neither Technician A nor Technician B

_____ 3. Technician A says that in hydraulically controlled Allison transmissions, modulator pressure is high at wide-open throttle. Technician B says that in hydraulically controlled Allison transmissions, high modulator pressure causes harsh shifting. Who is correct?
   A. Technician A
   B. Technician B
   C. Both Technician A and Technician B
   D. Neither Technician A nor Technician B

_____ 4. Technician A says that downshifting in hydraulically controlled Allison transmissions is caused by spring force. Technician B says that a downshift can be made at higher road speed by pushing the throttle to the floor. Who is correct?
   A. Technician A
   B. Technician B
   C. Both Technician A and Technician B
   D. Neither Technician A nor Technician B

_____ 5. Technician A says that all of the pressures found in hydraulically controlled Allison transmissions are derived from main or control pressure. Technician B says that hydraulically controlled Allison transmission lubrication circuits are at main pressure. Who is correct?
   A. Technician A
   B. Technician B
   C. Both Technician A and Technician B
   D. Neither Technician A nor Technician B

_____ 6. Technician A says that in the Allison 500 series transmission, the center planetary gear set is involved in four out of the five gear ranges. Technician B says that the center planetary gear set is not involved in first range. Who is correct?
   A. Technician A
   B. Technician B
   C. Both Technician A and Technician B
   D. Neither Technician A nor Technician B

_____ 7. Technician A says that the Allison AT 500 series transmission uses five hydraulic clutches. Technician B says the Allison AT 500 series transmission use three interconnected planetary gear sets. Who is correct?
   A. Technician A
   B. Technician B
   C. Both Technician A and Technician B
   D. Neither Technician A nor Technician B

_____ **8.** Technician A says that in the Allison AT 500 series transmission, the connecting drum is attached to the front carrier, the center carrier, and the rear carrier. Technician B says that in the Allison AT 500 series transmission, the front sun gear is part of the main shaft. Who is correct?
   A. Technician A
   B. Technician B
   C. Both Technician A and Technician B
   D. Neither Technician A nor Technician B

_____ **9.** Technician A says that the center ring gear is attached to the connecting drum in the Allison AT 500 series transmission. Technician B says that the rear carrier is attached to the output shaft in the Allison AT 500 series transmission. Who is correct?
   A. Technician A
   B. Technician B
   C. Both Technician A and Technician B
   D. Neither Technician A nor Technician B

_____ **10.** Technician A says that in fourth range in the Allison AT 500 series transmission, the two rotating clutches are turning at the same speed. Technician B says that in fourth range in the Allison AT 500 series transmission all three planetary gear sets are turning at the same speed. Who is correct?
   A. Technician A
   B. Technician B
   C. Both Technician A and Technician B
   D. Neither Technician A nor Technician B

Maintaining Automatic Transmissions

Chapter Review

The following activities have been designed to help you refresh your knowledge of this chapter. Your instructor may require you to complete some or all of these activities as a regular part of your training program. You are encouraged to complete any activity that your instructor does not assign as a way to enhance your learning.

Matching

Match the following terms with the correct description or example.

A. Aeration

B. Cavitation

C. Friction modifier

D. Supplemental additive

E. TranSynd fluid

_____ **1.** Additive in transmission fluid designed to enhance the traction characteristics of certain clutch materials.

_____ **2.** A full synthetic fluid produced by Castrol to Allison specification; the recommended fluid for all Allison transmissions.

_____ **3.** Aftermarket additive available for automatic transmissions but not recommended by manufacturers.

_____ **4.** Air in the fluid.

_____ **5.** The formation of air bubbles in the transmission fluid as a result of low pressure at the pump inlet.

Multiple Choice

Read each item carefully, and then select the best response.

_____ **1.** Using fluids with friction modifiers in transmissions that are not designed for them can lead to _____.

    A. severe oxidation issues

    B. clutch pack slippage

    C. transmission failure

    D. All of the above

_____ **2.** If _____ is being used, the fluid will require preheating if ambient temperatures are below −22°F (−30°C).

    A. ethylene glycol

    B. TranSynd

    C. C-type fluid

    D. severe duty fluid

_____ **3.** A typical oil and filter change interval for the MT series non-electronic control transmissions would be _____ when using non-synthetic TES-389TM fluids.

    A. 25,000 miles (40,240 km)

    B. 50,000 miles (80,500 km)

    C. 75,000 miles (120,700 km)

    D. 100,000 miles (161,000 km)

_____ **4.** Never use a container that has held _____ to transfer transmission fluid; it will quickly destroy clutch plate material leading to complete failure of the transmission.

    A. TranSynd fluid

    B. synthetic fluid

    C. ethylene glycol

    D. oil-type fluids

_____ **5.** Most manufacturers warn that any use of _____ may void the transmission warranty and should not be used.
  A. synthetic fluids
  B. oil-type fluids
  C. supplemental additives
  D. Either A or C

_____ **6.** A _____ can be used to determine if a transmission problem is mechanical or hydraulic.
  A. stall test
  B. pressure test
  C. road test
  D. fluid analysis

_____ **7.** High system hydraulic pressure could indicate a _____.
  A. seized main pressure regulator valve
  B. failed pump
  C. twisted shift linkage
  D. failed clutch seal

_____ **8.** A special tool made by Kent Moore called a J-24314 is designed to be used on _____.
  A. shift linkage
  B. valve adjusting cams
  C. vacuum modulators
  D. support mounts

_____ **9.** A failed _____ will allow excessive movement of the power train and can lead to damage and/or erratic vehicle operation.
  A. modulator cable
  B. line or hose
  C. mount
  D. vacuum modulator

_____ **10.** Transmission fluid that has a milky or light pink color can indicate _____.
  A. engine coolant contamination
  B. failure of one or more of the transmissions clutch packs
  C. significant metal deposits
  D. torque converter failure

True/False

If you believe the statement to be more true than false, write the letter "T" in the space provided. If you believe the statement to be more false than true, write the letter "F".

_____ **1.** Aeration can lead to burned out clutches and a loss of converter efficiency.

_____ **2.** The temperature of the transmission fluid is not an important factor when obtaining a fluid level reading.

_____ **3.** Universal transmission fluid works with all models and types of transmissions.

_____ **4.** Allison highly recommends that only synthetic fluids be used in all of their transmissions.

_____ **5.** The Commercial Vehicle Service Alliance specifies out-of-service criteria for automatic transmissions.

_____ **6.** A clogged vent can lead to fluid aeration from pump cavitation.

_____ **7.** The transmission oil pan must be removed to replace the filter.

_____ **8.** The valve body test stand supplies pressurized transmission fluid and drives the governor, simulating a vehicle drive cycle.

_____ **9.** Diagnosing an issue with the transmission on the bench is easier than trying to pinpoint the problem before the transmission is removed.

_____ **10.** Most transmissions today have mechanical shift cables or linkage that may require adjustment.

Fill in the Blank

Read each item carefully, and then complete the statement by filling in the missing word(s).

1. Transmission _____ is the life blood of all automatic transmissions.

2. All transmissions have a transmission _____ that allows atmospheric pressure to enter the transmission.

3. A pump experiencing _____ will usually be extremely noisy and will eventually fail.

4. Allison electronically controlled transmissions have cold operation inhibits in their _____ to prevent the transmission from shifting below certain temperatures.

5. When Allison's _____ is turned on, the service interval is controlled entirely by the software.

6. When operating conditions vary from the norm, fluid _____ can optimize transmission longevity and service scheduling.

7. The Allison World Transmission models include _____ test points for each of the individual clutch apply circuits.

8. Allison transmission models and certain other hydraulically controlled transmissions do allow for some adjustment of shift _____.

9. Cracks in the _____ _____ will usually form near the torque converter mounting hardware or the bolts securing it to the crankshaft.

10. After transmission failure, it is common to find debris in the transmission _____ system.

Skill Drills

Test your knowledge of skill drills by filling in the correct words in the photo captions.

1. Checking Fluid Level and Inspecting Fluid Loss:

Step 1: Look up the procedure for checking the transmission fluid level in the appropriate service information.

Step 2: Locate the transmission _____ (if equipped). Most but not all, transmissions are checked with the engine at _____ temperature, _____, and the transmission in _____. If the transmission has a dipstick, wipe it off and reinsert it into the _____ before checking the level of _____ on the dipstick. Check both sides of the dipstick; the side that is the _____ is the accurate fluid level. On some transmissions, the fluid returning to the transmission _____ will splash up on one side of the dipstick, resulting in a _____ reading on that side.

Step 3: If the transmission fluid level is _____, add the recommended _____ and _____ of transmission _____. Be careful not to _____ the transmission.

Step 4: Inspect the transmission for signs of _____. Some places to check are the transmission _____, area around the entrance of the _____ _____ to the transmission, extension housing _____, output shaft _____, selector _____ seal, area around the _____ connectors that go into the transmission _____, front _____ seals, fluid _____ lines, and the fittings. Also, if the vehicle has a vacuum _____, remove the _____ _____ from the modulator and see if there is any transmission fluid in the hose. If there is, the modulator is _____. Be sure to remove the _____ _____ (with vehicle cold) and check for any transmission fluid in the _____; if present, it is an indication that the transmission _____ is leaking.

Step 5: If the transmission has a large amount of _____ _____ or _____ _____ covering it, you may need to _____ it with a _____ _____, some engine _____, or use a leak detection _____ in the transmission fluid.

Step 6: Restart the vehicle and allow it to _____ for a while. The leak detection dye will be easy to spot using a _____ _____, or look for _____ transmission fluid leaking.

Step 7: Record the _____ of the _____ and inform the _____ to obtain _____ for repairs.

2. Performing Automatic Transmission Pressure Tests:

Step 1: Refer to the appropriate _____ information to find the _____ to test the transmission's _____ pressures. Verify the correct transmission _____ _____ in the transmission.

Step 2: Place a _____ _____ under the transmission and _____ the correct pressure _____ _____ plug(s). Place the test port _____ (s) off to the side where they will not be _____.

Step 3: Install a transmission _____ _____ (s) capable of measuring the _____ pressure into the _____ _____ (s) on the transmission.

Step 4: Start the vehicle and place the vehicle in the correct operating _____ to _____ the pressure according to the _____ (for example, transmission hot, in drive, idling). Record the _____ (s).

Step 5: Shut off the engine, _____ the transmission pressure tester(s), _____ the _____, and _____ the test port _____ (s).

Step 6: Clean off any transmission _____ that dripped onto the transmission, _____ the vehicle to _____ for _____, and _____ _____ the _____ if necessary.

3. Removing the Transmission and Checking the Condition of Transmission Mounts, Insulators, and Mounting Bolts:

Step 1: Locate and _____ the appropriate _____ in the service _____.

Step 2: Complete the accompanying _____ _____ or _____ _____ with all pertinent information.

Step 3: Move the vehicle into the _____, apply the _____ _____, and _____ the vehicle wheels. Observe _____/_____ procedures.

Step 4: Since this is a procedure for a vehicle with an _____ transmission, place it in "_____" or "_____." Note: Some vehicles with _____ transmissions do not have "_____."

Step 5: Drain the _____ from the transmission by removing the _____ _____ from the _____ _____. Note: The transmission _____ _____ may have to be _____ if it interferes with transmission removal.

Step 6: Disconnect any hydraulic _____ from the transmission and _____ all openings.

Step 7: Drain _____ from the _____, if present, and _____ all _____.

Step 8: Disconnect the _____ and _____ speed _____, _____ sensors/connectors, the _____/_____ from the transmission, and the _____ harness from the _____-_____ harness.

Step 9: Remove any _____ that may be _____.

Step 10: Mark the driveshaft _____ or _____ on the transmission's _____ shaft. The marks will ensure that the _____ is properly _____.

Step 11: Place a transmission _____ tightly against the transmission's _____.

Step 12: Remove the _____ _____ flex plate _____ that hold the transmission to the _____ _____.

Step 13: Slide the transmission away from the engine approximately _____ to _____" (100 to 125 mm) and _____ the _____ _____, if used.

Step 14: Lower the _____ to the _____.

Step 15: Check the transmission _____, bolts, and _____ for wear. _____ if required.

Step 16: List the _____ _____ and recommendations on the _____ _____ or _____ _____, clean the _____ _____, and return _____ and materials to their proper _____.

4. Inspecting the Torque Converter and Flex Plate:

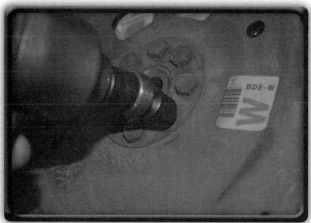

Step 1: Remove the _____ securing the _____ _____ to the _____.

Step 2: Inspect the bolt _____ used for mounting the _____ _____ to the crankshaft and the flex plate to the _____ _____ for _____ and bolt hole _____.

Step 3: Inspect the _____ or _____ used for connecting the flex plate to the _____ and the flex plate to the _____ _____ for damaged _____.

Step 4: Inspect the _____ _____ _____ for signs of damage.

Step 5: Inspect the _____ _____ _____ for signs of damage.

Step 6: Inspect the torque converter _____ _____ for damage.

Step 7: Inspect the _____ _____ _____ for damage.

Step 8: Install the required tool into the _____ to check for torque converter _____ _____. Use a _____ _____ to measure the amount of _____ movement.

5. Inspecting and Flushing Cooler Lines:

Step 1:   First, look up the recommended transmission _____ service _____ in the appropriate service
information, and _____ the instruction _____ for the flush _____ you are using or for the _____
can of transmission cooler _____. Remove the fluid _____ _____ from the transmission if the
transmission is still in the _____.

Step 2:   Using _____ _____ (do not exceed _____ psi [207 kPa]), _____ into one cooler line while
catching the _____ in a _____ as it comes out of the other line. Switch _____ and _____.

Step 3:   Install the cooler _____ _____ or _____ _____ lines onto the transmission _____ _____ so
that the flow is in the _____ direction. If using the _____ cooler _____ can, place the other cooler
line into a _____ can.

Step 4:   Start the _____ _____ or _____ _____ and allow it to _____ for the recommended _____.

Step 5:   If necessary, _____ directions on the _____ so they can be _____ in the other direction.

Step 6:   Remove the flush machine and _____ out the lines _____ so no _____ remains inside the lines.

Step 7:   Reinstall the _____ onto the transmission or _____ them if the transmission is _____ from the
vehicle.

Step 8:   After properly _____ the transmission with _____, start the vehicle and _____ the lines and
_____ for any signs of _____.

Step 9:   Check _____ the _____ for signs of the transmission _____ leaking into the _____.

Crossword Puzzle

Use the clues in the column to complete the puzzle.

Across

1. Steel backed rubber support that holds the power train components.
4. Small cam on the end of the shift signal valves that, when turned, increase the shift point.
5. A mechanical cable connected to the driver's shift lever and the transmission manual valve.

Down

2. A switch operated by the transmission shift linkage that prevents the vehicle from being started except when in park or neutral. Also known as the PRNDL switch on some transmissions.
3. The ability by some transmission ECUs to predict fluid and filter change intervals.

ASE-Type Questions

Read each item carefully, and then select the best response.

_____ 1. Technician A says that all automatic transmission fluids are the same. Technician B says that all synthetic automatic transmission fluids are compatible. Who is correct?

A. Technician A

B. Technician B

C. Both Technician A and Technician B

D. Neither Technician A nor Technician B

_____ 2. Technician A says using synthetic fluids greatly extend automatic transmission fluid change intervals. Technician B says that transmission vocation can influence fluid change intervals. Who is correct?

A. Technician A

B. Technician B

C. Both Technician A and Technician B

D. Neither Technician A nor Technician B

_____ 3. Technician A says that automatic transmission fluid should usually be checked with the vehicle running and the transmission at operating temperature. Technician B says that automatic transmissions using synthetic fluid can be topped up with regular fluid as long as it is not more than 2 quarts (1.9 liters) low. Who is correct?

A. Technician A

B. Technician B

C. Both Technician A and Technician B

D. Neither Technician A nor Technician B

_____ 4. Technician A says that automatic transmission fluid that looks milky or pink can mean a failed transmission cooler. Technician B says that transmission fluid that has a shiny look to it can mean internal failure of transmission components. Who is correct?

A. Technician A

B. Technician B

C. Both Technician A and Technician B

D. Neither Technician A nor Technician B

_____ 5. Technician A says that shift points can be adjusted in most of today's automatic transmissions. Technician B says that most of today's automatic transmissions are drive by wire and the only adjustment that may have to be done is the manual shift linkage and the neutral safety switch. Who is correct?

A. Technician A

B. Technician B

C. Both Technician A and Technician B

D. Neither Technician A nor Technician B

_____ 6. Technician A says that most hydraulically controlled transmissions require regularly scheduled oil and filter changes. Technician B says that some electronically controlled transmissions can indicate when an oil change is required. Who is correct?

A. Technician A

B. Technician B

C. Both Technician A and Technician B

D. Neither Technician A nor Technician B

_____ 7. Technician A says that shift point adjustment can be performed on most hydraulically controlled transmissions. Technician B says that shift point adjustment on hydraulically controlled Allison transmissions involves removal of the transmission oil pan. Who is correct?

A. Technician A

B. Technician B

C. Both Technician A and Technician B

D. Neither Technician A nor Technician B

_____ **8.** Technician A says that loss of transmission oil is the most common cause of automatic transmission failure. Technician B says that slight loss of transmission fluid over time is normal and just needs topping up from time to time. Who is correct?

    A. Technician A

    B. Technician B

    C. Both Technician A and Technician B

    D. Neither Technician A nor Technician B

_____ **9.** Technician A says that "TranSynd" is the fluid that Allison recommends for all its transmissions. Technician B says that, if a transmission has "TranSynd" installed, it can only be topped up with "TranSynd." Who is correct?

    A. Technician A

    B. Technician B

    C. Both Technician A and Technician B

    D. Neither Technician A nor Technician B

_____ **10.** Technician A says that each notch of the adjustment cam on an Allison transmission shift signal valve will change the shift point by 2 mph (3.2 kph). Technician B says that the cam is turned clockwise to increase the shift point and counterclockwise to decrease the shift point. Who is correct?

    A. Technician A

    B. Technician B

    C. Both Technician A and Technician B

    D. Neither Technician A nor Technician B

Electronically Controlled Automatic Transmissions

Chapter Review

The following activities have been designed to help you refresh your knowledge of this chapter. Your instructor may require you to complete some or all of these activities as a regular part of your training program. You are encouraged to complete any activity that your instructor does not assign as a way to enhance your learning.

Matching

Match the following terms with the correct description or example.

A. Adaptive control
B. Cab harness
C. Duty cycle
D. Failsafe operation
E. Prognostics

F. Pulse-width modulation
G. Ramp-off rate
H. Retarder
I. Synchronous speed
J. Transmission control module

_____ **1.** The specific reduction in clutch applys pressure for the clutch that is being released during a shift in the Allison World Transmission.

_____ **2.** Connects the shift selector to the electronic control unit.

_____ **3.** Any system used to slow a vehicle's momentum and augment the service brake.

_____ **4.** An electrical signal that varies in on and off time.

_____ **5.** The point at which the on-coming clutch has applied and there is no more slippage.

_____ **6.** A self-diagnostic maintenance schedule that informs the driver when the oil, filters, or the transmission itself requires service.

_____ **7.** A feature that senses topography and vehicle load and adjusts shift control to obtain maximum economy and comfort.

_____ **8.** The electronic controller that issues commands to the solenoids inside the transmission to obtain the desired range.

_____ **9.** The minimal transmission function that occurs when electrical power is lost.

_____ **10.** The percentage of time a PWM signal is ON in comparison to OFF time.

Multiple Choice

Read each item carefully, and then select the best response.

_____ **1.** All automatic transmissions require a _____ in order to be able to shift properly.
    A. driver's gear selection
    B. load sensitive signal
    C. speed sensitive signal
    D. All of the above

_____ **2.** The _____ is the brains of the control system.
    A. transmission control unit
    B. throttle position sensor
    C. transmission electronic control unit
    D. Either A or C

_____ **3.** The _____ ECU includes a connector, which allows a remotely mounted operator interface for remote power take-off operation.
A. Sealed Standard
B. Splash Proof
C. Sealed-Plus
D. Either A or C

_____ **4.** The _____ sensor is bolted to the electro-hydraulic control and uses pressurized lube oil directed to a small orifice in the body of the sensor.
A. fluid temperature
B. low oil level/pressure
C. throttle position
D. vehicle speed

_____ **5.** ATEC/CEC transmissions use _____ to control fluid flow.
A. solenoids
B. pressure valves
C. spool valves
D. Both A and C

_____ **6.** The _____ series Allison World Transmissions are available with a transfer case for four-wheel drive operation.
A. 1000
B. 2000
C. 3000
D. 4000

_____ **7.** The _____ of the World Transmission is an electro-hydraulic valve body attached to the bottom of the main housing module.
A. control module
B. torque converter
C. rotating clutch
D. charging pump

_____ **8.** In _____ mode, the WTEC transmission makes small changes to the shifts designed to make up for transmission clutch wear and solenoid drift or degradation.
A. slow adaptive
B. primary
C. fast adaptive
D. secondary

_____ **9.** The period of monitoring and adjusting during a shift in progress on a World Transmission is known as _____.
A. open-loop control
B. range verification
C. closed-loop control
D. pulse-width modulation

_____ **10.** A _____ is performed at the beginning and end of a shift in process.
A. range verification test
B. ratio test
C. modulation test
D. fluid flow test

_____ **11.** The Allison fifth-generation controllers include an integral _____ to allow further refinement of transmission shifting based on topography and operating conditions.
A. inclinometer/accelerometer
B. overdrive knock-down valve
C. hydraulic retarder
D. accumulator

_____ **12.** The letter "U" in an SAE J-2012 code indicates the trouble is located in the _____ system.
 A. chassis
 B. power train
 C. body
 D. network

_____ **13.** The _____ is the first Allison transmission targeted specifically to the Class 8 on-highway tractor market.
 A. DIWA
 B. TC-10-TS
 C. WTEC
 D. EcoLife

_____ **14.** The Voith _____ transmission is used in over 200,000 transit buses and coaches worldwide
 A. DIWA
 B. EcoMat
 C. TC-10-TS
 D. WTEC

_____ **15.** The CX28, CX31, and CX35 are electronically controlled transmissions made by _____ for the off-road market.
 A. ZF
 B. Voith
 C. Allison
 D. Caterpillar

True/False

If you believe the statement to be more true than false, write the letter "T" in the space provided. If you believe the statement to be more false than true, write the letter "F".

_____ **1.** The PROM chip is the only serviceable part in the ECU.

_____ **2.** The transmission shift control can be a push button unit used to activate gear changes.

_____ **3.** The cab harness is the wiring that connects the transmission, the TPS, and the VSS to the transmission ECU.

_____ **4.** Latching solenoids do not stay in an open position unless they have a constant voltage supply.

_____ **5.** Allison 1000, 2000, and 2400 series transmissions use the same control system design as the original World Transmission electronic control systems.

_____ **6.** The function of the rear cover module of the World Transmission is to contain and provide support to the output shaft.

_____ **7.** Since the original model was launched, WTEC has gone through three revisions, including WTEC11 and WTEC111.

_____ **8.** A normally closed solenoid will allow fluid flow while deenergized and stop flow when energized.

_____ **9.** Sub-modulation allows the ECU to provide a constant average current to the solenoids.

_____ **10.** Open-loop ramp rate means that clutch pressure is being increased at a fixed rate.

_____ **11.** The on-going ratio test is performed during the beginning of a shift in progress and assures that the off-going clutch actually released.

_____ **12.** In the Allison fourth-generation electronic control the transmission ECU has been renamed the transmission control module and the clutch control solenoids have been renamed pressure control solenoids.

_____ **13.** The overdrive knock-down valve was a new control feature introduced in the Allison fourth-generation electronic control.

_____ **14.** World Transmission shift controllers perform a diagnostic function when a transmission diagnostic trouble code is set or when maintenance is required.

_____ **15.** The counter-rotating torque converter is the heart of the TC-10-TS transmission's operation.

Fill in the Blank

Read each item carefully, and then complete the statement by filling in the missing word(s).

1. The _____ _____ sensor replaces the modulator throttle valve used on hydraulically controlled transmissions.

2. The vehicle _____ sensor provides a road-speed signal used with the throttle position sensor to determine shift timing.

3. The most common _____ sensors monitor pressure and temperature.

4. The diagnostic _____ _____ connector is the place on the vehicle where the technician can plug in diagnostic software.

5. The _____ _____ housing module of the World Transmission bolts the transmission to the rear of the engine flywheel housing.

6. A normally _____ solenoid will allow fluid flow when energized and stop fluid flow when energized.

7. The solenoids used with the WTEC controlled transmission are controlled by the transmission ECU using a _____-_____-modulated circuit.

8. The _____ adaptive mode of the WTEC is used when the transmission is new and makes large changes to bring the shift close to the optimal profile quickly.

9. Turbine _____ _____ is the reduction in turbine speed as the on-coming clutch starts to squeeze its clutch plates and the transmission is starting to attain the next range.

10. When no shifts are in progress, the transmission controller initiates a range _____ test to ensure that the transmission is in a selected range.

11. The WTEC transmission utilizes two latch valves to assure _____ operation during electrical failure.

12. The Allison fourth-generation electronic control introduced the _____ _____ solenoid; it is used by the transmission control module to reduce main pressure when desired.

13. A hydraulic _____ is used as a supplement to the vehicle braking system to minimize service-brake use and keep brake temperatures down.

14. The DIWA.5 transmission with the Intelligent Control Unit E-300 comes equipped with SensoTop, a(n) _____ control feature that senses topography and vehicle load and adjusts shift control to obtain maximum economy and comfort.

15. The _____ is ZF's latest six-speed transmission model, which can handle up to 1,475 ft-lb (2,000 Nm) of input torque.

Labeling

Label the following diagrams with the correct terms.

1. Identify the components of a latching solenoid:

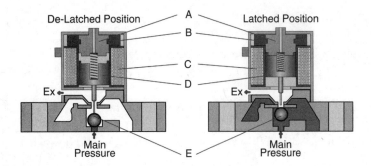

A. _____

B. _____

C. _____

D. _____

E. _____

2. Identify the modules of the Allison World Transmission:

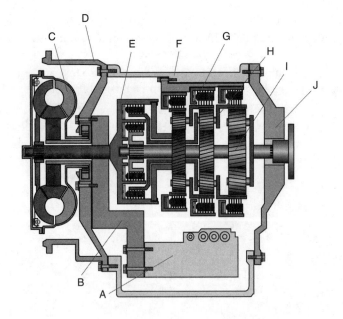

A. _____

B. _____

C. _____

D. _____

E. _____

F. _____

G. _____

H. _____

I. _____

J. _____

3. Identify the components of the Voith DIWA drive transmission:

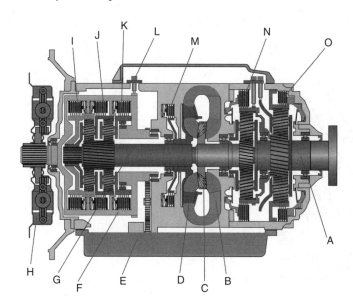

A. _____

B. _____

C. _____

D. _____

E. _____

F. _____

G. _____

H. _____

I. _____

J. _____

K. _____

L. _____

M. _____

N. _____

O. _____

Skill Drills

Test your knowledge of skill drills by filling in the correct words in the photo captions.

1. Scanning the TCM:

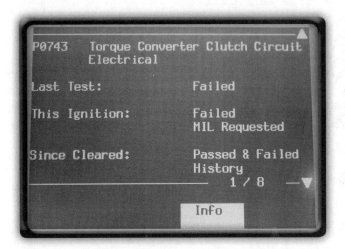

Step 1: Install a _____ _____ onto the vehicle's _____ _____ connector. For the location of the DLC, consult the service information.

Step 2: Retrieve any _____ _____ _____ from the vehicle. Record the codes.

Step 3: Using the _____ information, research the diagnostic _____ for any codes found.

Step 4: If there are _____ _____, evaluate the service information to see if codes are _____ to each other.

Step 5: Follow the diagnostic procedure step by step until you have completed the diagnostic procedure and _____ the _____ of the DTC.

Step 6: Consult with the _____ before completing any _____.

Crossword Puzzle

Use the clues in the column to complete the puzzle.

Across

1. A test performed at the beginning and end of a shift in process.
5. The pulse-modulated signal sent to a solenoid to initiate fluid flow.
6. The logical process created by the transmission controller using data gained from the vehicle to determine when and how shifting should occur.

Down

2. An accumulator used in the ATEC/CEC systems to smoothen out the shift process.
3. Solenoids that need only a short burst of electricity to move to an open or closed position and they remain in that state until they are energized again.
4. The unit that Allison uses to describe throttle position based on the variable voltage signal from a TPS (throttle position sensor).

ASE-Type Questions

Read each item carefully, and then select the best response.

_____ 1. Technician A says that the Allison transmission's TCU switches to slow adaptive mode after optimum shift quality has been attained. Technician B says that the TCU must be switched to fast adaptive mode after transmission replacement. Who is correct?
   A. Technician A
   B. Technician B
   C. Both Technician A and Technician B
   D. Neither Technician A nor Technician B

_____ 2. Technician A says that the Allison World Transmission series is a true "drive by wire" transmission. Technician B says that the World Transmission series still has a mechanical gear-shift linkage. Who is correct?
   A. Technician A
   B. Technician B
   C. Both Technician A and Technician B
   D. Neither Technician A nor Technician B

_____ 3. Technician A says the Allison World Transmission is capable of inhibiting neutral to range shifts if the engine RPM is too high. Technician B says that the TCU is capable of inhibiting downshifts if the road speed is too high. Who is correct?
   A. Technician A
   B. Technician B
   C. Both Technician A and Technician B
   D. Neither Technician A nor Technician B

_____ 4. Technician A says that the Voith DIWA drive transmission has two inputs to the transmission gear train: mechanical and hydrodynamic. Technician B says in the Voith DIWA drive transmission, torque converter doubles as a retarder. Who is correct?
   A. Technician A
   B. Technician B
   C. Both Technician A and Technician B
   D. Neither Technician A nor Technician B

_____ 5. Technician A says that the Allison TC-10 has two countershafts. Technician B says that the Allison TC-10 uses both countershafts for each power flow like the Eaton Fuller Twin countershaft transmission does. Who is correct?
   A. Technician A
   B. Technician B
   C. Both Technician A and Technician B
   D. Neither Technician A nor Technician B

_____ 6. Technician A says that prognostics in an Allison World Transmission can alert the driver when an oil or filter change is required. Technician B says that prognostics in an Allison World Transmission can alert the driver when the transmission clutches are in danger of failing. Who is correct?
   A. Technician A
   B. Technician B
   C. Both Technician A and Technician B
   D. Neither Technician A nor Technician B

_____ 7. Technician A says that the Caterpillar CX-28 transmission power flow is identical to the Allison World Transmission. Technician B says that the Caterpillar CX-28 uses two rotating clutches. Who is correct?
   A. Technician A
   B. Technician B
   C. Both Technician A and Technician B
   D. Neither Technician A nor Technician B

_____ **8.** Technician A says that the four-speed Voith DIWA drive transmission has three hydraulic clutches in its rotating clutch module. Technician B says that the four-speed Voith DIWA has three planetary gear sets in the front section. Who is correct?

    A. Technician A

    B. Technician B

    C. Both Technician A and Technician B

    D. Neither Technician A nor Technician B

_____ **9.** Technician A says that the four-speed Voith DIWA drive transmission has five hydraulic clutches in total. Technician B says the four-speed Voith DIWA drive transmission has four planetary gear sets in total. Who is correct?

    A. Technician A

    B. Technician B

    C. Both Technician A and Technician B

    D. Neither Technician A nor Technician B

_____ **10.** Technician A says that the Voith DIWA drive transmission uses a differential input in reverse. Technician B says that the Voith DIWA drive transmission uses a differential input in all forward gears. Who is correct?

    A. Technician A

    B. Technician B

    C. Both Technician A and Technician B

    D. Neither Technician A nor Technician B

Driveshaft Systems

Chapter Review

The following activities have been designed to help you refresh your knowledge of this chapter. Your instructor may require you to complete some or all of these activities as a regular part of your training program. You are encouraged to complete any activity that your instructor does not assign as a way to enhance your learning.

Matching

Match the following terms with the correct description or example.

A. Drive line   **D.** Slip joint

B. Gimbals   **E.** Trunnion

C. Jack shaft

_____ **1.** The smooth ends of the U-joint cross that accepts the bearing caps.

_____ **2.** A splined shaft and tube assembly that allows driveshaft length changes.

_____ **3.** Two or more concentric circles used to support an item; while the circles can move, the supported object will remain stationary.

_____ **4.** A series of driveshafts, yokes, and support bearings used to connect a transmission to the rear axle.

_____ **5.** A short shaft usually at the front of a drive line.

Multiple Choice

Read each item carefully, and then select the best response.

_____ **1.** The invention of the universal joint is generally attributed to mathematician _____, who described the operation of the joint in detail in 1545 but never produced it.
   A. Robert Hooke
   B. Gerolamo Cardano
   C. Clarence Spicer
   D. John Gimbal

_____ **2.** The term _____ refers to the inherent vibration effects caused by the acceleration and deceleration of the rotating driveshaft.
   A. excitation
   B. brinelling
   C. resonance
   D. phasing

_____ **3.** A(n) _____ is designed to be installed over the splined output shaft of the transmission, or the splined input shaft of the drive axle.
   A. tube yoke
   B. flange yoke
   C. end yoke
   D. companion yoke

_____ **4.** A _____ is used to support a multiple piece driveshaft.
   A. center bearing
   B. flange yoke
   C. hanger bearing
   D. Either A or C

_____ **5.** Maximum driveshaft low gear torque is calculated by multiplying the net engine torque by the _____.
   A. transmission lowest gear ratio
   B. transmission efficiency
   C. torque converter stall ratio
   D. All of the above

_____ **6.** Without proper lubricant the needle bearings will start to dig into the trunnions causing an effect known as _____.
   A. phasing
   B. tempering
   C. false brinelling
   D. splining

_____ **7.** The preferred method for cancelling out non-uniform velocity is called the _____ arrangement.
   A. broken back
   B. parallel joint
   C. intersecting angle
   D. Either A or C

_____ **8.** Drive line angles should not cause vibration if _____.
   A. there is at least one-half to one degree of operating angle
   B. the angles at opposite ends of a shaft are equal within one degree
   C. working angles are kept to less than three degrees
   D. All of the above rules are met

_____ **9.** In a _____ joint the drive angle always bisects a series of six balls, leading to perfect cancellation of the angles and constant velocity of the driven shaft.
   A. Rzeppa joint
   B. double Cardan joint
   C. Hooke joint
   D. Spicer joint

_____ **10.** What type of vibrations are caused by an out-of-balance driveshaft or system and occur once per shaft revolution?
   A. Torsional vibrations
   B. Secondary couple vibrations
   C. Transverse vibrations
   D. Critical speed vibrations

True/False

If you believe the statement to be more true than false, write the letter "T" in the space provided. If you believe the statement to be more false than true, write the letter "F".

_____ **1.** The primary function of a driveshaft is to provide the strength needed to withstand the peak torque delivered from the engine while providing an ample safety margin.

_____ **2.** A driveshaft must be capable of transmitting torque to the rear axle while operating through constantly changing drive angles.

_____ **3.** Most heavy truck drive lines consist of a single driveshaft connecting the output of the transmission to the input of the drive axle.

_____ **4.** A tube yoke allows the driveshaft to lengthen or shorten in order to accommodate length changes caused by suspension oscillation.

_____ **5.** The universal joint allows the two connected yokes to rotate at different angles to each other.

_____ **6.** Operating angles at either end of a driveshaft must be equal to within one degree to obtain acceptable cancellation of the non-uniform velocity created by joint working angles.

_____ **7.** Waterfall installations are usually only found between the two axles of a tandem drive because driveshaft length changes are minimal in this location.

_____ **8.** If the component slope goes higher as it moves to the back of the vehicle, it is an upward slope and recorded as a positive angle.

_____ **9.** Secondary couple vibrations are vibrations that are passed through or coupled through the hanger bearing in a heavy-duty driveshaft.

_____ **10.** Driveshaft runout can be caused by a bent driveshaft, damaged yokes, or worn U-joints.

Fill in the Blank

Read each item carefully, and then complete the statement by filling in the missing word(s).

1. The scientific community traces the universal joint back to the _____ used by the ancient Greeks as early as 220 B.C.

2. Sometimes, a(n) _____ flange is matched with a flange yoke and used instead of an end yoke.

3. A phenomenon called _____-_____ velocity happens when any shaft with a universal joint operates at an angle different from the axis of rotation of the drive component.

4. An out-of-_____ driveshaft causes the accelerations and decelerations of the joints on either end of the shafts to be out of sync with each other.

5. Drive line _____ simply refers to the angles at the universal joints.

6. Compound drive line angles involve angles in two planes—the side view and the _____ or top view.

7. If proper cancellation is not achieved by correct angles and phasing, the driveshaft will be subjected to _____ vibrations.

8. Contaminated lubricant or lack of lubricant in a joint leads to _____.

9. End _____ of the trunnions is usually caused by excessive joint operating angles.

10. Lack of proper _____ is one of the most common causes of universal joint and driveshaft failures.

Labeling

Label the following diagrams with the correct terms.

1. Identify the components of a universal joint:

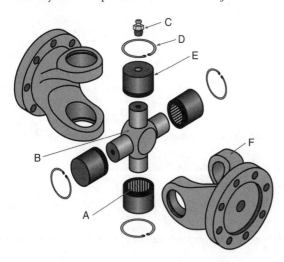

A. _____

B. _____

C. _____

D. _____

E. _____

F. _____

Skill Drills

Test your knowledge of skill drills by filling in the correct words in the photo captions.

1. Disassembling and Inspecting a Universal Joint with a Bolted End:

Step 1:   Locate and follow the appropriate _____ in the _____ _____.

Step 2:   Complete the accompanying _____ _____ or _____ _____ with all pertinent information.

Step 3:   Remove the U-joint from _____:

    a. Bend _____ of lock _____ away from cap screw _____.

    b. Remove _____ _____ and _____ _____.

    c. Remove bearing caps from _____ and _____. Note: If caps have to be driven out with a _____, be careful not to damage the _____ or _____.

Step 4:   Inspect _____with _____ ends:

    a. Clean all _____ parts.

    b. Check bearing _____ for evidence of _____ or _____ damage; also, check _____ of _____.

    c. Make sure _____ _____ in _____ are clean.

    d. Check for missing, worn, or damaged _____ _____.

    e. Apply the recommended _____ to _____ in caps.

    f. Turn _____ on _____ to check for wear. Note: If any parts are worn or damaged, _____ the entire _____.

Step 5:   List the _____ _____ and/or recommendations on the _____ _____ or _____ _____, clean the _____ _____, and return _____ and _____ to their proper _____.

2. Installing Universal Joints:

Step 1: With all of the _____ removed from the _____, position it in the _____ _____ with one of the _____ protruding above the yoke _____. Install the _____ in the _____, one _____ at a time.

Step 2: Place the _____ _____ over the trunnion, making sure that the _____ remain properly _____ in the cap. Then, _____ the cap into position while holding the _____ so that the _____ remain engaged with the trunnion. If the cap _____ in the yoke, tap it lightly with a _____ _____ hammer until it is _____. Always tap the _____ of the cap only—not the _____.

Step 3: Install the cap retaining bolts with the _____ _____ if equipped, but do not _____ the lock strap _____ to secure the _____ at this time. (Wait until the joint is properly _____.)

Step 4: With one _____ installed correctly, turn the _____ over and _____ the cross sufficiently to engage the _____ of the second _____ with its trunnion. Do not raise the cross so high that the other _____ comes out of its cap. Then, _____ the second cap into position and _____ it.

Step 5: Rotate the _____ on its _____ to be sure there is no _____. If it binds, the joint should be _____ to find the cause.

Step 6: If the _____ is being installed into a _____-_____ end _____, place the two other _____ on their trunnions and _____ the exposed caps together with _____ _____ so they do not fall off when positioning the _____ for installation. Install the _____ and the attaching _____.

Step 7: If installing the shaft into a _____-_____ yoke, repeat the installation instructions used on the _____ by lifting the first _____ through the _____ _____ then installing its _____ so the rollers are _____. Push the _____ into place. Depending on the type of _____, it may be necessary to use a _____ installation _____ to install the caps. Lift the last _____ through the _____ _____ just enough so that the _____ of the bearing cap are held in place by the trunnion as the _____ is installed. _____ it into position.

Step 8: After the _____ is _____, follow the lubricating instructions in the Lubrication section of this chapter. It may be necessary to _____ the attaching _____ during the lubrication procedure. If your _____ bolts have _____ _____, do not fold over the lock strap _____ until you have correctly _____ the U-joints. After lubricating the joints, correctly fold up the lock strap _____, if equipped, to _____ the attaching _____.

3. Removing and Reinstalling the Driveshaft:

Step 1: Locate and follow the appropriate _____ in the _____ _____.

Step 2: Complete the accompanying _____ _____ or _____ _____ with all pertinent information.

Step 3: Move the vehicle into shop, apply _____ _____, and _____ the vehicle wheels. Observe _____/_____ procedures.

Step 4: If the vehicle has a _____ transmission, place it in "_____." If it has an _____ transmission, place it in "_____" or "_____."

Step 5: Jack up the _____ of vehicle and place _____ _____ under _____.

Step 6: Mark all _____ and _____ with a _____ _____ or _____ marker to retain _____ and _____.

Step 7: Support the _____ with a suitable _____ and remove the driveshaft _____ _____. Study the driveshaft to determine how it is _____.

Step 8: Remove the _____ support bearing if a _____-_____ driveshaft is used. Check between center support and frame for _____. If _____ are used, they must be _____ when the driveshaft is reinstalled.

Step 9: Remove the _____ from vehicle. Tape the U-joint _____ _____ to prevent loss of _____ _____. The _____ _____ should also be protected to prevent _____ during removal. When removing, replacing, or servicing a driveshaft, careless _____ can _____ the shaft and U-joints.

Step 10: Service the _____ according to the _____ _____.

Step 11: Reinstall _____:

a. Place in position and check _____ marks. All mounting surfaces should be _____ and free of _____ before assembly.

b. Position all _____ correctly and _____ evenly.

c. Replace _____ in center _____ _____, if used.

d. _____ all _____ to manufacturer's _____.

Step 12: Jack up the _____ of the vehicle and remove _____ _____.

Step 13: Lower the _____ to _____.

Step 14: Grease each _____. Continue to grease until the _____ is removed and _____ comes from the bearing cap _____. Once grease is _____ from seals, _____ seals of all grease with a _____ _____.

Step 15: List the _____ _____ and/or recommendations on the _____ _____ or _____ _____, clean the _____ _____, and return _____ and _____ to their proper storage.

4. Inspecting and Servicing Center Support Bearings:

Step 1: Safely _____ the vehicle on an approved _____. Inspect the _____ bearing components for any major _____, such as _____ or _____.

Step 2: Inspect the _____ _____ for proper _____.

Step 3: Inspect the bearing mount _____ _____ for _____ _____ and _____.

Step 4: If the bearing must be _____, follow the manufacturer's _____ and _____ for proper installation of a new bearing. Typical bearing replacement may go as follows:

   a. Mount the _____ in an approved _____.

   b. Mark the _____ so they may be properly _____ when put back together.

   c. Separate the two _____.

   d. Remove the U-shaped metal _____ _____.

   e. Remove the _____ _____ from around the _____ _____.

   f. Remove any _____ _____ or _____ that may be holding the _____ in place.

   g. Use an appropriate _____ or _____ to remove the _____ from the driveshaft.

   h. Check the _____ of the _____ _____ for any defects.

   i. Check the slip yoke on the _____ _____ for _____ and _____.

   j. Press on a new _____.

   k. Reinstall any necessary _____ _____ or _____.

Step 5: Install a new _____ _____ around the new _____. Reinstall the _____ _____.

Step 6: Put the two _____ back together, paying attention to driveshaft _____.

Step 7: Remove the _____ from the _____, and reinstall it into _____.

Crossword Puzzle

Use the clues in the column to complete the puzzle.

Across

3. A splined flange attached to a vehicle component, such as a drive axle pinion shaft, that bolts to a flange yoke on a driveshaft.

5. The rotational speed at which a driveshaft starts to bow off its center line due to centrifugal force, leading to vibration and shaft failure.

Down

1. An inherent vibration that occurs at precisely 50% of a shaft's critical speed.

2. A yoke with two ears to hold a U-joint and a flat flange to bolt to a companion flange.

4. Lining up the inboard yoke ears of driveshaft so that the non-uniform velocity cancellation occurs in the proper quadrant of the circle.

ASE-Type Questions

Read each item carefully, and then select the best response.

_____ 1. Technician A says that when a driveshaft operates at an angle, the driven shaft accelerates and decelerates once per revolution. Technician B says that using a U-joint at the front and back with equal angles cancels the non-uniform velocity. Who is correct?
  A. Technician A
  B. Technician B
  C. Both Technician A and Technician B
  D. Neither Technician A nor Technician B

_____ 2. Technician A says that a drive line is made up of more than one driveshaft. Technician B says that multi-shaft drive lines must have a center or hanger bearing. Who is correct?
  A. Technician A
  B. Technician B
  C. Both Technician A and Technician B
  D. Neither Technician A nor Technician B

_____ 3. Technician A says that that drive line attaching bolts should not be reused. Technician B says that Spicer Life series spring clips can be reused as long as they are not bent. Who is correct?
  A. Technician A
  B. Technician B
  C. Both Technician A and Technician B
  D. Neither Technician A nor Technician B

_____ 4. Technician A says that some driveshafts are cross phased or phased at 90 degrees. Technician B says that, when a driveshaft slip yoke is removed, you should mark its position so that it is reassembled correctly in phase. Who is correct?
  A. Technician A
  B. Technician B
  C. Both Technician A and Technician B
  D. Neither Technician A nor Technician B

_____ 5. Technician A says that critical speed is when a driveshaft starts to bow off its center line due to centrifugal force. Technician B says that a driveshaft operating at or above critical speed will vibrate violently. Who is correct?
  A. Technician A
  B. Technician B
  C. Both Technician A and Technician B
  D. Neither Technician A nor Technician B

_____ 6. Technician A says that driveshaft angularity is the first thing to check when diagnosing driveshaft vibrations. Technician B says that a driveshaft out of phase will vibrate. Who is correct?
  A. Technician A
  B. Technician B
  C. Both Technician A and Technician B
  D. Neither Technician A nor Technician B

_____ 7. Technician A says that as long as a driveshaft has canceling angles, it will not vibrate. Technician B says that driveshaft operating angles are limited by the speed the shaft must rotate. Who is correct?
  A. Technician A
  B. Technician B
  C. Both Technician A and Technician B
  D. Neither Technician A nor Technician B

_____ 8. Technician A says that a dent in a driveshaft may cause the shaft to vibrate. Technician B says that foreign material on the driveshaft may cause vibration. Who is correct?
  A. Technician A
  B. Technician B
  C. Both Technician A and Technician B
  D. Neither Technician A nor Technician B

_____ **9.** Technician says that small amounts of rust purging from the U-joint while greasing it is expected and that you should keep greasing the joint until all the rust is gone. Technician B says that a couple of drops of water escaping the U-joint grease seals while lubricating the joint is normal. Who is correct?
   A. Technician A
   B. Technician B
   C. Both Technician A and Technician B
   D. Neither Technician A nor Technician B

_____ **10.** Technician A says that, when checking U-joints, end play between the U-joint trunnions and the bearing cap should be no more than 0.006" (0.15 mm). Technician B says that slip yoke radial play should not exceed 0.030" (0.76 mm). Who is correct?
   A. Technician A
   B. Technician B
   C. Both Technician A and Technician B
   D. Neither Technician A nor Technician B

Heavy-Duty Truck Drive Axles

Tire Tread:
© AbleStock

Chapter Review

The following activities have been designed to help you refresh your knowledge of this chapter. Your instructor may require you to complete some or all of these activities as a regular part of your training program. You are encouraged to complete any activity that your instructor does not assign as a way to enhance your learning.

Matching

Match the following terms with the correct description or example.

A. Bevel gears

B. Differential gear

C. Hypoid gearing

D. Pinion gear

E. Worm wheel

_____ **1.** An older drive axle gear arrangement capable of very high gear reductions in a compact space.

_____ **2.** A small driving gear.

_____ **3.** A gear arrangement that splits the available torque equally between two wheels while allowing them to turn at different speeds when required.

_____ **4.** A type of spiral bevel gear set that mounts the pinion gear below the centerline of the crown gear.

_____ **5.** Gears that intersect at an angle—usually 90 degrees.

Multiple Choice

Read each item carefully, and then select the best response.

_____ **1.** A self-steering axle that is located in front of the drive, or main axles, on trucks and/or trailers is called a _____.
   A. pusher axle
   B. drive axle
   C. tag axle
   D. Either A or C

_____ **2.** Drive axles can be arranged as a _____, where the driving force is divided between multiple drive axles.
   A. tandem
   B. triangle
   C. tridem
   D. Either A or C

_____ **3.** A _____ axle is used with certain types of trailers with low floors, such as furniture vans.
   A. drop center tubular
   B. crank
   C. steering
   D. live

_____ **4.** The _____ gear is attached to the differential case.
   A. pinion
   B. worm
   C. ring
   D. Both A and C

_____ 5. The _____ tooth design implements non-symmetrical tooth flanks.
   A. durapoid
   B. spiral bevel
   C. hypoid
   D. topoid

_____ 6. On _____ gears, the pinion gear is mounted above the centerline of the crown gear.
   A. hypoid
   B. amboid
   C. generoid
   D. All of the above

_____ 7. The removable carrier housing is also known as a _____ housing because of the shape of the housing.
   A. guitar
   B. drum
   C. banjo
   D. tuba

_____ 8. The _____ gears are fitted to the four legs of the differential cross, so they must rotate with it.
   A. spider
   B. amboid
   C. side
   D. worm

_____ 9. In any driving situation, when you add the speed of the two axles of a differential gear set together, the total will always equal _____ of case speed.
   A. 50%
   B. 100%
   C. 150%
   D. 200%

_____ 10. In a _____ differential, two sets of plates are interleaved to form a clutch pack similar to the clutch packs found in automatic transmissions.
   A. double reduction
   B. controlled traction
   C. locking
   D. biased torque

_____ 11. A _____ differential is capable of sending more torque to one wheel than the other when a wheel slip condition is encountered.
   A. biased torque
   B. controlled traction
   C. proportional
   D. Either A or C

_____ 12. A _____ two-speed drive axle uses a double reduction to achieve a low range ratio through the drive axle, and a single reduction in high range.
   A. planetary
   B. biased torque
   C. helical double reduction
   D. Both A and C

_____ 13. The _____ drives the pinion gear of the front drive axle in a tandem drive arrangement.
   A. generoid gear
   B. helical drop gear
   C. spider gear
   D. topoid gear

_____ 14. Spinout can occur while _____.
   A. starting on a slippery surface
   B. backing under a trailer
   C. driving in slippery conditions
   D. All of the above

_____ **15.** A _____ axle shaft does not carry any of the vehicle weight on either end on the shaft.
- **A.** two-piece
- **B.** semi-floating
- **C.** full-floating
- **D.** All of the above

True/False

If you believe the statement to be more true than false, write the letter "T" in the space provided. If you believe the statement to be more false than true, write the letter "F".

_____ **1.** A dead axle can be raised or lowered by the driver in the cab when needed in order to allow the vehicle to carry more payload.

_____ **2.** Plain bevel gears are inherently noisy and only have one set of teeth in mesh at any time.

_____ **3.** A topoid gear is simply an amboid system mounted below the centerline of the crown wheel.

_____ **4.** The term differential is a synonym for drive axle.

_____ **5.** Most differential locks are air operated and consist of a differential lock switch on the dashboard.

_____ **6.** The most famous biased torque main differential is the Eaton/Dana TruTrac.

_____ **7.** Adding two-speed capability to a double reduction drive axle effectively doubles the transmission ranges available to the driver for vehicle and road conditions.

_____ **8.** Planetary double reduction axles are usually only found in articulated busses.

_____ **9.** Electric shift systems are much simpler than using an air shift control system.

_____ **10.** When poor traction conditions are encountered, the Mack design can automatically send 75% of available torque to the drive axle wheels with the best traction.

Fill in the Blank

Read each item carefully, and then complete the statement by filling in the missing word(s).

1. A(n) _____-_____ axle contains wheels that will automatically follow the curve of a turn to prevent tire scrubbing.

2. The _____ _____ is a rod with two ball joint style ends and its length is usually adjustable so the steering can be set up properly.

3. A(n) _____ _____ tubular axle is concave in the middle and commonly found in situations when product-handling tubes and pipes are required to run under the trailer.

4. The development of _____ bevel gears helped reduce the noise associated with plain bevel gearing because of the wiping or sliding effect of the tooth contact.

5. In a(n) _____ carrier housing the carrier is not removable.

6. Heavy-duty _____ differentials can be engaged or disengaged by the vehicle operator when required.

7. A(n) _____ _____ drive axle uses two gear reductions at all times.

8. An inter-axle differential, also called a(n) _____ _____, works in exactly the same way as a drive axle differential.

9. The _____ shaft exits the rear of the power divider housing and connects to a short driveshaft, which in turn, connects to the rear-rear drive axle pinion gear.

10. Most drive axles are lubricated by _____ caused by the rotation of the crown wheel.

Labeling

Label the following diagrams with the correct terms.

1. Identify the components of a controlled traction differential:

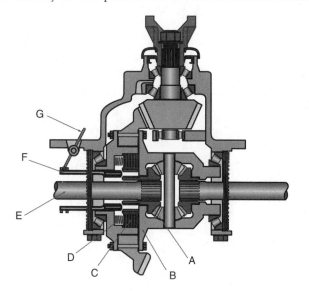

A. _____

B. _____

C. _____

D. _____

E. _____

F. _____

G. _____

2. Identify the components of a planetary drive axle:

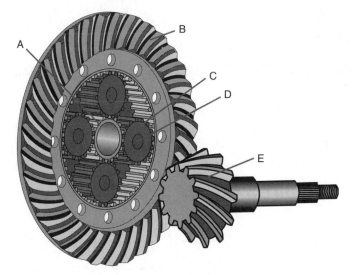

A. _____

B. _____

C. _____

D. _____

E. _____

3. Identify the components of an electric shift system:

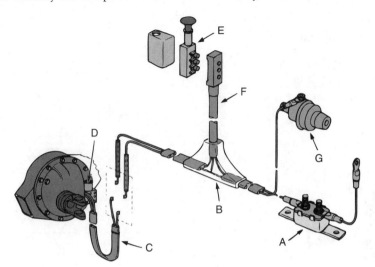

A. _____

B. _____

C. _____

D. _____

E. _____

F. _____

G. _____

4. Identify the major components of a power divider:

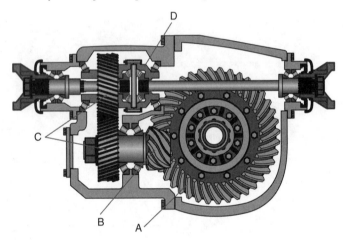

A. _____

B. _____

C. _____

D. _____

5. Identify the components of a full-floating axle shaft:

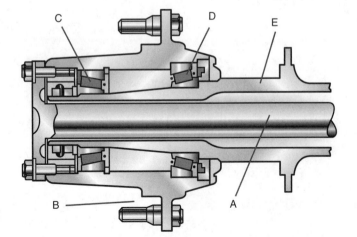

A. _____

B. _____

C. _____

D. _____

E. _____

Crossword Puzzle

Use the clues in the column to complete the puzzle.

Across

4. A rear, non-drive rear mounted axle, ahead of the drive axle.

5. The component that holds the support bearings for the drive axle gearing.

Down

1. A large bevel gear that is driven by a smaller pinion gear in the bevel gear set. Also known as a crown gear.

2. Two drive axles connected by a power divider.

3. A type of amboid gear set with the pinion gear mounted even higher than a normal amboid set.

ASE-Type Questions

Read each item carefully, and then select the best response.

_____ 1. Technician A says that drive axles allow the power from the engine to turn 90 degrees to turn the wheels. Technician B says that a drive axle usually provides the last gear reduction in a drive train system. Who is correct?
  A. Technician A
  B. Technician B
  C. Both Technician A and Technician B
  D. Neither Technician A nor Technician B

_____ 2. Technician A says that a hypoid gear set has the pinion gear mounted above the centerline of the crown wheel. Technician B says that a generoid gear set uses a stronger tooth design. Who is correct?
  A. Technician A
  B. Technician B
  C. Both Technician A and Technician B
  D. Neither Technician A nor Technician B

_____ 3. Technician A says that a differential gear set allows for drive axle wheel speed difference in turns. Technician B says that a differential gear set can allow a single wheel on a drive axle to spin wildly while the other wheel remains stationary. Who is correct?
  A. Technician A
  B. Technician B
  C. Both Technician A and Technician B
  D. Neither Technician A nor Technician B

_____ 4. Technician A says that a controlled traction differential allows the engine to build more torque in poor traction conditions. Technician B says that controlled traction differentials prevent any differential action from occurring while engaged. Who is correct?
  A. Technician A
  B. Technician B
  C. Both Technician A and Technician B
  D. Neither Technician A nor Technician B

_____ 5. Technician A says that in a tandem drive vehicle most of the driving effort is provided by the front-rear axle. Technician B says that the rear-rear drive axle only receives 50% of the available driving torque. Who is correct?
  A. Technician A
  B. Technician B
  C. Both Technician A and Technician B
  D. Neither Technician A nor Technician B

_____ 6. Technician A says that two-speed drive axles offer more speed ranges to a vehicle operator. Technician B says that two-speed helical axles use a smaller crown gear so are less apt to flex under load. Who is correct?
  A. Technician A
  B. Technician B
  C. Both Technician A and Technician B
  D. Neither Technician A nor Technician B

_____ 7. Technician A says that an inter-axle differential divides the available power between the front and rear axles of a tandem drive. Technician B says that an inter-axle differential can split the torque between the front and rear axles of a four-by-four vehicle. Who is correct?
  A. Technician A
  B. Technician B
  C. Both Technician A and Technician B
  D. Neither Technician A nor Technician B

_____ **8.** Technician A says that a durapoid bevel gear tooth is stronger than a regular bevel gear tooth. Technician B says that a durapoid bevel gear set is a spiral bevel gear set. Who is correct?
   A. Technician A
   B. Technician B
   C. Both Technician A and Technician B
   D. Neither Technician A nor Technician B

_____ **9.** Technician A says that an amboid gear set has the pinion mounted below the center line of the crown gear. Technician B says that an amboid gear set's crown gear teeth are concave on the drive side. Who is correct?
   A. Technician A
   B. Technician B
   C. Both Technician A and Technician B
   D. Neither Technician A nor Technician B

_____ **10.** Technician A says that most inter-axle differentials today are pressure lubricated. Technician B says that the inter-axle differential lock can be engaged while the vehicle is moving as long as there is no wheel spin occurring. Who is correct?
   A. Technician A
   B. Technician B
   C. Both Technician A and Technician B
   D. Neither Technician A nor Technician B

Servicing and Maintaining Drive Axles

Chapter Review

The following activities have been designed to help you refresh your knowledge of this chapter. Your instructor may require you to complete some or all of these activities as a regular part of your training program. You are encouraged to complete any activity that your instructor does not assign as a way to enhance your learning.

Matching

Match the following terms with the correct description or example.

A. Heel

B. Root

C. Toe

D. Tooth face

E. Top land

_____ **1.** The area that actually comes into contact with a mating gear and is parallel to the gear's axis of rotation.

_____ **2.** The radius shape between the bottoms of two teeth.

_____ **3.** The apex of a tooth.

_____ **4.** The end of a crown gear tooth furthest from the center of its axis.

_____ **5.** The end of a crown gear tooth closest to the center of its axis.

Multiple Choice

Read each item carefully, and then select the best response.

_____ **1.** The recommended SAE grade for drive axle lubricant used in ambient temperatures of 10° F (–12° C) and above is _____.

  A. 85W-140

  B. 74W-140

  C. 80W-90

  D. 75W-80

_____ **2.** Dana Spicer recommends checking the drive axle fluid level and inspecting for leaks every _____.

  A. 5,000 miles (8,000 km)

  B. 10,000 miles (16,000 km)

  C. 12,000 miles (19,300 km)

  D. 15,000 miles (24,000 km)

_____ **3.** The recommended change interval for a heavy-duty line haul vehicle using a mineral-based SAE J-2360 lubricant is _____.

  A. 100,000 miles (161,000 km)

  B. 120,000 miles (193,000 km)

  C. 180,000 miles (290,000 km)

  D. 250,000 miles (402,000 km)

_____ **4.** A tandem drive axle with a nomenclature of D C 40 4 – (P) would indicate a _____.

  A. single reduction with controlled traction differential

  B. design level of 40

  C. rear tandem axle

  D. standard lube pump

_____ **5.** A straddle mount pinion is supported by two opposing tapered roller bearings and also by a small _____ that supports the pinion at the inside end.
- **A.** spigot bearing
- **B.** pinion bearing cage
- **C.** pinion pilot bearing
- **D.** Either A or C

_____ **6.** The pinion depth setting must be accurate to within _____.
- **A.** 0.001" (0.025 mm)
- **B.** 0.025" (0.635 mm)
- **C.** 0.003" (0.076 mm)
- **D.** 0.005" (0.127 mm)

_____ **7.** After the differential case and crown gear are installed, crown gear _____ should be checked.
- **A.** contact patterns
- **B.** runout
- **C.** profile
- **D.** preload

_____ **8.** If the contact pattern is too close to the toe of the crown gear the problem can be corrected by _____.
- **A.** increasing the backlash
- **B.** tightening the thrust screw
- **C.** decreasing the backlash
- **D.** adjusting the pinion bearing preload

_____ **9.** What type of fatigue failure, characterized by beach marks, usually occurs with gear teeth?
- **A.** bending stresses
- **B.** torsional stresses
- **C.** surface fatigue
- **D.** abuse stresses

_____ **10.** Twisted main-shafts in the transmission or broken universal joints caused by dumping the clutch are examples of _____.
- **A.** lubrication failure
- **B.** manufacturing failure
- **C.** fatigue failure
- **D.** abuse failure

True/False

If you believe the statement to be more true than false, write the letter "T" in the space provided. If you believe the statement to be more false than true, write the letter "F".

_____ **1.** Most manufacturers recommend a synthetic formulation for their drive axle lubricant.

_____ **2.** Lube change intervals are universal.

_____ **3.** Manufacturers recommend an initial fluid drop at 3,000 to 5,000 miles to remove metal particles produced by the axle gearing during the break-in period regardless of the type of lubricant used.

_____ **4.** If the axle is removed from the vehicle when the axle is in the unlocked position, the lock will drop and it will be difficult to reinstall the axle shaft.

_____ **5.** A positive pinion variation number indicates a distance further away from the crown gear centerline.

_____ **6.** The nominal shim pack is one that would be used if the pinion had a zero variation.

_____ **7.** Side bearing preload is controlled by the hardened steel spacer between the inner and outer pinion bearings.

_____ **8.** The two elements of drive axle assembly that affect contact pattern are the gear set backlash and the pinion depth setting.

_____ **9.** If the drive axle has a thrust screw it must be adjusted before the gear set contact pattern is correctly adjusted.

_____ **10.** Step one of diagnosing drive axle failures is to determine the cause of the failure.

Fill in the Blank

Read each item carefully, and then complete the statement by filling in the missing word(s).

1. Manufacturers suggest using change intervals for _____ duty service on any vehicle that consistently operates at or near maximum GCW or GVW ratings, in dusty or wet environments, or on grades greater than 8%.

2. All axles have the _____ _____ stamped on the axle or on a plate attached to the drive axle.

3. Heavy-duty driveshafts can be extremely heavy. Use a(n) _____ to support the shaft before removal.

4. The differential case has two halves: the plain case half and the _____ case half.

5. If there is no spigot bearing, the pinion mounting is known as a(n) _____ mount pinion.

6. The pinion bearing _____ is a plate at the front of the differential carrier that holds the two outer cups of the pinion bearings.

7. Never use a(n) _____ gear from one set with the pinion gear from another—it is a recipe for disaster.

8. Gear set _____ allows the gears to expand while they are running.

9. The design of the gear set calls for the pinion to run at a set _____ distance from the crown gear's centerline.

10. Pinion bearing _____ ensures that the pinion remains rigid in the axle and will not move away from the crown gear as load is applied.

11. The contact pattern itself will consist of a lengthwise bearing along the tooth face from the toe to the heel and a(n) _____ bearing between the top land and the root.

12. A(n) _____ contact pattern is used for durapoid and hypoid generoid gear sets.

13. The _____ _____ has two components: the inter-axle differential and the main differential.

14. A(n) _____ _____ failure occurs when a component is momentarily overloaded to a level that surpasses the base strength of the material, causing it to fail immediately.

15. Small imperfections known as _____ _____ can occur during the casting process when the metal of the entire tooth is not uniformly fused together with the metal of the rest of the gear.

Labeling

Label the following diagrams with the correct terms.

1. Identify the nomenclature found on a crown and pinion gear set:

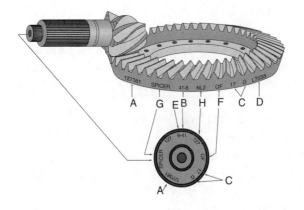

A. _____

B. _____

C. _____

D. _____

E. _____

F. _____

G. _____

H. _____

2. Identify the different parts of a gear tooth:

A. _____

B. _____

C. _____

D. _____

E. _____

F. _____

Skill Drills

Test your knowledge of skill drills by filling in the correct words in the photo captions.

1. Inspecting Drive Axles for Leaks and Determining the Cause:

Step 1: Put the vehicle on an approved _____ and make sure it is _____. Visually inspect around the _____ where the _____ seats for any _____.

Step 2: Inspect the _____ _____ for any _____.

Step 3: If necessary, remove the _____ wheels and install a _____ _____ on the axle _____ to check for any _____.

Step 4: Check and clean the _____ or _____ for any _____ that may cause a _____ build-up to occur.

Step 5: Check the _____ rear cover for a leaking _____, if so equipped. Tighten it if it is _____ or _____ as necessary.

Step 6: Check the fluid _____ for _____ of fluid or _____ of the _____, as either one can indicate that a _____ is present.

2. Disassembling the Differential Carrier:

Step 1: Mark with _____ marks _____ of the differential side bearing _____ _____ (the bore in the casting that holds the side bearing races) and the bearing _____ _____ (semicircular caps that clamp the side bearing into the casting). This allows the _____ to be reinstalled on the _____ _____.

Step 2: If the differential carrier has a _____ _____, loosen the _____ _____ and back out or _____ the thrust screw. The thrust screw (circled) will be located on the _____ _____ side of the differential carrier _____.

Step 3: Remove the bearing adjuster _____ (cotter pins, lock plates, and so on that stop the adjusters from turning) and _____ the four (or more) _____ _____ retaining cap screws. Back out the bearing _____ (threaded rings that position the side bearings) _____ to _____ turns. Remove the bearing _____ _____ (A), _____ _____ (B), and the _____ (C). Keep each side together as a _____ to ensure you will be able to reinstall them in the correct location.

Step 4: Using a _____ and a _____, remove the differential _____ and _____ _____ as an assembly and place it on a work bench. Remove the _____ _____ _____ from either the differential case or the _____ _____ using a wedge-type _____ _____. Place the assembly in the _____ with the puller _____ at first. This will allow the puller to _____ the bearing.

Step 5: After the bearing has been loosened, _____ the wedge-type _____ and install the assembly into the press _____ to finish the removal procedure.

Step 6: Remove the _____ _____, if replacing, by removing the retaining cap screws or _____ and _____ out the _____. The crown gear may need to be _____ off or lightly _____ off the differential case with a soft _____. Always _____ the crown gear from damage from _____.

3. Setting Pinion Bearing Preload:

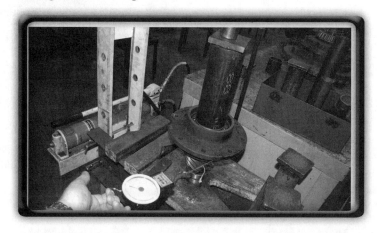

Step 1: Support the _____ under a _____. Then, using a correctly sized _____, press on the outer bearing _____ _____. Increase the press _____ to the amount recommended in the overhaul manual, typically _____ to _____ tons (9 t, 72 kg to 18 t, 144 kg). This load will accurately represent the load placed on the _____ when the pinion _____ or _____ is properly _____.

Step 2: Tie a length of _____ to one of the cage _____ _____ and _____ the _____ around the pinion _____ several times. Attach a _____ _____ that reads in _____ or _____ to the _____ end of the string. In a steady motion, start rotating the _____ by _____ and keep it rotating by _____ the scale.

Step 3: Record the _____ required to keep the cage _____, _____ the force required to _____ it rotating.

Step 4: Multiply the pounds or kilograms _____ by the _____ of the cage where the string was attached. This will indicate the _____ _____ of the _____ in inch-pounds or kilograms per _____. Typical settings are between _____ and _____ inch-pounds or _____ and _____ kilograms/centimeter. Always check the _____ _____ for the correct specification.

Step 5: After installing the two _____ _____, oil the _____ and place them into the _____ with the original _____ between them. Use the press to the correct press _____, supporting the rear bearing _____ _____, and pressing on the _____ bearing inner race. Measure the _____ _____ as above, and keep adjusting the size of the bearing _____ until the torque is correct. Then select a spacer _____" (0.025 mm) thicker to allow for bearing _____ the bearings will _____ slightly as they are pressed onto the _____. This should result in the _____ rotating torque on final assembly.

4. Measuring Crown Gear Runout:

Step 1: Locate and follow the appropriate procedure in the _____ _____.

Step 2: Complete the accompanying _____ _____ or _____ _____ with all pertinent information.

Step 3: Place a _____ _____ with _____ base to the differential carrier's _____.

Step 4: Position the _____ or _____ against the back of the _____ _____, and set the dial indicator to _____. Make sure the indicator is _____. If not stable, you may get an _____ reading.

Step 5: Rotate the _____ _____ and _____ while reading the _____ _____.

Step 6: Record the _____ _____ _____ by adding the _____ and _____ spots. For example [+ 0.010" (0.254 mm)] + [−0.003" (0.0762 mm)] would be 0.013" (0.330 mm) TIR.

Step 7: Check total against manufacturer's specifications. Total _____ should not normally exceed _____" (0.2 mm). If runout exceeds _____, the _____ and _____ _____ assembly must be _____ from the _____, and Steps 8, 9, and 10 must be completed. If runout is within _____, the procedure is _____.

Step 8: Check all parts of the _____ and _____ for the _____ that caused the runout to _____ specifications.

Step 9: Repair or _____ parts.

Step 10: Reinstall _____ and _____ _____ into the _____ and recheck _____.

Step 11: List the test _____ and/or recommendations on the _____ _____ or _____ _____, clean work area, and return _____ and materials to proper _____.

5. Checking Input Shaft End Play:

Step 1: With the _____ _____ cover installed, remove the _____ _____ bearing retainer and the _____
_____. Hold the bearing retainer against the power divider cover with _____ pressure and _____
the _____ between the _____ and the cover with a _____ _____.

Step 2: Add _____" (0.127 mm) to the measurement above if _____ gearing is installed and _____" (0.381
mm) if the _____ gearing was reused. This will result in the proper _____ of _____ to _____"
(0.076 to 0.178 mm) for _____ gearing and _____ to _____" (0.330 to 0.432 mm) for _____
gearing.

Step 3: Install the correct amount of _____, then _____ the bearing retainer cap screws to specification and
_____ the _____ _____. If the end play is in the correct range, install an _____ _____ washer
and torque the _____ _____ to specification.

Crossword Puzzle

Use the clues in the column to complete the puzzle.

Across

3. Negative end play, or less than zero clearance.

4. Small inclusion in a cast or formed metal that weakens it.

5. A stamped steel ring used to throw lubricant in a certain direction.

Down

1. Semi-circular mark in a fracture indicating repeated overload.

2. A point where the diameter of a shaft or thickness of a component changes.

ASE-Type Questions

Read each item carefully, and then select the best response.

_____ 1. Technician A says that drive axles do not usually require any regular maintenance, as they are sealed units. Technician B says that some drive axles with synthetic lube will not need any maintenance for 500,000 miles. Who is correct?
   A. Technician A
   B. Technician B
   C. Both Technician A and Technician B
   D. Neither Technician A nor Technician B

_____ 2. Technician A says that a drive axle must always be filled from the plug at the rear of the housing to the correct level. Technician B says that some drive axles have more than one fill plug. Who is correct?
   A. Technician A
   B. Technician B
   C. Both Technician A and Technician B
   D. Neither Technician A nor Technician B

_____ 3. Technician A says that the pinion depth adjustment influences the drive axle's contact pattern. Technician B says that the gear set backlash influences the drive axle's contact pattern. Who is correct?
   A. Technician A
   B. Technician B
   C. Both Technician A and Technician B
   D. Neither Technician A nor Technician B

_____ 4. Technician A says that most power dividers today have lubrication pumps to lubricate the inter-axle differential. Technician B says that single axle drive axles rely on splash from the crown gears rotation to provide lubrication. Who is correct?
   A. Technician A
   B. Technician B
   C. Both Technician A and Technician B
   D. Neither Technician A nor Technician B

_____ 5. Technician A says that bearing growth refers to the increase in a bearing's size as it is pressed onto a shaft. Technician B says that bearing growth has no effect on pinion bearing preload as long as the original pinion bearing shim is used while installing a new pinion gear. Who is correct?
   A. Technician A
   B. Technician B
   C. Both Technician A and Technician B
   D. Neither Technician A nor Technician B

_____ 6. Technician A says that two-speed drive axles offer more speed ranges to a vehicle operator. Technician B says that two-speed helical axles use a smaller crown gear so are less likely to flex under load. Who is correct?
   A. Technician A
   B. Technician B
   C. Both Technician A and Technician B
   D. Neither Technician A nor Technician B

_____ 7. Technician A says that pinion bearing preload can be measured with a string and a fish scale. Technician B says that pinion bearing preload in heavy-duty axles is controlled by the torque on the pinion nut. Who is correct?
   A. Technician A
   B. Technician B
   C. Both Technician A and Technician B
   D. Neither Technician A nor Technician B

_____ 8. Technician A says that side bearing preload causes a slight flexing of the bearing mounts. Technician B says that gear set backlash is set after side bearing preload. Who is correct?
   A. Technician A
   B. Technician B
   C. Both Technician A and Technician B
   D. Neither Technician A nor Technician B

_____ **9.** Technician A says that side gear support bearings should always be changed when overhauling a drive axle. Technician B says that spinout damage is usually visible as excess heat stress on the differential components. Who is correct?

A. Technician A

B. Technician B

C. Both Technician A and Technician B

D. Neither Technician A nor Technician B

_____ **10.** Technician A says that, after replacing the pinion seal, installing the pinion yoke nut with a 1-inch air gun is sufficient. Technician B says that some pinion nuts require as much as 1,500 ft-lb (2,034 Nm) of torque. Who is correct?

A. Technician A

B. Technician B

C. Both Technician A and Technician B

D. Neither Technician A nor Technician B

Hybrid Drive Systems and Series-Type Hybrid Drives

Chapter Review

The following activities have been designed to help you refresh your knowledge of this chapter. Your instructor may require you to complete some or all of these activities as a regular part of your training program. You are encouraged to complete any activity that your instructor does not assign as a way to enhance your learning.

Matching

Match the following terms with the correct description or example.

A. Electric vehicle (EV)

B. Hybrid electric vehicle (HEV)

C. Parallel drive

D. Series drive

E. Series-parallel drive

_____ **1.** A vehicle in which both the engine and electric motor work together, blending motor and engine torque, to propel the vehicle.

_____ **2.** A type of vehicle that combines an internal combustion engine with an electric propulsion system.

_____ **3.** A vehicle in which only an electric traction motor supplies torque to propel the vehicle.

_____ **4.** A vehicle in which only electric motors are used to move a vehicle.

_____ **5.** A more complex system enabling an engine only, an electric motor only, and a combined engine-motor operation.

Multiple Choice

Read each item carefully, and then select the best response.

_____ **1.** Hybrid propulsion systems use a _____ engine assisted by an electric motor to accelerate the vehicle.

    A. natural gas

    B. diesel

    C. reciprocating

    D. Any of the above

_____ **2.** Studies have shown that approximately _____ of energy used to accelerate a city bus is quickly dissipated into heat by frequent braking.

    A. 35%

    B. 50%

    C. 65%

    D. 75%

_____ **3.** All of the following are advantages to using a hybrid drive train, *except*:

    A. Smoother acceleration

    B. Lower purchase cost

    C. Increased brake life

    D. Quieter vehicle operation

_____ **4.** What type of hybrid drive configuration is also called a power-split configuration?

    A. Series drive

    B. Parallel drive

    C. Series-parallel drive

    D. Plug-in hybrid

_____ **5.** A _____ system works best in frequent stop-and-go service conditions.
- **A.** conventional
- **B.** series drive
- **C.** parallel drive
- **D.** series-parallel drive

_____ **6.** Shock hazard to the human body is a function of the _____.
- **A.** type of current
- **B.** skin resistance
- **C.** voltage
- **D.** All of the above

_____ **7.** Class _____ lineman gloves are recommended for use on high voltage hybrid circuits and offer protection from 1,500 to 5,000 volts.
- **A.** 0
- **B.** 1
- **C.** 2
- **D.** 3

_____ **8.** Connected directly to the flywheel of the engine is the _____, which converts mechanical energy produced by the engine into electrical current for the propulsion system.
- **A.** intuitive drive system
- **B.** propulsion control system
- **C.** alternating current traction generator
- **D.** energy storage system

_____ **9.** During _____, the vehicle is powered only—or almost only—by the energy stored in the battery.
- **A.** charge-sustaining mode
- **B.** charge-depleting operating mode
- **C.** intuitive operating mode
- **D.** Both A and C

_____ **10.** A(n) _____ type current inverter is used in the HybriDrive system.
- **A.** DC-to-AC
- **B.** resolver
- **C.** AC-to-DC
- **D.** Both A and C

True/False

If you believe the statement to be more true than false, write the letter "T" in the space provided. If you believe the statement to be more false than true, write the letter "F".

_____ **1.** Vehicles operating under long-haul highway conditions are best suited to hybrid use.

_____ **2.** A series system requires a larger electric motor and battery pack, but a smaller internal combustion engine than a parallel system.

_____ **3.** Hydraulic launch assist systems are a series-parallel hybrid system.

_____ **4.** In HLA performance mode, energy stored in the accumulator during braking is used only to initially accelerate the vehicle.

_____ **5.** Under the right conditions, 5 milliamps of AC current can be dangerous, and 500 milliamps can be lethal.

_____ **6.** When working on the battery storage system, two persons are required in case one person is harmed or becomes incapable of removing themselves from a live electrical circuit.

_____ **7.** A Class B fire extinguisher is recommended for any fire that involves a hybrid vehicle.

_____ **8.** In charge-sustaining mode, the batteries' state of charge may rise and fall slightly.

_____ **9.** The brake pressure signal on HybriDrive regenerative brakes can be adjusted using a scale of 1 to 10.

_____ **10.** With the engine test switch in the test position, only the alternating current traction motor responds to the throttle pedal.

Fill in the Blank

Read each item carefully, and then complete the statement by filling in the missing word(s).

1. A feature called _____ braking uses generators to recover energy during braking.

2. A(n) _____-_____ hybrid electric vehicle contains a battery storage system that uses an external source to recharge the battery when the vehicle is not in operation.

3. The _____ _____ _____ system uses hydraulic regenerative braking to capture braking energy and help launch the vehicle during acceleration.

4. In HLA _____ mode, both the engine and accumulator will provide driveline torque until the accumulator empties.

5. Disconnecting and _____ any residual current in EV components is imperative before performing any service work.

6. Many buses using the BAE _____ system are coupled to a Cummins diesel engine to obtain the highest fuel efficiency with the lowest emissions.

7. The _____ _____ system module is the system element controlling the operation of the entire HybriDrive System.

8. To maximize acceleration energy, the _____ _____ system supplies current to the ACTM when current demand exceeds availability from the ACTG.

9. A(n) _____ _____ _____ located in the battery compartments enables technicians to disconnect the power circuit for maintenance or emergencies.

10. An optional regenerative braking _____ switch is located near the driver for use during slippery road conditions.

Labeling

Label the following diagrams with the correct terms.

1. Identify the components of a series hybrid power train configuration:

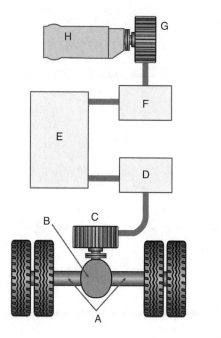

A. _____

B. _____

C. _____

D. _____

E. _____

F. _____

G. _____

H. _____

2. Identify the components of a parallel-drive hybrid configuration:

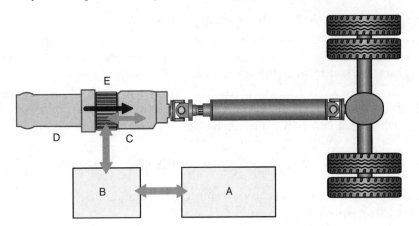

A. _____

B. _____

C. _____

D. _____

E. _____

Crossword Puzzle

Use the clues in the column to complete the puzzle.

Across

3. A special sensor that measures the rotor position and speed for the PCS to properly manage the motor operation by reducing current flow and shutting down the system as needed.

4. A motor that functions as an electrical generator in a hybrid drive system.

Down

1. An electric motor that provides propulsion to a vehicle.

2. A device that changes the shape of electrical current waves.

ASE-Type Questions

Read each item carefully, and then select the best response.

_____ 1. Technician A says that a hybrid electrical vehicle is one that has an electrical motor to drive the vehicle only and an engine to charge the vehicle batteries when necessary. Technician B says that the type of a hybrid that Technician A is describing is known as a series hybrid. Who is correct?

A. Technician A

B. Technician B

C. Both Technician A and Technician B

D. Neither Technician A nor Technician B

_____ 2. Technician A says that a parallel-drive hybrid is one in which both the engine and the electric motor combine to drive the vehicle at all times. Technician B says that series-parallel drive hybrid can use the engine, the electric motor, or both together to drive the vehicle. Who is correct?

A. Technician A

B. Technician B

C. Both Technician A and Technician B

D. Neither Technician A nor Technician B

_____ 3. Technician A says that not all hybrid drive vehicles are electric. Technician B says that hybrid drive electrical systems can be serviced in the same way as regular vehicle electrical systems. Who is correct?

A. Technician A

B. Technician B

C. Both Technician A and Technician B

D. Neither Technician A nor Technician B

_____ 4. Technician A says that electrical hybrid drive systems require an electrical storage system. Technician B says that most electrical hybrid drive systems use regenerative braking. Who is correct?

A. Technician A

B. Technician B

C. Both Technician A and Technician B

D. Neither Technician A nor Technician B

_____ 5. Technician A says that regenerative braking means that the foundation brakes can regenerate themselves after they wear. Technician B says that foundation brakes last longer when regenerative braking is used. Who is correct?

A. Technician A

B. Technician B

C. Both Technician A and Technician B

D. Neither Technician A nor Technician B

_____ 6. Technician A says that the original BAE HybriDrive system is a series hybrid. Technician B says that the original BAE HybriDrive system has two electric traction motors. Who is correct?

A. Technician A

B. Technician B

C. Both Technician A and Technician B

D. Neither Technician A nor Technician B

_____ 7. Technician A says that lead–acid batteries are used to store electricity on the latest hybrid drive systems. Technician B says that the BAE Gen 2 HybriDrive system uses nickel–metal hydride batteries as a power storage system. Who is correct?

A. Technician A

B. Technician B

C. Both Technician A and Technician B

D. Neither Technician A nor Technician B

_____ 8. Technician A says that electrical hybrid drive systems use a very high voltage traction motor to propel the vehicle. Technician B says that electrical hybrid drive systems require high voltage disconnect systems to shut off the high voltage for service. Who is correct?

A. Technician A

B. Technician B

C. Both Technician A and Technician B

D. Neither Technician A nor Technician B

_____ **9.** Technician A says that AC current is used to power the traction motor in BAE HybriDrive systems. Technician B says the nickel–metal hydride batteries in the BAE Gen 2 HybriDrive systems are AC batteries. Who is correct?

    A. Technician A

    B. Technician B

    C. Both Technician A and Technician B

    D. Neither Technician A nor Technician B

_____ **10.** Technician A says that, when a hybrid drive vehicle is brought into the shop for service, the high voltage system should be locked out. Technician B says that, when a hybrid vehicle must be towed, both axles should be removed so that the driveshaft does not rotate or damage the hybrid drive components. Who is correct?

    A. Technician A

    B. Technician B

    C. Both Technician A and Technician B

    D. Neither Technician A nor Technician B

Chapter Review

The following activities have been designed to help you refresh your knowledge of this chapter. Your instructor may require you to complete some or all of these activities as a regular part of your training program. You are encouraged to complete any activity that your instructor does not assign as a way to enhance your learning.

Matching

Match the following terms with the correct description or example.

A. Compound split operation

B. Dual-mode hybrid drive train

C. EP 40/50 system

D. High-voltage interlock loop (HVIL)

E. Smart electrification

_____ **1.** A hybrid system that combines both mechanical and electrical propulsion systems.

_____ **2.** Blending torque from the motors and engine together.

_____ **3.** A device that prevents access to potentially hazardous energized electrical circuits.

_____ **4.** A feature that enables the EP 40/50 system's motors to switch over to generating mode to produce as much as 300 amps at 24 volts at idle.

_____ **5.** Models of Allison's electric propulsion system. Also known as Allison's electrically variable (EV) drive.

Multiple Choice

Read each item carefully, and then select the best response.

_____ **1.** The Allison H-EP 40/50s offers a feature referred to as _____ that uses a highly efficient solid-state DC-to-DC converter eliminating the need for a traditional belt-driven alternator.
   A. energy storage
   B. smart electrification
   C. dual power inversion
   D. battery boost control

_____ **2.** Most of the EP system operation is directly controlled by the _____, which collects input signals to determine electrical outputs controlling the EV transmission operation.
   A. vehicle control module
   B. hybrid control module
   C. transmission control module
   D. dual power inverter module

_____ **3.** Which of the following is an **output** of the transmission control module?
   A. Transmission output speed
   B. Remote shutdown
   C. Accelerator interlock
   D. Engine brake enable

_____ **4.** Which of the following is an **input** of the vehicle control module?
   A. Dash indicator lamp control
   B. Reverse warning
   C. Propulsion system inhibits
   D. Brake pressure sensor

_____ **5.** Two parallel-connected battery subpacks form a _____ having approximately 312 volts DC.
   A. tub
   B. substring
   C. module
   D. group

_____ **6.** The _____ is a DC-AC and AC-DC electronic wave inverter used to power the EP drive propulsion system and charge the batteries in the energy storage system.
   A. dual power inverter module
   B. vehicle control module
   C. high-voltage interlock loop
   D. transmission control module

_____ **7.** In the dual power inverter module's _____ state, both high-side and low-side relays are closed, allowing 85% of total ESS voltage to reach the DPIM.
   A. initial
   B. pre-charge
   C. operational
   D. post-charge

_____ **8.** The _____ consists of a 12V relay control circuit routed in series to switches on cover plates located on all hybrid components where potential electrical hazards exist.
   A. insulated gate bipolar transistor
   B. high-voltage interlock loop
   C. vehicle control module
   D. dual power inverter module

_____ **9.** The EP control maintains _____ operation until the vehicle's speed is under 20 or 25 mph (32 to 40 kph).
   A. Mode 1
   B. Mode 2
   C. Mode 3
   D. dual mode

_____ **10.** What is the advantage to using the Meritor dual-mode hybrid drive train?
   A. Fuel efficiency
   B. The electrification of accessories
   C. Smaller engines
   D. All of the above

True/False

If you believe the statement to be more true than false, write the letter "T" in the space provided. If you believe the statement to be more false than true, write the letter "F".

_____ **1.** A parallel drive hybrid allows you to choose between engine only, electric motor only, or combined engine-motor operation.

_____ **2.** The Allison EP system has adjustable acceleration rates to balance fuel economy with performance.

_____ **3.** The transmission control module and vehicle control module are identical looking modules that perform very different functions.

_____ **4.** Energy storage system batteries remain fully charged at all times.

_____ **5.** One advantage of using NiMH batteries is their ability to be charged and discharged repeatedly without a shortened life cycle.

_____ **6.** In the pre-charge state of the dual power inverter module all battery relays are open, and no current flows into or out of the ESS.

_____ **7.** An open high-voltage interlock loop circuit detected during forward or reverse operation will log a fault code and result in an active system shutdown.

_____ **8.** At speeds in excess of 48 mph (77 kph), the dual-mode hybrid drive train transitions to an all-electric power system, supplemented occasionally by the diesel engine.

_____ **9.** A stop system warning light indicates the propulsion system will shut down with a 30-second warning period.

_____ **10.** Four separate hydraulic filters are located in the EP drive transmission.

Fill in the Blank

Read each item carefully, and then complete the statement by filling in the missing word(s).

1. When decelerating, the EP system uses _____ braking to recover braking energy.

2. The EV drive transmission unit provides a pathway for transmitting electric motor or engine torque (or a blend of both) using three _____ gear sets.

3. The TCM and VCM both communicate over the SAEJ-1939 _____ network with other control modules.

4. Induction of a magnetic field in a(n) _____ motor is caused by the change in current flow in the stator winding.

5. Electrical energy to charge the _____ _____ _____ is generated by both drive motors during regenerative braking and from Motor A in mode one when not in use for propulsion.

6. The energy storage system battery _____ contains 240 nickel–metal hydride modules weighing under 1,000 lbs (455 kg) operating at a voltage range of 432–780 VDC.

7. A specialized field effect transistor called a(n) _____ _____ bipolar transistor inverts DC current to three-phase, variable-frequency, and variable-voltage AC current.

8. Meritor produces a(n) _____-_____ hybrid drive train specifically designed for line haul trucks.

9. Allison EP systems use a(n) _____ fault detection monitor to identify high voltage circuit shorts to the vehicle chassis.

10. A(n) _____ system warning light alerts the operator that an EP system fault has occurred but does not lead to a system derate or shut-down.

Labeling

Label the following diagrams with the correct terms.

1. Identify the standard modules of an Allison EV transmission:

A. _____

B. _____

C. _____

D. _____

E. _____

F. _____

Crossword Puzzle

Use the clues in the column to complete the puzzle.

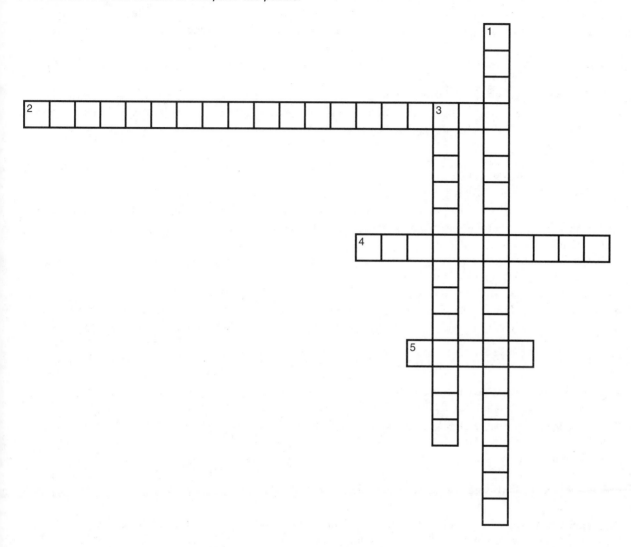

Across

2. A motor in which the magnetic field in the rotor is induced by induction of the magnetic field in the stationary stator.

4. PC-based service software for Allison's EP system.

5. In split-mode operation, the mode that is for low-speed operation.

Down

1. A system that stores and distributes electrical current to the various components of a hybrid drive system.

3. An electric motor that provides propulsion to a vehicle.

ASE-Type Questions

Read each item carefully, and then select the best response.

_____ **1.** Technician A says that the Allison EP drive hybrid systems are series-parallel systems. Technician B says that the Allison EP drive can operate as a parallel system if required. Who is correct?

    A. Technician A
    B. Technician B
    C. Both Technician A and Technician B
    D. Neither Technician A nor Technician B

_____ **2.** Technician A says that the Allison EV drive transmission has one electric traction motor. Technician B says that the Allison EV drive has three planetary gear sets. Who is correct?

    A. Technician A
    B. Technician B
    C. Both Technician A and Technician B
    D. Neither Technician A nor Technician B

_____ **3.** Technician A says that the battery modules used in the Allison EP system contain 40 cells of 1.2 volts each. Technician B says that the energy storage system has 40 battery modules. Who is correct?

    A. Technician A
    B. Technician B
    C. Both Technician A and Technician B
    D. Neither Technician A nor Technician B

_____ **4.** Technician A says that traction motors used in the Allison EP hybrid system use DC voltage. Technician B says that the Allison EP hybrid energy storage system operates at a voltage range of 480 to 780 VDC. Who is correct?

    A. Technician A
    B. Technician B
    C. Both Technician A and Technician B
    D. Neither Technician A nor Technician B

_____ **5.** Technician A says that the DPIM converts AC to DC. Technician B says that the DPIM converts DC to AC. Who is correct?

    A. Technician A
    B. Technician B
    C. Both Technician A and Technician B
    D. Neither Technician A nor Technician B

_____ **6.** Technician A says that the Allison EP hybrid system has two modes of operation—Mode 1 and Mode 2. Technician B says that, in the Allison EP system, Mode 2 is for low-speed operation. Who is correct?

    A. Technician A
    B. Technician B
    C. Both Technician A and Technician B
    D. Neither Technician A nor Technician B

_____ **7.** Technician A says that the Allison EV drive transmission has six forward ratios. Technician B says that the Allison EV drive transmission has five hydraulic clutches. Who is correct?

    A. Technician A
    B. Technician B
    C. Both Technician A and Technician B
    D. Neither Technician A nor Technician B

_____ **8.** Technician A says that Allison EP hybrid systems are capable of logging fault codes when a problem occurs. Technician B says that Allison EP hybrid system fault codes are two-digit main codes followed by a second two-digit sub code. Who is correct?

    A. Technician A
    B. Technician B
    C. Both Technician A and Technician B
    D. Neither Technician A nor Technician B

_____ **9.** Technician A says that the Allison EP 40 and 50 save more fuel when compared to the BAE HybriDrive system. Technician B says that the late-model Allison transmission EV drive can generate electricity at idle. Who is correct?

   A. Technician A

   B. Technician B

   C. Both Technician A and Technician B

   D. Neither Technician A nor Technician B

_____ **10.** Technician A says that the Allison EP hybrid system uses information from up to 12 microprocessors to function. Technician B system the TCM is the most important microprocessor for the EV drive operation. Who is correct?

   A. Technician A

   B. Technician B

   C. Both Technician A and Technician B

   D. Neither Technician A nor Technician B

CHAPTER

51

Tire Tread:
© AbleStock

Principles of Heating and Air-Conditioning Systems

Chapter Review

The following activities have been designed to help you refresh your knowledge of this chapter. Your instructor may require you to complete some or all of these activities as a regular part of your training program. You are encouraged to complete any activity that your instructor does not assign as a way to enhance your learning.

Matching

Match the following terms with the correct description or example.

A. British thermal unit

B. Condensation

C. Convection

D. Latent heat

E. Specific heat

_____ 1. The quantity of heat required to produce a change of state from a solid to a liquid or a liquid to a gas.

_____ 2. The amount of energy required to heat or cool 1 pound of water 1°F (–17°C).

_____ 3. The amount of heat a substance must absorb to undergo a temperature change of 1°F (–17°C).

_____ 4. The transfer of heat through a gas.

_____ 5. Moisture that collects on cooler surfaces as a result of hot vapors coming into contact with the cooler surface.

Multiple Choice

Read each item carefully, and then select the best response.

_____ 1. In 1928, Thomas Midgley, Jr., aided by Charles Kettering, invented a colorless, odorless, nonflammable, and noncorrosive gas or liquid refrigerant called _____.
   A. chlorofluorocarbon
   B. Freon
   C. methyl chloride
   D. sulfur dioxide

_____ 2. In a vehicle's heating ventilation and air-conditioning system heat transfer takes place via _____.
   A. conduction
   B. convection
   C. radiant heat transfer
   D. All of the above

_____ 3. When heat is transferred through a solid, such as a body panel, the metal fins of a condenser, or an evaporator it is called _____.
   A. conduction
   B. convection
   C. migration
   D. radiation

_____ 4. How many Btu are required to change 1 pound of water to 1 pound of ice or vice versa?
   A. 1
   B. 144
   C. 212
   D. 252

_____ **5.** A gauge that uses vacuum as a reference point is calibrated to read _____ psi at sea level.
   A. 0
   B. 10
   C. 14.7
   D. Either A or C

_____ **6.** For every 1-psi increase in cooling system pressure, there is a _____ increase in the boiling point.
   A. 1°F (−17.2°C)
   B. 2°F (−16.7°C)
   C. 3°F (−16.1°C)
   D. 4°F (−15.6°C)

_____ **7.** All refrigeration systems use _____ to move heat from one place to another.
   A. latent heat of vaporization
   B. latent heat of radiation
   C. latent heat of condensation
   D. Both A and C

_____ **8.** Compressor pistons are arranged in a(n) _____ design inside the compressor housing.
   A. in-line
   B. axial
   C. radial
   D. Any of the above

_____ **9.** Outside air flows over the fins of the _____ and absorbs heat from the refrigerant as it converts from a liquid to a gas.
   A. evaporator
   B. condenser
   C. receiver
   D. expansion valve

_____ **10.** There are two common types of _____ used in commercial vehicle air-conditioning systems: the fixed orifice tube and the thermostatic expansion valve.
   A. expansion devices
   B. condensers
   C. compressor clutches
   D. evaporators

_____ **11.** The _____ is a heat exchanger located inside the cab or passenger compartment containing the chamber where refrigerant boils and converts to a vapor.
   A. condenser
   B. radiator
   C. evaporator
   D. compressor

_____ **12.** In a cycling clutch orifice tube system, the _____ will collect liquid refrigerant leaving the evaporator and separate vapor from liquid before the refrigerant enters the compressor.
   A. condenser
   B. accumulator
   C. evaporator
   D. receiver-dryer

_____ **13.** Which of the following refrigerant compositions are currently in use today?
   A. Hydrofluorocarbons
   B. Chlorofluorocarbons
   C. Hydrochlorofluorocarbons
   D. Both A and C

_____ **14.** The DuPont refrigerant number _____ is used in trailer refrigeration.
   A. R-12
   B. R-134a
   C. R-404a
   D. Both A and C

_____ **15.** What type of refrigerant oil is used in all R-134a systems?
  A. Polyalkylene glycol oil
  B. Mineral oil
  C. Polyalphaolefin oil
  D. Either A or C

True/False

If you believe the statement to be more true than false, write the letter "T" in the space provided. If you believe the statement to be more false than true, write the letter "F".

_____ **1.** Dirt and condensed moisture are purged from the evaporator through a drain in the bottom of the evaporator plenum.

_____ **2.** There is technically no such concept as cold, only a difference in heat energy between objects.

_____ **3.** Convection takes place through a medium, such as a gas or vacuum, but the medium itself does not heat up.

_____ **4.** Latent heat of vaporization is a term for the amount of energy required to raise the temperature of water by 1°F (–17°C).

_____ **5.** The heating capacity of a truck's heating system is approximately the same as an average furnace of a medium-sized home.

_____ **6.** Pressures above atmospheric pressure are considered to be absolute pressures, and pressures below atmospheric pressure are considered gauge pressures.

_____ **7.** To obtain a change in state—solid to liquid or liquid to gas, and vice versa—requires much more heat than is required simply to increase the temperature by a single degree.

_____ **8.** Nothing can stop the movement of heat; the transfer of heat can only be slowed down.

_____ **9.** The thermostatic expansion valve controls pressure by cycling the compressor clutch on and off.

_____ **10.** A simple, plastic tube with a calibrated brass orifice is used on current cycling clutch orifice tube systems to produce refrigerant pressure drop in the evaporator.

_____ **11.** The temperature of the refrigerant vapor at the evaporator outlet will be approximately 4 to 16°F (–15.6–8.9°C) higher than the temperature of the liquid refrigerant at the evaporator inlet.

_____ **12.** Receiver-dryers are used primarily on cycling clutch orifice tube air-conditioning systems.

_____ **13.** Refrigerant used in the air-conditioning system of a truck, bus, or automobile is the same as the refrigerant used to freeze food products, make ice, or cool an office building.

_____ **14.** Leak-tracing dye is the most common refrigerant additive and is often added during manufacturing.

_____ **15.** The APADS/air-conditioning protection unit is an electronic microcontroller-based device that operates both air-conditioning controls and diagnostic systems.

Fill in the Blank

Read each item carefully, and then complete the statement by filling in the missing word(s).

1. Air-conditioning systems transfer heat to the atmosphere using a heat exchanger called a(n) _____.

2. Most late-model vehicles are equipped with a(n) _____ _____ located at the cab air inlet to help maintain a cleaner, dust-free cab interior.

3. The transfer of heat through a gas is known as _____.

4. The process of changing water to ice is called latent heat of _____.

5. The _____ is an engine-driven pump that increases refrigerant pressure and circulates refrigerant through the system.

6. In addition to being compact in design, the primary advantage of _____ piston compressors is their minimization of noise, vibration, and harshness.

7. Mobile HD air-conditioning compressors have an electromagnetic _____ that enables the compressor to easily shut off when compressor operation is not required.

8. The terms high side and low side refer to the two different _____ found in the air-conditioning system.

9. The pressure cycling switch is located on the _____ of a cycling clutch orifice tube system.

10. Rather than using a pressure cycling and thermostatic switch, the Navistar system uses three _____ as input to the electrical system control module.

11. The _____ draws warm air from the passenger compartment, over the evaporator, and sends the cooled air into the passenger area.

12. In order to inspect the condition of the refrigerant, a(n) _____ _____ at the receiver-dryer outlet allows the technician to detect contaminated or undercharged refrigerant.

13. A(n) _____ is placed in the accumulator to absorb moisture.

14. A refrigerant's _____ _____ potential is a measure of a refrigerant's contribution to global warming over 100 years for a given mass compared to the same mass of carbon dioxide.

15. The _____ switch is mounted in the high-pressure refrigerant line.

Labeling

Label the following diagrams with the correct terms.

1. Identify the components of a heavy-duty mobile air-conditioning system:

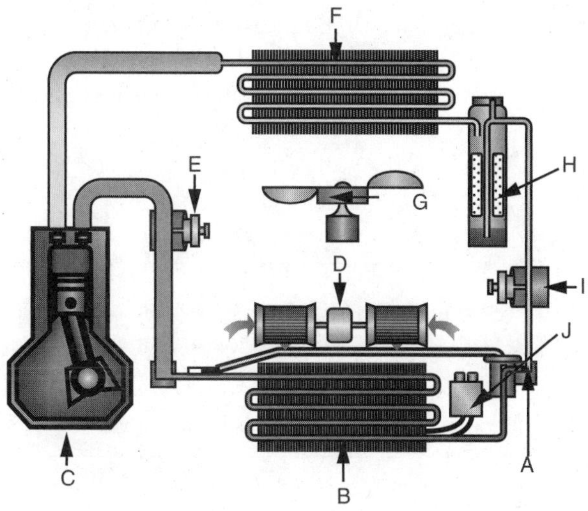

A. _____

B. _____

C. _____

D. _____

E. _____

F. _____

G. _____

H. _____

I. _____

J. _____

2. Identify the components of the heating and defroster system:

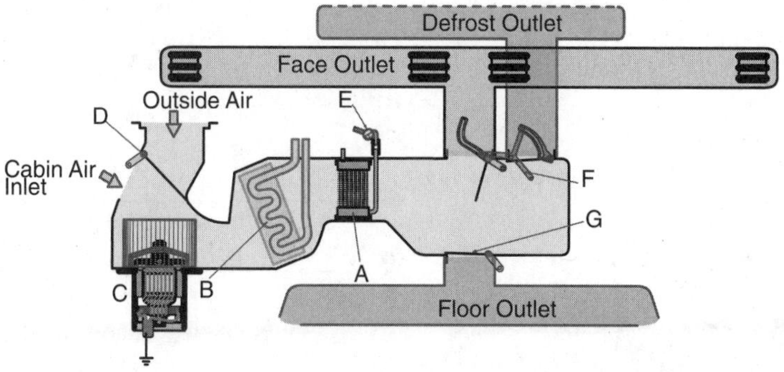

A. _____

B. _____

C. _____

D. _____

E. _____

F. _____

G. _____

3. Identify the components of an electromagnetic compressor clutch:

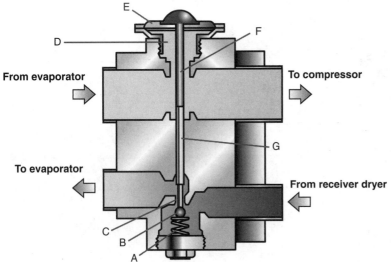

A. _____

B. _____

C. _____

D. _____

E. _____

4. Identify the components of an H-type TXV:

From evaporator

To compressor

To evaporator

From receiver dryer

A. _____

B. _____

C. _____

D. _____

E. _____

F. _____

G. _____

5. Identify the components of a fixed-orifice tube:

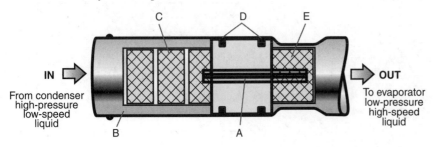

IN

From condenser
high-pressure
low-speed
liquid

OUT

To evaporator
low-pressure
high-speed
liquid

A. _____

B. _____

C. _____

D. _____

E. _____

Crossword Puzzle

Use the clues in the column to complete the puzzle.

Across

3. A heated component that operates to clear the windows.

5. The unit of energy that reflects the amount of energy required to raise the temperature of 1 gram of water by 1°C.

6. Heat that can be sensed or felt.

Down

1. A condition in which excess refrigerant floods the evaporator.

2. An in-cab heat exchanger that regulates heating by circulating engine coolant.

4. The temperature differential between the refrigerant vapor and at the evaporator and the refrigerant vapor at the evaporator inlet.

ASE-Type Questions

Read each item carefully, and then select the best response.

_____ 1. Technician A says that heat, like all forms of energy, can be transferred from one place to another. Technician B says that the air-conditioning system's condenser removes heat from the cab and transfers it to the atmosphere via the evaporator. Who is correct?
  A. Technician A
  B. Technician B
  C. Both Technician A and Technician B
  D. Neither Technician A nor Technician B

_____ 2. Technician A says that a British thermal unit, or Btu, is a common term for heating and air conditioning. Technician B says that 1 ton of refrigeration (TR) is the amount of heat required to change 1 ton of ice to water in 12 hours. Who is correct?
  A. Technician A
  B. Technician B
  C. Both Technician A and Technician B
  D. Neither Technician A nor Technician B

_____ 3. Technician A says that simply changing the pressure of a liquid will allow a change of state to take place. Technician B says that changing refrigerants back and forth between a gas and liquid state is accomplished by compressing a gas refrigerant or lowering the pressure of a liquid refrigerant. Who is correct?
  A. Technician A
  B. Technician B
  C. Both Technician A and Technician B
  D. Neither Technician A nor Technician B

_____ 4. Technician A says that air-conditioning and refrigeration systems transfer heat from the cab and passenger compartment to the air stream outside the vehicle. Technician B says that air-conditioning and refrigeration systems also remove moisture from the air passing through the evaporator and channel it to a drain leading outside the vehicle. Who is correct?
  A. Technician A
  B. Technician B
  C. Both Technician A and Technician B
  D. Neither Technician A nor Technician B

_____ 5. Technician A says that outside air flows over the fins of the condenser and absorbs heat from the refrigerant as it converts from a gas to a liquid. Technician B says that the condenser typically consists of coiled tubing mounted in a series of thin cooling fins. Who is correct?
  A. Technician A
  B. Technician B
  C. Both Technician A and Technician B
  D. Neither Technician A nor Technician B

_____ 6. Technician A says that the thermostatic expansion valve controls refrigerant flow by the action of a spring-loaded control valve. Technician B says that roughly an 8°F (–13.3°C) temperature difference between evaporator inlet and outlet is required to open the valve. Who is correct?
  A. Technician A
  B. Technician B
  C. Both Technician A and Technician B
  D. Neither Technician A nor Technician B

_____ 7. Technician A says that the refrigerant R-404a is used in vehicle air-conditioning systems. Technician B says that the refrigerant R-143a is used in trailer refrigeration. Who is correct?
  A. Technician A
  B. Technician B
  C. Both Technician A and Technician B
  D. Neither Technician A nor Technician B

_____ **8.** Technician A says that the low-pressure cutout switch is connected in the compressor clutch electrical circuit. Technician B says that when a predetermined low charge is sensed, the switch stops compressor operation. Who is correct?
  A. Technician A
  B. Technician B
  C. Both Technician A and Technician B
  D. Neither Technician A nor Technician B

_____ **9.** Technician A says that the pressure-cycling switch is used on CCOT (cycling clutch orifice tube) systems and located on the accumulator. Technician B says that it is not possible to remove and replace the switch without having to discharge the system. Who is correct?
  A. Technician A
  B. Technician B
  C. Both Technician A and Technician B
  D. Neither Technician A nor Technician B

_____ **10.** Technician A says that the APADS module receives information from the vehicle data link and the evaporator thermostatic switch. Technician B says that the APADS module receives information from the high-pressure and the low-pressure system switches. Who is correct?
  A. Technician A
  B. Technician B
  C. Both Technician A and Technician B
  D. Neither Technician A nor Technician B

Servicing Heating and Air-Conditioning Systems

Chapter Review

The following activities have been designed to help you refresh your knowledge of this chapter. Your instructor may require you to complete some or all of these activities as a regular part of your training program. You are encouraged to complete any activity that your instructor does not assign as a way to enhance your learning.

Matching

Match the following terms with the correct description or example.

A. Charge

B. Pressure transients

C. Reclaiming

D. Refrigerant identifiers

E. State of charge

_____ **1.** The process of removing refrigerant from the air-conditioning system by using an air-conditioning machine; also called recovering.

_____ **2.** The amount of refrigerant in a system compared to how much should be in it.

_____ **3.** The amount of refrigerant present in the system or the process of installing refrigerant in the system.

_____ **4.** Devices used to check for impurities in the air-conditioning system.

_____ **5.** Minor fluctuations on the gauges that may indicate a problem.

Multiple Choice

Read each item carefully, and then select the best response.

_____ **1.** Section 609 of the _____ outlines standards and requirements for servicing motor vehicle air conditioners.

    A. Ozone Depletion Act

    B. Environmental Protection Act

    C. Clean Air Act

    D. OSHA regulation handbook

_____ **2.** The _____ can be found listed on the OEM AC decal in the engine compartment.

    A. oil capacity

    B. charge amount

    C. type of refrigerant

    D. All of the above

_____ **3.** Extremely high-pressure readings on the high side indicate that there is a blockage on the high side or an airflow restriction across the _____.

    A. compressor

    B. condenser

    C. restriction

    D. drain hose

_____ **4.** Unusual smells when running the air conditioner are most likely caused by _____.

    A. contaminated refrigerant

    B. a failed compressor

    C. a blocked or plugged drain

    D. dirty filters

_____ **5.** A _____ is a protective device designed to shut down air-conditioning operations in the event of an electrical overload to prevent further damage.
   A. circuit breaker
   B. thermal unit
   C. fuse
   D. All of the above

_____ **6.** A _____ hooks up to the air-conditioning service ports on the vehicle and can check pressures, but also has a storage tank to hold refrigerant.
   A. refrigerant identifier
   B. pressure gauge set
   C. reclaim/recycle machine
   D. sealant detector

_____ **7.** The most accurate way to test airflow velocity is to use a(n) _____.
   A. ohmmeter
   B. anemometer
   C. micron gauge
   D. vacuum gauge

_____ **8.** What method of leak detection is considered the safest and the most accurate?
   A. Electronic detection
   B. Heated diode
   C. Nitrogen testing
   D. Dye testing

_____ **9.** What method of leak detection requires that the air conditioning system be full of refrigerant?
   A. Dye testing
   B. Nitrogen testing
   C. Electronic detection
   D. Both A and C

_____ **10.** For testing discharged systems or prechecking for a leak after repairs have been made and before recharging the system you would use _____.
   A. dye testing
   B. nitrogen testing
   C. electronic testing
   D. Both A and C

True/False

If you believe the statement to be more true than false, write the letter "T" in the space provided. If you believe the statement to be more false than true, write the letter "F".

_____ **1.** The only way to determine the type of refrigerant in a system is with the aid of a refrigerant identifier.

_____ **2.** Undercharging the air-conditioning system will affect both orifice tube and TXV systems in the same manner.

_____ **3.** Allowing sealant to be drawn into a refrigerant identifier or air-conditioning machine can ruin them.

_____ **4.** Manifold gauge sets come in both mechanical and digital styles and are used to diagnose and service air-conditioning systems.

_____ **5.** Oil-filled gauges are designed to help identify pressure transients.

_____ **6.** A retrofit kit has the fittings and oil to change an R-12 unit over to R-134a.

_____ **7.** If a small leak is detected in the system a small amount of sealer may be used to stop the leak.

_____ **8.** New virgin refrigerant tanks are a one-use-only tank and have a one-way check valve in the valve stem to prevent refilling of the tank.

_____ **9.** The refrigerant R-134a uses polyalkylene glycol oil.

_____ **10.** The only tool needed to charge the air-conditioning system is a refrigerant charging unit, with the correct type and amount of refrigerant in it.

Fill in the Blank

Read each item carefully, and then complete the statement by filling in the missing word(s).

1. A(n) _____ air-conditioning system contains less refrigerant than the system calls for.

2. A refrigerant _____ hooks to the low-side fitting of the air-conditioning system to determine whether the refrigerant is pure or whether it is contaminated with another refrigerant or air.

3. A(n) _____ gauge is an electronic device designed to precisely measure vacuum.

4. Using _____ light and refrigerant dye is a common way to test for leaks in an air-conditioning system.

5. The air-conditioning system should be _____ if the compressor comes apart or if the desiccant bag breaks open.

6. Any time lines are loosened, the _____-_____ in the fittings must be replaced or there is potential for leaks.

7. The receiver/drier or _____ needs to be removed and inspected whenever there are leaks or the desiccant is failing to dry the refrigerant.

8. After all repairs are made, the air-conditioning system needs to be _____ to remove all of the moisture from the air introduced into the lines from opening up the air-conditioning system.

9. The oiler uses _____ pressure to push oil into the air-conditioning system.

10. Leaks from the _____ _____ can result in coolant misting out of the vents or coolant dripping onto the passenger-side carpet, or both.

Labeling

Label the following diagrams with the correct terms.

1. Identify the tools and equipment required to maintain and repair air-conditioning systems:

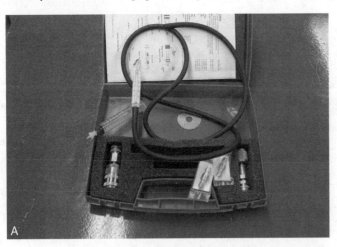

A. _____

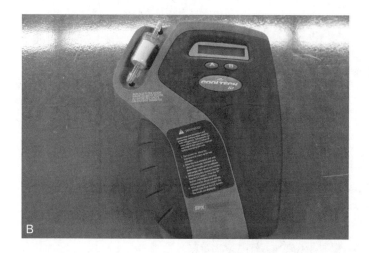

B. _____

C. _____

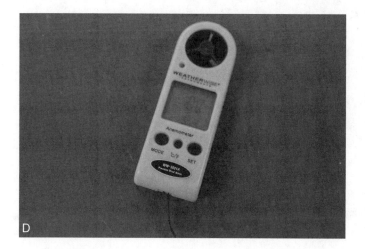

D. _____

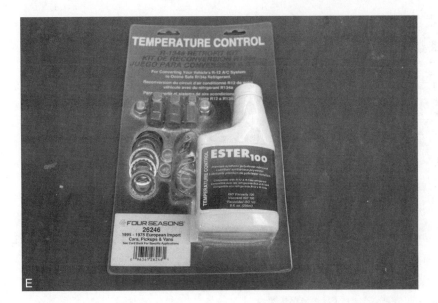

E. _____

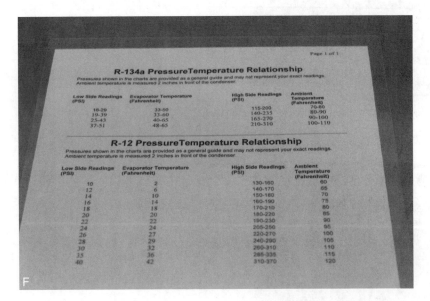

F. _____

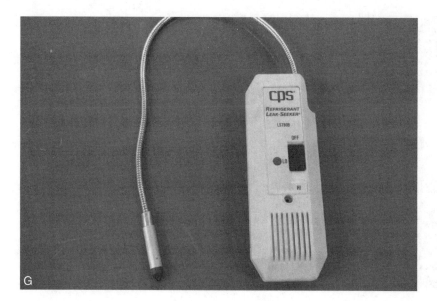

G. _____

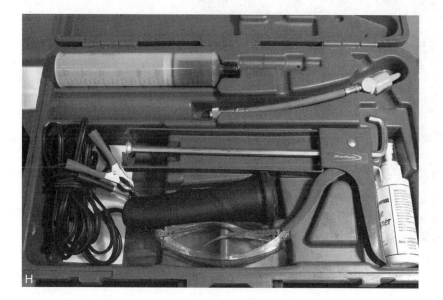

H. _____

I. _____

J. _____

Skill Drills

Test your knowledge of skill drills by filling in the correct words in the photo captions.

1. Performance Testing an Air-Conditioning System:

Step 1:   Turn on the vehicle. Place a _____ in front of the vehicle to simulate the _____ that occurs when driving.

Step 2:   Close all _____. Turn the air conditioner to its _____ setting.

Step 3:   Raise the engine rpm to _____ _____.

Step 4:   Check the vent temperature in the cabin using a _____. Compare the temperature recorded to the _____ _____ in the manufacturer's service manual.

2. Testing for Leaks Using an Electronic Leak Detector:

Step 1:   Make sure the air-conditioning system has _____ by installing a _____ _____ set and checking the readings against the _____ chart.

Step 2:   Select a fairly sensitive setting for the _____. Slowly move the _____ around and under all of the air-conditioning _____ and _____. If a leak is detected, turn the sensitivity down and _____ the exact location of the leak. Once the leak is located, move the wand _____ from the leak to outside the vehicle. This allows the detector to "breathe" clean air, cleaning out its _____ and stopping the alarm.

Step 3:   Reclaim the _____ and _____ the leak.

Step 4:   Always _____ for a leak after the system has been properly _____.

3. Reclaiming and Recovering the Air-Conditioning System:

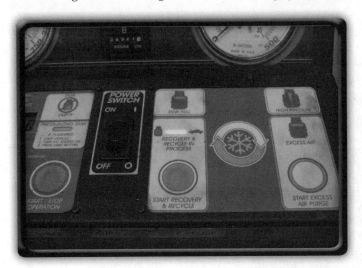

Step 1: Identify the refrigerant using the _____ _____, and verify that there is no _____ in the system.

Step 2: Start the _____ process by hooking up the air-conditioning _____ to the low- and high-side _____ _____.

Step 3: Open the _____ and turn on the air-conditioning machine. Select the _____ mode and follow the _____ on the screen.

Step 4: When the refrigerant has been _____, record the _____ and compare it to the _____ on the vehicle.

Step 5: The air-conditioning machine will drain any excess oil that might have been reclaimed. The refrigerant oil that is drained should be _____ or _____. Record the amount of oil that is discharged, and install the _____ _____ if the total oil removed is less than 30 mL. If the oil drain discharges more than _____ mL, the air-conditioning system will need to be _____ using a _____ machine, removing all of the oil from the system.

Step 6: After the old oil is flushed, reinstall the _____ _____ of _____ oil to the system.

4. Removing, Inspecting, and Reinstalling the Condenser:

Step 1: After _____ the air-conditioning system, remove all necessary components to access the _____. This may include removing the _____, _____, _____, and coverings. Refer to the manufacturer's specific procedures on component removal.

Step 2:   Remove the _____ and _____ lines on the _____.

Step 3:   Remove the _____-_____ bolts for the condenser.

Step 4:   Install the new _____. Fasten the condenser with the _____ _____.

Step 5:   Install new _____-_____ on the air-conditioning _____.

Step 6:   Install the _____ and _____ lines.

Step 7:   Replace all of the components in _____ _____ from removal. _____ the air-conditioning system if all other air-conditioning _____ are complete.

5. Using a Micron Gauge to Evacuate an Air-Conditioning System:

Step 1:   Refer to the boiling point _____ for the boiling point _____ in _____. Connect the _____ _____ and _____ _____.

Step 2:   Turn the _____ _____ on to begin the _____ process. Evacuate for a minimum of _____ minutes. Time the _____ _____ reading.

Step 3:   The _____ _____ should reach the _____ _____ pressure from the boiling point _____ within _____ minutes.

Step 4:   If the pressure gauge hits the _____ within _____ minutes, continue to allow the machine to _____ the air-conditioning system until the micron gauge reaches _____ microns. When the _____ _____ reaches _____ _____, the air-conditioning system is _____ free.

Crossword Puzzle

Use the clues in the column to complete the puzzle.

Across

5. Overfilling of the air-conditioning system; may result in poor cooling or mechanical failure of the system.

6. A device to quiet the pipes of the air-conditioning system with baffles placed inside to deaden the sound of refrigerant moving.

Down

1. A device used to add oil to the air-conditioning system.

2. Flexible line used to direct liquids or gases.

3. A pressure–temperature chart that shows the relationship between air-conditioning pressures and evaporator temperature.

4. A device placed between the evaporator and the compressor to collect liquid refrigerant and prevent it from entering the compressor.

ASE-Type Questions

Read each item carefully, and then select the best response.

_____ 1. Technician A says that the wider the gap on an air-conditioning clutch, the greater the ohm reading when checking the windings. Technician B says that the air-conditioning clutch is electromagnetically operated. Who is correct?

A. Technician A

B. Technician B

C. Both Technician A and Technician B

D. Neither Technician A nor Technician B

_____ 2. Technician A says that an air-conditioning performance test usually requires that an auxiliary condenser fan be used during the test. Technician B says that a performance test will show if the air-conditioning system is contaminated with sealer. Who is correct?

A. Technician A

B. Technician B

C. Both Technician A and Technician B

D. Neither Technician A nor Technician B

_____ 3. Technician A says that refrigerant in a vehicle should be identified before recovering the refrigerant. Technician B says that refrigerant doesn't need to be identified if you are only topping up a system with refrigerant. Who is correct?

A. Technician A

B. Technician B

C. Both Technician A and Technician B

D. Neither Technician A nor Technician B

_____ 4. Technician A says that when evacuating an air-conditioning system, the vacuum should be maintained for approximately 10 minutes after the system reaches the boiling point pressure of water. Technician B says that the primary purpose of evacuating an air-conditioning system is to remove any moisture from the system. Who is correct?

A. Technician A

B. Technician B

C. Both Technician A and Technician B

D. Neither Technician A nor Technician B

_____ 5. Technician A says that the system should be flushed if the compressor came apart. Technician B says that the system should be flushed if the oil is contaminated. Who is correct?

A. Technician A

B. Technician B

C. Both Technician A and Technician B

D. Neither Technician A nor Technician B

_____ 6. Technician A says that when using pressurized nitrogen to locate a leak, an electronic detector should be used. Technician B says that electronic detectors are used when the system has at least a minimal refrigerant charge. Who is correct?

A. Technician A

B. Technician B

C. Both Technician A and Technician B

D. Neither Technician A nor Technician B

_____ 7. Technician A says that microns are a much more accurate unit of measuring vacuum than inches of mercury (Hg). Technician B says that microns are a much more accurate measure of time than seconds. Who is correct?

A. Technician A

B. Technician B

C. Both Technician A and Technician B

D. Neither Technician A nor Technician B

_____ **8.** Technician A says that to determine how much Freon is needed in a system, you must refer to identifying labels on the vehicle or the service manual. Technician B says that to determine the amount of Freon needed, you just charge the system until the pressures look correct. Who is correct?
   A. Technician A
   B. Technician B
   C. Both Technician A and Technician B
   D. Neither Technician A nor Technician B

_____ **9.** Technician A says that when removing any part of an air-conditioning system, the oil should be drained from it and measured so that the same amount can be reinstalled. Technician B says that oil should only be in the compressor, and if any oil is found in any other components, it means that the receiver dryer is faulty. Who is correct?
   A. Technician A
   B. Technician B
   C. Both Technician A and Technician B
   D. Neither Technician A nor Technician B

_____ **10.** Technician A says that if moisture enters the air-conditioning system, acid will be created. Technician B says that evacuating an air-conditioning system will boil moisture, which will be removed from the system as a gas. Who is correct?
   A. Technician A
   B. Technician B
   C. Both Technician A and Technician B
   D. Neither Technician A nor Technician B

Trailer Refrigeration

Tire Tread:
© AbleStock

Chapter Review

The following activities have been designed to help you refresh your knowledge of this chapter. Your instructor may require you to complete some or all of these activities as a regular part of your training program. You are encouraged to complete any activity that your instructor does not assign as a way to enhance your learning.

Matching

Match the following terms with the correct description or example.

A. Multi-temp unit

B. Reefer

C. Self-powered refrigeration units

D. Transport temperature control

E. Vehicle-powered refrigeration units

_____ **1.** A transport refrigeration system powered by a small horsepower diesel engine.

_____ **2.** A transport refrigeration system that is powered by a compressor located in the vehicle's engine.

_____ **3.** A reefer configured to control multiple temperatures in different areas of the trailer.

_____ **4.** A truck-trailer refrigeration temperature-control system.

_____ **5.** Heating or cooling over a wide range of outside temperatures and product storage temperatures.

Multiple Choice

Read each item carefully, and then select the best response.

_____ **1.** The process of transferring heat away from a product storage container to achieve a temperature of 65°F (18°C) or colder is called _____.

A. air conditioning

B. chilling

C. refrigeration

D. dehumidification

_____ **2.** To remove the ice that freezes on an evaporator's fins and tubes, the _____ is heated.

A. condenser

B. evaporator

C. ambient air

D. expansion valve

_____ **3.** Insulation in the ceilings and walls of a refrigerated truck or trailer minimizes heat transfer through _____.

A. radiation

B. conduction

C. evaporation

D. convection

_____ **4.** The cooling or heating capacity of a reefer is measured in _____ per hour.

A. Btu

B. F°

C. C°

D. joules

_____ **5.** Which of the following trailer refrigeration components would **NOT** be used in a standard air-conditioning system?
  A. Accumulator
  B. Expansion valve
  C. Condenser
  D. Three-way valve

_____ **6.** The purpose of the _____ cycle is to remove ice from the evaporator.
  A. heating
  B. cooling
  C. defrost
  D. Both A and C

_____ **7.** Reefers transfer heat from the cargo compartment to the atmosphere using _____ to move large quantities of heat.
  A. latent heat of evaporation
  B. latent heat of radiation
  C. latent heat of condensation
  D. Both A and C

_____ **8.** The _____ service valve is located on top of the compressor.
  A. discharge
  B. expansion
  C. suction
  D. Both A and C

_____ **9.** The _____ located after the receiver tank operates like a filter and a device to remove moisture and other contaminants from the refrigerant during unit operation.
  A. evaporator
  B. receiver tank
  C. liquid line dryer
  D. thermostatic expansion valve

_____ **10.** All current truck–trailer refrigeration systems use _____ refrigerant.
  A. R-134a
  B. R-404a
  C. R-502
  D. R-12

True/False

If you believe the statement to be more true than false, write the letter "T" in the space provided. If you believe the statement to be more false than true, write the letter "F".

_____ **1.** Blower fan speeds are more important in refrigeration systems then they are in air-conditioning systems.

_____ **2.** To defrost a reefer's evaporator, the major components for heating and cooling reverse jobs.

_____ **3.** The water content of the load has a major influence on how quickly a reefer can reach optimal temperatures.

_____ **4.** The efficiency of any refrigeration system will remain constant even with variations in outside temperature.

_____ **5.** Vehicle-powered refrigeration units are self-contained units integrating the compressor, evaporator, blower fans, and motors, control valves, and so on into a single module that can be suspended from a truck box or trailer body.

_____ **6.** The direction of refrigerant flow determines whether the reefer is in cooling or heating mode.

_____ **7.** During the cooling cycle, the evaporator is used to release heat into the product compartment and the condenser is used to absorb heat from the outside air.

_____ **8.** Reciprocating-piston compressors are the most common type used in self-powered refrigeration systems.

_____ **9.** Flexible braided copper lines connect the compressor inlet and outlet to the system.

_____ **10.** The thermostatic expansion valve regulates the flow of liquid refrigerant into the evaporator to produce the low evaporator temperatures.

Fill in the Blank

Read each item carefully, and then complete the statement by filling in the missing word(s).

1. In a truck–trailer refrigeration system, _____ is a critical function needed to defrost evaporators.

2. During defrosting, the _____, which transfers heat from the product to the atmosphere, absorbs heat.

3. To reduce heat loads from _____ heat and prevent heat absorption, trailers are often painted white or remain as reflective bright metal.

4. In _____-_____ mode, the reefer requires a supply of electric current to operate, and that current comes from a connection to a power grid or shore power source.

5. A(n) _____-_____ unit can regulate temperature using additional evaporators mounted in the trailer ceiling.

6. The position of the _____-_____ valve spool is electrically controlled using a combination of spring and gas pressure.

7. During the _____ cycle, the refrigeration cycle is identical to one found in conventional AC systems.

8. During the _____ mode, a damper door is closed to control air flow from the evaporator to the container.

9. A refrigerant _____ _____ at the condenser outlet allows refrigerant to flow during the cool mode and blocks refrigerant flow during the heat mode.

10. The _____ tank often has a sight glass on the top and/or bottom to provide a means of checking the system refrigerant level.

Components of a Trailer Refrigeration Unit

Match the component of the trailer refrigeration unit to its correct location on the diagram.

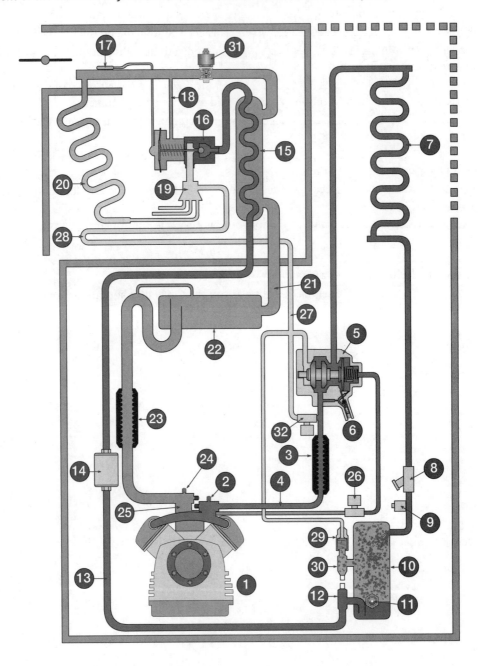

A. Three-way valve

B. Heat exchanger

C. Receiver tank

D. Accumulator

E. Compressor

F. Evaporator coil

G. Pilot solenoid

H. Discharge line

I. Bypass service valve

J. Liquid line

K. Equalizer line

L. Defrost check valve

M. Condenser pressure bypass check valve

N. Suction service valve

O. Expansion valve

P. Hot gas bypass valve

Q. Condenser coil

R. Distributor

S. High pressure relief valve

T. Modulator valve

U. Discharge service valve

V. Throttling valve

W. Receiver tank sight glass

X. Suction line

Y. Condenser check valve

Z. Liquid line dryer

AA. Bypass check valve

BB. Suction vibrasorber

CC. Discharge vibrasorber

DD. Expansion valve feeler bulb

EE. Hot gas line

FF. Receiver tank outlet valve (RTOV)

1. _____

2. _____

3. _____

4. _____

5. _____

6. _____

7. _____

8. _____

9. _____

10. _____

11. _____

12. _____

13. _____

14. _____

15. _____

16. _____

17. _____

18. _____

19. _____

20. _____

21. _____

22. _____

23. _____

24. _____

25. _____

26. _____

27. _____

28. _____

29. _____

30. _____

31. _____

32. _____

Crossword Puzzle

Use the clues in the column to complete the puzzle.

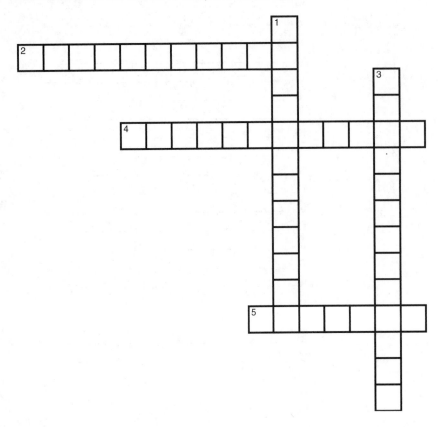

Across

2. A reefer operating mode during which the engine is not driving the compressor.

4. Flexible stainless steel lines that connect the compressor inlet and outlet to the trailer refrigeration system and absorb compressor movement and vibration.

5. Very damp products.

Down

1. A situation in which the evaporator releases heat instead of absorbing it, and the condenser absorbs heat instead of transferring it.

3. A valve that directs hot refrigerant gas to either the condenser (in cool mode) or directly to the evaporator (in heat or defrost modes).

ASE-Type Questions

Read each item carefully, and then select the best response.

_____ 1. Technician A says that most engines require oil and filter changes at 1,500 hours, or about once every 3 to 6 months. Technician B says that the use of synthetic oil lengthens the interval between oil drains to between 2,000 and 2,500 hours. Who is correct?
   A. Technician A
   B. Technician B
   C. Both Technician A and Technician B
   D. Neither Technician A nor Technician B

_____ 2. Technician A says that a number of manufacturers distribute refrigeration temperature-control systems that are installed in trailers, shipping containers, or truck boxes. Technician B says that these systems are more familiarly called reefers, a common term for truck–trailer refrigeration temperature-control systems. Who is correct?
   A. Technician A
   B. Technician B
   C. Both Technician A and Technician B
   D. Neither Technician A nor Technician B

_____ 3. Technician A says that the cooling or heating capacity is measured in Btu per hour. Technician B says that Btu per minute is the amount of heat required to change the temperature of 1 pound of water 1° F. Who is correct?
   A. Technician A
   B. Technician B
   C. Both Technician A and Technician B
   D. Neither Technician A nor Technician B

_____ 4. Technician A says that vehicle-powered refrigeration units are used in smaller delivery vans and trucks. Technician B says that self-powered refrigeration units use a powerful electric motor to power the refrigeration system. Who is correct?
   A. Technician A
   B. Technician B
   C. Both Technician A and Technician B
   D. Neither Technician A nor Technician B

_____ 5. Technician A says that controlling the direction of refrigerant flow essentially determines whether the reefer is in cooling or heating mode. Technician B says that the three-way valve directs hot refrigerant gas to either the evaporator (when in cool mode) or directly to the condenser (when in the heat or defrost mode). Who is correct?
   A. Technician A
   B. Technician B
   C. Both Technician A and Technician B
   D. Neither Technician A nor Technician B

_____ 6. Technician A says that heating capabilities are not as high as cooling capacity. Technician B says that electric heaters cannot supplement heating capacity of the refrigeration system in heat mode. Who is correct?
   A. Technician A
   B. Technician B
   C. Both Technician A and Technician B
   D. Neither Technician A nor Technician B

_____ 7. Technician A says that most units will not enter the defrost mode unless the evaporator coil temperature is below approximately 45°F (7.2°C). Technician B says that timed defrosts can be scheduled to defrost the evaporator automatically every 1, 3, or 5 hours of operation. Who is correct?
   A. Technician A
   B. Technician B
   C. Both Technician A and Technician B
   D. Neither Technician A nor Technician B

_____ **8.** Technician A says that trailer refrigeration systems contain the same basic components as an air-conditioning system. Technician B says that some of the basic components are compressors, condensers, evaporators, expansion valves, and refrigerant. Who is correct?
  A. Technician A
  B. Technician B
  C. Both Technician A and Technician B
  D. Neither Technician A nor Technician B

_____ **9.** Technician A says that, because the amount of refrigerant needed during reefer operation depends on a variety of factors, such as ambient and container temperature, storage of extra refrigerant by the receiver tank is needed for efficient reefer operation. Technician B says that often the tank has a sight glass on the top and or bottom to provide a means of checking the system refrigerant level. Who is correct?
  A. Technician A
  B. Technician B
  C. Both Technician A and Technician B
  D. Neither Technician A nor Technician B

_____ **10.** Technician A says that refrigeration compressors are much like engines, with moving parts that require constant lubrication. Technician B says that without oil, a compressor quickly overheats and destroys itself. Who is correct?
  A. Technician A
  B. Technician B
  C. Both Technician A and Technician B
  D. Neither Technician A nor Technician B

Chapter Review

The following activities have been designed to help you refresh your knowledge of this chapter. Your instructor may require you to complete some or all of these activities as a regular part of your training program. You are encouraged to complete any activity that your instructor does not assign as a way to enhance your learning.

Matching

Match the following terms with the correct description or example.

A. Cavitation
B. Chafing
C. Diaphragm
D. Flow
E. Land

F. Plunger
G. Pressure
H. Swaging
I. Trunnion
J. Undercuts

_____ **1.** A mechanical device that provides a thrusting motion, such as a piston.

_____ **2.** A flexible partition separating two cavities.

_____ **3.** The smallest diameter in a spool; used to create a flow path when the valve is open.

_____ **4.** The formation of air bubbles in the transmission fluid as a result of low pressure at the pump inlet.

_____ **5.** A method of joining a fitting to a fluid conductor by deforming either the fitting or the conductor to form a strong joint.

_____ **6.** How much fluid is being moved in relation to the work that is being done.

_____ **7.** The largest diameter in a spool; used to block flow paths.

_____ **8.** Wear or abrasion due to prolonged or constant friction.

_____ **9.** Paired cylindrical projections used for support, as on a cannon.

_____ **10.** The force per unit area applied to the surface of an object.

Multiple Choice

Read each item carefully, and then select the best response.

_____ **1.** Phosphateester is the most common type of _____ hydraulic fluid.
  A. petroleum-based
  B. fire-resistant
  C. synthetic
  D. biodegradable

_____ **2.** By multiplying the working pressure by the surface area of the output piston, you can determine the _____.
  A. input force
  B. flow rate
  C. output force
  D. displacement

_____ **3.** The volume of fluid moved by a pump in one complete revolution is called its _____.
  A. displacement
  B. rate of flow
  C. working pressure
  D. output force

_____ 4. A(n) _____ filter is used to clean the oil before it enters the pump.
   A. pressure
   B. suction
   C. return
   D. off-line

_____ 5. Schedule specifications refer to a table of specifications that define the _____ for a specific size of pipe.
   A. wall thickness
   B. pressure rating
   C. inside diameter
   D. Both A and C

_____ 6. The use of _____ is intended for industrial applications requiring long, straight runs in fixed, permanent systems.
   A. pipe
   B. hoses
   C. tubing
   D. Both A and C

_____ 7. A _____ is used to connect a tube to a component or device such as a valve block, pump, or actuator.
   A. flare fitting
   B. permanent hose end
   C. compression fitting
   D. Either A or C

_____ 8. A _____ pump is typically limited to operating pressures of 2,000 psi (13,800 kPa) and is used in applications such as dump trucks and loading shovels.
   A. gear
   B. vane
   C. piston
   D. lobe

_____ 9. The pump's displacement and the input shaft speed are used to calculate the _____.
   A. theoretical flow rate
   B. volumetric efficiency
   C. actual flow rate
   D. maximum hydraulic power

_____ 10. A _____ pump can have a variable-displacement capability.
   A. vane
   B. gear
   C. piston
   D. Both A and C

_____ 11. A _____ has two oil ports; oil flows into one port to extend the cylinder, and oil flows into the other port to retract the cylinder.
   A. telescoping cylinder
   B. single-acting cylinder
   C. double-acting cylinder
   D. Both A and C

_____ 12. Needle valves are the most common type of _____ valve.
   A. check
   B. flow control
   C. pressure control
   D. directional control

_____ 13. The most common directional control valve mechanism for hydraulic applications is the _____.
   A. cartridge
   B. rotating plate
   C. spool-type
   D. sliding plate

_____ **14.** The lowered parts of a spool-type directional control valve are called _____ and provide the flow paths between the valve ports.
  A. lands
  B. retainers
  C. guides
  D. undercuts

_____ **15.** A _____ accumulator provides constant pressure, and therefore allows all the fluid from the accumulator to be used.
  A. gas-charged
  B. spring-loaded
  C. weight-loaded
  D. All of the above

True/False

If you believe the statement to be more true than false, write the letter "T" in the space provided. If you believe the statement to be more false than true, write the letter "F".

_____ **1.** In a closed-loop hydraulic system, fluid flows from a reservoir to the pump, through the system and back to the reservoir, where it is directed to the pump again.

_____ **2.** All hydraulic fluids will burn under certain circumstances.

_____ **3.** Modern hydraulic systems are almost exclusively hydrostatic systems.

_____ **4.** When velocity increases, the pressure must also increase if the flow is to remain constant.

_____ **5.** All rigid lines and fittings used for hydraulic system applications are galvanized to prevent corrosion.

_____ **6.** Flexible hoses are designated by a dash number that indicates the inside diameter of the hose in 16ths of an inch or multiples of 1.58 mm.

_____ **7.** There are three types of hose ends: permanent, reusable, and quick-disconnect.

_____ **8.** A positive displacement pump is designed in such a way that a buildup of pressure at the outlet causes the fluid to recirculate or leak back inside the pump housing.

_____ **9.** Pump displacement is commonly shown on the pump identification label.

_____ **10.** In bent-axis piston pumps, the pistons operate perpendicular to the axis of the pump.

_____ **11.** Contaminated fluid is the most common cause of pump failure.

_____ **12.** Double-acting cylinders have two or more sections that are extended sequentially.

_____ **13.** Rotary actuators provide a limited rotation, usually up to a maximum of 360 degrees.

_____ **14.** Hydraulic motors use a mechanical power input to produce a fluid power output.

_____ **15.** Although springs are not actuators, they are used to return valve spools to their unactuated positions.

_____ **16.** Three-position valves will normally have a spring on each end of the spool to return it to its center position when the valve is not actuated.

_____ **17.** There are two types of pressure-relief valves: direct acting and pilot operated.

_____ **18.** Oxygen is commonly used to fill gas-charged accumulators.

_____ **19.** Regular preventative maintenance will help prevent longer, more expensive repairs in the future.

_____ **20.** Fluid should be changed only if it has had its chemical structure damaged to the point that it cannot be returned to its original condition.

Fill in the Blank

Read each item carefully, and then complete the statement by filling in the missing word(s).

1. Hydraulic systems can be designed to lift very heavy objects through the use of _____ _____ using the fluid as a transfer medium.

2. _____ law states that, "pressure applied to a fluid in one part of a closed system will be transmitted without loss to all other areas of the system."

3. The _____ pressure of the hydraulic fluid is expressed as the amount of force per specified area.

4. A(n) _____ is a mechanical device, like a hydraulic cylinder or rotary motor, that moves or controls a mechanism that does the work.

5. The hydraulic fluid tank, or _____, holds excess hydraulic fluid to accommodate volume changes caused by cylinder extension and contraction.

6. A hydraulic _____ stores hydraulic energy and can act as an emergency power source in the event of pump or engine failure.

7. Normally used for on-machine plumbing, _____ is designed to be bent and shaped to accommodate the installation on the machine.

8. Hydraulic _____ normally consist of three layers: an inner tube, a reinforcement layer, and an outer cover of synthetic rubber or thermoplastic.

9. The correct internal diameter of a hydraulic line will create a smooth flow, described as _____ flow.

10. The purpose of a hydraulic _____ is to provide the system with a constant supply of hydraulic fluid by producing flow in the system.

11. Volumetric _____ is the comparison of theoretical pump flow to the actual flow that can be measured.

12. In an inline axial piston pump, the pistons are connected to a(n) _____ _____ in order to make them move in their pumping chambers.

13. True _____ can be caused by a clogged suction filter, a suction line that is too small or too long, or a clogged reservoir breather.

14. Cylinders used for _____ motion are trunnion or mounted so that the cylinder is free to move from its original alignment.

15. Rack-and-pinion actuators convert linear motion to _____ motion.

16. A(n) _____ valve provides a back pressure to hold a vertical load in place until certain pressure requirements are met.

17. The plunger in an electrical _____ is used to push the valve spool into position.

18. With a two-position directional control valve, the actuator cannot be stopped and held except at the ends of its _____.

19. Always _____ stored hydraulic fluid from the accumulator before removing it from the system.

20. Predict maintenance needs and schedule planned _____-_____ to accommodate them.

Labeling

Label the following diagrams with the correct terms.

    1. Identify the components of a rotary vane pump:

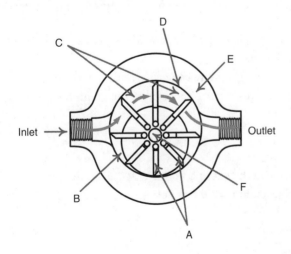

A. _____

B. _____

C. _____

D. _____

E. _____

F. _____

2. Identify the components of an axial piston pump:

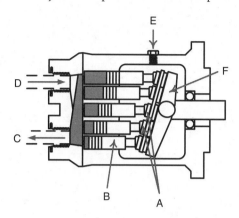

A. _____

B. _____

C. _____

D. _____

E. _____

F. _____

3. Identify the components of a radial piston pump:

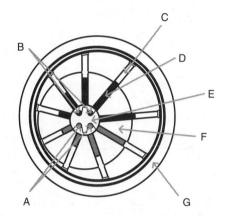

A. _____

B. _____

C. _____

D. _____

E. _____

F. _____

G. _____

4. Identify the components of a single-acting cylinder:

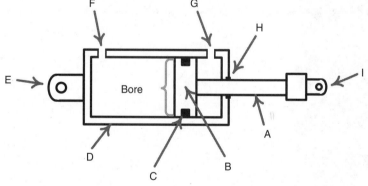

A. _____

B. _____

C. _____

D. _____

E. _____

F. _____

G. _____

H. _____

I. _____

5. Identify the components of a bladder-type gas-charged accumulator:

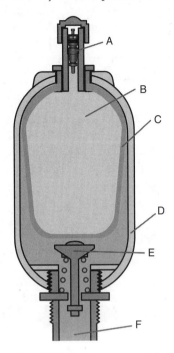

A. _____

B. _____

C. _____

D. _____

E. _____

F. _____

Skill Drills

Test your knowledge of skill drills by filling in the correct words in the photo captions.

1. Changing Hydraulic Fluid:

Step 1: Assemble the following tools and materials:
- Appropriate tool to fit hydraulic _____ _____
- Clean, lint-free _____ _____
- Hydraulic _____ according to manufacturer's specifications
- Safety _____ or _____
- _____

Step 2: Put on _____ _____ or _____, and _____.

Step 3: Operate the _____ to release _____ _____.

Step 4: Slowly open the _____ filler cap to relieve _____ on the _____.

Step 5: Drain the hydraulic fluid by removing the _____ _____ in the _____.

Step 6: Open the _____ _____ on the reservoir.

Step 7: Remove any _____ and _____ _____ that has settled to the _____ of the _____.

Step 8: Replace the _____ _____ and _____ _____.

Step 9: Remove, clean, and replace the _____ _____, if present.

Step 10: Fill the reservoir to the _____ _____ with _____ hydraulic fluid.

Step 11: _____ the system if necessary.

Step 12: Operate the system and check for _____.

Step 13: Check the _____ _____ to ensure it is still within _____.

Step 14: Clean the _____ _____, and return _____ and materials to their proper _____.

2. Changing a Hydraulic Filter:

Step 1: Assemble the following tools and materials:
- Wrench for removing _____
- Clean, lint-free _____ _____
- Appropriate _____ _____
- Safety glasses or _____
- _____

Step 2: Put on safety _____ or _____, and _____.

Step 3: With the system _____ _____, operate the _____ to relieve system _____.

Step 4: Clean the area around the _____.

Step 5: Remove the _____ _____.

Step 6: Clean the filter _____ (if it is a _____ type filter).

Step 7: Install a new _____ and _____ to the manufacturer's _____.

Step 8: Operate the system and _____ for _____.

Step 9: Clean the _____ _____, and return tools and _____ to their proper _____.

Pump Symbols

Match the pump symbol to the correct definition.

1   2   3   4   5

A. Variable displacement

B. Pressure compensated

C. Fixed displacement

D. Bidirectional variable displacement

E. Bidirectional fixed displacement

1. _____
2. _____
3. _____
4. _____
5. _____

Hydraulic Actuator Symbols

Match the hydraulic actuator symbol to its correct type.

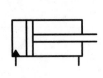 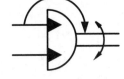 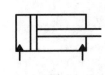

1   2   3   4

   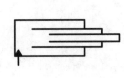

5   6   7   8

A. Rotary actuator

B. Bidirectional hydraulic motor

C. Double-acting cylinder

D. Fixed-displacement hydraulic motor

E. Rack-and-pinion rotary actuator

F. Telescoping cylinder

G. Variable-displacement hydraulic motor

H. Single-acting cylinder

1. _____
2. _____
3. _____
4. _____
5. _____
6. _____
7. _____
8. _____

Directional Valve Actuator Symbols

Match the directional valve actuator symbol to its correct type.

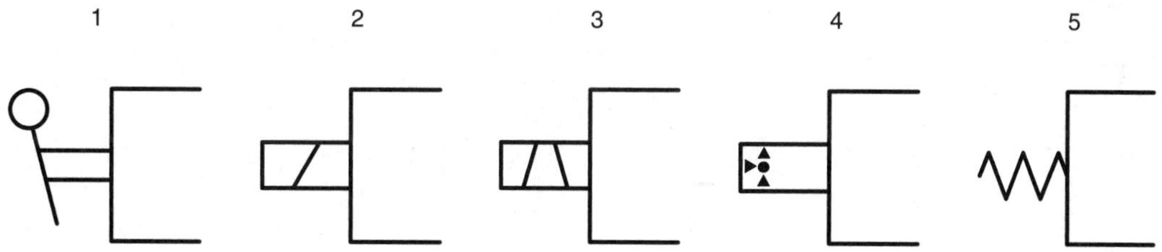

1   2   3   4   5

A. Spring

B. Manual

C. Servo

D. Solenoid

E. Proportional solenoid

1. _____

2. _____

3. _____

4. _____

5. _____

Crossword Puzzle

Use the clues in the column to complete the puzzle.

Across

4. An inflatable bag, or sack, that contains fluids or gas.
5. The measurement of the thickness of a liquid.
6. To pare, or cut, thin layers off an object to reduce its thickness.

Down

1. Movement of the hydraulic fluid not related to speed.
2. Coated with zinc for rust protection.
3. A solid disk that moves within a tube (or cylinder) under fluid pressure.

ASE-Type Questions

Read each item carefully, and then select the best response.

_____ 1. Technician A says that a single-acting cylinder relies on the weight of the load to return it to the original position. Technician B says that a double-acting cylinder is also load dependent. Who is correct?
   A. Technician A
   B. Technician B
   C. Both Technician A and Technician B
   D. Neither Technician A nor Technician B

_____ 2. Technician A says that check valves allow flow in both directions. Technician B says that check valves prevent flow in one direction and allow free flow in the opposition direction. Who is correct?
   A. Technician A
   B. Technician B
   C. Both Technician A and Technician B
   D. Neither Technician A nor Technician B

_____ 3. Technician A says that oxygen should be used to charge an accumulator. Technician B says that the accumulator should be fully charged before it is removed from the system. Who is correct?
   A. Technician A
   B. Technician B
   C. Both Technician A and Technician B
   D. Neither Technician A nor Technician B

_____ 4. Technician A says that spring-loaded accumulators can hold a constant pressure. Technician B says that only weight-loaded accumulators can hold a constant pressure. Who is correct?
   A. Technician A
   B. Technician B
   C. Both Technician A and Technician B
   D. Neither Technician A nor Technician B

_____ 5. Technician A says that angular motion is used to extend the bed of a garbage truck. Technician B says that rams can produce both angular and linear motion. Who is correct?
   A. Technician A
   B. Technician B
   C. Both Technician A and Technician B
   D. Neither Technician A nor Technician B

_____ 6. Technician A says that positive-displacement pumps are mostly used as fluid power pumps. Technician B says that dynamic pumps are primarily used as fluid power pumps. Who is correct?
   A. Technician A
   B. Technician B
   C. Both Technician A and Technician B
   D. Neither Technician A nor Technician B

_____ 7. Technician A says that long runs of hydraulic pipe should not need to be supported at regular intervals. Technician B says that it is okay to run hydraulic lines near hot exhaust components. Who is correct?
   A. Technician A
   B. Technician B
   C. Both Technician A and Technician B
   D. Neither Technician A nor Technician B

_____ 8. Technician A says that the same pressure applied over different sized surface areas produces the same level of force. Technician B says that the same pressure applied over different sized surface areas produces the different levels of force. Who is correct?
   A. Technician A
   B. Technician B
   C. Both Technician A and Technician B
   D. Neither Technician A nor Technician B

_____ **9.** Technician A says that most hydraulic systems are open-loop systems. Technician B says that most hydraulic systems are closed-loop systems. Who is correct?
  A. Technician A
  B. Technician B
  C. Both Technician A and Technician B
  D. Neither Technician A nor Technician B

_____ **10.** Technician A says that petroleum-based hydraulic fluids need additives to work well. Technician B says that fire-resistant hydraulic fluids will actually burn under certain circumstances even though they are made mostly of water. Who is correct?
  A. Technician A
  B. Technician B
  C. Both Technician A and Technician B
  D. Neither Technician A nor Technician B

Preventative Maintenance and Inspection

Chapter Review

The following activities have been designed to help you refresh your knowledge of this chapter. Your instructor may require you to complete some or all of these activities as a regular part of your training program. You are encouraged to complete any activity that your instructor does not assign as a way to enhance your learning.

Matching

Match the following terms with the correct description or example.

A. North American Standard Out-of-Service Criteria (OOSC)

B. PM-A

C. Proactive maintenance

D. Reactive maintenance

E. Return on investment (ROI)

_____ **1.** Reflects the understanding that the cost of repairing an unexpected breakdown is usually much greater than preventative maintenance.

_____ **2.** Defects that require a vehicle to be taken out of service until repaired.

_____ **3.** The ratio of dollars spent on a vehicle for its purchase and maintenance compared to how much the vehicle earns.

_____ **4.** Visual assessment of all safety-related items such as brakes, tires, horn, wipers, steering components, suspension components, and lighting.

_____ **5.** Service is only performed after equipment is broken, temporarily keeping vehicle and fleet operating costs low.

Multiple Choice

Read each item carefully, and then select the best response.

_____ **1.** Preventative maintenance _____.
  A. adds resale value to a vehicle
  B. increases productivity
  C. lowers overall lifetime cost of operation
  D. All of the above

_____ **2.** Companies that operate commercial vehicles within the United States to move freight, passengers, or transport any cargo interstate, must be registered with the _____.
  A. United States Department of Transportation
  B. Federal Motor Carrier Safety Administration
  C. Commercial Vehicle Safety Alliance
  D. North American Standards Alliance

_____ **3.** Which preventative maintenance inspection is often referred to as an annual safety inspection or DOT inspection required to maintain operational certification?
  A. PM-A
  B. PM-B
  C. PM-C
  D. PM-D

_____ **4.** Which type of preventative maintenance is based on a statistical analysis of when equipment and component failures are likely to occur and replacing parts or equipment before that point?

A. Predictive maintenance

B. Scheduled maintenance

C. Proactive maintenance

D. Reactive maintenance

_____ **5.** Which of the following is an example of a severe service operating condition?

A. Delivery

B. Towing or hauling heavy loads

C. Multiple drivers

D. All of the above

_____ **6.** The _____ is a nonprofit organization dedicated to improving the safe operation of commercial vehicles in North America by establishing a uniform, reciprocal enforcement of commercial vehicle safety standards.

A. Federal Motor Carrier Safety Commission

B. Commercial Vehicle Safety Alliance

C. United States Department of Transportation

D. North American Standards Alliance

_____ **7.** The original or a copy of a regulation 49 CFR, part 396.21 mandated inspection report must be retained by the entity responsible for the inspection for a period of _____.

A. 6 months

B. 12 months

C. 14 months

D. 24 months

_____ **8.** Oils are classified by the _____.

A. American Society of Automotive Engineers

B. National Highway Traffic Safety Administration

C. American Petroleum Institute

D. Both A and C

_____ **9.** Engine monitoring information should be extracted during a _____.

A. walk-around inspection

B. internal cab key-off inspection

C. internal cab key-on inspection

D. internal cab engine-on inspection

_____ **10.** The under-vehicle inspection should focus mainly on the _____ of the vehicle.

A. transmission

B. suspension system

C. drive train

D. Both A and C

True/False

If you believe the statement to be more true than false, write the letter "T" in the space provided. If you believe the statement to be more false than true, write the letter "F".

_____ **1.** Preventative maintenance and inspection is critical to making sure heavy-duty vehicles conform to federal, state, and local laws for roadworthiness and safe operation.

_____ **2.** The United States Department of Transportation number functions as a unique identifier used to collect and monitor a company's safety information.

_____ **3.** The normal interval for a PM-B is approximately halfway between normal oil change intervals or approximately every 10,000 miles or 16,000 km.

_____ **4.** Federal Motor Carrier Safety legislation demands that every motor carrier and equipment provider must systematically inspect, repair, and maintain all motor vehicles and intermodal equipment subject to its control.

_____ **5.** Mechanics are the first persons responsible for identifying potential safety issues and the possibility of imminent breakdowns.

_____ **6.** Dusty conditions, extreme cold or heat, stop-and-go driving, and off- or on-road operations all influence preventative maintenance service intervals.

_____ **7.** The only difference between the U.S. and Canadian editions of the North American Standard Out-of-Service Criteria is that the U.S. edition references the Federal Motor Carrier Safety Regulation violation codes.

_____ **8.** The use of software-based record keeping is almost universal in fleet operations.

_____ **9.** In the United States, an inspector must have a combination of training and/or experience totaling at least 5 years.

_____ **10.** Failure to use the correct tool or piece of equipment could result in personal injury and damage to equipment.

Fill in the Blank

Read each item carefully, and then complete the statement by filling in the missing word(s).

1. Regular preventative maintenance ensures operators that they will get the maximum _____ _____ _____ when they trade the vehicle for a replacement.

2. Preventative maintenance is generally _____, which means maintenance work is scheduled to prevent unexpected breakdowns from occurring.

3. The CSA 2010 _____ _____ is a calculated rating based on compliance, safety, and accountability initiated by the Federal Motor Carrier Safety Administration.

4. A Driver Post-Operation Vehicle _____ _____ supplies useful data for preventative maintenance work and alerts management to any unsafe operating condition.

5. It's helpful to a fleet operation for drivers to also report _____ items such as misfires, rough idle, and check engine and other warning lights.

6. A preventative maintenance service _____ should include an itemized task list of procedures that includes mechanical safety items related to braking, steering, suspension, lighting, mirrors, wipers, horns, tires, wheels, and so on.

7. A commercial vehicle may qualify for a Commercial Vehicle Safety Alliance (CVSA) _____ if it passes a Level I or V inspection and no defects are found in critical inspection items listed in the CVSA North American Standard Out-of-Service Criteria.

8. When carrying out an inspection, it is good practice to identify whether the vehicle you are inspecting has been subject to a(n) _____ and whether the repair has been completed.

9. Always obey the shop and vehicle _____ and principles, consider how the shop is laid out, and educate yourself on specialty tools that make the job easier and prevent damage.

10. A(n) _____-_____ inspection should be undertaken prior to beginning a preventative maintenance inspection to assess the general condition of the vehicle.

Skill Drills

Test your knowledge of skill drills by filling in the correct words in the photo captions.

1. Performing a Walk-Around Inspection:

Step 1: Identify _____. Look around for _____ from the various vehicle systems, including:
- _____
- _____
- Engine _____
- _____ fluid
- _____ _____ fluid
- _____ fluid
- _____ fluid

Step 2: Both the inspector and operator should look for, and document, obvious problems such as _____ _____.

Step 3: Both the inspector and operator should look for, and document, obvious problems such as _____ _____.

Step 4: Both the inspector and operator should look for, and document, obvious problems such as _____ or _____ out of _____.

Step 5: Both the inspector and operator should look for, and document, obvious problems such as _____ or _____ frames or _____.

Step 6: Both the inspector and operator should look for, and document, obvious problems such as _____ in the _____ or _____.

Step 7: Both the inspector and operator should look for, and document, obvious problems such as _____ or _____ parts.

Step 8: Both the inspector and operator should look for, and document, obvious problems such as improper _____ connections.

Step 9: Both the inspector and operator should look for, and document, obvious problems such as _____ _____.

2. Performing an Internal Cab Key-On Inspection:

Step 1: First, check the _____ _____ condition and operation of the ignition _____, making sure it operates in all _____.

Step 2: Leave the _____ in the _____ in the _____ position.

Step 3: Now check all the _____ indicators:
- The low _____ _____ light, for example, should be illuminated and a _____ should sound if it is part of the dash design.
- Check the _____ of any electronic engine or _____ system _____ lights. It is important to remember that these lights will normally _____ through various stages, so make sure you _____ their _____ and compare the results to the original equipment manufacturer's (OEM) guidelines.
- Check the system _____. Note the reading on the _____ _____ and record it on the checklist. Then _____ the engine, which should show a gauge reading _____. When the engine _____, check the system voltage again. When _____ the revolutions per minute (rpm), the gauge reading should _____.

Step 4:   Shut down the engine and then return the _____ back to the _____ position.
- Check the operation of _____ _____ and washers by moving the _____ through its positions; check also that the wipers _____ correctly when turned _____. Ensure that the washer _____ _____ function and are adjusted properly.
- Check the operation of all other accessories and controls such as _____ mirrors, _____ mirrors, _____ control (the on and off function only), powered _____, and any other installed accessories.

Step 5:   Extract the engine _____ information. The correct method of retrieving such vehicle _____ _____ varies with each manufacturer.
- Some vehicles are equipped with a diagnostic _____ switch, while others may require the use of a _____ _____, a _____ _____, a _____, or some other device. Make sure you extract any monitoring information from the vehicle computer using the method prescribed in the _____ _____.

3. Inspecting Electrical Components, Exhaust, and Lubrication (Including Fifth Wheel):

Step 1:   Check _____ _____ and _____ to ensure that the license has not _____ and that the brackets are securely _____. Ensure that license plate _____ are working.

Step 2:   Check the _____ system for _____, proper _____, and damaged or missing components by inspecting the _____ and _____.
- It is especially important that the exhaust system not be _____ at a point forward of, or directly below, the _____/_____ compartment. Ensure that the exhaust outlet is _____ or _____ any part of the vehicle designed to be _____.
- Check that the exhaust system does not _____ or _____ any other objects and that no part of the exhaust system is positioned in a location that could result in _____, _____, or damaging the _____ _____, fuel supply, or any _____ part of the vehicle.

Step 3:   Check _____ for looseness and damage, and check that _____ are securely mounted to the _____ and to their associated _____ or exhaust _____.
- Check for any missing _____ on the exhaust _____ and _____, and inspect any supports for excessive _____ or _____.
- Check the muffler for _____, _____, or other damage or _____ components.

Step 4:   Check front and rear _____ _____ for wear and secure attachment to the _____ and cab _____, and ensure that all _____ are _____ and _____.
- Check the cab rear _____ _____ height and _____ if fitted. In such cases, the cab should sit approximately in the _____ of its limits of travel.
- Check the cab _____ and _____ for secure attachment, _____, or _____ and for _____ and secure attachment.

Step 5:   Check _____ _____ for deterioration, _____/_____, hardening, missing _____ parts, and secure attachment to the _____ assembly. Operate wipers/washers to make sure the wipers cover the whole _____ with no _____.

- Wiper _____ should be inspected for _____, looseness, or wear in _____ and for _____ and spring _____.
- Windshield washer _____ should be examined for _____ of foreign material and their hoses for attachment, _____, and proper _____.

Step 6: Check the headlight _____ using a marked _____ wall, mechanical headlight _____, or _____ aimer.

Step 7: Lubricate all _____ and _____ grease fittings and wipe grease fittings. _____ any fittings that are _____.
- All grease fittings should take _____; if they do not, they should be _____.
- Lubricate door and hood hinges, _____, _____, lock _____, safety latches, _____ and cables.

Step 8: Lubricate all _____-_____ grease fittings and _____. Wipe grease fittings and _____ any fittings that are _____.
- All _____ fittings should accept _____; if they do not, they should be _____. This process should be undertaken while _____ the fifth wheel _____ to _____ to disperse the lubricant evenly on the _____.
- Lubricate the fifth wheel _____ (unless it is _____ coated) by applying a liberal amount of lubricant to the _____ and _____ _____ of the plate. _____ the lubricant over the back half of the plate, from about the front edge of the _____ to the back of the _____.

4. Inspecting Tires and Wheels:

Step 1: First, check _____ for irregular _____ patterns.
- Run your _____ over the _____ and feel for areas of _____ wear and confirm with a _____ inspection.
- Take note of any _____ _____ on the _____.
- Irregular tire wear patterns may indicate other problems such as loose front-end _____, worn wheel _____, over- or underinflated _____, bad _____ _____, out-of-balance _____, or poor _____.

Step 2: Next, look for the proper mounting of _____ tires. This involves noting any missing _____ _____ and making sure the tires are a _____ set. Note any discrepancies.
- You will need to make sure the tire _____ and _____ are the _____ on all tires on each _____. This is particularly important on _____ tire installations.
- Ideally, all _____ across the same _____ should be matched in _____ design and by manufacturer. You can still operate the vehicle safely if _____ tires on one side of the _____ are different from the _____ set on the _____ _____ of the _____.
- NOTE: _____ and _____ tires should _____ be _____ on any vehicle, regardless of tread design.

Step 3: Check the overall condition of the _____, _____, and _____.

Note any of the following:

- _____
- _____
- _____
- _____
- _____ edges
- Spotty or excessive _____ on the outside _____
- Excessive _____ and _____ wear on _____-_____ tires
- Broken wheel _____

Step 4:   Check the valve _____ and _____.
- Note any loose or leaking _____, oxidized or rotted _____, or _____ caps.
- Make sure valve _____ are properly _____ (_____ degrees apart on dual wheels).

Step 5:   Check and record tread _____, and probe for embedded _____.
- Check the tread depth by measuring in _____ places with a tread depth _____ at equal intervals around the _____ of the tire.
- Record the tread depth on a _____ sheet. The minimum depth allowed by the FMCSA is _____/_____" (3.175 mm) on the steering axle and _____/_____" (1.5875 mm) on drive trailer _____.
- In all cases, your local government _____ will have all the _____ technical specifications.
- Next, check the tire _____ for embedded _____, and remove the _____ where appropriate.

Step 6:   You will also need to check and record _____ _____. Find the recommended tire pressure _____ or _____ (usually mounted on a door post) and _____ the maximum and minimum tire pressures.
- Use an appropriate tire pressure _____ to measure the pressure on each _____, recording the pressure on the _____ checklist.
- A vehicle should not be driven if the tire pressure is _____ than _____% of the _____ recommended pressure.

Step 7:   Next, inspect _____, _____, wheels, and mounting _____.
- Look and feel for _____, _____, missing lugs, broken _____, and _____ streaks between _____ surfaces and the wheels around the studs.
- Note any oil or grease _____ from the _____, slipped _____, loose _____, and any other obvious damage.
- It is important that the lugs are _____ to the manufacturer's specifications, so use a _____ _____ to verify the correct _____ on the _____.

Step 8:   On vehicles with _____ wheels, check dual mating with a _____. Measure the difference in _____ between the two _____ on each _____ set using the _____ square.
- The difference in _____ should not be more than a _____/_____" (6.35 mm), and the _____ tire must be on the _____.
- Mismatched dual tires overload the _____ diameter tire, causing it to _____ and _____. The _____ diameter tire, lacking proper road _____, wears faster and _____. Tread or ply _____, tire body _____, and _____ may result from mismatched tires.

5. Inspecting Engine-Off Engine Compartments:

Step 1: Check the _____, _____, and _____.
- Check the belts for _____, _____, jagged or streaked _____, tensile breaks in the _____ body, and uneven _____ on serpentine belts.
- Check that the _____ ride slightly _____ the pulley, not down _____ the pulley.
- Worn out _____ will wear out _____ quickly.
- Stretched _____ indicate a _____ _____ pulley.
- Check that the _____ are holding _____ on the _____. If the vehicle has an _____-tensioner and the belt is _____, the belts and the tensioner will need to be _____ as the belts cannot be adjusted.
- Check that the pulleys do not have excessive _____ or _____ and that they are _____.
- Ensure that the _____ do not have embedded _____ _____.

Step 2: Check the engine _____.
- Always clean around the _____ with a clean _____ before _____ the dipstick to check the _____.
- Check that the oil is at the proper _____ and check the dipstick for signs of _____ and _____ contamination (e.g., _____, _____ color, _____).
- Check the entire engine compartment for any visible signs of _____, focusing on _____, _____, _____, _____, and drain _____. NOTE: It can be _____ to determine where _____ fluids are coming from.

Step 3: If the _____ mileage/km specifications have been _____, take an _____ _____.
To take an oil sample:
1. Start and _____ the vehicle to _____ temperature.
2. Drain the _____ and check the magnetic _____ _____ for _____.
3. Take an oil _____ following recommended _____ _____ _____ [TMC] procedures using the oil sample _____.
NOTE: Samples should be taken from oil _____ through the draining. Evidence of _____ shavings or other contamination on the magnetic _____ _____ could indicate problems within the engine.

Step 4: If the servicing mileage/km specifications have been reached, _____ the engine _____ in accordance with the manufacturer's _____.
- Inspect and _____ the magnetic _____ _____.
- Replace the oil _____ and _____ with oil to the correct _____.

Step 5: Check _____ wiring, routing, and hold-down clamps, including the engine control _____ (ECM) and _____ control module (PCM). Check that the _____ is clear of _____ parts and _____-producing sources such as the _____, and that it is not _____.
- Wire _____ should be free of _____ and should not show _____ or _____.
- Wires should also not _____ together.
- Hold-down _____ should be _____ and should not _____ the wiring.
- For ECMs and PCMs, check that all sensor wires are no closer than _____" (15.24 cm) to any _____ surfaces. NOTE: If any wires are closer than _____" (15.24 cm) and cannot be _____, make sure they are protected by _____ _____.
- Also check all _____ and _____ on _____ units.

Step 6: Check the _____ linkages and return _____, making sure that the linkages do not _____ when applied and that return springs are not _____ and have retained their _____.
- Check the _____ mounting and _____ to be sure they are securely mounted.
- All electrical _____ should be _____, and wiring should not be _____ or _____.
- Check the _____ mounting, _____, and wire _____ to make sure all the electrical connections are _____ and not _____ and that there is no _____ or _____.
- Check that the windshield _____ fluid _____ is _____ to the proper level.

Step 7: Check the hydraulic clutch _____ and _____ cylinders' fluid levels and look for any indication of _____ (if fitted). Also look for any leaks on _____, _____, and _____, and make sure the lines are properly _____.

Step 8: Check _____ _____ booster(s), hoses, and check/control _____ for secure mounting. Inspect all _____ and _____ for _____ or _____.

Crossword Puzzle

Use the clues in the column to complete the puzzle.

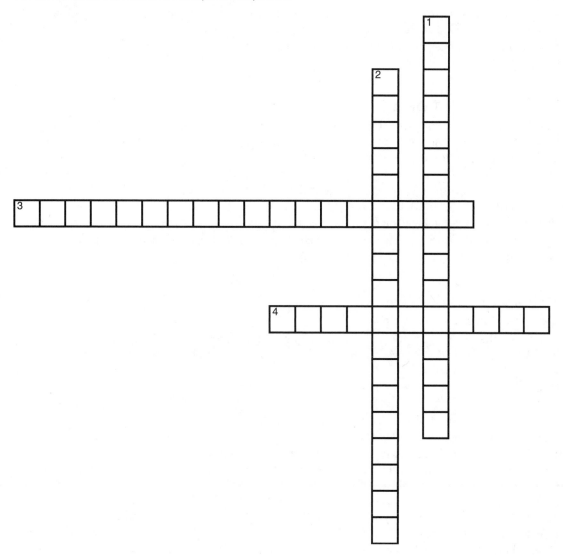

Across

3. The frequency of a PM schedule.

4. Preventative maintenance that is typically based on distance traveled, engine hours, time, or fuel used.

Down

1. Warning lights such as misfires, rough idle, and check engine.

2. An itemized task list of mechanical safety procedures.

ASE-Type Questions

Read each item carefully, and then select the best response.

_____ 1. Technician A says that the type of checklist as well as the inspection schedule will vary with vehicle type and operating service. Technician B says that inspection of fire protection, emergency exit, and evacuation equipment is critical for buses and motor coaches. Who is correct?
   A. Technician A
   B. Technician B
   C. Both Technician A and Technician B
   D. Neither Technician A nor Technician B

_____ 2. Technician A says that a DVIR is a driver vehicle inspection report. Technician B says that a DVIR covers vehicle safety items such as the tires, rims, wipers, horn, brakes, steering, trailer brake connections, coupler condition, and parking brake. Who is correct?
   A. Technician A
   B. Technician B
   C. Both Technician A and Technician B
   D. Neither Technician A nor Technician B

_____ 3. Technician A says that the CVSA is the commercial vehicle safety alliance. Technician B says that the CVSA does not include a training curriculum. Who is correct?
   A. Technician A
   B. Technician B
   C. Both Technician A and Technician B
   D. Neither Technician A nor Technician B

_____ 4. Technician A says that the use of software-based record keeping is almost universal for fleet operation. Technician B says that managers can accurately monitor the cost of PM and associated vehicle costs to make decisions. Who is correct?
   A. Technician A
   B. Technician B
   C. Both Technician A and Technician B
   D. Neither Technician A nor Technician B

_____ 5. Technician A says that record keeping is an essential component of the PMI process. Technician B says that inspections have to be carried out by duly authorized inspectors who can demonstrate both training and experience. Who is correct?
   A. Technician A
   B. Technician B
   C. Both Technician A and Technician B
   D. Neither Technician A nor Technician B

_____ 6. Technician A says that, in most countries, an inspector carrying out this work is required to be registered and appropriately qualified. Technician B says that, in the United States, the requirements include, in part, at least 5 years of experience as a commercial vehicle mechanic. Who is correct?
   A. Technician A
   B. Technician B
   C. Both Technician A and Technician B
   D. Neither Technician A nor Technician B

_____ 7. Technician A says that flammable liquids and oily rags should be stored in an EPA-approved container. Technician B says to use the right tool for the right job. Who is correct?
   A. Technician A
   B. Technician B
   C. Both Technician A and Technician B
   D. Neither Technician A nor Technician B

_____ **8.** Technician A says that it is very important that the shop be set up for functionality. Technician B says that some manufacturers specify maximum wear limitations before a vehicle out-of-service criteria (OOSC) is reached. Who is correct?
- **A.** Technician A
- **B.** Technician B
- **C.** Both Technician A and Technician B
- **D.** Neither Technician A nor Technician B

_____ **9.** Technician A says that the PMI process should begin with a walk-around inspection. Technician B says that you should perform the walk-around inspection alone so that you can concentrate on your inspection. Who is correct?
- **A.** Technician A
- **B.** Technician B
- **C.** Both Technician A and Technician B
- **D.** Neither Technician A nor Technician B

_____ **10.** Technician A says that you should check all exterior lights, lenses, covers, and reflectors for secure mounting and correct location. Technician B says that you should check any visible wiring for general condition. Who is correct?
- **A.** Technician A
- **B.** Technician B
- **C.** Both Technician A and Technician B
- **D.** Neither Technician A nor Technician B